Touring the Backroads of North Carolina's Upper Coast

ALSO BY DANIEL W. BAREFOOT

Touring the Backroads of North Carolina's Lower Coast

OTHER TITLES IN JOHN F. BLAIR'S *TOURING THE BACKROADS* SERIES

Touring the Western North Carolina Backroads by Carolyn Sakowski
Touring the East Tennessee Backroads by Carolyn Sakowski
Touring the Coastal South Carolina Backroads by Nancy Rhyne
Touring the Coastal Georgia Backroads by Nancy Rhyne
Touring the Backroads of North Carolina's Lower Coast by Daniel W. Barefoot
Touring the Middle Tennessee Backroads by Robert Brandt

Touring the Backroads of North Carolina's Upper Coast

Daniel W. Barefoot

John F. Blair
Publisher
Winston-Salem,
North Carolina

BOOK DESIGN BY DEBRA LONG HAMPTON
MAPS BY LIZA LANGRALL
PRINTED AND BOUND BY R. R. DONNELLEY & SONS

*The paper in this book meets the guidelines
for permanence and durability of the
Committee on Production Guidelines for Book Longevity
of the Council on Library Resources.*

Photographs on front cover, courtesy of North Carolina Division of Travel & Tourism
Clockwise from top left—
Lake Mattamuskeet, from The Pamlico Sound Tour
Cape Hatteras Lighthouse, from The Cape Hatteras Tour
River Forest Manor, from The Pamlico Sound Tour
Pea Island National Wildlife Refuge, from The Cape Hatteras Tour
Elizabethan Gardens, from The Roanoke Island Tour
Chicamacomico Lifesaving Station, from The Cape Hatteras Tour

Library of Congress Cataloging-in-Publication Data
Barefoot, Daniel W., 1951—
Touring the backroads of North Carolina's upper coast / by Daniel W. Barefoot.
p.   cm. — (Touring the backroads series)
Includes bibliographical references and index.
ISBN 0-89587-125-4
1. North Carolina—Tours.   2. Automobile travel—North Carolina—Guidebooks.
I. Title. II. Series.
F252.3.B37   1995
917.5604'43—dc20   94-40668

To my wife, Kay,
for her love, patience, and encouragement

Table of Contents

Preface   ix

Acknowledgments   xiii

The Land of Currituck Tour   3

The Great Dismal Swamp Tour   37

The Northern Albemarle Tour   73

The Southern Albemarle Tour   111

The Roanoke Island Tour   147

The Heart of the Outer Banks Tour   175

The Cape Hatteras Tour   201

The Ocracoke Tour   235

The Pamlico Sound Tour   261

The Northern Pamlico River Tour   285

The Southern Pamlico River Tour   313

Appendix   338

Bibliography   342

Index   353

Preface

*We have discovered the maine to be the goodli-
est soile under the cope of heaven.*

Letter from Ralph Lane
to Richard Hakluyt,
September 3, 1585

My earliest memory of the North Carolina coast dates to a vacation with
my parents in 1956, some 371 years after Ralph Lane described the incom-
parable beauty of the coast in the very first letter written in English in the
New World. Yet my first impression of the coast as a five-year-old boy was
much like that of Ralph Lane.

Over the past four decades, I have been witness to the myriad natural and
man-made changes that have come to the region. Nonetheless, my first
impression of the coast remains unchanged. Quite simply, Ralph Lane said
it best.

Despite the lavish praise conferred upon the area by Lane and other British explorers, the North Carolina coast remained the Rip Van Winkle of
the Atlantic seaboard in terms of development until the second half of the
twentieth century. During the intervening three and a half centuries, the
other Atlantic states witnessed the birth and growth of the great American

cities, ports, and resorts along their shores, while North Carolina, because of its unique geography, saw its beautiful barrier islands preserved in their natural state. Treacherous offshore shoals, shallow sounds, and hundreds of nooks and crannies along the irregular North Carolina coast won it dubious acclaim as a pirate haven and a graveyard for ships.

But the centuries of isolation and relative obscurity have now proved to be a blessing. Whereas much of the Atlantic coastline displays the telltale signs of rampant, unplanned development, the North Carolina coast has been largely spared the engineering nightmares evident on the coast of the states to the north and south.

Millions of people travel to coastal North Carolina annually to enjoy the land which has enchanted visitors since the early European explorers. Much of the attraction lies with the unspoiled conditions. Tourists from throughout the United States and from distant parts of the globe revel in the miles of majestic, uncrowded strand, the vast public parks and wildlife refuges, the multitude of family-oriented resorts, and the historic cities and towns, all of which seem to exist in harmony with the natural forces at work on the slender barrier islands and along the sounds, creeks, and other estuaries.

North Carolina possesses the sixth-largest coastline in the United States, following only Alaska, Florida, Louisiana, Maine, and California. Its 301-mile-long coast comprises more than a fourth of the total coast of the original thirteen English colonies. Accordingly, the vast size of the North Carolina coast has necessitated the publication of two volumes of tours.

This volume contains eleven tours of the upper coast—tours of the barrier islands lying north of Ocracoke Inlet and the portion of the mainland north of the Neuse River.

It was on the upper coast of North Carolina that English America took its first breath. Not surprisingly, then, the area is steeped in history and legend. Over the past fifteen years, I have traveled extensively over the backroads of this unique region to collect stories and bring coastal history to life.

Too often, coastal visitors in a hurry to reach the beach resorts speed by fascinating towns, historic sites, and natural areas without understanding their significance, without partaking of their beauty and charm, and without sampling their briny flavor. And even at the beach resorts, there are intriguing backroads with stories that have either been neglected by historians or forgotten as the region has grown more sophisticated.

As you travel the backroads on these tours, please remember that *change* is a watchword along the coast. While I have taken great care to make the information presented herein as accurate as possible, road numbers change, roads and bridges are rerouted, and historic buildings and other landmarks vanish almost overnight.

This volume and its companion volume on the lower coast are not meant to be exhaustive histories of the North Carolina coast. Nor have they been written to provide details on lodging, dining, and shopping facilities. Such information changes constantly and is available from the sources listed in the appendix. Rather, the purpose of these volumes is to introduce the coastal visitor—whether armchair or automobile—to the places, the people, and the events that have indeed made the North Carolina coast "the goodliest soile under the cope of heaven."

Acknowledgments

This book is the realization of one of my fondest dreams: a great, abiding desire to tell the fascinating stories of the North Carolina coast. The realization of my dream has not been achieved without the dedication, assistance, and kindness of many people. To name everyone who has helped in this effort would be impossible, but there are some special people to whom I am especially indebted.

In the entire world, there are no more gracious people than those who live on the North Carolina coast. Whether I was in a library researching local history, on a backroad seeking directions, or at a rural church hoping to get inside on a weekday, the people of the coast were always genuinely interested in lending a helping hand.

The staffs at the North Carolina Collection and the Southern Historical Collection at the University of North Carolina at Chapel Hill and at the State Archives in Raleigh have been helpful and considerate on each of my many visits.

The folks at John F. Blair, Publisher, have been a real pleasure to work with throughout this project. In the fine tradition begun by Mr. Blair more than forty years ago, they are truly dedicated to publishing quality books on the history, geography, and culture of North Carolina and the Southeast.

Carolyn Sakowski, the president of Blair and the author of the first book in the *Touring the Backroads* series, saw merit in my manuscript from the outset and has given much of her time and attention to the project from day one. Steve Kirk, my editor, has provided his professional advice and expertise with patience and a smile. Debbie Hampton, Judy Breakstone, Anne Schultz, and the rest of the staff at John F. Blair have worked to make this book a success.

In my hometown, I am grateful to my dear friends Judge John R. Friday and Darrell Harkey for their never-ending support and loyalty.

My family—my wife, my daughter, and my parents—have been a constant source of inspiration and encouragement.

Much of the original manuscript, written in my favorite No. 3 pencils, was typed by my daughter, Kristie. Since her birth, Kristie has been a great travel companion for her parents, and the coast will always be a very special place for the three of us.

Above all, no one deserves more credit for this book than my wife, Kay. Over the course of this long project, she has traveled thousands of miles of coastal backroads and helped make the book as accurate as possible. She has endured hurricanes, torrential rainstorms, howling winds, sweltering heat, and pesky insects; she has asked for directions innumerable times; she has made hotel and ferry reservations; she has missed meals to get from one point to another; and she has read every word of the manuscript over and over and acted as my sounding board. In the bleak moments as well as the good, she has always been there with love, compliments, and patience.

Touring the Backroads of North Carolina's Upper Coast

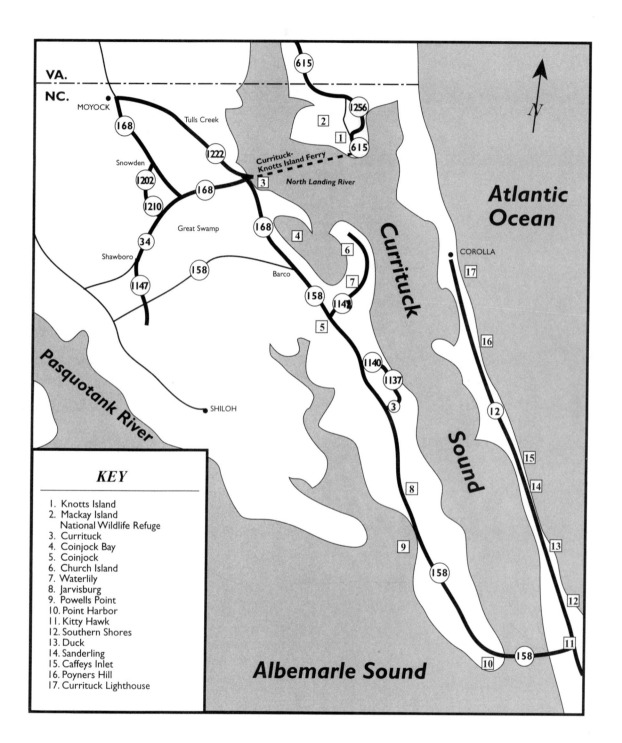

VA.
NC.

MOYOCK

Tulls Creek

168

1222

Snowden

1202

1210

168

34

Shawboro

1147

158

Great Swamp

Barco

Pasquotank River

SHILOH

615

1256

2

1

615

Currituck-
Knotts Island Ferry

3

North Landing River

168

4

6

7

158

1141

5

1140

1137

3

8

9

158

10

158

11

12

13

14

15

16

12

17

COROLLA

Currituck Sound

Atlantic
Ocean

Albemarle Sound

N

KEY

1. Knotts Island
2. Mackay Island
   National Wildlife Refuge
3. Currituck
4. Coinjock Bay
5. Coinjock
6. Church Island
7. Waterlily
8. Jarvisburg
9. Powells Point
10. Point Harbor
11. Kitty Hawk
12. Southern Shores
13. Duck
14. Sanderling
15. Caffeys Inlet
16. Poyners Hill
17. Currituck Lighthouse

The Land of
Currituck Tour

This tour begins at Knotts Island, the "Forgotten Province of North Carolina," and proceeds by ferry or road to the quaint, historic villages of Currituck, Tulls Creek, Moyock, Snowden, Shawboro, Sligo, Bell's Island, Maple, Coinjock, Waterlily, Aydlett, Poplar Branch, Grandy, Jarvisburg, and Powells Point, all clustered on the mainland peninsula of Currituck County. From Point Harbor, the tour crosses Currituck Sound via the Wright Memorial Bridge. It then turns north on N.C. 12 and passes through the Outer Banks villages of Southern Shores, Duck, and Sanderling en route to historic Corolla, the village outpost at the terminus of the state-maintained road.

Among the highlights of the tour are Mackay Island National Wildlife Refuge, the Currituck County Courthouse, the wreck of the USS *Metropolis*, the ponies of Currituck, the story of Betsy Dowdy's ride, the Currituck Beach Lighthouse, and the fabulous Whalehead Club.

Total mileage: approximately 90 miles.

The tour begins at the Currituck–Knotts Island Ferry landing on the southern end of Knotts Island in Currituck County. In this far northeastern corner of North Carolina, bordered by the vast Atlantic Ocean and the state of Virginia, lies the land of Currituck. Taken from the Indian word *coratank*, meaning "land of the wild goose," the name *Currituck* has been bestowed upon a county, an expansive sound, several inlets, and a barrier island.

Currituck County is the home of all of the geographic features of that name. It is an ancient political subdivision of North Carolina, having been formed as a precinct of Albemarle County in 1681. When Currituck County celebrated its centennial anniversary, America was fighting for its independence, and fewer than fifty of the state's counties had been created. Long before the popular phrase "from Murphy to Manteo" was coined, nineteenth-century Tar Heels described their state as having "one foot upon the shores of Currituck and the other on the mountains of Buncombe." Even so, while the western part of the state was being opened, old Currituck faded into obscurity. Over time, the county gained the dubious nickname "Lost Province of North Carolina," a title it has been unable to renounce. For that nickname, Currituck has only geography to thank.

At the ferry landing, you can see many of the distinct geographic features that have determined the destiny of Currituck County. As with all of the state's coastal counties, water has been important in shaping the growth of Currituck. Of the 469 square miles in the county, almost 200 are covered by water. Three large bodies of water—Currituck Sound, on the southern side of the ferry landing; the North Landing River, on the western side of the landing; and the North River, out of sight to the south—have carved Currituck into three distinct parts.

Beyond the North Landing River lies the triangular-shaped mainland peninsula, created by the North River on the west and the sound on the east.

To the east, Knotts Island Channel and Knotts Island Bay separate Knotts Island from Currituck Banks, the long, narrow strip of sand which helps protect Knotts Island and the mainland peninsula from the fierce, destructive Atlantic storms.

Knotts Island, the third distinct land segment of Currituck County, is a true enigma. Though it has long been referred to as an island, this teardrop-shaped piece of land on the edge of North Carolina is in reality a peninsula. Although it is isolated from the remainder of North Carolina and Currituck County by water, Knotts Island is connected to Virginia to the north by a 2-mile-wide land bridge.

Visitors who desire to make their way to Knotts Island by road quickly discover why its citizenry feels out of touch with the rest of the state. To reach the peninsula, which is about 7 miles long and 3.5 miles wide, the motorist must use roads in Princess Anne County, Virginia. Knotts Islanders who want to shop in North Carolina face a drive of an hour or more to Elizabeth City. A 40-mile motor trip to the county seat of Currituck takes even longer. While telephone calls to the Virginia mainland are free, Knotts Island residents must pay long-distance charges to phone their county seat.

To this land of forests, swamps, and marshes came some of the state's first permanent settlers. Now, more than three hundred years later, Knotts Island is referred to by its 750 or so residents as "North Carolina's Forgotten Child."

From the ferry landing, drive north on N.C. 615 for 2.5 miles to the intersection with S.R. 1256. Scattered along this route are the modest frame farm homes of island residents, all of whom live on the eastern third of the island. Just west of the road, most of the remaining two-thirds of the island is consumed by the vast Mackay Island National Wildlife Refuge.

No one is exactly sure how Knotts Island came to be named. Some historians and geographers believe that it was named for James Knott, who owned land in the southern part of Virginia in the first half of the seventeenth century. Others argue that the name came from a group of Huguenots that settled in the area. According to this theory, Huguenots Island later became known as Knotts Island, Knots Islet, and Notts Island. The peninsula appears as Knots Isle on the Comberford map of 1657.

There is no certainty as to the exact date when the first permanent settlers made their way onto Knotts Island from Virginia. Most research indicates that the initial settlement was organized between 1675 and 1692. These first settlers were truly people without a state or colony. For a half-century or so, both Virginia and North Carolina issued land grants and attempted to levy taxes on Knotts Island. In 1728, when the line between the two colonies was established, the bulk of the peninsula was placed within the boundaries of North Carolina.

From the junction of N.C. 615 and S.R. 1256, turn northeast onto S.R. 1256 and proceed 0.2 mile to Knotts Island United Methodist Church.

Most of the early inhabitants of the peninsula were fishermen. After Currituck Inlet closed in 1828, farming and fishing came to be the chief means of livelihood.

By 1811, the population of Knotts Island had grown to such an extent that a Methodist church was constructed. A hundred years later, the Methodists replaced the original building with the existing structure, a handsome white frame edifice with a tall steeple and beautiful stained-glass windows. A Baptist church was constructed in 1876. Today, these two structures remain the only houses of worship on Knotts Island.

Near the churches stands Knotts Island Elementary School. Until the last quarter of the nineteenth century, there were no public schools on Knotts Island. Local and county taxes were used to build the first schools—one-room structures at the northern and southern ends of the peninsula. A three-room elementary school opened in 1908 and was replaced seventeen years later by the existing brick building, donated by Joseph Palmer Knapp, a generous benefactor of the citizens of Currituck County.

Knotts Island United Methodist Church

To obtain a high-school education, the teenagers of Knotts Island have always had to overcome significant obstacles. Before World War I, the only secondary school in the county was on the mainland at Poplar Branch. Students from Knotts Island were forced to board in homes on the mainland during the school year. After the war, the high school in Creed, Virginia, opened its doors to students from the peninsula. Subsequent improvements in the public road system allowed Currituck County to educate the Knotts Island youngsters at Moyock High School until 1960, when the new county high school at Currituck opened. The long overland trip to Moyock meant an arduous school day lasting from dawn to dusk. When the state established ferry service between Knotts Island and the county seat in 1962, the students' travel time was reduced to a twice-a-day fifty-minute ferry ride.

The first post office at Knotts Island was established on January 5, 1833, only to be discontinued and reestablished on at least four occasions. Since April 27, 1874, it has remained in continuous operation. Today, the post office remains a focal point of village activity.

Continue north on S.R. 1256 as it loops 1.5 miles to rejoin N.C. 615. State and county maintenance of the roads on the peninsula did not begin until the twentieth century. Prior to that, residents of Knotts Island saw to it that the one road through the marsh was kept passable at all times. All able-bodied men were required to give one day each month toward maintenance of the road.

Virtually all visitors to Knotts Island are day visitors, for there are no motels or hotels. There is only one store, Knotts Island Market, a well-stocked grocery and local meeting place. While some of the residents earn their livelihood from traditional sources, such as farming, decoy making, crabbing, and teaching, many work at the nearby military installations, shipyards, and factories in the Norfolk area. Despite their isolation from the rest of North Carolina, most Knotts Islanders treasure the tranquility of their remote enclave and are willing to forgo many modern conveniences.

From the intersection of S.R. 1256 and N.C. 615 on the northeastern end of Knotts Island, N.C. 615 heads north 4.8 miles through a desolate, virtually uninhabited area to the Virginia line. Much of the roadside is lined by drainage canals. Rather than taking the northern route, turn south onto N.C. 615 at the intersection.

After 1 mile on N.C. 615, turn west at the entrance to Mackay Island

National Wildlife Refuge. Mackay Island, now a portion of southwestern Knotts Island, was once separated from Knotts by Indian Creek and Back Creek. Both creeks have virtually dried up.

Of the nearly 8,000 acres in the refuge, all but 842 lie within North Carolina. The primary purpose of the refuge is to provide a winter home for snow geese. A population of up to 50,000 of these beautiful waterfowl has been observed here. More than 174 species of birds winter at the refuge, which is administered by the United States Fish and Wildlife Service.

Although much of the refuge borders Currituck Sound and the North Landing River, there are expansive areas of brackish marsh. Beyond the marsh is a young swamp forest of mixed loblolly pine, red maple, black gum, and sweet gum. Information about the various refuge roads, the hiking trails, fishing, hunting, and water access is available at the refuge office. An observation tower is open to the public, but visitors are urged to avoid walking in the marsh because of the cottonmouth snakes found there.

When the refuge was established in 1960, most of its acreage was a gift from Joseph Palmer Knapp.

For more than a century, Currituck County has reaped tangible benefits from wealthy waterfowl hunters who have come from far and wide. On both sides of the sound, magnificent lodges bear testimony to the hunters' opulence. But there was one Currituck hunter who made an impact on the county the likes of which most likely will never be witnessed again.

Joseph Palmer Knapp was fifty-two years old when he first visited the county on a duck-hunting trip in 1916. Knapp was an affluent magazine publisher and printer who had been born into a wealthy Brooklyn family. His father was the founder of the Metropolitan Life Insurance Company. With his vast inheritance, Joseph Palmer Knapp made wise investments in the printing industry. Among his innovations was the development of multicolor printing at the close of the nineteenth century. He became the largest stockholder and chairman of the board of Crowell-Collier Publishing Company, the publisher of the nation's leading magazines in the early part of the twentieth century.

For Joseph Palmer Knapp, Currituck County was love at first sight. Soon after his initial hunting expedition, he decided to adopt the county as his home. Negotiations led to the purchase of Mackay Island from Thomas

Dixon, the celebrated North Carolina writer who penned *The Clansman*. In 1920, Knapp completed a Mount Vernon–style mansion on the island overlooking the North Landing River. Included in the complex were a nine-hole golf course and a swimming pool. Until his death, Knapp split time between his New York apartment and his island mansion. The structure was torn down in the 1960s. A barn and a small house built by Thomas Dixon are all that remain of the estate.

Once he adopted Currituck as his home, Knapp took an interest in the welfare of the local people. He chose public education as his first cause to champion. Because of his generosity, the Currituck school system was transformed from one of the poorest in the state to one of the best in the nation.

His concern for the people of Currituck prompted Knapp to help the county in many other ways: he brought in agricultural experts to improve farming; he provided funds for a local farm credit bank; he contributed to the county welfare system; and he assisted in the organization of a regional hospital in Elizabeth City.

After his death on January 30, 1951, Knapp was buried in his beloved Currituck County. His grave is located in Bagley Memorial Cemetery on the mainland near Moyock. His benevolence to his adopted state continued after his death, in the form of a foundation that provided funds to construct the building that now houses the Joseph Palmer Knapp Institute of Government at the University of North Carolina at Chapel Hill.

From the refuge, return to N.C. 615 and proceed south for 2.5 miles to the ferry landing. The tour makes its way to the Currituck mainland via this toll-free ferry, owned and operated by the state.

On Tuesday, September 4, 1962, Governor Terry Sanford welcomed Knotts Island "back into North Carolina" when the ferry service was instituted between the island and the county seat of Currituck. For the first time in its history, Knotts Island had a direct link to the North Carolina mainland.

Today, the modern twenty-vehicle, 150-passenger ferry makes five daily round trips during daylight hours. During the fifty-minute, 4-mile crossing, passengers are afforded an unobstructed view down the length of Currituck Sound.

Covering 166 square miles, the sound is by no means the largest in coastal North Carolina. From the Virginia line, it stretches 30 miles south, and at no point is it much more than 4 miles wide. By comparison, nearby Albemarle Sound is 51 miles long and 11.5 miles wide, and Pamlico Sound is 80 miles long and 30 miles wide. However, because of its unique geographical history, Currituck Sound can lay claim to being the state's most unusual sound.

The shells of oysters and other shellfish can be seen on the bottom of the sound today. Some of them were deposited long ago by Indians and early white settlers, and others were dropped by birds. But for the most part, the shells came to rest on the floor of the sound when the animals encased in them died from a cataclysmic event more than 150 years ago.

Prior to 1828, Currituck Sound was a saltwater body. Several inlets poured seawater into the sound, causing it to teem with shellfish. During his visit to Currituck to survey the dividing line between North Carolina and Virginia, William Byrd raved about the oysters in the sound, declaring them to be "as savory and well-tasted as those in England." But in 1828, New Currituck Inlet, approximately 6 miles north of Corolla, and Caffeys Inlet, just north of present-day Duck, suddenly closed, completely choking off the ocean water from the sound.

Once the sound changed to fresh water, it took on a new look and new characteristics. Bass, rockfish, perch, and other fish made their way into the waters. Saw-grass, giant cordgrass, cattails, and other marine vegetation that could not survive in salt water began to grow in profusion. Migrating waterfowl discovered the change in the sound and chose the area as a wintering ground.

There have been times since 1828 that the sea has threatened to invade the sound again. On several occasions, storms have forced salt water through Back Bay in Virginia, and some of the vegetation essential to the diet of the waterfowl has begun to die. To remedy the impending disaster, a lock was installed at Great Bridge, Virginia, at the direction of Joseph Palmer Knapp. Consequently, the modern sound has remained virtually salt-free.

Currituckers are quite fond of the sound that divides their county into three pieces. It resembles a vast, shining freshwater lake, lying but a hundred yards from the ocean at some points. For decades, it has been a beautiful playground for locals and visiting sportsmen alike. On hot summer days, the calm, dark waters of the lagoon reflect images like a gigantic mirror.

Although lunar tides have no effect on the sound waters, winds from coastal storms can create a two- to three-foot chop.

Since 1962, the tiny county seat of Currituck has been a modern port of sorts, serving as the mainland terminal for the Currituck–Knotts Island Ferry. When you depart the ferry, park at the public spaces at the landing.

Along the historic Currituck waterfront, there is scant evidence of the important role this once-bustling port played in the colonial history of North Carolina. As one of the five original ports of the colony, the village of Currituck thrived commercially until Currituck Inlet closed. A custom house was constructed between the village and nearby Bell's Island to handle the heavy volume of trade that passed in and out of the sound. A few weathered pier heads are all that remain from the prosperous era when large ships from ports all over the world called on Currituck.

Since 1722, Currituck has been the seat of county government. However, its diminutive size and easygoing pace make this venerable village on the sound unlike most of the other county seats in the state. The businesses and residences that commonly grow up around a county government complex are not to be found in Currituck.

Within sight of the ferry landing are the historic county government structures. Walk north along S.R. 1242 (Courthouse Road) to the courthouse district. Located between the ferry landing and the courthouse is the frame, two-story Granberry House. Built in 1847 in the late Federal style, the house is listed on the National Register of Historic Places.

Currituck County Courthouse

Portions of the existing brick courthouse are remnants of the original courthouse, erected in 1842. Listed on the National Register of Historic Places, the present Romanesque Revival structure is the result of a remodeling and construction project in 1897. Further enlargement and remodeling took place in 1953. A western wing was added in 1968 to connect the building to the Currituck Jail.

A small war memorial monument on the courthouse lawn bears the inscription "To Our Confederate Dead." This unusual marker rests on the spot where Union soldiers camped in 1862. During their occupation of the county seat, some of the soldiers burned county records. Still other records were stolen and transported to the North. In 1976, a batch of old deeds was returned to the courthouse from Ohio.

County residents provided funds for the base of the monument, which was erected in 1923. Money was not available to pay for the casting of a Confederate soldier that was to surmount the base. When Joseph Palmer Knapp subsequently saw the need to landscape and beautify the courthouse grounds, he engaged a New York sculptor to craft the 2,397-pound marble globe that now rests upon the base. Knapp felt that it would be a fitting tribute to Currituck soldiers in all wars.

Located adjacent to the courthouse, the ancient county jail is the oldest jail in the state. Although the exact date of its construction is uncertain, some historians believe that it was erected in 1786. The brick Tudor building is listed on the National Register of Historic Places.

Return to your car at the ferry landing and drive south 0.2 mile on S.R. 1242 to its junction with U.S. 168. At the junction stands a state historical marker for circuit rider Joseph Pilmoor, the man who preached the first Methodist sermon in North Carolina, an event that took place on September 28, 1772. On the western side of S.R. 1242 near the junction stands Pilmoor Methodist Church, a historic church named in honor of the Methodist pioneer.

Proceed north on U.S. 168 for 1.1 miles until the highway forks. Take the S.R. 1222 fork as it curves gently to the west for 5 miles to the small community of Tulls Creek. This scenic route passes through fertile farmland

Pilmoor Methodist Church

that has been cultivated by Currituck County farmers for more than 250 years.

Tulls Creek, a handsome farming and fishing hamlet located just south of the bridge over the creek of the same name, displays little of its past glory. Founded during the colonial period by Thomas Tull, a French Huguenot, the village grew along the creek that empties into Tull Bay on the nearby sound. Archaeologists have found evidence that Indians occupied the town site before the arrival of white settlers. In addition to an Indian burial site several centuries old, there are traces of an oyster-shell road that Indians attempted to build across the sound long ago.

Prior to the closure of Currituck Inlet, an important port existed at Tulls Creek. Trading ships were able to make their way into Tull Bay, where they were loaded with agricultural and forest products for markets in the North and in the West Indies.

From the bridge over Tulls Creek, you can look north to Gibbs Point, a peninsula stretching into the sound. Gibbs Woods, a community on that peninsula, is accessible only by roads extending south from Virginia. Captain John Gibbs, who in 1690 maintained a claim as governor of the Albemarle region, lived in the area.

From the bridge, S.R. 1222 (Tulls Creek Road) stretches 4.4 miles to Moyock in the northern central portion of the mainland peninsula of Currituck. Whatever the season, magnificent vistas are offered along this route. In summer, the lush green fields are ripe with corn, wheat, and other crops, while in the winter, the same fields are white—not from snow, but from thousands of snow geese in their seasonal habitat.

The Marina at Tulls Creek

On the northern side of the road 2 miles east of Moyock, the Sanderson House is of historic significance. This Federal-style brick structure was built around 1800.

Moyock is the commercial center of northern Currituck. Settled early in 1753, the village now offers a wide variety of shopping facilities and public services in this predominantly rural county. In the downtown district, a fine ensemble of late-nineteenth- and early-twentieth-century store buildings, including the first bank in the county, graces Main Street.

At Moyock, S.R. 1222 intersects N.C. 168. For a brief tour, turn north on N.C. 168 and proceed 0.6 mile to the intersection with S.R. 1229, then turn around and proceed south on N.C. 168 as the highway parallels the railroad tracks on the run to the village of Snowden.

From Moyock, the tour moves south down the triangular mainland Currituck peninsula. Just north of Moyock at the Virginia line, the peninsula is 20 miles wide. As it extends south, the slender finger of land narrows to less than a mile at its tip. Except for a high ridge running down the center, mainland Currituck is low and level. Both of the major highways in the county—U.S. 158 and N.C. 168—run along the ridge, and most of the small villages and farming communities that dot the mainland Currituck landscape were built upon the high ground. Various streams and creeks flow east and west from the ridge toward the sound and the river, providing irrigation and drainage for the productive farms surrounding the settlements. Beyond the fertile farmlands is the vast acreage of the Great Dismal Swamp, the Great Swamp, the Maple Swamp, and numerous other smaller swamps.

Railroad crossing at Snowden

Turn southwest off N.C. 168 onto S.R. 1202 approximately 4.6 miles south of Moyock. Snowden, nestled off the highway 0.8 mile west of the intersection, was named for its first postmaster, Milton Snowden, in 1881. Almost at the same time, the railroad came to the community, bringing with it a train depot, a telegraph agency, and related businesses. As many as six passenger trains a day called at Snowden in the late nineteenth century. Now, almost a century later, Snowden has settled into a peaceful sleep. Only freight trains rumble along the tracks, and the post office and the telegraph office were closed long ago.

On the northwestern side of S.R. 1202, the James Bell House is an interesting late Federal dwelling erected in the village before 1850.

From Snowden, continue south on S.R. 1202 for 0.7 mile to the junction with S.R. 1210. Turn left on S.R. 1210. It is 1.3 miles to the hamlet of Gum Corner, situated at the junction with N.C. 34. Three houses of historic interest are located along the route. On the southwestern side of S.R. 1210, the Haywood Bell House predates the Revolutionary War. Nearby are the Samuel Ferebee House, a Federal-style home constructed by a local Methodist Episcopal minister around 1820, and the W. H. Cowell House, a Victorian residence built for a local physician in 1870.

Turn right on N.C. 34 and drive south 1.8 miles to the old village of Shawboro. Two historic churches are located along the route. Perkins Chapel Methodist Church, on the eastern side of the road 0.4 mile south of Gum Corner, was constructed in 1856. It originally had a division down its center, so that men sat on the right while women sat on the left. Providence Baptist Church stands 1 mile south of Perkins Chapel Methodist Church on the eastern side of N.C. 34. Constructed in 1817, the church building has been substantially enlarged and modernized.

Shawboro is located 0.4 mile south of Providence Baptist Church. Originally named Bayley, the community was settled before the American Revolution. After the Civil War, the name was changed in deference to the town of Bailey in Nash County, and also to honor a local hero, Henry Shaw, a Confederate colonel. An army surgeon, Shaw was killed during the Civil War.

Built on an old Indian trail stretching from Albemarle Sound to Chesapeake Bay, the community boasts some of the most historic houses in the county. Several are listed on the National Register of Historic Places.

Located on N.C. 34 just north of its junction with S.R. 1203, the Cupola House, also known as the Shaw House, is an Italianate Victorian structure erected around 1888 by William Shaw. This white frame house is known for its distinctive cupola, which rises from the front center.

Nearby, in the heart of Shawboro on N.C. 34, the Twin Houses offers an unusual appearance true to its name. Built before 1797, the house is one of the best-preserved Federal structures in the county. Colonel Henry Shaw purchased the house in 1856.

In Shawboro, turn south onto S.R. 1147. During the next 3.5 miles, you will pass a magnificent assemblage of historic houses. Culong, the third of

The Cupola House in Shawboro

the Shawboro houses listed on the National Register of Historic Places, is located 3 miles south of the village on the eastern side of the road. Constructed in 1812, it survives as the earliest and most outstanding example of Greek Revival architecture in the county. Among the other homes of interest on this route are the Humphries-Roberts House, a Federal structure built around 1820, and the much-altered Etheridge House, built around 1820 in the same style as Culong.

The Twin Houses in Shawboro

At the Currituck County–Camden County line, turn around and retrace your route to Shawboro. In Shawboro, turn east onto S.R. 1203 and drive 5.1 miles through the Great Swamp, the once-vast morass that covered much of the central portion of the mainland peninsula, to the junction with N.C. 168.

Sligo, a crossroads community at the intersection of N.C. 34, N.C. 168, and S.R. 1203, owes its name to Edward Drumgoole, a Methodist circuit rider from Sligo, Ireland, who visited the area in 1783. Myriad beautiful creeks and branches lace their way through the village. Of architectural interest is the Flora House, a Victorian structure constructed around 1880.

At Sligo, turn right onto N.C. 168 and follow it as it veers south to parallel the sound. After 4.5 miles, turn east onto S.R. 1245 and drive 2.9 miles to the end of the road on Bell's Island.

Connected to the mainland by a causeway, this irregularly shaped body of land has changed in size and shape over the past two centuries. It takes its name from John Bell, to whom the land was granted before the Revolutionary War. When viewed from a map, the peninsula, which now measures 1.5 miles long and 0.5 mile wide, resembles the head of a horse. The majestic waters of Currituck Sound and Coinjock Bay have made this neck of land one of the most appealing sites for residential development in Currituck County. A fishing pier and campground have been constructed near the southern tip of the peninsula to accommodate the fishermen who come seeking the excellent fishing in the adjacent waterway.

Retrace your route to N.C. 168. Turn south and drive 1.5 miles to the small community of Maple. Settled in the nineteenth century, Maple takes its name from the *Maple Leaf*, a Federal transport loaded with 101 Confederate prisoners that grounded on nearby Currituck Banks during the Civil War.

Continue on N.C. 168 for 2 miles to the tiny farming hamlet of Barco.

Just south of Barco, N.C. 168 merges with U.S. 158. Follow U.S. 158 for 2.9 miles to the boating center of Coinjock. Here, the Intracoastal Waterway slices the mainland in two. In the 1980s, the Joseph Palmer Knapp Bridge, a high-rise span, replaced an old swing bridge. Before crossing the bridge, turn left off U.S. 158 onto S.R. 1143 (old U.S. 158) and drive into the heart of the community. The road terminates at the base of the old bridge overlooking the Intracoastal Waterway.

At least four bridges have spanned this old canal, which was in existence long before the Intracoastal Waterway was conceived. By the time the popular water route for pleasure craft was completed, the great ditch in Coinjock had carried freight and passengers for more than a half-century. It was constructed as a part of the famous Albemarle and Chesapeake Canal in 1859.

Ever since its construction, the canal has been a source of income for Coinjock residents. In the late nineteenth century and the early part of the twentieth century, lumbermills and related industries operated along the canal. Steamboats and barges made it a busy commercial highway. But once the old mills closed, there was a distinct change in water traffic. "White collar" yachts replaced the old "blue collar" workboats of the past. From this change emerged modern Coinjock.

The Joseph Palmer Knapp Bridge at Coinjock

To profit from the large volume of pleasure craft plying the Intracoastal Waterway, the village has developed a sizable collection of service facilities, including marinas, stores, and restaurants. On the eastern side of U.S. 158 on the banks of the Waterway stands the old Bray Store, House, and Inn. Constructed around 1820, the rambling structure was used as a commissary during the Civil War.

Around 1880, the federal government constructed a lighthouse station at Long Point, located on the canal 2 miles north of Coinjock. A small plant at the station produced the first illuminating gas ever made in the United States. This gas was used to light America's lighthouses until 1910, when it was replaced by electricity. President Grover Cleveland anchored his yacht at the Long Point station on one of his hunting trips to Currituck. In 1922, the lighthouse station was moved to Coinjock, where it was taken over by the Coast Guard in 1939. Today, the Coast Guard Light Attendant Station is located several hundred yards north of the bridge.

Retrace your route to U.S. 158, turn left, and proceed south over the Waterway. On the southern side of the bridge, turn left onto S.R. 1142 and follow this scenic route as it winds its way east onto Church Island.

Much like Bell's Island to the north, this island is actually a large peninsula bounded by the waters of Coinjock Bay and the sound. Shaped like a giant court jester laughing at the mainland, this vast neck of land stretches 5 miles long and 1 mile wide. More than half of Church Island is marshland.

Waterlily, the only village on the peninsula, is located 3.1 miles east on the sound at the southern end of Church Island, near the junction of S.R. 1142 and S.R. 1154. Named for the profusion of water lilies growing in the local ponds and ditches, it is an ancient place, having been settled around 1750. Long before the first white settlers put down roots in and around the present village site, Church Island was shown on maps as Emperors Island and White Island.

Water lilies en route to Church Island

On the waterfront at Waterlily, the 150-year-old Alphonso Barco House features its original cistern.

At Waterlily, S.R. 1142 turns north. For the next 3.2 miles, the drive overlooks the sound from the high banks of its western shore. Because most of the houses and cottages stand on the western side of the road, the spectacular vistas of the expansive body of water are almost uninterrupted. On the northern end of the island at the terminus of the state road are a campground, fishing piers, a boat landing, and similar facilities. Nearby is Hampton Lodge, built around 1840, which rivals the Alphonso Barco House as the oldest home on Church Island.

From the northern end of the island, retrace your route on S.R. 1142 to U.S. 158. Turn south onto U.S. 158 and drive 1.4 miles to the intersection with S.R. 1140. Turn left onto S.R. 1140, which traverses the Maple Swamp under a canopy of tall trees.

The road terminates 1.7 miles east of U.S. 158 at the sound-side village of Aydlett. Originally known as Narrow Shore, the village was given its present name, as were many other coastal communities, by federal postal authorities. Its post office opened on August 10, 1900. In the years before the Great Depression, Aydlett was a popular summer resort, complete with a public bathhouse, a concession stand, and a fishing pier. Erosion long ago erased all traces of the former amusement spot.

Turn south off S.R. 1140 onto S.R. 1137. A pleasant 3.1-mile sound-side drive will lead you to the old fishing community of Poplar Branch. This route passes several of the hunt clubs that have long been synonymous with Currituck County.

A post office opened at the present site of Poplar Branch on January 5, 1829. The settlement was then known as Currituck Narrows. A sizable commercial district grew up around the post office by the turn of the twentieth century. One of the unique features of the pre-Depression village was a floating luxury hotel. It operated on the Poplar Branch waterfront until a powerful hurricane drove it ashore.

Turn left off S.R. 1137 onto N.C. 3 for the 0.3-mile drive east to the waterfront. Much of the activity in the village is centered around Poplar Branch Landing, a picturesque old boating center where fishermen launch small boats into the sound.

Turn your car around at the waterfront in Poplar Branch and head west on N.C. 3. It is 1.7 miles to the hamlet of Bertha, where N.C. 3 intersects U.S. 158. Head south on U.S. 158. It is 3 miles to Grandy, a village that caters to the hordes of hunters and fishermen who flock to mainland Currituck.

Although the post office at Grandy, established April 19, 1898, was a Johnny-come-lately compared to those in many of the other mainland villages, the community is one of the oldest on the giant peninsula. White settlers reached the present site of Grandy around 1650.

There are several reminders of old Grandy about the village. Mount Zion Methodist Church is located on U.S. 158 at the intersection with S.R. 1131. The main portion of the present sanctuary was constructed in 1828. Just north of the church on the western side of the highway stands a century-old frame building that originally housed the Grandy School. Believed to be the oldest existing school building in Currituck County, the late-nineteenth-century frame structure retains its bell tower.

Continue south on U.S. 158 for 2.7 miles to Jarvisburg. During the summer months, this stretch of highway is known for its large number of fruit-and-vegetable stands. Currituck farmers use the heavy Outer Banks traffic from Virginia to their advantage by hawking crops from nearby fields at these local markets, which dot the roadside all the way to the southern end of the peninsula.

Permanent settlers began arriving in the Jarvisburg area before 1750. Located midway between the sound and the North River, the community has remained a quiet farming and fishing hamlet over the past 250 years. Today, in physical appearance, Jarvisburg has little to distinguish it from other villages on this tour. Indeed, were it not for a state historical marker at the site of his birthplace on U.S. 158, there would be nothing in Jarvisburg to honor Currituck's most famous son, Thomas Jordan Jarvis, a North Carolina governor.

Even though the Jarvis home no longer stands, there are several historic structures of note in the village. Located on the eastern side of the highway, the Sykes–New Bern House was constructed after the Civil War by Captain James Sykes on property once owned by the Reverend Edward Hardy, the great-grandfather of General Douglas MacArthur. On the opposite side of the highway, the Mager Woodhouse House, a well-maintained Federal residence, also has a connection with the great-grandfather of General MacArthur. Two of the Reverend Hardy's four wives were buried in the family cemetery near the house.

Continue south on U.S. 158. Corinth Baptist Church, located 0.7 mile

Jarvisburg takes its name from Thomas J. Jarvis

south of Jarvisburg on the western side of the road, was established by local black residents in 1867. It features an unusual pew construction—the pews are progressively narrower toward the pulpit.

Two miles south of the church, the old village of Powells Point offers a view of the North River. Turn right off U.S. 158 onto S.R. 1120 (Newbern's Landing Road) and proceed west 0.5 mile to the eastern shore of the river.

Here at Newbern's Landing, an important commercial center at the turn of the century, are two nineteenth-century homes of note. Although it has been remodeled into a two-story Greek Revival dwelling, the Scott Newbern House was constructed in 1860 as a one-story cottage. South of the old harbor is the Walter Scott Newbern House, a turn-of-the-century Victorian dwelling. It was built by W. S. Newbern, whose son, Dr. Walter R. Newbern of Palm Beach, Florida, was the personal physician of Joseph P. Kennedy and singer Kate Smith.

From the river, retrace your route on S.R. 1120 to U.S. 158. Turn right onto U.S. 158 and proceed south. East of the highway, at a spot virtually inaccessible to the public, four round holes, long known in the area as the Indian Kettles, punctuate the earth. For years, local legend has held that the unusual pits were used by Indians to make tar to keep their canoes watertight. However, archaeologists for the North Carolina Division of Archives and History have concluded that the kilns at Powells Point were built by colonists to collect tar that came from burning trees.

Five of the dome-shaped, claylike structures, each measuring four feet across and three feet deep, survive on a small rise fifty feet from the marsh bordering the sound. Similar kilns were used well into the twentieth century all over tidewater North Carolina. Most have either been plowed under or have eroded.

As U.S. 158 nears the end of mainland Currituck, it passes the tiny farming and fishing settlements of Mamie, Spot, and Harbinger. Seven miles south of Powells Point, it reaches the point of the long peninsula. At the village of Point Harbor, Currituck and Albemarle sounds merge to form a popular spot for boating and fishing.

From Point Harbor, continue on U.S. 158 as it makes the 3-mile crossing of Currituck Sound via the magnificent Wright Memorial Bridge. When it was completed by a group of Elizabeth City businessmen in 1930, the Wright

Currituck Sound, near Jarvisburg

TOURING THE BACKROADS OF NORTH CAROLINA'S UPPER COAST

Memorial Bridge was a toll span. In order to alleviate the traffic congestion that often occurs on the venerable bridge today, the state began work on a new two-lane bridge parallel to the original structure in 1994.

On the other side of the bridge, the highway enters Dare County and skirts the northern limits of Kitty Hawk. One mile east of the bridge, U.S. 158 intersects N.C. 12. Turn north onto N.C. 12 and drive through the town of Southern Shores, one of the oldest planned developments on the Outer Banks.

In the late 1940s, Frank Stick, coastal artist and father of well-known author David Stick, purchased twenty-six thousand acres in the area, from ocean to sound. From his careful planning emerged the modern town of Southern Shores, a blend of residential and vacation homes. Many of the older homes—flat-topped concrete bungalows—are evident on the route north.

Continue north on N.C. 12. Modern home and cottage development dominates both sides of the road on the 5-mile drive up the Outer Banks from Southern Shores to the village of Duck. Midway between the two communities, Martins Point Creek, better known to locals as Jean Guite Creek, empties into Currituck Sound. Somewhere under the silt and sand of the creek may lie a treasure that was unwittingly buried during the Civil War.

In the years leading up to the war, Hodges Gallop, a North Carolinian, developed a lucrative enterprise by hauling lumber from Martins Point Creek to the West Indies on his schooner. Much to his consternation, the war disrupted regular shipping, forcing Gallop to seek business where he could. His schooner happened to be in Baltimore during the early part of the war when a serious fire broke out in businesses near the waterfront. Terrified shopkeepers and clerks, attempting to save their money from the conflagration, rolled their safes onto Gallop's ship. The following morning, after the flames had been quenched, the local proprietors returned to the harbor to discover that the schooner had disappeared.

Captain Gallop made his way to Martins Point Creek, where he planned to enjoy his windfall. Once again, however, the war altered his plans. He looked across the sound and saw Union troops making their way down the Currituck mainland. To avoid possible arrest and the loss of his newfound wealth, Gallop decided to put out to sea, but the weight of the loaded safes made it impossible to sail at low tide. After he dumped the safes, the schooner was able to bear Gallop to safety.

Gallop returned to Martins Point Creek after the enemy troops left the area. He carried out a laborious but unsuccessful search for the safes. Apparently, they had sunk deep into the mud on the bottom of the creek.

Tales of Gallop's treasure brought others to the creek. One treasure hunter reported making contact with the bed of the creek, yet there is no reliable record that the safes have been recovered.

Today, the village of Duck is a bustling resort community of shops, restaurants, and vacation cottages set amid a canopy of live oaks. Since the early 1980s, increasing numbers of visitors have been "finding" Duck as they drive the winding road up the Outer Banks. At several spots throughout the village where the trees have been cleared for development, the sparkling waters of Currituck Sound are visible.

Prior to World War II, most of the residents of Duck worked as caretakers and guides for the many hunt clubs prevalent in this area, a popular stopover on the Atlantic flyway for many kinds of waterfowl. In fact, most historians believe that the village was named for the wild ducks that have long populated the nearby sound. Following the war, many of the clubs never reopened, and Duck settled into an obscurity that lasted for nearly forty years.

On a secluded stretch of beach just north of Duck, the Corps of Engineers operates a sophisticated research station—the United States Army Coastal Research Facility—where the forces that create and destroy beaches are monitored. Most of the research is conducted from an imposing steel-and-reinforced-concrete pier that extends more than 0.25 mile out to sea.

State-of-the-art instruments have been installed on the pier to collect continuous data on waves, tides, and beach changes during all kinds of weather, including storms. Among the marvels of technology at the facility is a wave radar unit that periodically photographs wave directional patterns up to 15 miles at sea. Instrument readouts are recorded simultaneously at the Dare County facility and at the Coastal Engineering Research Center, located at Fort Belvoir, outside Washington, D.C.

Because of the sensitive nature of the equipment and the importance of the ongoing research, the pier and other areas of the facility are not generally open to the public. However, from early June to early August, public tours of the pier are offered weekdays at 10:00 A.M.

It is approximately 5 miles from Duck to Sanderling, one of a number of vacation-home resorts that have proliferated north of Duck since the mid-1980s. Some of the majestic homes constructed on the strand at Sanderling in recent years have had price tags in excess of a million dollars.

Sanderling is best known as the site of the Caffeys Inlet Lifesaving Station. Constructed in 1889, the building was listed on the National Register of Historic Places in 1981. In 1985, it was incorporated into the Sanderling Restaurant and Bar.

Just north of the old station, you will enter Currituck County at one of the narrowest spots on the ribbon of sand that is the Outer Banks. It was here that Caffeys Inlet was open until 1828.

Former Caffeys Inlet Lifesaving Station

Until the 1970s, the 26-mile strip of sand banks from Sanderling north to the Virginia line was the last frontier for real-estate developers on the Outer Banks. Prior to that time, Currituck Banks had never been very hospitable to human inhabitants. No settlement other than Corolla, the only commercial village on Currituck Banks, was able to attract more than two dozen residents.

In 1974, motorists hoping to make their way up the Banks from Sanderling discovered that there was no public road access to the north. That year, developers of the Ocean Sands resort declared that the old 11-mile stretch of rutted pathway—known locally as Pole Line Road because of its use by power-company trucks to service electrical lines in Corolla—was no longer a public road. Ignoring state highway maps that as late as 1970 showed a portion of the road as S.R. 1152, the developers erected a barbed-wire fence across the road near the Currituck County line. They subsequently paved the entire stretch of road and erected a gatehouse manned by armed security guards at its entrance. Only resort property owners and their guests were allowed past the gatehouse.

The years of controversy that followed culminated in action by the North Carolina General Assembly in March 1983 to reopen the road to public use. Eighteen months later, the gatehouse was demolished and the road was brought into the state highway system as a portion of N.C. 12.

A small wooden sign near the county line marks the entrance to the National Audubon Society Sanctuary. This waterfowl preserve extends a mile north along the road and encompasses five thousand acres of marsh, wetland, and oceanfront. Society members consider it one of the best preserves in the United States.

Approximately 2.5 miles from Sanderling, and just north of the sanctuary, a planned community called Pine Island is being developed along 3.5 miles of oceanfront. Nearby on the shore of the sound stands the Pine Island Hunt Club, one of the surviving private hunt clubs once prevalent in the area.

Continue 3 miles north from the Pine Island Hunt Club to Ocean Sands, an oceanfront resort development of vacation homes. The roof of the Currituck Shooting Club is visible on the western side of the road. Established in 1857, this private hunt club is the second-oldest continuously operating club of its kind in the United States. Its massive clubhouse is listed on the National Register of Historic Places. Much of the undeveloped land of beautiful rolling dunes on the sound side of N.C. 12 is part of the two-thousand-acre tract owned by the club.

On the strand just north of Ocean Sands is the former site of the Poyners Hill Lifesaving Station. A sound-side community named for Poyners Hill— the sand dune that once dominated the local landscape—grew up around the station in the last quarter of the nineteenth century. When the Coast Guard base at Poyners Hill closed following World War II, the final chapter of the community was written. The old buildings vanished long ago, and elegant vacation homes have been built on the site of the village.

It was the most famous shipwreck in the history of Currituck Banks that prompted the construction of the lifesaving station at Poyners Hill. In the nearby offshore waters, the 879-ton, 198-foot *Metropolis* broke apart after hitting the outer bar of Currituck Beach on January 31, 1878. Of the 235 passengers aboard, 102 died in the tragedy. Portions of the old ship, a Civil War gunboat refitted for commercial service, survive at the wreck site, located about 100 yards off the beach in the surf zone.

Continue north for 5.5 miles from Ocean Sands to Corolla. Much of this stretch is characterized by the rampant resort development that has invaded Currituck Banks since the early 1980s. Well-planned resorts with names like Timbucktu and Monteray Shores have introduced banks and shopping centers to an area that was once known for its isolation and solitude.

For many years, developers and property owners on Currituck Banks have clamored for a new bridge across the sound north of the Wright Memorial Bridge. In May 1994, plans were announced for the construction of a 5-mile toll bridge by the year 2000. Proponents argue that the new span, which would be the longest bridge in the state, would save tourists about 50 miles and, in summer, a three-hour drive from northern Currituck County to Corolla. Three routes are under consideration for the bridge.

Corolla is the venerable village at the end of N.C. 12. Originally, the fledgling village was known as Whalehead, named for a giant dune to the south. Village residents referred to the oceanfront as Currituck Beach. In 1895, when the federal government announced plans to establish a post office in the village, three prospective names were sent to Washington, as was the custom at that time. Of the three—Jones' Beach, Whalehead, and Currituck Beach—postal officials did not like the first two and were reluctant to choose the third because of its similarity to the post office at the county seat, just across the sound. A local schoolteacher, in recognition of the fondness of villagers for the many beautiful violets growing in the area, offered the name *Corolla*, the botanical term for the inner circle of petals of a flower. Officials at the Post Office Department liked the suggestion, and Corolla officially came into existence.

For most of its existence, Corolla has not been a populous place. Until recent times, it numbered fewer than a hundred residents. Now, the village is in the midst of an unprecedented population and building boom. As you enter the village, you will see vacation villas and other modern structures dotting the landscape in the shadow of the tall, brick Currituck Beach Lighthouse. Shopping centers, video arcades, restaurants, and an indoor sports center seem out of place with the weathered frame structures from Corolla's past.

Unlike most of the old communities on the Outer Banks, Corolla was never a fishing village. Most of its early residents earned their livelihood from government jobs associated with the nearby lifesaving stations and the lighthouse. Others acted as guides for the wealthy sportsmen who were attracted to Currituck Sound.

Without question, the most famous residents of modern Corolla are its oldest residents—the beautiful, wild "Banker ponies" that often greet visitors as they drive into the village. Of the thousands of these magnificent animals that once roamed the Outer Banks from the Virginia line to Beaufort Inlet on the central North Carolina coast, fewer than two hundred survive. By far the largest population is found on the northern Currituck Banks.

These Currituck ponies are clustered in two herds, the larger of which numbers more than a hundred head and lives in the wildlife refuges north of Corolla. The smaller but more visible herd of approximately twelve horses can often be seen roaming the village streets or grazing on the green lawns of the elegant vacation homes.

Although the beautiful animals delight visitors and residents alike, the growth enjoyed by Corolla in recent years has put the herd in great danger. In a two-month span during the summer of 1989, a half-dozen ponies were killed when vehicles collided with them on N.C. 12 in the village. One motorist crashed into three of the animals in one night.

Quite naturally, concern grew for the safety of the small herd. Fearing that the ponies might become extinct, villagers began to seek ways to preserve the remaining horses. A nonprofit organization, the Corolla Wild Horse Fund, was formed in October 1989. From Sanderling north to Corolla, Wild Horse Crossing signs have been erected along N.C. 12 to warn motorists of the dangers posed by the horses.

Although various attempts have been made to contain the Corolla herd, the village horses continue to roam freely. Not only do they graze in yards, but they often seek shelter from harsh winter winds under the decks of houses. Visitors often approach the majestic animals supposing that they are tame. To the contrary, none of the horses is used to human handling. Both studs in the Corolla herd have charged humans on occasion, and all of the mature horses can deliver deadly kicks with any leg.

Preservation of the Currituck herds is important, because the horses are the direct descendants of Spanish mustangs left on the Outer Banks by early Spanish explorers or by Sir Walter Raleigh's men, who are known to have purchased the Spanish breed of horse in the Caribbean before swinging north toward the North Carolina coast. In 1989, the Spanish Mustang Registry voted unanimously to include on its list the remaining mustangs on the Outer Banks. Registry inspectors have examined the horses in both Currituck herds and have pronounced them to be of the original Spanish strain.

A wild horse at Corolla

It was a Banker pony that played a pivotal role in one of the beloved legends of Currituck County and coastal North Carolina.

Throughout America's long quest for independence, the residents of Currituck talked often among themselves about the constant threat of British invasion. In late 1775, Lord Dunmore, the royal governor of Virginia, began marching British forces south from Norfolk in preparation for an invasion of northeastern North Carolina. Only North Carolina colonel Robert Howe's meager Continental Army forces at Great Bridge, Virginia, stood in the way of the invasion.

In the meantime, on a cold December night on Currituck Banks, a courageous sixteen-year-old girl, Betsy Dowdy, overheard a neighbor tell her father that a British invasion of Currituck was imminent unless Howe's men could be reinforced. From the conversation, Betsy learned that General William Skinner and his American forces encamped in Perquimans County knew nothing of Dunmore's secret advance. And then the neighbor expressed a fear that brought chills to Betsy: British invaders would round up all the Banker ponies and ship them away.

In a flash, Betsy scrawled a note to her father, walked outside into the frigid night, and mounted her favorite Banker pony, Black Bess. She galloped up the Banks, then turned west and swam the cold waters of Currituck Sound to the mainland peninsula. Through the Great Dismal Swamp she rode as fast as she could. Her route took her through Camden, Elizabeth City, and Hertford. As the new day dawned, the loyal mare and her rider arrived at General Skinner's camp.

No sooner had Betsy relayed the intelligence to Skinner than his army was on the march. His forces arrived in time to unite with Howe's soldiers to defeat Dunmore's army at the Battle of Great Bridge. To this day, Currituckers are proud to relate the story of the 51-mile ride of Betsy Dowdy on a frigid winter night to save her homeland.

The two most famous landmarks of Corolla—the Currituck Beach Lighthouse and the Whalehead Club—lie in the heart of the village just off N.C. 12. Turn west on the sandy lane between the landmarks and park in the spaces provided. Walk across the road to the lighthouse grounds.

In 1992, the Corolla tower earned the distinction of being the only lighthouse on the North Carolina coast open to the public. Since that time, the Cape Hatteras Lighthouse has also been opened.

For a nominal fee, visitors may climb the 214 steps of the spiral staircase leading to the top of the stately Currituck Beach Lighthouse. From the metal gallery circling the beacon, they are treated to a magnificent vista of the Whalehead Club, the village, the sound, and Currituck Banks.

In stark contrast to the other active lighthouses on the North Carolina coast, which are brightly painted with distinctive patterns, the Currituck Beach Lighthouse retains its natural red-brick color. But the lack of paint does not render the tower any less appealing than its neighbors to the south. Rather, many people believe that the least-visited of the state's sentinels of the sea is the most aesthetically pleasing.

In April 1873, while the lighthouse at Corolla was in its planning stages, the United States Lighthouse Board made its decision to paint the existing structures at Bodie Island, Cape Lookout, and Cape Hatteras in the patterns that continue to identify them. Subsequently, the decision was made to leave the new lighthouse unpainted.

The need for the Currituck tower had become apparent in October 1872 with the lighting of the new lighthouse at Bodie Island. Between Bodie Island and Cape Henry, Virginia, there remained an 80-mile stretch of coast without a lighthouse—the last dark spot for shipping on the southern Atlantic coast of the United States. To remedy this problem, the light at Currituck Beach was constructed in 1874–75. Using the prototype Cape Lookout Lighthouse as a pattern, workmen used 1.5 million red bricks barged in from Norfolk to craft the tower.

On December 1, 1875, the first-order lens of the new lighthouse was illuminated. Now fully automated, the light is maintained by the Coast Guard. Its 160,000-candlepower beacon, which flashes on for three seconds and off for seventeen, is visible for up to 19 miles.

From a hexagonal masonry base, the lighthouse rises 158 feet. It features an unusually large, elaborate entrance building, which once served as a keeper's workshop and fuel-storage area.

Three keeper's houses have served the lighthouse. One of them survives. A private, nonprofit organization has been granted a fifty-year lease in exchange for its restoration of the multistory Victorian house. Aided by the

Currituck Lighthouse

original blueprint of the house, which was located in the National Archives, workers are meticulously returning the structure to its past splendor.

Return to the parking area and walk south onto the grounds of the Whalehead Club.

From the top of the lighthouse, the Whalehead Club, named for a large sand dune that once towered nearby, resembles an elegant dollhouse. From the parking area, it looks out of place in one of the most remote villages of the Atlantic coast. Although time, the elements, and years of neglect have exacted a heavy toll on the magnificent estate, the Whalehead Club remains an imposing monument to a romantic bygone era of coastal North Carolina history.

Overlooking Currituck Sound, the mansion stands on property once owned by the Lighthouse Club, a hunt club founded by a group of Northern sportsmen in 1874. Years later, Edward Collins Knight, a wealthy businessman from Philadelphia, became a member of the club. By the time Knight was fifty years old, he had amassed a fortune from his holdings in the Pennsylvania Railroad, the American Sugar Refinery, and Knight's Publishing Company. Soon thereafter, he met a young French artist-actress, Amanda Marie Louise Label, who became his second wife. Their relationship was based not only on a mutual love of art, but also on a fondness for hunting. Knight attempted to have his wife admitted into the membership of the Lighthouse Club, but like all the other shooting clubs in the area, it steadfastly maintained a "no women allowed" policy.

When the opportunity presented itself in 1922, Knight purchased the Lighthouse Club property so that he could bring his bride to Currituck Banks to enjoy the fall hunting season. His purchase included the old clubhouse, as well as nearly eight thousand acres of sound-to-ocean land in a 5-mile stretch down the beach.

After the clubhouse was torn down, construction commenced on a mansion the likes of which the Outer Banks had never seen before, and has never seen since. The Knights selected a site within view of the lighthouse. A hydraulic dredge was brought in to create an artificial island with a promontory on which the mansion was to be erected. Nearly three years and more than $383,000 went into the completion of the grand estate. No ex-

The Whalehead Club

TOURING THE BACKROADS OF NORTH CAROLINA'S UPPER COAST

pense was spared. If a portion of the house did not meet with Mrs. Knight's approval, her husband would have it rebuilt to suit her tastes.

The three-story, 20,000-square-foot structure contained features never before heard of on the Outer Banks. Knight's private swimming pool mystified village residents, who could not understand why anyone would go to such an expense with the soothing waters of the sound and the ocean just a short walk away. And the full basement was an engineering marvel in an area where the water table is so high.

Knight's lavish mansion was built in the Italian style. Its five reddish brown chimneys were built at the request of Mrs. Knight, who wanted one more hearth than the club that had refused her admission. The copper-tile roof, now green with age, was punctuated by eighteen gables with handsome dormer windows. Four oversize picture windows, two on each side, provided unbounded views of the surrounding countryside. Patios were located on either side of the house on the first and second levels.

As impressive as the exterior was, the interior was even more breathtaking. Twenty rooms and twelve bathrooms were laid out on the three main floors. The walls were covered with corduroy panels, the floors with cork tiles; fine rugs were laid on top of the tiles. Sixty-three original oil paintings adorned the walls. Priceless antiques, including five grandfather clocks and Tiffany lamps and chandeliers signed by their maker, were located throughout the house.

Each of the bedrooms boasted a private bathroom fitted with solid brass plumbing, from which flowed fresh and salt water for the bathtubs. Edward Knight had a fancy for doors, as evidenced by the multitude of portals found within the mansion. Each of the interior doors was a special creation, artistically carved with a unique design. Some rooms had as many as four doors. Craftsmen also carved water lilies on the handsome molding around the twelve-foot ceilings, on the banister that climbs the wide stairway to the second floor, and on the elegant mahogany paneling found throughout the mansion.

To handle the household chores and to ensure the comfort of the Knights and their guests, a full-time staff of twelve servants was employed. All rooms were wired with bell buttons. An elevator carried baggage and other items to the upper floors and to the sixteen-room basement.

Two spectacular wooden-arch English-style bridges were constructed across the moatlike canal encircling the mansion. Just across the canal was a twelve-room caretaker's house. A large boathouse, built over the sound, was located a short distance from the caretaker's house.

Until they died within a month of each other in 1936, the Knights divided their time between their Northern home and their palace on Currituck Banks.

After the mansion had been vacant for four years, Ray T. Adams, a Washington, D.C., businessman, purchased it, all of its furnishings, and two thousand acres from ocean to sound for twenty-five thousand dollars. Local legend has it that Adams sold more than thirty thousand dollars' worth of antiques and silver from the mansion.

During World War II, Adams leased the estate to the Coast Guard for use as a training facility and patrol base. More than three hundred military personnel were housed in the old mansion. Adams's postwar plans to develop the property never came to fruition, and at his death, the property was sold to George T. McLean, an industrialist from Portsmouth, Virginia.

In 1959, McLean leased the mansion to a nonprofit foundation for use as a boys' summer school, known as Corolla Academy. Fifty to seventy-five boys from all over the nation attended the school during each of the three

The Whalehead Club

summers it operated at the estate. After the 1961 session, the academy suspended its operations at Corolla due to the apparent danger to which students would be exposed from rocket tests conducted nearby. In 1964, the foundation opened a similar school in Essex, England. Corolla-in-England continues to keep its doors open to students.

The rocket experiments that led to the demise of the school at the Whalehead Club provided a new use for the graceful mansion and grounds. The Atlantic Research Corporation, an aerospace firm from Alexandria, Virginia, acquired the property in 1962 for use as a headquarters for the development of gel-propellant fuel for the nation's fledgling space program. Working under a government contract, the company conducted top-secret rocket tests at the site for eight years. Launching pads from the operation are still visible in the area.

From 1969 until 1991, various owners proposed plans to develop the property, but none got much farther than the drawing board. But now, after many years of failed plans, there appears to be a bright future for the estate. When the mansion and the 28.5 acres of land around it went on the market in 1991, the Currituck County commissioners made the purchase for $2.4 million in order to preserve the historic structure and the significant salt marshes around it. Funds for the purchase came from revenues produced by the county's public-lodging occupancy tax.

Although the mansion, listed on the National Register of Historic Places, is badly in need of paint and other cosmetic improvements, it remains structurally sound. Once it is restored, it will be opened to the public, most appropriately, as the Currituck County Wildlife Museum. Mrs. Knight's hunting lodge will have come full circle.

On selected days, while workmen are busy restoring the tired old palace, guided tours of the safe portions on the first and second floors are offered for a small charge. Inside, the cork-covered floors show the effect of years of neglect, and the hallways, once covered with great works of art, are barren passageways to rooms that once knew happier days. Of the original furnishings, only three significant pieces remain: Mr. Knight's safe, the dining-room table, and a modified Louis XV grand piano. Of the three, the piano is the most important. Although it is in a terrible state of disrepair, the piano is being restored by the Steinway Company, its maker. When the

Edward Knight's safe, Whalehead Club

$21,000 restoration project is completed, the 1903-vintage instrument will be a certified museum piece with an anticipated value of $82,000.

Return to the lighthouse parking lot and drive west on the sandy road as it loops back around to N.C. 12. On this short route stands the village school that served the children of Corolla from 1903 to 1958. At the junction with N.C. 12 stands the original Kill Devil Hills Lifesaving Station, now restored as a real-estate office.

Proceed north on N.C. 12 to the end of the state road at the Ocean Hill subdivision. Here ends the tour.

To the north lies the Currituck Banks National Estuarine Research Reserve. This 960-acre tract of islands, marshes, maritime forest, dunes, and oceanfront was donated to the state by the Nature Conservancy in 1984. It is used for research. Adjoining the reserve is a portion of the 1,787-acre Currituck National Wildlife Refuge.

Former village school of Corolla

Still farther north, the remote developments of Swan Beach, North Swan Beach, and Carova Beach are clustered 13 miles from Corolla. At those remote spots, accessible only by four-wheel-drive vehicles at low tide, some property owners have chosen to build homes.

Although little evidence remains of its existence, a small community flourished near the current site of the three beach developments during the second half of the nineteenth century and the first half of the twentieth. Wash Woods, named for the hundreds of stumps of old cedar trees that may still be seen in the surf at low tide, was settled by some twenty families as a farming community before the Civil War. A lifesaving station and a United States Weather Bureau station, both established in 1879, provided employment for village residents and attracted new villagers. On January 27, 1907, a post office opened under the name of Deals. It was discontinued ten years later, and thereafter the community gradually became a ghost town. Only the stumps and the old lifesaving station survive from the days of Wash Woods.

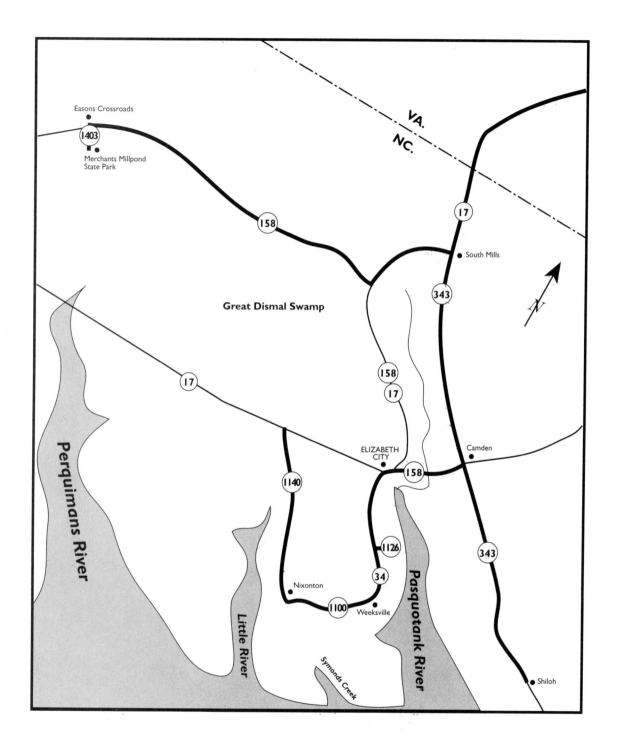

The Great Dismal Swamp Tour

This tour begins at Easons Crossroads, visits Merchants Millpond State Park, and moves east through the Great Dismal Swamp to the historic town of South Mills at the locks of the Dismal Swamp Canal. It then heads to Camden and Shiloh and leads visitors on a brief walking tour of Elizabeth City before turning south to Weeksville and the historically significant village of Nixonton.

Among the highlights of the tour are the geography, history, and legends of the Great Dismal Swamp, a Civil War love story from South Mills, the Camden County Courthouse, Shiloh Baptist Church, the historic district of Elizabeth City, and the Museum of the Albemarle.

Total mileage: approximately 102 miles.

This tour begins at the intersection of S.R. 1403 and U.S. 158 at the Gates County community of Easons Crossroads, located 8 miles south of the Virginia line.

Because of its remote, rural location on the western fringes of the Great Dismal Swamp, Gates County attracts fewer tourists than do most counties of the North Carolina coastal plain. Consequently, many coastal visitors miss the opportunity to enjoy one of the rarest ecological communities in the state at Merchants Millpond State Park.

Proceed south 1.1 miles on S.R. 1403 to the Millpond Access Area, one of the two entrances to the state park. Located here are two of the primary attractions of the 2,659-acre park: Merchants Millpond, a 760-acre impoundment on Bennetts Creek, and Lassiter Swamp, a beautiful, undisturbed, remote swamp. Though its botanical composition is different, this preserved swamp is as ecologically important as the famed Corkscrew Sanctuary in Florida and the Four Holes Swamp in South Carolina.

Located close to the parking lot at the Millpond Access Area are a number of visitor facilities, including a picnic ground, a boat ramp, an interpretive center with exhibits, and trailheads for canoe and hiking trails. This complex overlooks the beautiful millpond on the creek.

Bennetts Creek is formed by the junction of three swamps in the center of Gates County—Duke, Harrell, and Raynor swamps. It was named for Richard Bennett, governor of Virginia from 1652 to 1655. On the creek at the site of Merchants Millpond, Kinchen Norfleet built Norfleets Millpond in 1811. A year later, gristmills and a sawmill were completed, and by the turn of the century, the millpond had the largest complex of mills in the area. Although the wheat mill ceased operations after 1908, the other mills remained profitable, and a farmers' supply was constructed nearby. Quickly, the millpond site became the commercial center of the county. Thus, it acquired its present name.

The mills were successfully operated until World War II. After a succession of postwar owners, the millpond was purchased in 1961 by A. B. Coleman of Moyock. Coleman's concern over the wanton slaughter of swamp creatures led him to donate a 919-acre tract, including the millpond, to the state in June 1973. His public-spirited generosity led to the creation of the park. The Nature Conservancy acquired an additional tract of 925 acres for the park from Georgia-Pacific. Subsequent purchases by the state and an additional land gift from Coleman have brought the park acreage to its present total.

Since the park was opened to the public in April 1976, the state has done a masterful job of preserving the natural integrity of the area while improving access to the majestic wilderness. Two hiking trails at the pond

The Great Dismal Swamp

offer opportunities to see portions of the park. An excellent short loop trail near the picnic area leads hikers around a small peninsula jutting into the pond. And signs at the parking lot direct hikers to the trailhead for the 6.7-mile Millpond Loop Trail, which begins at the north end of the Bennetts Creek bridge; the dam and the concrete pilings of the old millhouse are visible from the bridge. From the old mill site, the trail follows the bank of the pond and then moves upland into a breathtaking forest of cypress, maple, oak, loblolly, pine, beech, and holly. At 1 mile, the trail crosses a boardwalk. A wide fire lane runs through the heart of the park, intersecting the circular route on the north and south.

Unquestionably, the best way to witness the splendor of the millpond and the swamp is by boat. Near the parking lot, canoe rentals are available at the edge of the millpond. A canoe tour of the millpond gives visitors a wonderful sample of the wide variety of flora and fauna within the park. Although the water depth is rarely greater than 8 feet, the millpond is the home of a complex of mature ecosystems. Much of the time, its dark, acidic waters are covered with a greenish red layer of floating duckweed. Small islands dot the placid pond, which is studded with heavily buttressed gum and cypress trees. One of the largest cypress trees in the entire South is located very close to the main channel of Bennetts Creek. It stands 117 feet tall and measures more than 8 feet in diameter.

Bats can be found roosting in clumps of Spanish moss hanging from the trees. And although they are rarely seen by humans, mink, black bear, and bobcats roam the shores. Beavers were introduced to the area in the 1930s, and their presence is apparent from the number of dams throughout the park. One beaver dam on the upper reaches of the pond near Lassiter Swamp measures twenty-one hundred feet in length.

A unique experience awaits the intrepid park visitor who is willing to paddle into the vast solitude of Lassiter Swamp. As the millpond begins to narrow, the forest closes in near the mouth of the swamp. Caution must be exercised in this isolated area, because the channel of Bennetts Creek becomes hard to ascertain. In the swamp, the water seems to have very little flow, appearing at times to be motionless.

Some 163 different species of plant life, including a virgin stand of bald cypress, are found within the recesses of the swamp. Many of the trees rising from the swamp tower more than a hundred feet. Most range in age from five hundred to a thousand years, though some of the oldest were standing when Jesus Christ lived.

One of the most awe-inspiring parts of the swamp is a place called the "Enchanted Forest." An ancient stand of tupelo gum contains the largest tree of the species in North Carolina. Knobs on the trunks and branches, caused by American mistletoe, which penetrates tree tissue, give the trees an eerie, distorted appearance.

From the Millpond Access Area, return to the intersection of S.R. 1403 and U.S. 158. Turn east on U.S. 158 and drive 0.3 mile to the main entrance of the park. An eye-appealing sign greets visitors at the highway. Rangers at the nearby park headquarters provide visitor information and maps. A family campground equipped with restrooms, a wash house, and drinking water is located beyond the headquarters building in a hardwood forest. Near the family campground, a short trail approximately 0.5 mile in length connects with Millpond Loop Trail. A primitive backpack camp is located on a short side trail.

Return to U.S. 158 and continue east for 19.6 miles to the Camden County town of South Mills. This scenic route passes through the heart of the Great Dismal Swamp.

More than two and a half centuries have passed since William Byrd gave America its first written description of the swamp with these words: "The ground of this swamp is a mere quagmire, trembling under the feet of those who walk upon it."

Though Byrd served as a commissioner of the historic survey of the dividing line between Virginia and North Carolina in 1728, he managed to avoid venturing into the swamp. He and the other commissioners made their way around its fringes and waited until the surveyors and their helpers came out the other side. Emerging from the great wilderness after an ordeal of several days, the haggard men of the survey crew became the first white men to have crossed the swamp. They reported that had it not been the dry season, the quagmire would have been impossible to pass over or through.

Despite his failure to penetrate the swamp, Byrd saw and heard enough about it to form an opinion about the "Dismal." He remarked, "Never was rum, that cordial of life, found more necessary than in this dirty place."

Today, the Great Dismal Swamp remains a forbidding place containing areas that have never been seen by the eyes of man. Many travelers on U.S. 158 and U.S. 17, the two primary highways that crisscross the vast jungle, pass through the swamp without ever knowing they have done so. Yet on either side of the roadway lies one of the most unexplored natural areas in North America, the northernmost link in the chain of large swamps of the mid-Atlantic coastal plain.

Drainage has reduced the size of the swamp from 2,200 square miles to its present size of 600 square miles. Nevertheless, the wet wilderness of marshes, peat bogs, lakes, and cypress forests encompasses a huge chunk of land in southeastern Virginia and northeastern North Carolina, measuring 20 miles long by 10 miles wide. Approximately the size of Rhode Island, the swamp engulfs nearly 300,000 acres.

There is an abundance of travel literature which leaves readers with the distinct impression that all or most of the Great Dismal Swamp is located in Virginia. To the contrary, nearly 60 percent of the swamp lies within the confines of the North Carolina counties of Gates, Perquimans, Pasquotank, Camden, and Currituck.

Scientists estimate the age of the Great Dismal at between six thousand and nine thousand years. Once under the sea, this natural treasure emerged as a landform when the continental shelf made its last significant shift.

Ironically, the Great Dismal is not a swamp in the true sense of the word. A conventional swamp is found in a low-lying area where flowing water collects and stagnates because of poor drainage. The stagnated water becomes polluted. Life abounds there, but it is parasitic in nature. However, the Great Dismal is higher than the surrounding countryside, resting on a hillside which is at least twenty feet above sea level. Rather than water flowing in, seven sizable rivers flow out.

Decay occurs in conventional swamps because of the warm, moist, and dark conditions characteristic of these areas. Warm and moist conditions also prevail in much of the Great Dismal. Water oozes from the spongy floor. Yet because of its high acidity, the chocolate-colored water does not promote decay. The tannic acid in the water comes from leaching from juniper and cypress trees.

Before the days of refrigeration, water from the swamp was a highly prized commodity on sailing ships. Chemically sterile, the water stayed fresh for long periods when stored in wooden kegs. When Admiral Perry made his famous "Open Door Trip to Japan" in 1852, he carried Dismal Swamp water on his ships. Union ships carried large quantities of Dismal Swamp water during the Civil War in order to avoid sailing back to Washington, D.C. Those who have tasted the dark brown water claim that it is quite drinkable. They liken its taste to sassafras tea, which is also rich in tannic acid.

Because the water in the Great Dismal inhibits decay, dead plant matter accumulates as it falls onto the floor of the wilderness. After countless years, the packed accumulation of plant debris forms peat. The Great Dismal is one of the few places in all of North America where peat is still being formed. Many large trees have fallen and become embedded in the peat, only to be dug out later and used as timber. Some of the preserved trees are believed to be centuries old. At some places in the swamp, scientists have even detected the formation of coal.

When the water table drops in the Great Dismal during times of drought, the peat dries out, making it susceptible to fire. Once the peat catches fire, the flames spread outward and downward until they reach water. Often, they burn underground for several feet.

Peat fires of several months' duration are not uncommon. A terrible conflagration erupted during a drought in 1923 and burned for three years. At the height of the Nazi U-boat menace during World War II, United States military officials were dismayed to discover that the battle against enemy submarines was being hindered by the peat fires. Smoke from smoldering peat bogs floated out over the North Carolina and Virginia coasts, thereby limiting the visibility of lookout aircraft. A virtual army of firefighters was sent into the Great Dismal to drown the fires with dark swamp water.

Naturalists and other scientists value the Great Dismal as one of the best outdoor laboratories in the world. A temperate climate characterized by long, humid summers and mild winters has caused contradictions of nature in the swamp and the surrounding countryside. Annual rainfall averages over fifty inches in the interior, but just over twenty inches on farmlands on the fringes of the swamp. Due to the swamp's location on the north-south isothermal line, certain plants and animals here are not found farther south, while others do not grow farther north. For example, the venomous cottonmouth water moccasin does not exist north of the James River. Plants which reach the limits of their range in the swamp include the longleaf pine, the cotton gum, the French mulberry tree, and Spanish moss.

Brave adventurers who dare to make their way into the junglelike interior of the swamp find a world of weird splendor. The varied plant life ranges from aromatic wildflowers to a log fern which traces its origins back to the Ice Age.

Strong concentrations of swamp forest trees are found throughout the wilderness. When men first entered the swamp with axes and saws to harvest timber, trees stood 150 feet tall and measured 16 feet or more around the base. Of all the indigenous trees of the Great Dismal, the Atlantic white cedar, known to locals as the juniper, has most often fallen prey to timber companies. Deep in the heart of the swamp, a few rare virgin stands of the tree can still be seen.

Close to the south end of the swamp, the area known as the "Green Sea" appears today much as it did when William Byrd so named it. Patches of green cane and rushes grow in profusion, some plants towering as high as fifteen feet. Some cane stalks measure an inch and a half in diameter.

The southern locks of the Dismal Swamp Canal

U.S. 158 merges with U.S. 17 near the Camden County village of South Mills. Follow U.S. 17 Business north into the village to the southern lock of the Dismal Swamp Canal.

South Mills has been an outpost in the great swamp since the eighteenth century. Organized before 1800, the community was originally called New Lebanon, because of the magnificent junipers that once grew in the adjacent portion of the Great Dismal Swamp; apparently, the name was a Biblical reference to the tall cedars of Lebanon. A post office was established under the name of New Lebanon in 1815 and operated as such until 1839, when the name was changed to South Mills. The new name was a reference to the mill wheels turned by the waters pouring over a spillway in the village.

South Mills is best known as the site of the southern locks of the Dismal Swamp Canal, an ancient 22-mile watercourse that today serves as an alternate route on the Intracoastal Waterway. Its wild, beautiful scenery makes the canal a worthwhile detour for pleasure boaters on their north-south pilgrimage on the Waterway.

On his visit to the fringes of the Great Dismal, William Byrd proposed the construction of a canal running completely through the swamp. Despite his exaggerated description of the desolate nature of the swamp, Byrd possessed great business acumen. He foresaw the value of a water outlet to Hampton Roads from the agricultural lands of the North Carolina and Virginia colonies. Nothing came of the proposal.

The seed for the actual Dismal Swamp Canal was planted by Hugh Williamson of Edenton in letters to George Washington while the Continental Congress was in session. After a commission appointed by Virginia governor Patrick Henry returned a favorable report on the canal project in 1785, President Washington gave his blessing. Following legislative approval by Virginia in 1787 and North Carolina in 1790, the Dismal Swamp Company was hired to construct the canal. Using slave labor, the private company began its work in 1793. Money appropriated for the project was exhausted in 1796. Nonetheless, parts of the canal had been completed at each end.

The canal was dug entirely by hand, without benefit of dynamite or dredges. During the construction process, muck was shoveled from the canal into a high bank adjacent to it. Workers packed the muck into a towpath, which became a toll road in 1804. Stagecoach service was commenced along the route from Norfolk to Elizabeth City.

When the British navy blockaded the Atlantic coast during the War of 1812, the fledgling American government quickly came to the realization that, if completed, the Dismal Swamp Canal could be an invaluable source of interstate transportation. Once again funds were appropriated, and the canal was completed. It connected Deep Creek, Virginia, at the southern end of the Elizabeth River, with Joyce's Creek, a tributary of the Pasquotank River.

In 1828, the canal was widened to forty feet and deepened to four and a half feet with funds provided by the federal government and Virginia. Two significant events occurred shortly after the completion of the improvements. Alexander Macomb, a high-ranking federal engineer, formulated a plan for an "inland waterway" which would run from Norfolk to Beaufort. His idea, ahead of its time, was the forerunner of the modern Intracoastal Waterway. Of more direct significance to the canal was the safe passage of the *Cordorus* through the locks. This ship was the first vessel with a metal hull built in the United States.

From 1839 to the beginning of the Civil War, the canal enjoyed its golden age as a commercial waterway. During that time, large freighters, stern-wheel steamboats, barges, and schooners plied its waters. As the Civil War loomed on the horizon, the canal began to suffer a decrease in traffic, the result of the completion of the rival Albemarle and Chesapeake Canal in 1859. This new cut, which ran from Great Bridge, Virginia, to Coinjock in Currituck County, was virtually free of locks and the customary delays that plagued the Dismal Swamp Canal.

During the Civil War, the Dismal route was an important highway for Confederate traffic until it fell under Union control. Following the war, and for much of the remainder of the nineteenth century, competition and neglect took their toll on the canal. But when the Lake Drummond Canal and Water Company purchased the canal in 1888, the new owner immediately set about dredging, widening, and improving it. Three locks were eliminated, leaving only the northern lock at Deep Creek, Virginia, and the southern lock at the current tour stop.

A short period of prosperity followed, until the federal government purchased the Albemarle and Chesapeake route in 1913, made it toll-free, and included it on the primary route of the Intracoastal Waterway. Sixteen years later, the Dismal route was likewise purchased by the federal government. Its depth was increased to nine feet and its width to fifty feet. New concrete and steel locks were installed at the northern and southern locations. Control and maintenance of the waterway fell to the United States Army Corps of Engineers.

In recent years, the very existence of the canal has been threatened. Due to dwindling usage and federal budget constraints, proponents of the Dismal route have found it increasingly difficult to get appropriations through Congress for its operation and maintenance. Earlier in the century, the lock at South Mills was manned twenty-four hours a day. Now, it is opened only four times daily.

From the lock, continue north on U.S. 17 Business, which merges back into U.S. 17.

Along the 8 miles to the Virginia line, the highway parallels the canal, which has survived war, competition, and economic woes for two centuries. In recognition of its historic importance, the canal was listed on the National Register of Historic Places in 1988.

The Welcome Center for traffic on the Dismal Swamp Canal and U.S. 17

To encourage travel on the canal, the North Carolina Division of Transportation opened a welcome center for canal traffic in May 1989. Located approximately 5 miles north of South Mills on a well-landscaped lot between the highway and the canal, the center has overnight docking facilities.

It is approximately 3 miles from the welcome center to the Virginia line. If you would like to make a brief side trip across the border, continue 5 miles north on U.S. 17 to the canal entrance to the 3,180-acre Lake Drummond. This magnificent oval-shaped lake is the centerpiece of the Great Dismal Swamp National Wildlife Refuge.

The Great Dismal Swamp National Wildlife Refuge is managed by the United States Fish and Wildlife Service. Encompassing 106,000 acres in Camden, Pasquotank, and Gates counties and two Virginia counties, it is the largest refuge of its kind from Maine to North Carolina. It was established in 1973 after Union Camp Corporation donated most of the acreage.

Annually, some fifteen thousand visitors come to the refuge. Public access to the Great Dismal Swamp is limited. No motor vehicles are allowed in the refuge. Visitor access is by foot, bicycle, or boat. There is a maze of more than 140 miles of unpaved roads in the vast wilderness. Primitive camping, boating, and picnic facilities are provided just north of the state line at the feeder canal for Lake Drummond.

Adjoining the Great Dismal Swamp National Wildlife Refuge is the Dismal Swamp Natural Area, owned and managed by North Carolina as part of its state parks system. Located primarily in Camden County, this natural area covers 14,344 acres of the swamp. Currently, there are no facilities and no resident staff. Prospective visitors must make an appointment with a ranger for a guided tour. Nearly 25 miles of trails have been laid out, but only experienced hikers should use them. Permits are required for hiking and camping in the interior portions of the preserve.

From the state line, turn around and begin retracing your route back to South Mills on U.S. 17.

Much of the human history of the Great Dismal Swamp has been played out in this area near the state line. Nearly thirty-five years after William Byrd got his first taste of the swamp, a thirty-one-year old soldier, surveyor, and businessman from Virginia made his first visit to the Great Dismal on

May 25, 1763. George Washington came to the swamp to inspect the nearly fifty thousand acres in Virginia and North Carolina granted to a group of land and timber speculators known as "Adventurers for Draining the Dismal Swamp." Among Washington's associates in the enterprise were a number of his relatives, as well as Patrick Henry and Richard Caswell, later governor of North Carolina. These men envisioned huge profits flowing from the reclamation of land from the swamp.

Access road to the Great Dismal Swamp National Wildlife Refuge

From 1763 to 1768, Washington made five trips to the swamp. Deeds for his Dismal Swamp holdings in North Carolina are recorded in Gates and Perquimans counties. His experience with the wilderness area produced an opinion in sharp contrast to that of Byrd. In a letter to a friend, Washington described the Dismal as "a glorious paradise, abounding in wildfowl and game." Although he never became a rich man from the venture, Washington's optimism about the area never waned.

A hotel, the Brickhouse Plantation, was built along the canal in Camden County in 1802. Located less than 3 miles south of the state line, its remote location in the swamp made it a popular place for honeymooners.

In January 1830, a second hotel, the Lake Drummond Hotel, was constructed on the canal. Built to straddle the state line, the structure soon acquired a notorious reputation as a place of rendezvous for gamblers, duelists, and elopers.

Throughout most of its existence, the Lake Drummond Hotel was better known as "The Halfway House." An early advertisement for the hotel read, "Marriage parties can at all times be accommodated to their utmost wish—in half an hour after their arrival, the blushing bride salutes her wedded lord."

Duelists were attracted to this swamp outpost because they could face each other and fire across the state line. Authorities discovered that it was nearly impossible to bring the combatants to justice. If arrest were threatened, the wanted man could simply step across the state line by walking across the hall or fleeing into the nearby swamp.

Since man's earliest entry into the Dismal, the swamp has been the origin of many strange legends. Unusual sights and bloodcurdling sounds reported throughout the morass have inspired an assortment of tales involving spirits, witches, ghosts, ghouls, and other supernatural beings.

One of the most intriguing legends of the Dismal involves a recurring theme of coastal legends: lost treasure. According to the legend, a lost French payroll is the cause of the strange French voices often heard emanating from the North Carolina portion of the swamp. During the American Revolution, a French warship laden with gold to pay French troops in America was forced to seek shelter at Hampton Roads because of a severe storm. Once inside the protected waters of the harbor, the ship hurried up the Elizabeth River to elude nearby British ships. In the process, a man-of-war sighted the enemy vessel. It began pursuit, forcing the French ship farther up the river. Finally, the water became so shallow that the captain ordered his crew to load the gold into smaller boats and burn the ship.

Relentlessly, the British pursued their adversaries. In order to avoid losing the treasure, the French sailors hid the gold in the river and on its banks. Fleeing into the Dismal, they were finally overtaken by their attackers. Furious hand-to-hand combat ensued, and none of the French sailors survived the fight to provide the location of the gold. Adherents of the legend caution that swamp visitors can still hear the voices of the French crew echoing across the forbidding wilderness on some evenings.

In addition to George Washington, William Byrd, and Patrick Henry, the Dismal has been visited by many famous people. Some experts have speculated that the first white man to see the swamp was Leif Ericson around 1000 A.D. Presidents Monroe and Jackson visited the swamp while they were in office.

The mystique of the swamp has lured many authors of renown. In 1796, the Duke de la Rochefoucauld, a world-famous writer and traveler, toured portions of the swamp and the new canal. Sir Thomas Moore, the Irish poet and British consul from Bermuda, traveled into the Dismal and visited "The Halfway House." From his experience, he wrote his famous poem "The Lake of Dismal Swamp."

American authors later enjoyed using the swamp as a subject. Henry Wadsworth Longfellow composed his poem "The Slave of Dismal Swamp" in 1842 aboard a ship on a transatlantic crossing. Fourteen years later, Harriet Beecher Stowe introduced her novel *Dred, A Tale of the Great Dismal Swamp*. And though the story has never been corroborated, it has long been reported that Edgar Allen Poe wrote "The Raven" while visiting the swamp.

Notwithstanding the fact that he never wrote anything about the swamp, the most famous American poet of the modern era owed his life to the Dismal. Robert Frost came to the swamp in 1894 a dejected man, having been recently jilted by his girlfriend. By the time he arrived, the disconsolate young man had decided to take his life. Fortunately, the budding poet fell in love with his surroundings and found the people kind and friendly. Consequently, Frost changed his mind about suicide and decided to sojourn in the wilderness. His repose in the Dismal provided the opportunity for him to take stock of his life. Fully restored and with a new zest for living, Frost returned to his home in Lowell, Massachusetts, where he married the girl who had earlier rejected him.

U.S. 17 intersects N.C. 343 in South Mills. Proceed south on N.C. 343. It is 3 miles to the site of a significant Civil War skirmish, though nothing is visible to travelers on N.C. 343.

In what is known as the Battle of South Mills, nine hundred Confederates forced the retreat of the brigade of Union general Jesse L. Reno after a spirited fight of four hours on April 19, 1862. By repelling Reno's forces, the Southern troops prevented the destruction of the lock at South Mills. A state historical marker in South Mills calls attention to the battle. Some of the breastworks and trenches of the battlefield can be found today.

Historical marker for the Battle of South Mills

It was among these entrenchments that a tragic and heartwarming story had its beginnings. During the height of the battle, as the two armies fought it out, a young woman with a baby in her arms ran toward an old house in the field that separated the two warring forces. From his vantage point in the Confederate works, Henry Dixon, the son of a wealthy South Carolina planter, watched in horror as the house was riddled by cannon fire about the time the woman reached it.

Dixon scampered across the battlefield in an attempt to rescue the helpless souls, but a cannon blast had struck the woman in the face, killing her instantly. Beside the woman, the Southern soldier found the baby covered in her mother's blood, but alive. He gathered up the child and placed her in the custody of the Confederate surgeon, Dr. R. A. Lewis. Following the skirmish, Dr. Lewis was busy on the battlefield treating the wounded. There, he discovered the lifeless body of the child's mother. From her neck, he removed a locket in order to save it for the infant.

At the conclusion of the war three years later, Dr. Lewis and Henry Dixon returned to their homes. In Richmond, Dr. Lewis busied himself with his profession and with rearing the orphan rescued at the Battle at South Mills. Henry Dixon's homecoming was less promising. He found the graves of his parents and the burned ruins of the family plantation—the result of Sherman's infamous March to the Sea. Even more tragic was the absence of his wife, Mary, and their child. Friends could only tell him that Mary had gone to Norfolk with the child during the war to find her husband.

A fruitless search ended in Norfolk when Dixon depleted his meager resources. Back in South Carolina, he worked tirelessly to resurrect the old plantation from the ashes. Renewed prosperity allowed Dixon to return to Norfolk to resume the search. A month of despair followed. As the dejected man prepared to depart for home, he stopped in Richmond to call on his old army buddy, Dr. R. A. Lewis.

En route to the Lewis home, Dixon paused at a school where a little girl was playing with other children. She told Dixon that her name was May Darling and that she lived with Dr. Lewis.

At the Lewis home, Dixon learned that May Darling was not the girl's real name. Dr. Lewis's wife had given her that name when the physician brought the orphan to Richmond. Dixon's army friend then handed him the locket taken from the dead woman on the North Carolina battlefield.

With shaking hands, quivering lips, and tears flowing down his cheeks, Dixon opened the locket. On one side was a picture of May Darling and on the other a picture of Henry Dixon. Henry and Mary Dixon had been reunited just seconds too late on that Camden County battlefield in the spring of 1862. The baby Henry had risked his life to save was his own daughter.

It is 10 miles from the battlefield site south to Camden, the county seat of Camden County. On this scenic route along the western edge of the county, it becomes evident that Camden is a very rural county. Were it not for its Albemarle neighbor, Chowan County, and Clay County in western North Carolina, Camden County would be the smallest county in land area in the state. Most of its 220 square miles is lowland ranging from two to twelve feet above sea level. Shaped like a finger pointing toward Albemarle Sound, Camden County is bounded by water on three sides: the North

Camden County Courthouse

River on the east, Albemarle Sound on the south, and the Pasquotank River on the west.

Located at the intersection of N.C. 343 and U.S. 158 near the eastern shore of the Pasquotank River, Camden—or Camden Courthouse, as the county seat is known—bespeaks the rural nature of Camden County. It is a rarity—an unincorporated seat of county government. Coastal visitors often hurry through Camden en route to the Outer Banks without stopping to take a look at the smallest county seat in the state.

An interesting ensemble of historic homes and buildings lines N.C. 343 and U.S. 158. There are, unfortunately, few reminders of the earliest days of the village. It was settled as early as 1740 and was known for the next fifty-two years as Plank Bridge. In 1790, Plank Bridge reached the zenith of its importance when it was made an official port of entry. Two years later, the village was incorporated as Jonesborough. With the loss of its port-of-entry status to Elizabeth City across the river, the village declined in importance. Its name was changed to Camden Courthouse in the 1840s.

The most prominent of the existing landmarks is the county courthouse, located on N.C. 343 just north of its intersection with U.S. 158. Completed in 1847, this magnificent Greek Revival structure is reminiscent of the architecture of the Deep South. Its front entrance, highlighted by four massive columns on brick piers, faces the road. For many years after the structure was built, the ground floor was used to quarter horses.

Located adjacent to the courthouse, the restored Camden Jail was constructed in 1910. Among its unusual features is an iron cellblock, or "bullpen," surrounded by a narrow catwalk on the second floor.

On the east side of the road within sight of the courthouse stands the imposing clapboard Masonic Lodge, built in 1856 as a combination lodge and school. Near the lodge is a dwelling erected by Noah Burfoot around 1856.

From the courthouse, proceed south on N.C. 343 for 6.3 miles through the fertile farmland bordering the Pasquotank River to the old village of Shiloh.

Originally known as Billet's Ridge, after Daniel Billet, who settled in the area before 1694, the name was changed to Danson's Manor after 1696.

The name change resulted from a grant of 3,640 acres of land to John Danson, the son-in-law of Governor John Archdale. From the middle of the eighteenth century until 1812, when the present name was adopted, the community was known as Mill Town, after a group of water mills that once stood on a nearby bluff overlooking the river.

Shiloh took its name from its most famous landmark: Shiloh Baptist Church. Organized in 1727, it is the oldest Baptist church in North Carolina. Paul Palmer, an itinerant Baptist minister and church organizer from Maryland, was the founder of the church. His evangelical work began in Chowan County, but a church predating the Shiloh church disbanded in 1732. Originally, the church at Shiloh was known as "the Church in the House of William Burgess." In the churchyard is the grave of Dempsey Burgess, an officer in the Continental Army and a member of the Continental Congresses of 1775 and 1779.

Retrace your route to Camden via N.C. 343. Along the way are side roads leading to the small riverfront communities of Elizabeth City Beach and Taylor Beach.

At the intersection of N.C. 343 and U.S. 158 in Camden, turn west on U.S. 158 for the 3.2-mile drive to Elizabeth City via an ancient causeway and the Pasquotank River Bridge.

Near the causeway is the old Sawyer Cemetery. Here lies the grave of Lemuel Sawyer, an eight-term United States congressman. Sawyer was the author of *Blackbeard*, an 1824 comedy about the infamous North Carolina pirate. He was the first native North Carolinian to write a drama using local materials. A state historical marker honoring Sawyer stands along the highway.

Adjacent to the cemetery is the site of Lamb's Ferry. From 1779—when a franchise was granted to Colonel Gideon Lamb—until 1912, the Lamb family operated a ferry providing access across the river at this point. Near the pecan orchard to the south stood the fine home of Enoch Sawyer, where President James Monroe was once a guest.

At the Pasquotank River, Camden County gives way to Pasquotank County. Much like its neighbor to the east, Pasquotank is a rather long, narrow strip of land extending into the sound. Much of its 229 square miles of land is extremely flat, averaging only three feet above sea level. Ironically, the highest point in the county is located in the Great Dismal Swamp near the Gates County line. The population base of the most populous county of the North Albemarle region lies in the southern half of the county.

From the bridge, you will enjoy a spectacular view of the Pasquotank River, which forms in northwestern Camden County at the junction of the dark swamp waters of two streams, Moccasin Track and The Horseshoe. The Pasquotank's 40-mile run to Albemarle Sound is relatively narrow until the river makes a horseshoe turn just north of the bridge. There, it widens substantially, taking on the appearance of a bay as it approaches the sound. From the time the North Albemarle region was settled, the Pasquotank has been the major access to the sound for inhabitants of the region. Today, mariners enter the Dismal Swamp Canal route of the Intracoastal Waterway through the river.

The bridge itself is a historic structure. Since the early 1930s, the concrete and steel drawbridge has provided the only vehicular access across the Pasquotank. To oversee the construction of the bridge, the state selected Sam Liles, a very able engineer who later achieved international fame. In the 1960s, he superintended the Chesapeake Bay Bridge–Tunnel project, a modern engineering feat without rival. Liles's engineering handiwork on the Pasquotank allows travelers to sample a postcard view of Elizabeth City during the crossing.

Before touring the historic streets of the downtown area, there are two significant stops on the outskirts of town.

After crossing the bridge, continue on U.S. 158 as it heads west along Elizabeth Street for six blocks, then turns north on North Road Street in the heart of the old river town. Approximately 0.9 mile from where U.S. 158 turns onto North Road Street, you will reach a junction with U.S. 17 (Hughes Boulevard). Turn left, or south, onto U.S. 17. It is 3.6 miles to the Museum of the Albemarle, a regional branch of the North Carolina Museum of History.

Crammed inside the one-story brick building is a wide array of interesting exhibits detailing the history of the Albemarle region. Included among the holdings are Indian artifacts, lumbering and farming relics, Coast Guard memorabilia, nautical antiques, old firefighting equipment, and wildfowl decoys. A slide presentation is available upon request. Admission is free,

Museum of the Albemarle

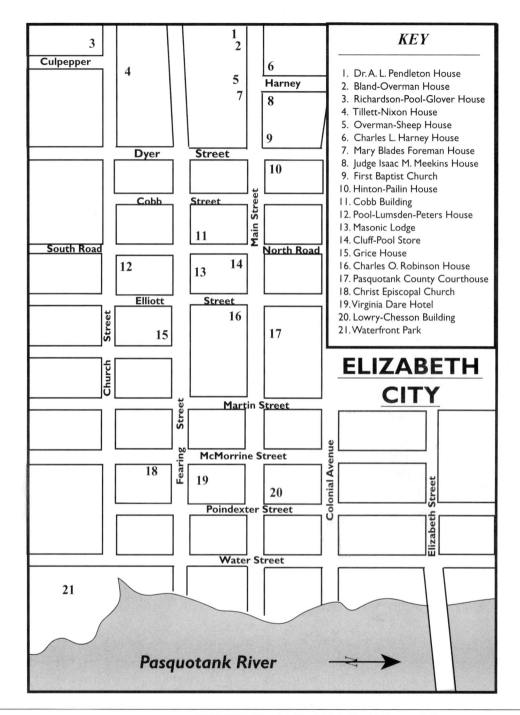

KEY

1. Dr. A. L. Pendleton House
2. Bland-Overman House
3. Richardson-Pool-Glover House
4. Tillett-Nixon House
5. Overman-Sheep House
6. Charles L. Harney House
7. Mary Blades Foreman House
8. Judge Isaac M. Meekins House
9. First Baptist Church
10. Hinton-Pailin House
11. Cobb Building
12. Pool-Lumsden-Peters House
13. Masonic Lodge
14. Cluff-Pool Store
15. Grice House
16. Charles O. Robinson House
17. Pasquotank County Courthouse
18. Christ Episcopal Church
19. Virginia Dare Hotel
20. Lowry-Chesson Building
21. Waterfront Park

ELIZABETH CITY

Pasquotank River

and workshops on local history and archaeology are offered from time to time.

Retrace your route on U.S. 17 and continue past the junction with U.S. 158. It is 5.2 miles from the Museum of the Albemarle to S.R. 1345 (Brickhouse Lane). Turn right onto S.R. 1345 and drive 0.6 mile to the end of the narrow lane. Take caution: the road leads directly into the Pasquotank River.

Here in this placid setting, at 182 Brickhouse Lane, stands the Brick House, one of the most historic houses in northeastern North Carolina. Because Edward Teach—Blackbeard—used the backwaters of the North Carolina coast as his base of operations during his reign of mayhem on Atlantic shipping, countless places up and down the coast have been rumored to be his former hiding spot. And so it is with the Brick House. Local tradition claims that this stately house was once the headquarters of Blackbeard. According to legend, the basement was used by the pirate as a dungeon for prisoners taken during sea raids. A secret tunnel, now closed, led from the basement to the adjacent river. Through this passage, Blackbeard is alleged to have escaped to his waiting ship.

Many historians disbelieve the Blackbeard legend, for architectural evidence indicates that the house was not built until well after the pirate's death. Only a small, circular slab of granite sunken near the steps appears to be from Blackbeard's time; it is dated 1709 and bears the initials *E. T.* (For more information about Blackbeard, see The Ocracoke Tour, pages 253–57, The Northern Pamlico River Tour, pages 291–94, and The Southern Pamlico River Tour, pages 329–30.)

Regardless of its possible connection to the pirate, the structure is an outstanding example of the home of a wealthy colonial planter and is of enormous historic significance. Experts believe it to be the oldest existing structure in Pasquotank County. It was added to the National Register of Historic Places in 1971.

Set on a low bluff overlooking the river, the one-and-a-half-story house is believed to have been built in the 1750s by Robert Munden, a member of the Colonial Assembly. It rests on a raised basement containing a massive fireplace and oven. Unfortunately, the interior of the main floor was removed in 1935 for use in a private residence in Delaware. Since that time, meticulous restoration efforts have brought the main floor back to its original appearance through the use of salvaged materials from existing Georgian- and Federal-style structures in the region.

The house takes its name from its end walls, which are built of mixed brick and stone. Its five-bay front and rear facades are covered with weatherboarding. This "brick-end" style was common in seventeenth-century Virginia. There is some evidence that the house was not originally meant to be of that design but so resulted when the end walls and massive chimneys consumed a quantity of brick that was supposed to have covered the entire house.

Great pains were taken in the planning of the house to provide for defense against Indian raids. On one side of the mantel in the spectacular banquet hall is a closet with a secret opening into the basement. Stalls in the basement, constructed of cedar and juniper from nearby forests, were used to shelter ponies and other valuable animals from Indian attacks. A smaller room to the rear of the banquet hall contains a closet equipped with an unusual sliding panel. When opened, the panel reveals the solid brick wall of a secret inner closet extending the entire length of the house. This inner sanctum provided a hiding place for the inhabitants and their valuables during Indian rampages.

Over the years, various tales that the house is haunted have circulated throughout the area. Privately owned, the house is not open to the public.

Return on U.S. 17 to its intersection with Road Street (U.S. 158). Turn left and follow Road Street south to its intersection with Ehringhaus Street. Turn east on Ehringhaus Street and drive 5 blocks to the historic Elizabeth City waterfront. Park near the scenic waterfront park to begin a brief walking tour.

Walk two blocks north on Water Street to the intersection with Fearing Street. During the late eighteenth century, Betsy Tooley's Tavern, the first combination inn and tavern in Elizabeth City, stood at the foot of Fearing Street.

No sooner had construction begun on the Dismal Swamp Canal in 1793 than the North Carolina General Assembly, meeting at Fayetteville, enacted legislature to establish a town at "the Narrows of the Pasquotank," where port facilities and a customs office had opened in 1722. Commissioners were appointed to purchase fifty acres of land from Adam and Elizabeth Tooley, and the town of Redding (sometimes shown as Reading) was laid out. Though the source of the name is uncertain, it is believed to have come from an early prominent family in the area. In 1794, the legislature changed the name to Elizabeth Town. The new name may have been intended to honor early settlers from Elizabeth County, Virginia. Or it may have been intended to honor Queen Elizabeth or Elizabeth Tooley. Tradition has it that it honors Elizabeth Tooley, the tavern owner who donated most of the land for the new town.

From Betsy Tooley's generosity has emerged the vibrant modern town on the Pasquotank. Construction began on a courthouse and jail in 1799, as a result of the town's selection as the seat of county government. Hotels, shops, and other commercial enterprises sprang up almost overnight to meet the needs of county residents who came to town for court and other governmental business.

By 1801, the North Carolina General Assembly came face to face with a growing problem confronting the Pasquotank county seat. Its name was identical to a town established in 1773 in Bladen County. Consequently, Elizabeth Town gave way to Elizabeth City.

Increased federal involvement in the construction of the Dismal Swamp Canal led to its completion in 1828. Elizabeth City was one of the primary beneficiaries of the project. In its edition of October 21, 1831, the *Elizabeth City Star* termed the city the "Eastern Emporium of North Carolina."

But completion of the Albemarle and Chesapeake Canal in the late 1850s brought devastating results to the Elizabeth City economy. Much of the ship traffic that had once called on Elizabeth City began choosing the new, deeper canal, located 25 miles northeast.

On the eve of the Civil War, the population of the town was approximately nine hundred. During the first year of the war, Elizabeth City was a beehive of activity. With the Union blockade off the North Carolina coast, badly needed supplies were funneled into Virginia through the North Carolina sounds and the Dismal Swamp Canal. This newfound economic prosperity was short-lived, however, because the defeat of the small North Carolina navy on February 10, 1862, just a few miles downriver resulted in the Federal occupation of the town for the duration of the war. So terrifying

was the approach of the enemy that the sheriff and many citizens torched their homes and some public buildings, including the courthouse. Ironically, this self-destruction was the only physical damage suffered by the town for the remainder of the war.

With the arrival of the railroad in 1881, Elizabeth City began to enjoy unparalleled industrial, commercial, and residential growth. At the time, its population was approximately twenty-five hundred, making it the tenth-largest city in the state.

In 1915, as its population neared nine thousand, local business leaders boasted that the bustling city could become the largest city in North Carolina within twenty-five years. Much of this optimism was fueled by Elizabeth City's status as a mini-metropolis in the heart of a rural region. Farmers not only shopped in the city, but brought their crops there as well. Soybeans, now one of the most significant cash crops in the state and nation, were processed commercially for the first time in the United States at a facility in Elizabeth City in December 1915. A state historical marker on Ehringhaus Street calls attention to the milestone.

Although the dynamic growth predicted for the town never materialized, Elizabeth City began to use its location to boost its appeal to tourists following World War II. As the 1940s melted into the 1950s, improved roads made the Outer Banks accessible to tourists from all parts of the country. Unable to compete with other coastal towns like Edenton, Bath, and Beaufort in terms of antiquity, Elizabeth City was finally able to offer a challenge for the tourist dollar.

Today, "Old Betsy," as she is sometimes called, remains the commercial, political, and social kingpin of the Albemarle region. Old and new stand side by side. Portions of the waterfront are picture perfect, while others are eyesores. The town's physical size and the quality and quantity of its amenities are far greater than would ordinarily be supported by a city of fewer than twenty thousand residents.

A large majority of the city's most important structures survived the conflagration started by citizens during the Civil War. Now, a magnificent assemblage of nineteenth-century houses and commercial buildings makes up the thirty-block Elizabeth City Historic District. Listed on the National Register of Historic Places, the district features a variety of architectural styles, including Greek Revival, Queen Anne, and Colonial Revival. A short walk along the streets of the district will give you a sense of the cosmopolitan atmosphere that has pervaded the city for many years.

From Water Street, turn west onto Fearing Street. After two blocks, you will reach McMorrine Street, where the Virginia Dare Hotel towers over the city. Since its opening on November 11, 1927, the nine-story, hundred-room building has claimed the honor as the first and only skyscraper of the Albemarle. William Lee Stoddard, a nationally prominent hotel architect from New York, designed the Colonial Revival structure, which was once among the finest hotels in the southeastern United States.

Valiant Decorations and Furniture of Baltimore, Philadelphia, and Paris decorated and furnished the interior of the once-grand hotel. Its spacious lobby, accented in brass, and its dining room remain virtually intact. However, the former ballroom was lost to history when the hotel was converted to apartments in the 1980s.

At the corner of McMorrine and Fearing streets stands Christ Episcopal Church. Not only is this the most beautiful church in the city, it is the oldest religious structure as well. Built in 1857, the handsome, ivy-clad Gothic Revival building was designed by J. Crawford Nelson of Baltimore.

Virginia Dare Hotel

Among its outstanding features are the three-story corner stair tower and the exquisite stained-glass windows illustrating the Beatitudes.

Continue 3 blocks west on Fearing Street to the Grice House, located at 207 East Fearing. This two-story Queen Anne house was constructed in 1885.

Follow Fearing Street 1 block farther west. At 100 East Fearing stands the city's first Masonic lodge. Now used for storage, this narrow, two-story late Federal–Greek Revival structure was built by the Masons in 1825.

At the intersection of Fearing and South Road streets, turn left on South Road. At 111 South Road, the L-shaped two-story Cobb Building is one of a small number of combination residence-store structures surviving from antebellum North Carolina. Historians believe the Greek Revival structure was erected in the late 1840s.

Proceed south for 1 block on South Road Street. Two of the finest homes in the city grace this block.

Perhaps the oldest structure in the district, the Grice-Fearing House, located at 200 South Road, is a magnificent two-and-a-half-story frame house dominated by four massive Doric columns. Its Federal–Greek Revival main block was constructed for Charles Grice, a shipbuilder from New England, around 1800.

Of all the wonderful antebellum residences in Elizabeth City, the Pool-Lumsden-Peters House, located at 204–206 South Road, is the most intact. This two-and-a-half-story Greek Revival house was constructed in 1840 for Mrs. Lovey Pool, the widow of a wealthy planter and merchant. Dr. William J. Lumsden, a subsequent owner, erected the one-and-a-half-story brick doctor's office on the corner of the lot in 1895.

Turn right onto Church Street. After 3 blocks, you will reach the Tillett-Nixon House, located at 400 West Church. This two-story Greek Revival structure was constructed in 1869 by Isaac Tillett, a Confederate officer.

Across the street at the intersection of West Church and Culpepper streets, the Richardson-Pool-Glover House is the largest antebellum house in the city. It was constructed in the 1850s by Daniel Richardson, a local merchant.

Continue 2 blocks west on Church Street to Selden Street. Turn right onto Selden and walk 2 blocks north. Notice the street's brickwork, which

Richardson-Pool-Glover House

dates from the late nineteenth century, when the West End Land Improvement Company paved the city's streets.

Turn right off Selden Street onto West Main Street. West Main is lined with an outstanding assortment of stately old homes.

At 503 West Main, the Dr. A. L. Pendleton House, built around 1891, is one of the finest Colonial Revival dwellings in Elizabeth City.

Although the Bland-Overman House, located at 501 West Main, has been extensively remodeled, it remains an excellent representative of the antebellum Greek residences built for merchants and businessmen during the 1850s.

Constructed in 1859, the Overman-Sheep House, at 401 West Main, is a massive, two-story Greek Revival mansion dominated by a full Doric portico.

Particularly noteworthy is the Charles L. Harney House, at 400 West Main. This magnificent Greek Revival structure is thought to be the only surviving nineteenth-century brick residence in the city. Constructed in 1853, the house possesses one of the finest interiors in Elizabeth City.

Two houses dominate the 300 block of West Main Street.

The Judge Isaac M. Meekins House

Constructed in 1903, the Judge Isaac M. Meekins House, at 310 West Main, is an impressively styled Neoclassical Revival structure. Its dignified, four-column portico dominates the street entrance. Meekins, a federal judge who grew up in Tyrrell County, North Carolina, presided over a crowded New York City docket during the Prohibition era. He is recognized as the first judge who made a serious attempt at enforcing New York laws relating to prohibition.

Just across the street, at 309 West Main, the Mary Blades Foreman House is equally impressive. Its pedimented Doric portico dominates the structure, which was built in 1912 for Mrs. Foreman after the sudden, tragic death of her husband, a local banker. Because the couple had planned the house before Foreman's death, the widow decided to follow through with the project. She insisted that builders follow her late husband's wishes—three nails were used where one was needed.

First Baptist Church, located at 300 West Main, houses one of the oldest congregations in Elizabeth City. Established in 1786, the congregation built the existing brick Gothic Revival structure in 1889 to replace a building destroyed by fire a year earlier. The cemetery behind the church on Colonial Avenue is the original church graveyard. Graves there date from 1814.

At 202 West Main, the Hinton-Pailin House, constructed around 1855, was built as a two-story Greek Revival dwelling; however, it was renovated and enlarged in the Neoclassical Revival style in the first quarter of the twentieth century.

Continue 2 blocks east from the Hinton-Pailin House to the Southern Hotel, located at the corner of East Main and Road streets. Since 1829, when the National Hotel was erected, a hotel of some kind has stood at this site. When the present structure was completed in 1887, it was one of the largest hotels in the entire state. Extensive renovations to the four-story brick Colonial Revival building resulted in the existing Art Deco look. On the interior, the lobby is highlighted by a beamed ceiling, Ionic columns, and handsome wainscoted walls. On the second floor, the old ballroom was partitioned into rooms during World War II.

Continue on East Main. Commercial buildings dominate the tour route as it makes its way toward the river.

Across the street from the Southern Hotel, the Cluff-Pool Building was erected in 1820, making it the oldest commercial structure in the district. In 1858, the two-story brick building was remodeled in the Italianate style. It served as the county courthouse from 1862 to 1882.

Nearby at 106 East Main stands the North Carolinian Building, built between 1871 and 1883 by Dr. Palemon John to house his newspaper, the *North Carolinian*, a strong advocate of the economic potential of the Albemarle. Since John's death in 1902, the two-story Victorian structure has been occupied by a variety of businesses, the most interesting of which was the Marriage Chapel of Harry B. Umphlett from the 1950s to the 1980s.

Located at 108 East Main, the Farmers Bank Building is one of the most notable antebellum buildings in the state. It was completed on October 15, 1855, but subsequent remodeling on the one-story structure in the early twentieth century transformed its exterior into a pedimented storefront. With only a photograph from 1870 to aid them, workmen meticulously rebuilt the original facade in 1984.

Ensconced among the commercial and governmental buildings on East Main is the most splendid private residence in the city. The Charles O.

Robinson House, at 201 East Main, was constructed in 1914 as a wedding gift from lumber magnate William Benjamin Blades to his daughter. Standing in dignity across the street from the Pasquotank County Courthouse, the Neoclassical Revival mansion is highlighted by pairs of tall Corinthian columns.

Charles O. Robinson House

Since it was constructed in 1882, the red brick county courthouse, at 206 East Main, has been enlarged twice. Its Victorian middle block is surmounted by a two-stage domed cupola which houses a clock tower and bell tower.

A block away, at 306 East Main, the three-story United States Post Office and Courthouse, built around 1906, is a handsome Neoclassical Revival structure of brick and stone. Its magnificent two-story courtroom features hand-carved mahogany wainscoting and a three-hundred-pound brass and milk-glass chandelier.

From the post office, continue east 2 blocks to the massive three-story Lowry-Chesson Building, at 514 East Main. Constructed by Dr. Freshwater W. Lowry in 1897, the building has always housed a department store on its first floor. Of special interest is an early electrical conveyor installed in 1924 to carry cash slips and cash to the mezzanine office from any of the sales stations. Even though replacement parts for the system have not been manufactured since 1946, it has been kept in working order with handmade parts.

Pasquotank County Courthouse

The Lowry-Chesson Building

After the building opened, the two upper floors became the home of the Academy of Music—better known as the Opera House—the first sizable theater in the town. Vaudeville shows and other entertainments once drew large, enthusiastic crowds. Such legendary performers as Clifton Webb and Thoms Mitchell (of *Gone With the Wind* fame) are reported to have played here at one time or another.

When modern theaters came to Elizabeth City in the second decade of the twentieth century, the Opera House closed. Although the last applause was heard long ago, the stage and balcony remain, bearing silent testimony to the performances once witnessed in the building. Doric columns support the proscenium arch, which is decorated with gold leaf.

At 117 North Water Street, near the corner of East Main and North Water, stands the three-story McMullan Building, one of the best-preserved Victorian stores in North Carolina. It still displays its original pressed-metal storefront, a style of architecture that was popular in the state during the latter part of the nineteenth century.

Nearby at the foot of East Main, Moth Boat Park is a small waterfront park that exemplifies the continuing efforts of civic leaders to beautify the historic business district on the river.

Turn south onto Water Street to return to the park where the walking tour began. New shops, restaurants, cafes, and public boat docks are gradually replacing the dilapidated, rotting structures that until recently marred the "front door" of Elizabeth City.

To celebrate local heritage and culture, several annual festivals are held in the city. Without question, the largest and most popular is Riverspree. Held annually in May, the extravaganza celebrates life along the Pasquotank River. One of the featured attractions is a replica of the James Adams Floating Theatre. During the early part of the twentieth century, the famous floating theater had its winter quarters in Elizabeth City. (For more information on the James Adams Floating Theatre, see The Northern Pamlico River Tour, page 306–7.)

On the street nearby stands a state historical marker honoring J. C. B. Ehringhaus, the only governor of North Carolina from Elizabeth City. He is buried in Episcopal Cemetery, located at 505 Ehringhaus Street, the oldest active burial ground in the city.

From the waterfront, drive south for 1 block; Water Street now becomes

Southern Avenue. At the intersection with Shepard Street/Riverside Drive, turn east on Riverside Drive and proceed over the Charles Creek Bridge, which overlooks the serene, picturesque Charles Creek Park. Drive approximately 1 mile to the end of Riverside Drive as the street makes its way through one of the beautiful, old riverfront residential sections of the city.

Of the many pleasant dwellings on this quiet street, the most interesting is the George W. Beveridge House, at 1006 Riverside. Although the wood-shingled, one-and-a-half-story bungalow is not old in a historical sense, it is one of the most storied homes in the city. Prior to its construction in 1926, Beveridge had always wanted to live on a houseboat. His wife would not acquiesce, so the couple compromised by building its home over the water, in the style of the sound-side cottage of Mrs. Beveridge's parents at Nags Head. Beveridge found the bungalow to be ideal: he did not have to mow grass, and he could fish from and tie his boat to the wooden deck at the rear of the house.

George W. Beveridge House

Retrace your route to the waterfront park at the foot of Ehringhaus Street. Turn west on Ehringhaus Street and drive 5 blocks to the intersection with Road Street. Turn left on Road Street, which becomes Weeksville Road (N.C. 34) as it makes its way south out of Elizabeth City.

Born during the pounding of war drums in Europe, the United States Coast Guard Air Station is located 2.9 miles south of the Elizabeth City waterfront on N.C. 34. It has been a dominant force in the life of the city from its inception. Construction of the facility on the site of an old river plantation restored some prestige to the city that was once the headquarters of the Seventh Coast Guard District.

Since World War II, the base has been enlarged several times. Its mission was expanded in 1947 from search and rescue to aviation service and supply. Twenty years later, a round barracks with a capacity for five hundred persons, only the second of its kind ever constructed, was completed at the base. At present, the Elizabeth City installation maintains the largest aircraft repair and supply center for Coast Guard aircraft in the nation.

Continue south on N.C. 34 for 0.3 mile to Bay Side, one of the most historic houses in southern Pasquotank County. This dignified two-and-a-half-story Greek Revival mansion is dominated by spectacular two-story porches on the front and rear, both supported by massive columns.

Constructed in 1856 by Christopher Wilson Hollowell, the thirteen-room house remained in the Hollowell family until it was sold at public auction in the summer of 1988. Margaret Hollowell, a descendant of the home's builder, was a historian and furniture collector while she lived here. At her death in 1951, her collection formed the basis for starting the Museum of the Albemarle.

Entertainer Wayne Newton purchased the eleven-acre plantation, sight unseen, at the auction for use as a vacation retreat. Newton, an avid collector of antiques, became interested in Bay Side through an advertisement in an antique magazine. He made his bid of $250,000 by telephone as the auctioneer stood on the front porch. Hopes that the Las Vegas star would be a part-time resident of Pasquotank County ended when Newton put the property on the market in the spring of 1992.

Stories of ghosts at Bay Side have circulated for years. It was well into the twentieth century when a beautiful houseguest was suddenly awakened by the apparition of a man sitting at the foot of her bed. She could even smell the cigar he was smoking. As the story goes, a bachelor uncle in the Hollowell family who loved cigars once farmed the plantation. After his death, members of the Hollowell family reported the sound of heavy footsteps in the empty house. At other times, they heard the creaking and rocking of empty chairs on the front porch.

Proceed south on N.C. 34 through the fertile Pasquotank farmlands. On this route, you cannot miss the behemoth hangars rising from the distant horizon. To reach these unusual structures, turn east onto S.R. 1126 (Toxey Road) 2.1 miles from Bay Side and drive 1.1 miles to the end of the road.

Military officials in Washington, D.C., scrambled to find ways to defend the Atlantic coast against the U-boat menace during the first year of World War II. A naval air station located at the current tour stop proved to be an invaluable aid in the fight. Construction of the facility began in 1940. The airships—more often called blimps—based here were especially effective in patrolling the vital shipping lanes of the Atlantic.

To accommodate the massive blimps, two gigantic hangars, known as Dock One and Dock Two, were put up in less than nine months. Dock One, the smaller of the two at 960 feet in length, resembles the Quonset hut of a giant. Its counterpart was built in the same general shape. However, Dock Two is 1,058 feet long and was built completely from wood. At the time it was constructed, this wooden hangar necessitated the use of the largest timber arches ever fabricated in the world.

During World War II, the airship squadron based here was officially known as Blimpron 14. Not one of the more than eighty thousand ships escorted by United States Navy blimps during the war was lost. In the 1950s and the early 1960s, the local airship fleet was used to guard against the Cold War missile threat. As East-West relations began to improve, the navy ended its blimp program, and the Pasquotank County facility was sold to Westinghouse.

Blimp hangar

About the time the navy gave up on the military use of blimps, the American public and private enterprise renewed a love affair with the strange-looking balloons. During the late 1960s, the popularity of the Goodyear Blimp convinced other companies that the airship business could be profitable. In 1984, Airships Industries USA, Inc., the largest blimp manufacturer in the world, began working with Westinghouse at the facility. Also around that time, the navy showed a new interest in the military potential of blimps. Work on military contracts has been performed at the Pasquotank hangars since 1985.

Retrace your route to N.C. 34 and drive south 0.5 mile to Union Chapel Baptist Church. Turn left onto the access road that loops around the front entrance of the church. This loop road represents the largest remaining portion of the Weeksville Brick Road. Constructed around 1920 by the county to connect rural Pasquotank with the outside world, the old brick roadway once ran 7 miles through the swamps to the county seat. Much of the existing route of N.C. 34 follows the old road.

Return to N.C. 34 and continue south 1.1 miles to Weeksville, a small community at the head of New Begun Creek that traces its origins to a trading settlement begun by early Quaker settlers. Near the intersection of N.C. 34 and S.R. 1100 in the heart of Weeksville stands Newbegun United Methodist Church, built around 1827. This large white frame structure was constructed in the popular temple form, but renovations in the 1920s gave the church its present appearance.

The Weeksville Brick Road

Turn west onto S.R. 1100 as the tour route winds toward the banks of the Little River and into the rural portion of Pasquotank County, the site of several significant firsts in the history of North Carolina.

Site of the first documented school in North Carolina

Near the head of Symonds Creek, located approximately 3 miles west of Weeksville on S.R. 1100, the Society of Friends organized the first religious meetings in North Carolina in the second half of the seventeenth century. By 1705, the growing strength and number of Quakers in Pasquotank resulted in the construction of a meeting house at Symonds Creek.

In 1706, cooperation between Quakers and Anglicans led to the first documented school in North Carolina. It was organized and conducted by Charles Griffin, an Anglican layman. Built on a site near the Friends' meeting house on Symonds Creek, the school remained open for several years, until Griffin moved to the Chowan precinct. Historical markers honoring these firsts are located along S.R. 1100 on the west side of the creek.

One of the most historic homes of southern Pasquotank County lies 1 mile west of Symonds Creek on S.R. 1100. Blackstock, a two-and-a-half-story house, was built in nearby Nixonton in 1810 and moved to its present site in the late nineteenth century. At one time, the handsomely styled structure served as a school.

Symonds Creek

Blackstock at Nixonton

Continue on S.R. 1100. It is 1.3 miles from Blackstock to the ancient village of Nixonton.

This historic village sleeps peacefully on the Little River, bearing little testimony to the prominence it once held in the colony. Early settlers chose this to be the site for the first commercial center of Pasquotank primarily because of its location on the Little River midway between Halls Creek and Symonds Creek. By 1746, streets were laid out and the village began taking shape. Twelve years later, it was incorporated as the first town in the county. It remained the only incorporated town for almost a half-century.

From 1785 to 1799, the town served as the county seat, complete with courthouse, jail, and pillory. Removal of the county seat to Elizabeth City at the dawn of the nineteenth century caused Nixonton to enter a decline from which it has never recovered.

Despite its loss of political stature two centuries ago, Nixonton is called the "Mother of North Carolina" by some historians, because the first governmental assembly and the first school in North Carolina were born within a mile or so of the town. In the village proper, the first custom house in North Carolina was constructed on a hill sloping toward the Little River. Built around 1745 by William Lane, a local merchant and shipper, the custom house was a small, one-story brick structure with three rooms. Two additional rooms and porches were subsequently added.

When the University of North Carolina was preparing a replica of an early Tar Heel room for its North Carolina Collection in the 1940s, the paneling from the great room in the custom house was removed and reassembled in the Wilson Library at the Chapel Hill institution. Stripped of its paneling, the old building in Nixonton fell into disuse and finally collapsed in the 1980s.

On the Nixonton waterfront, one home from the town's golden era survives. Turn left on S.R. 1137, a loop road less than a mile in length off S.R. 1100. Here stands the Nash House, constructed around 1790. This is one of two gambrel-roofed houses remaining in the once-thriving village. Continue on S.R. 1137 to rejoin S.R. 1100. Proceed in your original direction on S.R. 1100.

In Nixonton, S.R. 1100 intersects S.R. 1140. Turn north onto S.R. 1140 and drive 1.3 miles to Halls Creek United Methodist Church. Built in 1827,

Halls Creek
United Methodist Church

the picturesque Greek Revival structure is no longer used as a church. On the grounds near the waters of Halls Creek stands a small stone marker commemorating one of the earliest milestones in North Carolina history. It was here, on February 6, 1665, under the canopy of stately oak trees, that Governor William Drummond convened the first political assembly in North Carolina when he presided over the Assembly of Albemarle.

Continue 2.5 miles north on S.R. 1140. Few travelers give more than a glance to the large, vacant two-story frame dwelling set far off the west side of the highway. This obscure structure, portions of which date to 1800, is badly deteriorated, bearing little resemblance to the once-proud home which produced the first scholarly historian of North Carolina. Stephen Beauregard Weeks was born in the house in 1865.

After attending schools in Pasquotank County, Weeks, an orphan at age three, graduated from the University of North Carolina at Chapel Hill. He subsequently earned Ph.D. degrees from the University of North Carolina and Johns Hopkins University.

In his native state, Weeks embarked upon a remarkable career as an author, historian, and librarian. His fascination with North Carolina history led him to acquire a substantial and significant collection of books and other materials concerning the state. At his death, the invaluable collection was used to form the basis of the world-famous North Carolina Collection at the University of North Carolina at Chapel Hill.

Continue 0.6 mile north to U.S. 17, where a state historical marker honors Weeks. The tour ends here. Hertford is 8 miles to the west and Elizabeth City 6.9 miles to the east.

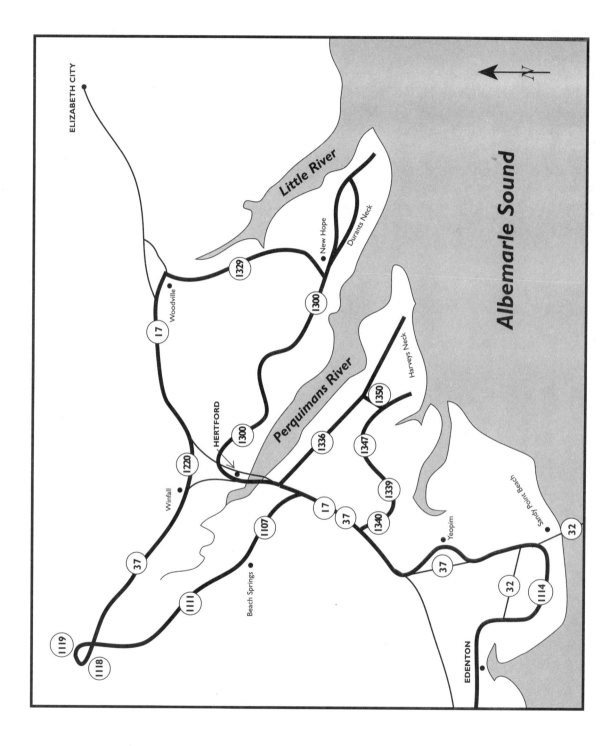

The Northern
Albemarle Tour

This tour begins on U.S. 17 on the banks of the Perquimans River at Hertford, then proceeds through much of the cradle of the early North Carolina colony, reaching deep into Durants Neck and Harveys Neck, the two large peninsulas in Perquimans County, before returning to Hertford for a walking tour. Finally, the tour heads to Edenton for a walking tour of one of the most beautiful and historic towns in North Carolina.

Among the highlights of the tour are the Newbold-White House, which is the oldest house in the state, the peninsula plantations, historic Hertford, the Albemarle Sound Bridge, and historic Edenton.

Total mileage: approximately 108 miles.

This tour begins on Church Street (U.S. 17 Business) in the historic town of Hertford, the county seat of Perquimans County. Perquimans is an ancient place, having been created as a precinct of Albemarle County in 1670. Its name came from Indians living in the area. Legend has it that the name means "Land of Beautiful Women."

Proceed north on Church Street as it leads away from the downtown area to the bridge over the Perquimans River. Rising from creeks in the surrounding Great Dismal Swamp, this breathtaking river begins to widen at Hertford and flows 12 miles on a southern route to Albemarle Sound. So majestic is the river that it inspired the world-famous ballad "Carolina Moon." Its writer is said to have composed the song in 1885 near the current tour stop while watching the moon from the old pontoon bridge which preceded the existing bridge.

The floating bridge was constructed in 1798 to span the river at this site, and it soon became a landmark in the region. Almost a century after its construction, a local newspaper editorialized, "We can justly claim the only float bridge in the world and we can also remark that we are the only people in the world that want one." By that time, concern had begun to mount about the bridge's safety. High water caused significant structural damage in 1897, and the county commissioners were forced to borrow funds from the state to build a replacement bridge that had a 270-foot trestle and a 153-foot draw span.

While lamenting the passing of the original bridge, the *Eastern Courier* provided a verbal picture of the century-old pontoon bridge: "We hate very much to give up the only real curiosity in the State, a wonder of the nineteenth century, a bridge floating on top of the water, supported by empty oil barrels and held in place with four guy lines, a relic left here by great grand sires."

After thirty years of service, the second bridge was replaced by the existing concrete-and-steel span. Like the original bridge, this 1928 structure is of unique design. Although the reasons for its remarkable S pattern are not known, it is believed to be the only structure of its kind in the United States and the largest S-type bridge in the world.

Proceed on U.S. 17 Business across the bridge and the adjoining causeway, where the river threatens to cover the roadway, to the intersection with U.S. 17 Bypass. Continue straight across U.S. 17 Bypass; the road becomes S.R. 1300. Drive south on S.R. 1300 for 0.7 mile to the Francis Nixon House. This dwelling, the first of many historic buildings on this tour, was built in three sections between 1830 and 1850 by Francis Nixon, a prominent planter who constructed the first summer home at Nags Head.

Near the Francis Nixon House once stood the Old Neck Meeting House, which served as the annual meeting site for North Carolina Quakers from 1706 to 1785.

The tour route will now begin making its way deep into Durants Neck, one of the two watery prongs of Perquimans County; Harveys Neck, to the west across the Perquimans River, is the other. Projecting into Albemarle Sound like a giant tooth, the county is divided into the two large peninsulas by three rivers: the Little, the Perquimans, and the Yeopim.

Durants Neck, the larger of the two peninsulas, is formed by the Perquimans and the Little rivers. Shown as Point Durant on the Hack map of 1684, this slice of Perquimans County was named in honor of George Durant (1632–1694), a pioneer settler of the Albemarle area who built his home on the peninsula. Accordingly, Durants Neck provides a scenic introduction to the North Albemarle, that venerable region of North Carolina which welcomed the first permanent settlers to the colony.

Perquimans River at Hertford

TOURING THE BACKROADS OF NORTH CAROLINA'S UPPER COAST

As is evident along much of the tour, most of the eleven thousand people who call Perquimans home earn their livelihood from the land. Few counties in North Carolina are more rural and agrarian. Though the county is blessed with the three rivers and Albemarle Sound, it has not been able to parlay these resources into tourist revenue. Perquimans rests in relative obscurity, surrounded by counties that have used their historic pasts to develop tourist industries. However, despite its apparent lack of tourist appeal, Perquimans is an undiscovered gem for coastal visitors who are interested in the history of the Albemarle.

Continue along S.R. 1300. Approximately 0.4 mile from the Francis Nixon House, turn right onto S.R. 1301 and proceed south 0.1 mile to the Jones House, sometimes called Riverside. This dwelling was erected in 1825 on the plantation of Francis Tomes, who entertained William Edmundson and George Fox, pioneer Quaker missionaries in North Carolina.

In 1672, Fox, the founder of the Society of Friends, came to the area to preach. Some historians claim that, along the Perquimans River, the Quakers held the first religious service of record in North Carolina. At the corner of Church and McCraney streets in Hertford, the Edmundson-Fox Memorial, erected in 1929 by the Quakers, bears an inscription asserting the claim. Yet somehow forgotten are the baptisms of Manteo and Virginia Dare on Roanoke Island almost a century earlier. At any rate, Quakers, spilling down from Virginia, quickly became entrenched in the North Albemarle and were responsible for much of the earliest organized religious activity in the colony.

The Edmundson-Fox Memorial

Continue 0.3 mile on S.R. 1301 to the Fletcher-Skinner House, which dates from 1815. Of particular interest are the original outbuildings, including the brick dairy at the rear of the two-story house. It now serves as a bed-and-breakfast inn.

Drive 1.1 miles south on S.R. 1301 to Cove Grove, one of the architectural treasures of Perquimans. Built between 1825 and 1830, this stately two-story white frame mansion is highlighted by Ionic porticoes and a front entrance with a large fanlight. Listed on the National Register of Historic Places, the plantation has remained in the Skinner family since it was built.

Proceed 0.2 mile south on S.R. 1301 to its junction with S.R. 1302. Turn left onto S.R. 1302 and drive east 0.5 mile to where Union Hall Academy

once stood. Erected around 1800, this private school educated area children before the first public schools were established in the county in 1839.

Continue on S.R. 1302 for 0.3 mile to the intersection with S.R. 1300. Turn right onto S.R. 1300 and proceed east 0.6 mile to Suttons Creek. Named for a family that settled in the county in the seventeenth century, this scenic waterway gradually widens on its southwesterly flow to the Perquimans River. Toms Mill, a large gristmill, once stood nearby on the creek.

It is 0.6 mile on S.R. 1300 from Suttons Creek to the Sutton-Newby House. Erected in the second quarter of the eighteenth century, this is one of the oldest homes in North Carolina. Despite modifications, the dwelling still exhibits Flemish-bond brick sides and glazed brick headers in a chevron pattern. The glazed bricks are distinguishable by their bluish color, which resulted from their being nearest the fire in the kiln.

As S.R. 1300 makes its way into the heart of the peninsula, you will pass Sumnerville 1.4 miles southeast of the Sutton-Newby House. This gambrel-roofed house of the American Revolution era features a floor plan common to country houses of that period—stairs ascend from a shed room through the smaller of two front rooms.

Continue 1.9 miles on S.R. 1300 to the Whedbee House, located just off the highway on Suttons Lane. Estimates as to the date of construction of this house range from 1722 to 1800. The old family cemetery at the rear of the house is characteristic of many rural homes in coastal North Carolina. A row of a dozen gravestones sadly chronicles the deaths of planter James Whedbee's twelve children.

It is 1.4 miles on S.R. 1300 from the Whedbee House to New Hope Methodist Church, organized in 1809. This is the oldest Methodist church in the county and is believed to be the oldest Methodist building in North Carolina. Ironically, the home of Clement Hall, a missionary for the Church of England who came to the Albemarle region in 1744, once stood nearby. Hall subsequently settled in Chowan County, where he penned *A Collection of Many Christian Experiences, Sentences, and Several Places of Scripture Improved*. When it was published in New Bern in 1753, Hall claimed the honor as the author of the first book written and published in North Carolina.

The Whedbee House

Continue on S.R. 1300 for 3.3 miles to the Jacocks House. En route, the road parallels the Little River. On the nearby riverbanks once stood Brickhouse Landing, where local farmers of the eighteenth and nineteenth centuries brought their crops and forest products to be loaded on waiting schooners and other river craft.

Built around 1845, the Jacocks House holds the distinction of having more rooms than any other dwelling in the county.

It is another 0.9 mile south to the site of the Hecklefield Farm. The colonial assembly met here in the early eighteenth century.

Continue 0.3 mile south on S.R. 1300 to the Thomas Newby House, built around 1835. When Union troops came ashore near this handsome Federal-style dwelling during the Civil War, they harassed Newby's wife, killed his son, stole his livestock, and drove away his slaves. During the final six months of 1863, local plantation owners were plagued by similar raids.

New Hope Methodist Church

Of all the war action in the county, the events in December 1863 were the most terrifying and irritating to county citizens. Union general Edward A. Wild, a fervent abolitionist from Massachusetts, led a rampage of eighteen hundred black troops, whom he had personally recruited, on several raids in the county. Planters and farmers branded Wild a "monster of humanity" and accused his forces of atrocities.

Upon receiving notice of the approach of the marauding enemy troops in late 1863, the wily citizens of Hertford decided to impede the progress of the invaders by removing the detachable portion of the pontoon bridge. The Yankees obliged their adversaries by promptly marching into the river. They subsequently retaliated by shelling the town.

As you continue 2.5 miles south to the terminus of S.R. 1300 near the tip of Durants Neck, you will be able to see the Little River at several places. Majestically set near the point where the Little River empties into Albemarle Sound is the largest plantation house in Perquimans County. Leigh's Farm, also known as Land's End, stands on part of the 1,000-acre tract that George Durant purchased from the Yeopim Indians in 1661. Erosion along the shore of the sound has reduced the original tract to 850 acres.

After fire destroyed his first two homes on the site, Colonel James Leigh resolved in 1825 to build a dwelling that "neither God nor man could destroy." From plans drawn by his grandfather, Gilbert Leigh, the man who designed the Chowan County Courthouse, James Leigh used slave labor and the sturdiest of materials to construct the massive Greek Revival masterpiece.

The bricks used in the construction of the house were fired on the plantation. The outer walls are eighteen inches thick. A double galley porch adorns the house front and rear. Granite steps approach the porches, which are supported by white Doric columns. A gambrel roof covers the third-story ballroom, which is lit at each end by a triple window topped with an elliptical fanlight. Though the half-buried cellar with arched windows is rumored to have been a dungeon, it was most likely a wine cellar.

Of special interest at Land's End is an old stone slab partially buried by an ancient elm tree. This slab is thought to be the gravestone of Seth Sothel, the most infamous colonial governor in North Carolina history.

In 1678, Sothel was appointed governor of Albemarle County, that sprawling, ancient political subdivision of the northeastern Carolina province. En route to his assignment, however, he was captured on the high seas by Turkish pirates and imprisoned in Algiers. Upon his release in 1681, Sothel was again commissioned governor. When he finally arrived in the colony in 1683, the new governor was met with immediate disfavor. Thereafter, he did little to endear himself to the people of the Albemarle region. Political opponents were imprisoned, property was illegally seized, and bribery and corruption were rampant throughout his administration. Ultimately, this behavior resulted in a number of charges being formally lodged against him. In 1689, Governor Sothel chose to be tried by the general assembly, rather than by the Lords Proprietors. Upon his conviction of thirteen charges ranging from extortion to tyranny, Sothel was temporarily banished, and Albemarle County faded into history as a political subdivision.

Retrace your route on S.R. 1300 for 1.5 miles to the intersection with S.R. 1321 (Muddy Creek Road). Turn left onto S.R. 1321 and proceed west 2.9 miles to Muddy Creek. This unpaved road is one of the many ancient county roads that were maintained by groups of local residents until the state took over maintenance.

Flowing into the mouth of the Perquimans River, Muddy Creek is home to a large flock of swans. Its ancient shores were once inhabited by the Yeopim Indians, who called the creek Awosoake. A wide variety of Indian artifacts have been found in the area.

Proceed north on S.R. 1321 for 2.6 miles. Lemuel Sutton Reed, a Methodist minister, lived in this area in the first half of the nineteenth century.

Land's End

His son, Dr. Walter Reed, gained worldwide recognition when he conquered yellow fever.

At the intersection of S.R. 1321 and S.R. 1300, turn left onto S.R. 1300 and drive 1 mile north to New Hope. Turn right onto S.R. 1329. After 4.7 miles, you will reach Stockton, an impressive nineteenth-century house that presents an interesting mixture of Greek Revival details and Roman temple forms. Constructed in 1840 and listed on the National Register of Historic Places, the house was the childhood home of Robert Welch, founder of the John Birch Society.

Continue 1.4 miles to Woodville, a small community that grew up near the point where the old stagecoach road crossed the Little River. From the early 1700s to 1854, the Little River Quaker Meeting House made the community a strong outpost for Quaker activities.

The tour leaves Durants Neck at Woodville. Turn left onto S.R. 1367 and drive 1.1 miles to the intersection with U.S. 17, then proceed west on U.S. 17 for 3.8 miles to the Thomas Nixon House.

On the south side of the road in this vicinity stood the Suttons Creek Meeting House, one of the seven Quaker meetings that existed in Perquimans in the eighteenth century. Founded in 1787, the Suttons Creek Meeting disbanded in 1835 in the midst of the great Quaker migration to the west, which began in 1812. Many Quakers left the county because of their opposition to slavery. By 1857, only one meeting house, Piney Woods, was left in Perquimans.

The Thomas Nixon House is a handsome, white two-story antebellum plantation house enclosed by a white wooden fence. From the south side of the highway, a cedar-lined driveway provides a graceful approach to the house, which was built after Francis Nixon gave the land to his son, Thomas, in 1848. Numerous plantation outbuildings and a windmill survive near the house.

Proceed 0.5 mile west on U.S. 17 to its junction with S.R. 1220. Turn north on S.R. 1220 and drive 0.7 mile to Cedar Grove Methodist Church, as the tour makes its way into the northern third of the county.

This Methodist congregation was organized in 1818; however, the existing building is the third at the site, built in 1911. Although Perquimans supplied manpower for the Confederate army, there was widespread local opposition to the war, particularly among the Quakers. Many influential citizens of Perquimans, including most of the doctors in the county, were in attendance at a peace meeting held at Cedar Grove Methodist Church on December 24, 1863. The attendees denounced "that species of business carried on here by private citizens for private game [sic] known as blockade running."

Continue northwest on S.R. 1220 for 0.9 mile to the crossroads village of Winfall. Although the community was known as Red House Fork in the early nineteenth century, it had become Winfall by the time the post office opened in 1873. Legend holds that Winfall acquired its name when a store at the crossroads was blown over by the wind. Today, the post office is housed in a two-story frame building located at the junction with N.C. 37. Built in 1890, the structure has changed little over the past century.

At the Winfall crossroads, turn northwest onto N.C. 37 and drive 1.2 miles to the junction with Nixon Bridge Road. Samuel Nixon constructed a float bridge near the end of the road that bears his name in 1797. Until the unusual span was burned by invading Union forces in January 1863, Perquimans owned the distinction of having two float bridges. Close to the bridge stood the Wells Meeting House, constructed in 1704. It was the first church in the county and the second in the state.

Continue on N.C. 37 for 4.6 miles as it passes through Bagleys Swamp en route to the riverside community of Belvidere. On the Moseley map of 1733,

Cedar Grove Methodist Church

Belvidere is shown as G. Newby's Ferry. A post office was established here under the name of Newby's Bridge in 1827; the name was changed to Belvidere in 1861.

In 1833, in the heart of town, the Quakers built Belvidere Academy, one of the most famous schools in eastern North Carolina. For the years until the county established high schools, the institution met the educational needs of many area students. When the new academy building was completed in 1903, the old structure was moved across the road, where it still stands as a private residence. When the academy closed in 1914, the newer building was used by the county as an elementary school until it burned in May 1935.

Belvidere Academy

Continue on N.C. 37. Less than 0.5 mile west of the academy site, you will cross Newby's Bridge. Here, the Perquimans is quite narrow, yet in the late nineteenth century, steamboats navigated the river between Belvidere and Hertford.

Nearby stands the majestic Belvidere Plantation. This eighteenth-century house has been renovated by one of America's most famous rock-and-roll personalities, Wolfman Jack, who now makes his home here. His wife, a native of Chowan County, had always dreamed of living in the house, so when it became available in the 1980s, the couple purchased it and began its restoration.

At the junction of N.C. 37 and S.R. 1118 approximately 0.2 mile west of Newby's Bridge, proceed west on S.R. 1118. After 0.6 mile, turn west onto S.R. 1119. It is 0.1 mile to the Piney Woods Meeting House. Constructed in 1854 and remodeled in 1928, this building houses the oldest religious congregation in Perquimans County and the oldest Quaker meeting in eastern North Carolina. It began in 1723.

Follow S.R. 1119 for another 0.6 mile, then turn left onto S.R. 1002, often called the County Line Road, because it runs along the Perquimans County–Chowan County line. At this intersection stands the deteriorating Mitchell-Ward House, built around 1835. Constructed by Dr. William Mitchell from Londonderry, Ireland, the structure exhibits an interesting gable fanlight.

Continue south on S.R. 1002 for 0.4 mile, then turn left onto S.R. 1118. After 1.1 miles, turn right onto S.R. 1111 and drive south 0.7 mile to the

Timothy Nicholson House, constructed in 1853. The builder, Timothy Nicholson, later acquired the title "Master Quaker" after he migrated to Indiana.

Proceed 3.7 miles south on S.R. 1111 to the community of Beach Springs. Standing in the village, which was named for a nearby spring, is a former school building, one of the largest in the county at one time. It has since been cut in two, with one section serving as a house and the other as a barn.

From Beach Springs, continue 0.5 mile on S.R. 1111 to its junction with S.R. 1113. Turn left onto S.R. 1113 and drive 0.4 mile to the junction with S.R. 1107 and S.R. 110. Proceed south on S.R. 1107 to the intersection with U.S. 17. Turn right onto U.S. 17 as it winds its way southwest onto Harveys Neck. After 2.8 miles, turn left on S.R. 1340. To the south and west lies the wilderness of Bear Swamp. Although much of the swamp has been drained for agricultural purposes, the morass once covered three-eighths of nearby Chowan County.

After 1.6 miles on S.R. 1340, turn right onto S.R. 1341 and proceed 0.1 mile west to Bethel Baptist Church. Erected in 1837 on land given to the Church of England a century earlier, the building is the home of the oldest Baptist church in Perquimans County. It was organized in 1806. Inside the sanctuary, the old slave galleries can still be seen. Visitors should take time to inspect the ancient cemetery behind the church, which contains some of the oldest accessible graves in the county.

Retrace your route to S.R. 1340 and continue 0.2 mile south to the junction with S.R. 1339. Turn left onto S.R. 1339 and drive 0.5 mile east to New Bethel Baptist Church. Organized in 1867, this is one of the oldest black churches in the county.

Proceed 0.5 mile east on S.R. 1339 to the John Gatling House, built around 1841. This two-story Greek Revival plantation house provided shelter for Confederate soldiers who escaped from the prison-bound USS *Maple Leaf* after it wrecked off the North Carolina coast in 1863.

Continue 1 mile on S.R. 1339 to the Isaac White House, a four-bay, two-story frame dwelling listed on the National Register of Historic Places. Constructed in 1760, the dwelling is noted for its massive chimneys and twin entrances.

Just east of the Isaac White House, S.R. 1339 intersects S.R. 1347. Turn right onto S.R. 1347 and proceed south 0.7 mile to the Myers-White House. This 1740-vintage gambrel-roofed structure with distinctive brick ends is listed on the National Register of Historic Places. It is one of only two eighteenth-century gambrel-roofed houses with brick ends in the state. Gambrel roofs were commonly used by early Albemarle settlers to avoid the higher taxes the Crown imposed on two-story structures. On the interior, the Myers-White House retains its original hand-hewn three-inch-thick pine floors, plaster walls, and heart-of-pine wainscoting. It is one of the oldest continuously occupied homes in the state.

The road crosses Yeopim Creek 0.3 mile south of the Myers-White House. The creek widens on its flow to the Yeopim River. Several large Indian pots have been found along the banks of the creek. Centuries ago, they were used for corn storage.

Moss-laden trees hide the Harrell House, located 0.2 mile south of the creek. It was constructed in 1840.

Continue south on S.R. 1347. It is 2 miles to where the road terminates on the northern shore of Albemarle Sound just west of the mouth of Yeopim Creek.

Resembling a large, multilegged, headless alligator, Albemarle Sound dominates the map of northeastern North Carolina. Like the geographic region and the ancient political subdivision of the same name, the sound was named for George Monck, the duke of Albemarle and one of the Lords Proprietors.

From the point where Albemarle Sound drains into Roanoke, Croatan, and Pamlico sounds, it extends almost 55 miles to the west. Though the average width is 7 miles, the northern and southern shores are separated by more than 14 miles near the eastern end of the sound. Depths up to 25 feet have been reported, but the sound is relatively shallow, rarely measuring more than 18 feet deep.

This massive, nontidal body of fresh water is fed primarily by the Chowan and Roanoke rivers. In recent years, the rising sea level and tides caused by the wind have resulted in shoreline recession at the rate of two to three feet per year. Boaters can now see banks of clay and sand as high as twenty feet along some portions of the sound. Most of the shoreline is still undeveloped, bounded by hardwood swamp forests.

Ralph Lane, Sir Walter Raleigh's lieutenant, is known to have explored the sound in 1586. In the early part of the seventeenth century, it was known as the "Sea of Rawnocke." On the Comberford map of 1657, it was shown as Roanoke Sound. Subsequently, it was known as the Carolina River and the Albemarle River. It first appeared as Albemarle Sound on the John Barnwell map, dating from around 1722.

Just west of the current tour stop, a shallow, muddy bottom near the mouth of the Yeopim River is all that remains of the island that was the home of the first permanent settler in North Carolina. Nathaniel Batts acquired the island that now bears his name on September 24, 1660. Prior to the arrival of this intrepid hunter, the Indians called the uninhabited island Kalola.

Batts became a living legend among the settlers who followed him to the Albemarle region. His fearless nature earned him the title "Captain Nathaniel Batts, Governor of Roanoke." He was also popular among the Chowanoke Indians. When he fell hopelessly in love with Kickowanna, the daughter of the Chowanoke chief, Kilcocanen, the Indian maiden returned his love, jilting Pamunky, the chieftain of a rival tribe. For his bravery and loyalty during the ensuing battle with their enemy, the Chowanokes adopted Batts into their tribe.

Although Batts and Kickowanna made their home north of the island after they married, Batts often stayed in his home on the beautiful island. On occasion, his wife traveled by canoe to visit him there. One night, a raging storm caused her canoe to capsize, and Kickowanna drowned. Her death devastated Batts. Forlornly, he vowed to never again leave his island, which subsequently became known as Batts Grave.

A deed recorded in Chowan Precinct in 1696 documented the sale of twenty-seven acres known as Batts Grave. On the Moseley map of 1733 and the Collett map of 1770, the island is shown as Bats Grave. It contained approximately forty acres in 1749. Over the next two centuries, the waters of the river and the sound eroded the island. Fishermen built a camp on the remaining portion in the early part of the twentieth century. By the 1930s, only one acre remained above water. When a hurricane ventured inland in the 1950s, the site of the home and bountiful gardens and orchards of the first permanent settler in the state vanished forever.

Legend has it that on stormy nights, the ghost of Nathaniel Batts can be seen sweeping about the shrieking sea gulls, searching and grieving for the lost Kickowanna.

Harvey Point
Defense Testing Area

Retrace your route north on S.R. 1347 for 1.4 miles to the intersection with S.R. 1350. Turn right onto S.R. 1350 and drive east 1.3 miles to the junction with S.R. 1336. Nearby stands the rotting Edmund B. Skinner House, a Greek Revival house built around 1840.

Turn right onto S.R. 1336 and drive south for 3 miles as the tour makes its way to the end of road near the southern tip of the 12-mile prong of land known as Harveys Neck. The road abruptly ends at the Harvey Point Defense Testing Area, a restricted national defense facility that now covers the tip of the neck.

Harveys Neck is named for some of the most prominent families in early North Carolina history. Thomas Harvey began a dynasty in the last quarter of the seventeenth century on a 931-acre tract in the area. By 1694, he was serving as deputy governor of the colony. Because the governor was often absent from the colony, Harvey acted as the chief executive much of the time. At his death in 1699, he was buried in a cemetery at his sound-side plantation. Erosion has long since claimed his burial spot.

Thomas Harvey, Jr., followed in his father's footsteps as a dynamic political figure. At his death in 1729 at the age of thirty-six, the younger Harvey was buried beside his father. As erosion began to take its toll on the cemetery, the decision was made in 1865 to move the grave and gravestone of Thomas Harvey, Jr., to the Harvey family cemetery at Belgrade Plantation. By that time, the grave of the elder Thomas Harvey was already underwater.

Although the Belgrade mansion burned during the Civil War, portions of its ruins and the cemetery remain. Now maintained by the Harvey Point military installation, the cemetery contains the oldest gravestone in the county—that of Thomas Harvey, Jr.

John Harvey was only four years old when his father, Thomas Harvey, Jr., died. Like his father and grandfather, John was destined to spend his life in public service. Elected by Perquimans County voters to the Colonial Assembly at age twenty-one, Harvey displayed great political savvy. In 1766, he was elected the last Speaker of the Assembly as the colony moved toward independence. Standing in the forefront of that movement was John Harvey. Because of his stalwart character, he became known throughout North Carolina as "Bold John."

When the royal governor dissolved the Colonial Assembly in 1769, Harvey nevertheless convened the legislature to transact business. He was elected moderator of the North Carolina First Provincial Congress at New Bern in August 1774 and of the Second Provincial Congress in April 1775. A month later, Harvey died at his home in Perquimans County, as a result of a fall from a horse.

For his undying devotion to the American cause, John Harvey was known as the "Father of the Revolution in North Carolina." He was laid to rest in a large granite tomb in the cemetery at Belgrade. Over the past two centuries, the eroding sound shoreline has caused the tomb to rest in the waters.

Retrace your route on S.R. 1336 to the intersection with S.R. 1350. Continue north on S.R. 1336 as the road parallels the western shore of the Perquimans River. The overgrown Skinner Cemetery, located 3.8 miles north of the intersection, contains the grave of General William Skinner, one of the most distinguished sons of Perquimans. During the Revolutionary War, Skinner gained widespread fame as the hero of the Battle of Great Bridge, Virginia.

Continue on S.R. 1336 for approximately 0.8 mile to the Newbold-White House, located on the northern extreme of Harveys Neck. Although the exact date of construction of the one-and-a-half-story brick structure is not known, many historians believe that it may have been built as early as 1664, which would make it the oldest house in the state.

During its more than three centuries of existence, the house has had approximately thirty owners, including farmers, carpenters, a mariner, and a congressman. Throughout the last quarter of the seventeenth century, it was a popular meeting place. In 1697–98, the Governor's Council General Court and a court of chancery met at the house. The Colonial Assembly convened here in 1697.

Architecturally, the structure exhibits medieval building practices and forms better than any existing structure in the state. Huge fireplaces at either end of the twenty-by-forty-foot house dominate the first floor, which contains a living room and kitchen. Upstairs, there are two bedrooms. Four closets lend some credence to the belief that the builder was a man of wealth. The first-floor walls are plastered, while those on the second floor are paneled in pine.

On the exterior, the eighteen-inch-thick brick walls are laid in Flemish bond, with the exception of the English-bond foundation. Shed dormers rise from the gabled roof, which is capped at each end by chimneys.

When the Perquimans County Restoration Association acquired the house from the family of the late Henry Newbold on February 20, 1973, it bore little resemblance to its original state. Vines covered the north end, and the other three walls were painted white. Through public grants and privately raised funds from twelve states, the association undertook the painstaking task of fully restoring the house. Once the project was completed in 1981, the refurbished house was opened to the public. Since that time, thousands of visitors have enjoyed a unique glimpse of the state's distant past.

The Newbold-White House is not only the oldest house in North Carolina, but also the oldest surviving seat of local government in the state and the only surviving building in which the Colonial Assembly met in proprietary times. Listed on the National Register of Historic Places, the house is open for tours Monday through Saturday from March 1 to Thanksgiving. A nominal admission fee is charged.

Newbold-White House

Proceed 2.3 miles north on S.R. 1336 to the Perquimans County Courthouse; S.R. 1336 becomes South Church Street in Hertford. Park near the courthouse to begin a walking tour of this scenic, historic river town of three thousand residents. A fine ensemble of nineteenth-century homes and buildings graces its streets, which bear names reminiscent of old England: Hyde Park, Covent Garden, and Punch Alley.

Of all the historic structures in Hertford, the most prominent is the courthouse on Church Street, in the heart of town. Construction on the original part of the structure was completed in 1732. At that time, it was a one-story building with a detached jury room. A second story was later added by the Masons under an agreement by which they could use the upper room as a meeting place. Subsequent renovations were made in 1825 and 1890.

Through the efforts and resources of Clinton W. Toms, a tobacco-manufacturing executive, the entire building was restored and modified in 1932. A clock cupola was added, and the original kiln-fired red bricks were painted ivory. Among the interior architectural features of the original portion of the building are raised paneled doors and wainscoting. Listed on the National Register of Historic Places, the building is one of the two surviving Federal-style courthouses in North Carolina.

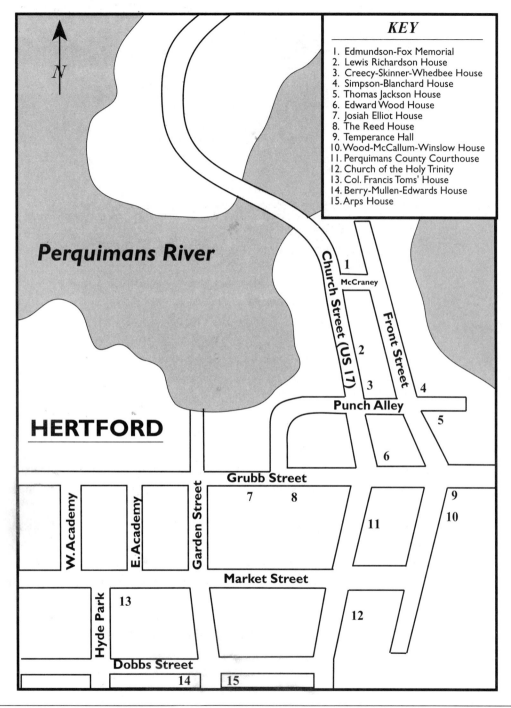

KEY

1. Edmundson-Fox Memorial
2. Lewis Richardson House
3. Creecy-Skinner-Whedbee House
4. Simpson-Blanchard House
5. Thomas Jackson House
6. Edward Wood House
7. Josiah Elliot House
8. The Reed House
9. Temperance Hall
10. Wood-McCallum-Winslow House
11. Perquimans County Courthouse
12. Church of the Holy Trinity
13. Col. Francis Toms' House
14. Berry-Mullen-Edwards House
15. Arps House

Perquimans River

Church Street (US 17)

McCraney

Front Street

Punch Alley

HERTFORD

Grubb Street

W. Academy

E. Academy

Garden Street

Market Street

Hyde Park

Dobbs Street

Perquimans County Courthouse

The Register of Deeds Office contains a wealth of historic information. Recorded here is the oldest surviving deed in North Carolina. Dated March 1, 1661, the instrument documents the transfer of a tract of land called Wecocomicke, sold by Chief Kilcocanen to George Durant. However, a reference in the deed to an earlier land purchase by one Samuel Pricklove lends credence to the contention that the earliest settlers in the colony took up residence at Durants Neck. Land records in the courthouse are unbroken from the Kilcocanen-Durant deed.

Two monuments on the courthouse lawn honor a pair of Hertford's favorite sons. One of the markers is dedicated to the memory of Dr. John Harris, the father of dental education in the United States. He died in Hertford in 1849. The other proclaims Hertford as the birthplace of Hall of Fame baseball player James "Catfish" Hunter.

Although the site of Hertford was settled as early as the last decade of the seventeenth century, attempts to incorporate the town as Phelps Point, in honor of a pioneer family, failed in 1746. Twelve years later, John Harvey used his political clout to obtain the incorporation of Hertford, named for a town in England.

From the courthouse, walk north on Church Street. The business district boasts an interesting assortment of shops housed in late-eighteenth- and early-twentieth-century buildings.

Turn left off Church Street onto Grubb Street. At this intersection, the famed Eagle Hotel and Tavern once covered six lots. From 1754 until it was destroyed in 1915, the rambling multistory hostelry served a variety of interesting guests. George Washington stayed at the tavern while surveying the Great Dismal Swamp. William Hooper, a North Carolina signer of the Declaration of Independence, once lived at the Eagle.

In the first block of West Grubb, there are two antebellum houses of interest.

Located at 106 West Grubb, the Reed House was built by Colonel Wilson Reed, a prominent planter, in 1850. An insurance policy dated May 12, 1851, reveals that the two-story Greek Revival structure was insured for three thousand dollars at the time.

Just down the street at 128 West Grubb, the Josiah Elliot House is named for a noted local Baptist minister. Built around 1832 by Edy Wood, a free black woman, it is the only surviving one-story coastal cottage in Hertford.

Return to the corner of Church and Grubb and proceed north on Church Street. At the northeast corner of the intersection, a commercial building occupies the site of the original town cemetery. Near the sidewalk are two sizable ballast stones that are said to mark the grave of Kiskitano, the king of the Yeopim Indians.

At 208 North Church, the Edward Wood House is dignified by a two-story porch supported by imposing columns. Constructed in 1818 of hand-hewn heart-of-pine timbers fastened together with wooden pegs, the Federal side-hall-plan dwelling exhibits an architectural style typical of its time. A tree close to the house is said to be the grave of Chief Kilcocanen.

The Creecy-Skinner-Whedbee House, at the corner of North Church and Punch Alley, is believed to be the oldest house in town. Although the actual date of construction has been lost to history, it may have been as early as 1775. Four-term United States congressman Thomas G. Skinner once lived in the two-and-a-half-story Federal-style house.

The Creecy-Skinner-Whedbee House

Located at 310 North Church, the Lewis Richardson House is a handsomely styled two-story Greek Revival dwelling. Its double-tier engaged porches on the front and rear were a common architectural feature in early-nineteenth-century structures in the Albemarle region.

Continue 1 block on North Church Street to McCraney Street. Here stands the Edmundson-Fox Memorial, erected by the Quakers in 1929 to honor early missionaries William Edmundson and George Fox.

Turn right onto McCraney and proceed east to the intersection with Front Street. Walk south on Front as it runs alongside the river.

Constructed in 1858, the Simpson-Blanchard House at 300 North Front is a majestic two-story Federal dwelling which was enlarged in the early twentieth century.

The impressive Thomas Jackson House, built around 1875, stands at 208 North Front near the site of the old ferry landing. From 1730 until the float bridge was built in 1798, the ferry ran across the Perquimans to Newbys Point.

In the original town plan, Front Street was not the waterfront street. Water Street once ran to the east of, and parallel to, Front Street, but the river claimed it many years ago. At the corner of Front and East Grubb, turn left onto Grubb and walk east to the end of the street for a panoramic view of the river near the site of old Water Street.

Return to Front Street and continue south. The Sons of Temperance built the two-story Temperance Hall, located at 116 North Front, in 1848. Less than a decade later, it was converted to a private dwelling.

Shells from Union naval vessels damaged the Wood-McCallum-Winslow House, located at 110 Front, during the Civil War. Although this New England–style house was completed in 1825, the lot at this site has been occupied continuously since Hertford was chartered.

Turn right off Front Street onto Market Street. Proceed 1 block to Church Street and turn left. On the left after 1 block is the Church of the Holy Trinity. This Episcopal church has stood on Church Street since 1850, making it the oldest church building in Hertford. Among its interesting architectural features are functional wooden buttresses, plaster ceiling decorations, and original stained-glass windows. Still functional, its 1854 Jardine organ is the oldest organ in the county. Its baptismal font was originally given to St. Paul's Parish in Edenton by Queen Anne in the early eighteenth century. The belfry and the vestibule were added to the building in 1894.

After you have seen the Church of the Holy Trinity, turn around and walk north on Church Street, then turn left, or west, onto Dobbs Street. Three handsome antebellum houses are located in a two-block section of Dobbs. Located at 113 West Dobbs, the Arps House dates from 1850. The

Berry-Mullen-Edwards House, at 201 West Dobbs, was constructed in 1821. And the Jacocks-Reed-Newbold House, at 217 West Dobbs, can be traced to 1851.

At the intersection of West Dobbs and Hyde Park streets, turn right on Hyde Park, then turn right onto West Market Street after 1 block. The store building at 308 West Market is believed to be the oldest commercial building in Hertford. Business has been conducted here since 1835.

The stately two-story Federal–Colonial Revival house at 215 West Market Street was erected in 1820 for Colonel Francis Toms, one of the county commissioners who was instrumental in the courthouse construction project of 1825.

A portion of the Toms-White House, located at 200 West Market, was built in 1819. Additions in the 1830s and 1900 brought about the present appearance. Clinton W. Toms, the benefactor who made the restoration of the courthouse possible, was born here.

At 130 West Market, just east of the Toms-White House, stands the Dr. C. Winslow House. This 1851-vintage structure served as the office of a prominent physician.

Located in the same block of West Market, Hertford Baptist Church, constructed in 1854, was extensively remodeled in 1923. The congregation traces its roots to Bethel Baptist Church at Harveys Neck.

At the corner of Market and Church streets, turn left onto Church and return to your car at the courthouse. Drive south on Church Street (U.S. 17 Business) for approximately 1 mile to its intersection with U.S. 17 Bypass. Head west on U.S. 17 Bypass as the tour passes along the southern edge of the Bear Swamp.

Six miles west of Hertford, U.S. 17 junctions with N.C. 37 near the Perquimans County–Chowan County line. Turn left on N.C. 37 and drive 0.7 mile south to the intersection with S.R. 1101. Turn left on S.R. 1101 and follow it south for 0.6 mile to its junction with S.R. 1102. Turn right on S.R. 1102 and drive 0.6 mile south to Yeopim Baptist Church.

Although the minutes of this first Baptist church in Chowan County began in 1791, the congregation can be traced back even farther. In its infancy, the church had some interesting rules and regulations. As early as

1803, women members were allowed to vote on church issues. However, from 1818 to 1845, any member who fished on Sunday faced excommunication. Dedicated on October 25, 1851, the existing church building replaced the original, which was destroyed by fire a year earlier.

Continue 0.5 mile south on S.R. 1102 to rejoin N.C. 37. Turn left on N.C. 37. After 2.4 miles, turn south on N.C. 32. Follow N.C. 32 for 1.5 miles and park in the parking area near the Albemarle Sound Bridge at Sandy Point Beach.

Until the twentieth century, the only way to cross Albemarle Sound from Edenton, 7 miles to the north, was by boat. In 1910, the Norfolk Southern Railway completed an engineering marvel when it opened a 5-mile-long railroad bridge across the sound, thereby linking Washington and Chowan counties by rail. Upon its completion, the wooden bridge was said to be the longest rail span over a body of water in the world.

On January 3, 1987, the railway bridge was closed and abandoned due to mounting maintenance costs. A year later, workmen began dismantling the landmark, which had been used by visitors to Edenton for much of the century. At the time it was torn down, the amazing structure was still one of the longest rail spans in the nation.

It was well into the twentieth century before Edenton was able to showcase the treasures of its glorious past to vast numbers of the motoring public. Before 1939, tourists on their way to the Outer Banks more often than not disdained a side trip to Edenton, because of the inconvenience and

Albemarle Sound Bridge

unreliability of the ferry service across Albemarle Sound. In the spring of 1936, the state began to formulate plans to bridge the sound. Just over two years later, the longest vehicular bridge in the state at the time was completed at a cost of $1.5 million. It was estimated that the building materials would have filled a freight train 7.5 miles long. Laid end to end, the pilings alone would have extended 50 miles.

After almost forty-five years of uninterrupted service, the long span began to exhibit serious signs of deterioration in the early 1980s. As a result, plans were formulated for the construction of a new bridge. Completed over a four-year period at a cost of $22.3 million, the new bridge is wider than its predecessor and features a sixty-five-foot arch that eliminates annoying traffic jams caused by the drawbridge portion of the old structure.

For most of 1985, the old and new spans paralleled each other. Late in the year, work began on the demolition of the wooden structure that had served the area so well. Despite the improvements embodied in the new bridge, the structure continues to elicit some of the same fear in tourists as did the old bridge. John Stillman, who operates a furniture store in the Pea Ridge community, located near the south approach to the bridge, was thirteen years old when the original span opened. He is well aware of the intimidating effect that the bridges have had on motorists. Numerous concerned drivers have stopped at his store over the years. "You wouldn't believe the number of times I've had people come in here and ask me to drive them over," Stillman once remarked.

You may want to make a quick side trip to experience the exhilarating bridge crossing.

From the parking area at Sandy Point Beach, retrace your route north on N.C. 32 for 1.2 miles to the junction with S.R. 1114. Turn west onto S.R. 1114 for a circular 7.2-mile drive along the sound. Numerous side roads provide spectacular views of the enormous body of water. Located approximately midway on this route is Edenton Municipal Airport, the outgrowth of a World War II military base.

As S.R. 1114 begins to swing northeast toward Edenton, the road parallels the Chowan River as it empties into the sound. In this area just south of Edenton, a number of ancient plantations survive. Located on the sound 5 miles from Edenton, Mulberry Hill is a beautiful four-story brick house built before the Revolution. A fan window with a radius of five feet in the west gable of the house was built from a single piece of wood.

At the northern junction of S.R. 1114 and N.C. 32, turn left onto N.C. 32 for the 2.5-mile drive north into Edenton. Among the plantation homes located nearby are Sycamore and Greenfield. Sycamore, built in the seventeenth century, contains its original floors, paneling, and mantels. Greenfield, built around 1752, is an excellent example of the double-galleried, low-ceilinged plantation houses of the Albemarle region.

Indeed, as the tour nears Edenton, you will begin to sense the timelessness of the place. Prominently situated at the mouth of the Chowan River, venerable Edenton stands proudly as the grand lady of northeastern North Carolina. Its downtown streets and tree-lined lanes are graced with scores of finely restored buildings from the colonial and antebellum periods. Though these antique architectural treasures bear testimony to the age of the town, they fail to convey the full story of the importance of Edenton to colonial North Carolina.

Over the past three centuries, much of the political prominence and power once enjoyed by Edenton has been eroded by the westward growth of North Carolina. Nevertheless, this small waterfront town with lingering colonial charm remains the unofficial capital of the Albemarle region.

N.C. 32 becomes Church Street on the eastern side of Edenton. Turn left off Church onto South Oakum Street and proceed south to the waterfront as Oakum merges into East Water Street.

Most every street in the oldest parts of Edenton bears a historic name. Water Street was known as George Street before the Revolution. Just north of Water Street and parallel to it is King Street. Before the rift developed between the colonies and England, a subject proceeding to the waterfront would thus be reminded of the British monarch as he crossed the two streets. Likewise, Queen Street was known as Queen Anne Street until the revolutionary spirit spread throughout the colony. Eden Street, located between King and Queen streets, was named to honor Charles Eden, the namesake of the town. Parallel to and north of Queen Street is Church Street, so named for ancient St. Paul's Church, which stands majestically nearby. Farther north, Gale Street honors Christopher Gale, the second chief justice of the North Carolina province, while Albemarle Street is named for George

Monck, the duke of Albemarle. Of the four primary north-south streets that dead-end at the waterfront, Granville, named for the earl of Granville, one of the Lords Proprietors, and Court Street, named for the splendid courthouse that has graced the town for more than two centuries, bear historic names.

And then there is the less-than-regal-sounding Oakum Street. A local legend explains the name. About the time of the Revolution, a beautiful young lady lived with her mother in a house on the street. She maintained what was considered to be the most beautiful flower garden in all of Edenton. When war came, her true love marched off to fight with the Continental Army. To help pass the time while he was away, the young lady and her mother sewed night and day, fashioning uniforms, blankets, and socks for the soldiers. Upon the surrender of Cornwallis, her boyfriend failed to return. Her heart was broken, and the forlorn young lady lost her mind. Daily, she walked the long porch of her home, her vacant eyes searching for her fallen sweetheart. Days melted into months as the bereaved woman screamed ceaselessly, "O come! O come! O come!" Residents of the neighborhood, sympathetic to her cries, came to speak of the street as the "O Come Street."

The chief attraction of Edenton is its treasure chest of historic architectural masterpieces. You need drive only a few blocks to get a glimpse of the many historic sites that have been restored. But the best way to take in everything that old Edenton has to offer is on foot. To begin the walking tour, park near the waterfront on Water Street.

Although vestiges of the town's proud past are evident in every part of Edenton, the heart of the old town is the waterfront. This delightful area is listed on the National Register of Historic Places as the Edenton Historic District.

Without question, one of the most picturesque spots on the waterfront is the gracefully sloping lawn known as the Village Green, or Edenton Green. Neatly manicured and landscaped with flowers, fountains, and walkways, this public area lies in the area bordered by King Street, Colonial Avenue, Court Street, and Water Street. It is maintained by the town of Edenton, even though there is no record of title or known owner. At one time, the green was called the "Public Parade." On the grounds were stocks, racks, and a pillory. Militia used the grounds for drills in the shadow of the courthouse.

Indeed, this scenic spot has been witness to the storied history of Edenton. While the first two towns in the colony—Bath and New Bern—were being humbled by the Tuscarora slaughter in 1711–12, the growing settlement on the Chowan River and Queen Anne's Creek took advantage of the relative peace existing between the settlers and Indians in the Albemarle region to raise its stature in the colony.

In the years before the Tuscarora uprising, the "Town on Matecomak Creek," as the community was known to the Indians, had already begun taking shape. The village grew into a town in 1712, when the Colonial Assembly enacted legislation "to build a Courthouse and House to hold the Assembly in the forks of Queen Anne's Creek."

From 1715 to 1722, the town was known officially as the "Town on Queen Anne's Creek." During that time, two significant developments took place to thrust the town into a preeminent position in the colony. First, Charles Eden, colonial governor from 1714 to 1722 and alleged conspirator of Blackbeard, located his home on the Chowan River near the town. As a result, it served as the first unofficial capital of North Carolina until 1740, when the political power of the Albemarle region was diluted. Additionally, it was recognized by the Colonial Assembly as an official port of entry. As the "Port of Roanoke," the town developed a thriving shipping trade. Wharves and warehouses sprang up on the waterfront. Upon Governor Eden's death in 1722, the town was incorporated as Edenton in his honor.

On the eve of the American Revolution, Edenton remained one of the leading towns in the colony, having virtually tripled in size since 1728. Thanks largely to a citizenry of unusual talents and abilities, the town was in the forefront of the call for independence in North Carolina. Several markers and monuments on the Village Green honor the revolutionary fervor in colonial Edenton.

Prominently displayed on the sea wall near the waterfront park at the foot of the Village Green are three Swiss cannon brought to Edenton in 1778 by Captain William Boritz on his ship, *The Holy Heart of Jesus*. They were among a shipment of forty-five cannon purchased in Marseilles, France, by Edenton patriots Thomas Benbury and Thomas Jones—through the assistance of Benjamin Franklin—for use in the defense of North Carolina.

Upon his arrival at Edenton in July 1778, Captain Boritz attempted to collect the transportation charges: 150 pounds of tobacco for every 100 pounds of cannon. State authorities tried to find enough tobacco to ensure delivery of the remaining twenty-three cannon on the ship. To their dismay, the guns weighed more than 100,000 pounds—a weight greater than all of the tobacco in the warehouses of Edenton.

The stalemate was finally broken when the cannon were dumped overboard into the murky waters of Edenton Bay. Two different stories surround the dumping of the cargo. One relates that the cannon remained on board the ship at anchor for half of the war; when British troops approached Edenton, the men of the town disposed of the weapons to prevent their capture by the enemy. However, the more widely accepted story is that Captain Boritz grew tired of waiting to collect his tobacco. His patience gone, Boritz threw the cannon off the ship.

Swiss cannon brought to Edenton in 1778

Regardless of who put them there, at least fifteen of the cannon remain in the mud under the waters of Edenton Bay. Six were recovered during the Civil War by patriotic citizens, who mounted them on wagon wheels for use in the defense of the town. Federal forces arrived in Edenton by water on February 12, 1862, and after an inspection of the cannon by the commanding officer, the weapons were declared unsafe and were subsequently spiked. Five of the six recovered cannon are on public display in North Carolina—three on the Edenton waterfront and two on Capitol Square in Raleigh.

From the waterfront, cross over to the north side of Water Street. Walk north on the west side of the Village Green to the bronze teapot monument, which commemorates the renowned Edenton Tea Party.

It was in Edenton, on October 25, 1774, that one of the most revolutionary acts in the American colonies prior to the Declaration of Independence took place. At the home of Mrs. Elizabeth King, fifty-one local ladies assembled to sign a resolution in support of the 1774 action of the First Provincial Congress that had banned the import and consumption of British tea. Presiding over the meeting was Mrs. Penelope Barker, who persuaded the group to refrain from drinking British tea until it was once again tax-free.

At their tea party, the women toasted their act of defiance with a concoction brewed from dried raspberry leaves. Their action is considered the earliest known instance of political activity on the part of women in the American colonies. This historic event inspired Edenton's town symbol: a brass teapot.

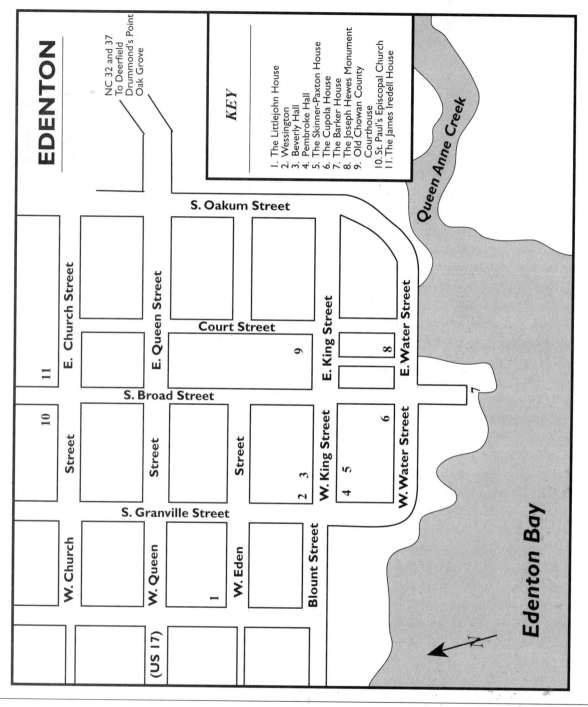

EDENTON

NC 32 and 37
To Deerfield
Drummond's Point
Oak Grove

KEY

1. The Littlejohn House
2. Wessington
3. Beverly Hall
4. Pembroke Hall
5. The Skinner-Paxton House
6. The Cupola House
7. The Barker House
8. The Joseph Hewes Monument
9. Old Chowan County Courthouse
10. St. Paul's Episcopal Church
11. The James Iredell House

S. Oakum Street

E. Church Street

E. Queen Street

Court Street

E. King Street

E. Water Street

S. Broad Street

Street

Street

Street

W. King Street

W. Water Street

S. Granville Street

W. Church

W. Queen

W. Eden

Blount Street

(US 17)

Queen Anne Creek

Edenton Bay

N

When a copy of the resolution made its way to Great Britain, it was published in a London newspaper. This caused such a stir there that the Edenton ladies were caricatured in a cartoon in the *London Adviser*.

Because it was an important event in the American struggle for independence, the tea party has been memorialized outside the confines of Edenton. An original mezzotint of the event is owned by the Metropolitan Museum of Art in New York City. In Raleigh, a plaque in the rotunda of the Capitol honors the brave women of Edenton.

Waterfront view of the Barker House

A photograph of a painting of the event is among the collection of the North Carolina Museum of History. The story behind the photograph is in itself fascinating. Just after the War of 1812, a young American naval officer, Lieutenant William T. Muse of nearby Pasquotank County, happened to be in a barbershop on a Mediterranean island when he was astonished to behold an unusual painting hanging on a wall. Entitled *The Edenton Tea Party*, the artwork was a 1775 caricature by a London artist. Muse prevailed upon the owner of the painting to allow him to take it home. In Edenton, it was prominently displayed in a barbershop and became the talk of the town. Subsequently, the painting was dropped and broke into numerous pieces. It was meticulously pieced back together in order that a photograph could be made by the Museum of History.

From the teapot monument, return to the south edge of the Village Green, where the Hewes Monument pays tribute to Joseph Hewes.

Because it was the most important town in North Carolina for most of the first half of the eighteenth century, Edenton attracted men of high intellect and great ability. An outsider observed that "within the vicinity of Edenton there was in proportion to its population a greater number of men eminent for ability, virtue, and erudition than in any other part of America." During and immediately after the Revolution, few American cities could boast a more remarkable group of statesmen of national import than Edenton. Among this elite group of Edentonians were some of the true champions of independence and builders of the new republic: Joseph Hewes, Samuel Johnston, Hugh Williamson, and James Iredell.

Hewes was one of the most celebrated members of the Continental Congress. In 1775, Congress assigned him to the Naval Board. His position as secretary of that board made him in essence the first secretary of the United

States Navy. It was Hewes who secured John Paul Jones's first commission in the Continental Navy.

On July 4, 1776, Hewes affixed his signature to the Declaration of Independence. Three years later, he died unexpectedly in Philadelphia at the age of forty-nine while serving in Congress. Its delegates voted to attend the funeral as a body and declared a one-month period of mourning. Among the many tributes paid to Hewes was the following: "His name is recorded on the Magna Carta of our liberty—his fame will lie until the last vestige of American history shall be blotted from the world."

Designed by Rogers and Poor and dedicated in 1932, the Hewes Monument is the only monument to a signer of the Declaration of Independence erected by congressional appropriation. This granite shaft is a solemn tribute to the man who made the first utterance for independence in the Continental Congress, when he presented the Halifax Resolves to that body on May 27, 1776.

Monument honoring Joseph Hewes

From the Hewes Monument, walk 1 block west on East Water Street. Turn left onto South Broad. Here on the waterfront at 509 South Broad stands the Barker House, a charming two-and-a-half-story frame house. Built in 1782, the clapboard structure originally stood at 213 Broad Street until it was moved to the end of Broad in 1952. Impressive in design, it features Federal and Greek Revival elements. Its original owners were Thomas and Penelope Barker. Thomas Barker served as a successful colonial agent for North Carolina in London prior to the Revolution, and his wife was one of the leading participants in the Edenton Tea Party.

By billing itself as the "most beautiful town on the Carolina coast," Edenton has thrown down the gauntlet to the other coastal towns in North Carolina which might challenge the claim: Wilmington, New Bern, Beaufort, and Oriental. With a population of approximately six thousand, Edenton is much smaller than Wilmington and New Bern, thus making a comparison with those cities unfair. Beaufort and Oriental are similar in size. Though neat, clean, and picturesque, Oriental lacks the historical charm and architectural treasures of Edenton. Beaufort rivals Edenton in its age and number of historic structures. Its renovated waterfront, a splendid sight indeed, represents a masterful job of blending old and new. Yet Edenton, by virtue of its almost unspoiled waterfront, provides a compelling visual argument for the title it proudly claims.

From the Barker House, walk north on South Broad Street. This wide main street, aptly named, contains an impressive array of commercial buildings dating from the late 1800s and early 1900s, some of which have cast-iron storefronts. Interesting shops, old-time hardware stores, and folksy diners offer a wonderful sample of small-town America in a historic setting.

Located at 408 South Broad Street, the two-and-a-half-story Cupola House was constructed in 1758. Part of the guided tour available at the Historic Edenton Visitor Center on Broad Street, this stately old house gives visitors the unique opportunity to inspect not only the oldest structure in Edenton but the oldest frame house in North Carolina. Listed on the National Register of Historic Places and preserved as a National Historic Landmark, it has been described as the finest Jacobean house in America. Its unusual second-story overhang is believed to be the only one of its kind in the South.

Edenton's most famous structure, Cupola House takes its name from the octagonal "lantern" atop its roof. In times long past, the cupola, reached by a circular stairway from the attic, was used to sight incoming ships.

Though the woodwork from one of the downstairs rooms was purchased by the Brooklyn Museum of Art, much of the original woodwork remains, including the hand-carved paneling, the chair rails, and the mantels. Visitors also marvel at the Chinese Chippendale staircase and the wavy glass windows.

At the intersection of South Broad and West King streets, turn west onto West King. Edenton has accepted change slowly, wisely, and gracefully. An air of tranquility pervades its streets, many of which have changed little over the past two hundred years. Majestic elm, pecan, and magnolia trees shade the narrow residential lanes, which are lined with homes featuring a variety of architectural patterns: Colonial, Georgian, Federal, Greek, Gothic Revival, Queen Anne, and Victorian.

Located at 104 West King, the James Iredell, Jr., Law Office was built in the transitional Georgian-Federal style in 1802. In the first third of the nineteenth century, James Iredell, Jr., was a leading politician in North Carolina. He was elected governor in 1828 and was subsequently appointed to fill the unexpired term of Nathaniel Macon in the United States Senate.

The 100 block of West King could well be called "Mansion Row," for there are no fewer than four mansions in the block.

Beverly Hall, at 114 West King, is a magnificent Federal-style mansion with Greek Revival details. Constructed in 1810 and enlarged in 1855, the dwelling served as the Edenton branch of the State Bank of North Carolina from 1816 to 1835.

Built in the 1820s, the Skinner-Paxton House, at 115 West King, is the largest and finest side-hall-plan house in town. In the interior of the two-and-a-half-story frame mansion is a spectacular folk-art mural painted in 1989 by Debra Darnall, an artist from Columbus, Ohio. This scenic wall painting, which illustrates the Edenton waterfront of the early eighteenth century, rises with the stairs to the attic.

At 120 West King stands Wessington, the grandest house in all of Edenton. Constructed of brick in 1850, this imposing mansion rises two stories over a full basement. Its elongated first-floor windows feature colorful transoms with panes of blue, red, yellow, green, and violet. Dr. Thomas Warren, one of the wealthiest men in the state, built the house. Most of his vast wealth was lost during the Civil War while he served as a surgeon for North Carolina troops. In 1869, Warren was forced to sell the house.

Pembroke Hall, the fourth of the mansions in this block, is located at

121 West King on a bluff overlooking Edenton Bay. Constructed for Dr. Matthew Page in 1850, the stately two-story frame house is considered one of the most impressive Greek Revival dwellings in the state. Matthew Page was the great-grandson of William Byrd, the surveyor of the North Carolina–Virginia border in 1728.

At the intersection of West King and South Granville, walk across South Granville to Blount Street. Located at 108 Blount, the rambling, frame West Custom House was built around 1772 on land originally set aside for the "governor's pasture." Swiss sea captain William Boritz owned this house from 1787 until 1798. A year later, the house acquired its name when it was purchased by the collector of customs.

Turn right off Blount Street onto Moseley Street, walk 1 block north, and turn right on West Eden Street.

Located at 218 West Eden, the Littlejohn House was built in 1791 by Sarah Blount Littlejohn, one of the signers of the Tea Party Resolutions.

Nearby, the Tredwell House, at 214 West Eden, was constructed around 1787. It was the home of Samuel Tredwell, collector of the port of Roanoke.

Near the end of the block, at 206 West Eden, stands the gambrel-roofed Charlton House, constructed in the 1760s by Jasper Charlton, an attorney and Revolutionary War firebrand. His wife was the first signer of the Tea Party Resolutions.

At the corner of West Eden and South Granville streets, turn left and walk 1 block north on South Granville, then turn right on West Queen

St. Paul's Episcopal Church

Street. Located in the middle of the block, at 120 West Queen, the gambrel-roofed Leigh House was constructed in 1756 by Gilbert Leigh, the architect of the Chowan County Courthouse. Lydia Bennett, a signer of the Tea Party Resolutions, lived in the house during the Revolution.

Proceed east on West Queen to the intersection with South Broad Street. Walk north on South Broad for one block, then turn left on West Church Street. Located at the northwest corner of Broad and Church streets, St. Paul's Episcopal Church ranks as one of the nation's most historic religious shrines. Here is the second-oldest extant church building in the state. Organized in 1701 under the first Vestry Act, the congregation is the oldest in the state.

Erected in 1736, the handsome brick structure with a distinctive semicircular apse is simple in design. Supporting the octagonal spire is a square, three-story tower. The original outer brick walls were twenty-one inches thick.

On the interior, the sanctuary is divided into nave and aisles by rows of wooden columns. Tablets on the walls memorialize faithful ministers and parishioners of the past.

In August 1936, the curator of fine arts and antiques at Yale University visited St. Paul's to inspect and photograph the ancient silver chalice and paten given to the church in 1725 by one of its earliest members, Edward Moseley. Moseley was an early settler of Edenton who served as surveyor general of the colony. The curator's inspection convinced him that the communion instruments were some of the rarest and most beautiful pieces of workmanship in the country. Only two similar communion services were known to exist in the world—one in the Louvre and the other in the British Museum in London.

On the afternoon of Wednesday, June 1, 1949, fire trucks from Edenton and the Edenton Marine Air Corps base hurried to the church to battle a disastrous fire. Thought to have originated near the old pipe organ, the fire reduced the building to a shell. Fortunately, at the time the fire struck, the church was undergoing renovation, and much of the interior furnishings had been removed.

A visit to the beautifully restored, vine-covered church is not complete without a walk through its ancient graveyard. Buried in the hallowed grounds are a number of famous North Carolinians, including colonial governors Charles Eden, Thomas Pollock, and Henderson Walker.

After 1 block on West Church, turn north onto Granville Street for 1 block. Located at 108 North Granville, near the intersection with Gale Street, the William-Flury-Burton House is one of the three surviving gambrel-roofed dwellings in town. It was constructed in 1779 on East Church Street and was moved to its present location in 1942.

Continue 1 block north on Granville, then turn right on West Albemarle. Located at the corner of West Albemarle and North Broad streets, St. Anne's Catholic Church was erected in 1858. For many years, the massive church was served by priests from as far away as Fayetteville and Wilmington.

Turn right onto North Broad and walk 2 blocks south to its intersection with East Church. Turn left onto East Church. Located at 105 East Church, the James Iredell House State Historic Site features the white frame Georgian-style house purchased by James Iredell, Sr., in 1776.

In 1788, North Carolina honored James Iredell by naming a new county for him. Two years later, President George Washington, without Iredell's knowledge, appointed him associate justice of the first United States Supreme Court.

As a member of the nation's highest court, Justice Iredell wrote the dissenting opinion in the case of *Chisholm v. Georgia*, which later became the basis for the Eleventh Amendment to the United States Constitution. Three electoral votes were cast for Iredell in the presidential election of 1796.

Iredell's son, James Jr., was born in the original part of the house.

It is also worth noting that James Wilson, a friend of the senior Iredell, died in one of the upstairs rooms in 1798. Wilson, a Pennsylvania native, was a signer of the Declaration of Independence and an associate justice of the United States Supreme Court.

Nearby, the Skinner-Elliott House, located at 113 East Church, was built in 1830. It was once the home of Thomas Courtland Manning, who later moved to Louisiana and served as a general in the Confederate army, as chief justice of the Louisiana Supreme Court, as a United States senator, and as a United States minister to Mexico.

After you have seen the James Iredell House and the Skinner-Elliott House, walk south for 3 blocks on Court Street, which intersects Church in the

Chowan County Courthouse

middle of the block. Near the intersection of Court and King streets stands the old Chowan County Courthouse, constructed in 1767 to replace the courthouse of 1719. Although the county dedicated a new courthouse in 1980, the courtrooms in the old building are still used when needed, making the structure the oldest courthouse in continuous use in North Carolina and possibly the nation. Indicative of its historic significance, the building is listed on the National Register of Historic Places.

This venerable building is one of the finest existing examples of Georgian public-building architecture in the nation. Both its exterior and interior plans have won acclaim from noted architects.

On the outside, the two-story brick structure is highlighted by a modified T-shaped hip roof and a cupola. Edenton patriots gathered in the courthouse to plan their strategy during the Revolution. When North Carolina ratified the United States Constitution in 1789, the cupola was illuminated.

Interior of the Courthouse

The interior features a combination assembly room and ballroom that was one of the largest completely paneled rooms of the colonial era. It was modeled after such rooms at Bath and Tunbridge Wells in England. President James Madison attended a banquet held in his honor in this room in 1819.

Turn east on East King Street. Located in the first block, the East Custom House, the Edmund Hatch House, and the Coffield House date from 1815,

1745, and 1837, respectively. Governor Charles Eden once owned the property on which the East Custom and Edmund Hatch houses stand.

Return to Court Street and proceed south. Governor Eden likewise once owned the property on which the handsome Old Bond House, with its double porch, is located. The structure was built in 1804.

Court Street dead-ends on the waterfront at East Water Street.

Near the east end of East Water Street, a private road leads to a bridge over Queen Anne's Creek. On the other side of the bridge is the entrance to the magnificent Hayes Plantation.

Samuel Johnston, the Edentonian who served as the de facto governor of North Carolina after the abdication of Royal Governor Josiah Martin, built the mansion in 1801. Named for the estate of Sir Walter Raleigh in England, Hayes Plantation consists of a white two-story section dominated by a large cupola. Single-story wings containing a library and kitchen are connected to the main building by curved, covered passages. On the mansion's southwest elevation, a two-story Doric portico faces Edenton Bay.

From the intersection of Court and East Water streets, return along East Water Street to your car to end the tour.

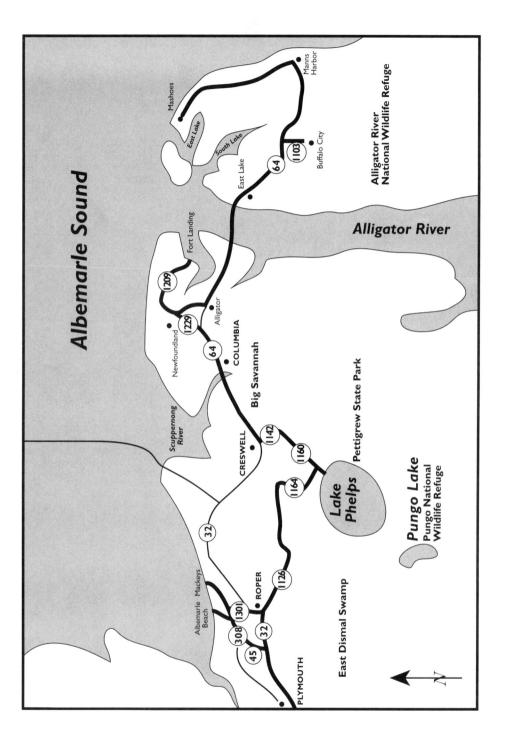

The Southern Albemarle Tour

This tour begins in the old Roanoke River town of Plymouth. It moves east into the sparsely populated coastal plain through the villages of Mackeys, Roper, and Creswell. Just south of Creswell, the tour reaches the shore of Lake Phelps and Pettigrew State Park before continuing east into Tyrrell County and the historic settlements of Columbia and Fort Landing. After crossing the enormous Alligator River, it proceeds through the communities of East Lake, Manns Harbor, and Mashoes.

Among the highlights of the tour are historic Plymouth, the former site of Buncombe Hall, Somerset Place State Historic Site, the Alligator River National Wildlife Refuge, and the former site of Buffalo City and Beechland.

Total mileage: approximately 117 miles.

This tour begins at the junction of U.S. 64 and Washington Street in the charming river town of Plymouth.

It is one of the quirks of coastal geography that county seats with the same names as counties are not the seats of the counties with which they share a name. Plymouth is the county seat of Washington County. Thirty-five miles to the south, Washington is the county seat of Beaufort County. Seventy-five miles south of Washington, Beaufort is the county seat of Carteret County.

Were it not for the route of U.S. 64 through Washington, Tyrrell, and mainland Dare counties, many of the present-day visitors to these counties on the south shore of Albemarle Sound would never pass through the region. Indeed, motorists who drive through Plymouth on their way to the Outer Banks usually see only the strip of fast-food restaurants, convenience stores, and shopping centers along the highway, which skirts the southern limits of town. Hidden beyond the view of the highway traveler is the old town resting tranquilly on the banks of the beautiful Roanoke River.

From the junction of U.S. 64 and Washington Street, proceed 4 blocks north on Washington, then turn right, or east, onto Fourth Street.

Approximately five thousand people live in Plymouth, making it comparable in population to Edenton, its historic neighbor across Albemarle Sound.

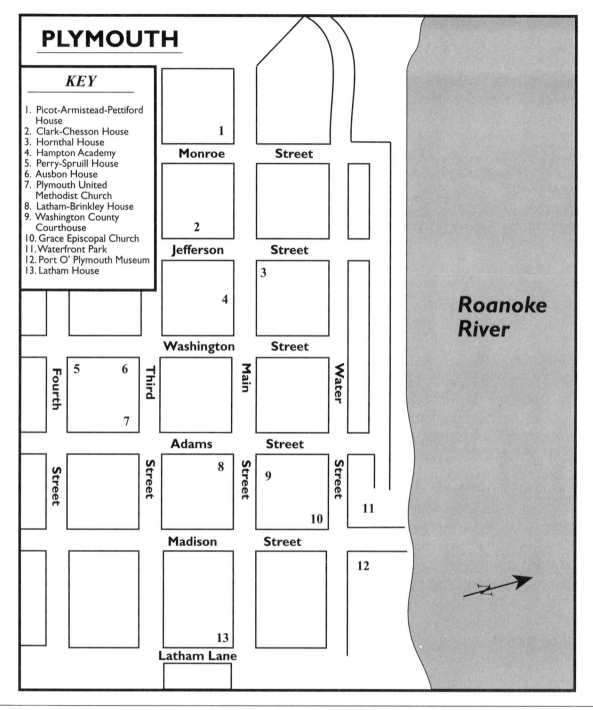

PLYMOUTH

KEY

1. Picot-Armistead-Pettiford House
2. Clark-Chesson House
3. Hornthal House
4. Hampton Academy
5. Perry-Spruill House
6. Ausbon House
7. Plymouth United Methodist Church
8. Latham-Brinkley House
9. Washington County Courthouse
10. Grace Episcopal Church
11. Waterfront Park
12. Port O' Plymouth Museum
13. Latham House

Monroe Street

Jefferson Street

Washington Street

Adams Street

Madison Street

Latham Lane

Fourth Street

Third Street

Main Street

Water Street

Roanoke River

Because of the damage it sustained during the Civil War, Plymouth is unable to boast as large an assemblage of antebellum structures as Edenton. Yet a handsome assortment of architectural prizes graces the quiet, shady streets of Plymouth.

Located at the northeastern corner of the intersection of Washington and Fourth streets, the Perry-Spruill House dates from 1883. This Greek Revival cottage is one of the finest buildings in Plymouth.

Drive 2 blocks on Fourth Street, then turn left, or north, on Madison Street for 1 block. Next, turn right, or east, on Third Street for 1 block, then turn north on Latham Lane for 1 block to the intersection with East Main Street.

Perhaps the most distinctive pre–Civil War house in Plymouth is the two-story Latham House, which stands near the intersection at 311 East Main Street. This Greek Revival frame dwelling was constructed in 1850 by Charles Latham, a prominent attorney and politician. While the Battle of Plymouth raged in 1864, many of the citizens of the town took refuge in the basement of this house. A close inspection of the house reveals musket-ball holes from the battle. After suffering from years of neglect, the house is presently being restored.

Latham House

Turn left, or west, onto Main Street. After 1 block, turn right, or north, on Madison Street and drive 1 block to its intersection with Water Street. Turn right, or east, on Water Street and park in the parking lot adjacent to the Port O' Plymouth Museum, at 302 Water Street.

Located on the majestic river in the former Atlantic Coast Line Railroad Station, constructed around 1923, the museum offers an attractive array of exhibits chronicling the history of Plymouth and the Roanoke River region. While much of the collection centers around the Civil War events in and around the town, exhibits are rotated on an annual basis. A nominal admission fee is charged.

The first known permanent settlers came to the present site of Plymouth around 1720, because of the area's strategic location near the mouth of the Roanoke River. However, there are some who believe the South Albemarle shores may have been settled as early as the year 1000 A.D., when King Olaf Triggvason ruled Scandinavia. Archaeological finds made in the 1940s along the shores of the Roanoke River in Mecklenburg County, Virginia, support the theory that the Vikings explored and lived on the banks of the Roanoke five hundred years before Columbus came to America and six hundred years before the ill-fated colonization attempts at nearby Roanoke Island. En route to upstream sites in present-day Virginia, the Vikings would have undoubtedly entered the river from Albemarle Sound near Plymouth. And according to the theory, they may have reconnoitered the river shoreline now occupied by the town.

During his exploration of the Albemarle region in the early eighteenth century, historian John Lawson made some startling discoveries, from which some have assumed that white people lived in the area long before the first known settlers arrived. In his *History of North Carolina*, printed in 1714, Lawson reported seeing iron-wrought timbers—timbers cut by metal implements—that had been found twenty-six feet below the surface of the earth in the Plymouth area.

Plymouth was established in 1787, when Arthur Rhodes, a former resident of Plymouth, Massachusetts, donated a hundred acres from his plantation on the river for a town site. Its advantageous location on the Roanoke River quickly vaulted Plymouth into a position of prominence in the Albemarle region. In 1790, though not yet incorporated, the town was designated a "port of delivery." A charter was granted to Plymouth in 1807, and the following year, the state recognized the growing importance of the town as a center of commerce by naming it a port of entry.

Washington County Courthouse

In 1823, Plymouth became the county seat of Washington County when the courthouse was moved west from Lees Mills. Two decades later, the thriving port was one of the leading shipping points in the entire state. As many as fifty ships and boats might be docked at one time at the riverfront wharves, where they were loaded with shingles and staves for shipment to the West Indies. During the early months of 1857, D. H. Strother, a writer for *Harper's New Monthly Magazine,* visited the town, then a place of more than a thousand residents. In the March issue of the magazine, he credited the town as being "the successful commercial rival of Edenton."

Following the vicious fighting during the Civil War, residents of Plymouth resurrected their town by using the plentiful natural resources in the nearby forests and the waterway. More than 130 years later, these resources continue to dominate the local economy.

Walk west from the museum to the adjacent waterfront park. This green, tree-sheltered area features picnic facilities, a boat-launching ramp, and a river overlook.

The Roanoke River

Perhaps Plymouth's greatest asset is the magnificent waterway that graces its downtown. To the casual observer, the Roanoke River does not appear large when compared to the other great coastal rivers in the state. Yet despite its relatively narrow width, this mighty river twists and turns for nearly 400 miles. It is formed by the junction of the North Fork and South Fork rivers in the hills of Montgomery County, Virginia. As it flows down the hills into the coastal plain of North Carolina, it steadily gains force. Along the North Carolina–Virginia border, the John H. Kerr Dam was constructed to tame the river.

Ralph Lane explored some portions of the river near its mouth in 1586. He noted that the Algonquin Indians who lived along its banks in the vicinity of present-day Plymouth called the river the Moratoc. Lane was dissuaded from further exploration on the river, because its current was so strong that little progress could be made against it with oars.

A legend along the river holds that the Indian word *roanoke* means "river of death." However, the word was used much earlier as a place name for the famous island in Dare County. Some historians have concluded that Roanoke means "Place of White Shells."

Because its narrow width prevented sailing ships from navigating very far upstream, the river did not take on early importance as a commercial waterway. Nevertheless, due to its location at the widest part of the Roanoke, Plymouth became a center for local water commerce. Although its days as a business waterway are long gone, the river continues to lend its grace and beauty to Plymouth. Its calm, glassy, black water gives the town an air of serenity.

From the riverbank in Plymouth, you can gaze upstream to catch a glimpse of the giant paper mill that seems to rise out of the depths of the river. Despite the large number of jobs the facility provides for residents of the Plymouth area, it has been the source of a number of controversies over river pollution in recent years.

Almost ten thousand acres of river land have been preserved and are managed by the North Carolina Wildlife Resources Commission as the Batchelor Bay Game Land. Batchelor Bay, formed at the mouth of the Roanoke and Cashie rivers at the head of Albemarle Sound just north of Plymouth, was the site of a famous naval standoff between the CSS *Albemarle* and a United States Navy task force on May 5, 1864.

After Roanoke Island fell to Union forces in February 1862, Plymouth and the rest of the Albemarle region were subjected to Federal occupation until April 1864. During the occupation, Union general W. H. Wessels and several thousand troops fortified Plymouth by constructing a network of forts and entrenchments that encircled the entire town. Plymouth became a large depository for Union supplies.

General Robert Frederick Hoke, a twenty-six-year-old North Carolinian, was handpicked by President Jefferson Davis and General Robert E. Lee to lead the joint Confederate army-navy expedition that stormed the town on April 18–20, 1864.

Finally, on the morning of April 20, the stage was set: the *Albemarle*, an ironclad ram built in a cornfield upriver at Hamilton, arrived with its guns blazing to play an instrumental part in the capture of the town. While the *Albemarle* assumed full control of the river, Confederate marksmen manned every window in the remaining houses and buildings in town. The beleaguered Union forces were holed up in Fort Williams, upon which was trained Confederate artillery. At ten o'clock that morning, General Wessels ordered his men to hoist the white flag. Moments later, he rode his beautiful black

*Historical marker
for the Ram* Albemarle

horse out to meet General Hoke, who graciously received him. Handing his sword to the handsome young North Carolinian, the fifty-five-year-old United States Army veteran remarked with gloom, "General, this is the saddest day of my life." The hero of the day replied, "General, this is the proudest of mine."

Indeed, the dashing Hoke had just won the most decisive, most important victory that the Confederacy would ever earn on North Carolina soil. To be sure, the spoils of the victory were sweet: twenty-five hundred prisoners, five hundred horses, twenty-eight pieces of artillery, five thousand stand of small arms, and a treasure trove of desperately needed supplies. Before the smoke cleared from the battlefield, many of these supplies were on their way upriver to Weldon for shipment to Lee's army on the battlefields of Virginia.

For Hoke's unparalleled success in North Carolina, President Davis awarded him with a battlefield promotion to major general, thus making Hoke the youngest soldier to hold that rank in the Confederate army during the entire war.

Yet the victory that Hoke and his forces gained in the second-largest Civil War battle in North Carolina was short-lived, as Union forces sabotaged and sank the *Albemarle* in the river on October 27, 1864. Soon thereafter, the town once again fell under Union control and remained that way for the duration of the war.

Nine state historical markers—located on Main, Washington, Campbell, Fort Williams, and Jefferson streets—detail various aspects of the Civil War struggle for Plymouth.

Every April, the Port O' Plymouth Museum hosts the Battle of Plymouth Living History Weekend to commemorate the historic events of 1864. During the three-day spectacular, a wide variety of events is featured. Highlighting previous festivals have been period plays, Civil War reenactments, torchlight tours, and lectures and speeches by historians and authors.

From the waterfront park, walk across Water Street, away from the river, to Grace Episcopal Church, which fronts on Madison Street.

Designed by Richard Upjohn, this majestic brick Gothic Revival structure with a pointed steeple was completed just before the outbreak of the Civil War. Many of the interior furnishings are not original, because the

The Port O' Plymouth Museum

congregation donated the pews and gallery for use in the construction of coffins for the young men who fell during General Hoke's assault on the town. Sometime later, twelve sycamore trees—each bearing the name of one of the Apostles—were planted around the church burial grounds on Main Street. Lightning subsequently killed the tree named Judas without causing harm to any of the others. This unusual event was featured in "Ripley's Believe It or Not."

Retrace your route to your car at the museum parking lot. Drive west on Water Street. On this street, which runs parallel to the river, the old business district remains vibrant despite the run-down appearance of some of its buildings and competition from newer businesses on the highway strip on the outskirts of town.

After 4 blocks, turn south onto Monroe Street. At 302 West Main, at the intersection of Monroe and Main, stands the Picot-Armistead-Pettiford House. Portions of this sixteen-room frame house date from 1815. From its commanding position overlooking the river, the structure was caught in the crossfire of the Civil War. A shell hole can be seen in the upper right-hand corner of the house. A tunnel once ran from the house under the street and into the river.

Turn left, or east, onto Main Street. After 1 block, turn right, or south, onto Jefferson Street. Located at 219 Jefferson, the two-story frame Clark-Chesson House is the oldest house in Plymouth. Constructed in 1810, it was subsequently owned by local shipbuilder Elijah Cornell, whose cousin founded Cornell University.

Return to Main Street and continue east. The Hornthal House, one of the most beautiful homes in Plymouth, is located at 109 West Main Street. It was constructed in 1870.

Across the street at 110 West Main Street is Hampton Academy, built around 1902. This was the first brick school building in Plymouth. It was used as a school until 1950.

Located at the northeastern corner of Main and Adams streets, the Washington County Courthouse is a handsome Neoclassical structure built in 1919. Like the nearby Latham-Brinkley House, the building is listed on the National Register of Historic Places. It is the fourth courthouse to stand here. A monument on the lawn honors General Hoke and his Confederate forces.

The Hampton Academy

On the corner directly across the street from the courthouse stands the Latham-Brinkley House, at 201 East Main. Built in 1883, this handsome Italian villa is one of Plymouth's architectural masterpieces.

Turn right, or south, off Main Street onto Adams Street. After 1 block, turn right, or west, on Third Street. Plymouth United Methodist Church, located at 109 Third, is one of the few buildings in town to survive the Civil War. Erected in 1832, the original frame structure was heavily damaged during the war. Its brick veneer was added in 1932.

Located at 302 Washington Street, on the southeastern corner of Third and Washington, the Ausbon House, built around 1840, is one of only four surviving antebellum houses in town. This neat two-story frame house was the site of fierce Civil War fighting. The exterior is marked by bullet holes from the combat. On the interior, the banisters and second-floor doorframes are carved with bullet grooves and a three-inch shell.

Turn left, or south, off Third Street onto Washington Street and drive 5 blocks to the intersection with U.S. 64 and N.C. 32. Proceed south from Plymouth on N.C. 32 for 0.6 mile, then turn east on S.R. 1112 and drive 1.8 miles, crossing N.C. 45 en route. Located on the south side of the road is Garretts Island House, a gambrel-roofed frame structure constructed in

The Ausbon House

1760. Not only is the abandoned farmhouse the oldest surviving dwelling in Washington County, but it is also one of the most mysterious places in the southern Albemarle region.

Garretts Island is a misnomer. In actuality, it is a high spot of fertile farmland surrounded by vast cypress swamps. Joseph Garrett built the farmhouse, which was later inherited by his son, Alfred (1807–1895).

On a windy, dark, overcast fall evening in 1853, Alfred Garrett was welcoming the last of his dinner guests from Plymouth when a tall, black coach pulled by six speedy, jet-black horses approached the farmhouse in reckless fashion. Suddenly, the driver, a dark figure draped in a dark cape and with his face covered by a black hood, swung the coach into the surrounding cotton fields, where it vanished without a trace. Unnerved by the episode, Garrett joined his guests for a dinner that began and ended in a somber, melancholy mood. Early the next morning, he awakened to the news that his forty-nine-year-old sister had died unexpectedly during the night. Little did Alfred Garrett realize that the previous evening had marked but the first of many visits by what the unfortunate family came to know as "the Coach of Death."

Over the next thirty years, the Coach of Death reappeared at Garretts

Garretts Island House

Island on various occasions, always followed by a tragic death. A second appearance came just months after the first, and Garrett's mother was the victim. Two years later, his forty-four-year old sister, a woman with no apparent infirmities, was claimed by the coach. On June 21, 1859, the coach's return was followed by the loss of Garrett's twenty-one-year-old son, Joseph. Over the years, young children died in the wake of the black omen of death.

Many of those who died were buried in the walled family cemetery across the road from the house. When the graveyard was full, family members were buried at Grace Episcopal Church in Plymouth. No one knows for sure, but the last appearance of the Coach of Death is thought to have occurred in 1882, when Alfred Garrett lost his twenty-three-year-old daughter, Mary Eliza.

But the strange happenings did not end with the last call of the Coach of Death. In the late 1940s, a bachelor brother and spinster sister moved into the Garretts Island house as tenant farmers. A few years later, they reported seeing a strange bluish orange figure in the parlor of the house. A short time later, while sitting on the cemetery wall during a pause from his plowing chores, the brother heard children singing. He later recalled, "Sometimes it would fade away and they'd laugh and then they'd be up close enough for me to touch them, only I never could see them."

Since the couple died in the 1980s, the house has remained vacant. Its doors and windows are now boarded up. Nearby, the cemetery remains a quiet, serene place, yet its gravestones are grim reminders of the days when a phantom black coach delivered tidings of sadness.

Retrace your route west for 1 mile on S.R. 1112 to the intersection with N.C. 45. Turn right, or northeast, onto N.C. 45 and drive 3.5 miles to N.C. 308. Turn right, or east, on N.C. 308 and proceed 4 miles to the junction with S.R. 1323. Just off the highway on this route are two historic plantation houses. Blount House, a two-story Greek Revival plantation house, faces Albemarle Sound. On the south side of the road stands Westover, a plantation house similar in architecture.

Turn left, or north, on S.R. 1323 for a 1.6-mile drive to the south shore of Albemarle Sound at Albemarle Beach. Previously known as Reas Beach, this local resort features summer cottages, swimming beaches, boathouses, and a boat-launching ramp.

Retrace your route to N.C. 308 and continue 1.4 miles northeast to the old ferry town of Mackeys.

Kendricks Creek, formerly known as Mackeys Creek, rises in the East Dismal Swamp in the center of Washington County and flows northward 9 miles into Albemarle Sound. At the mouth of the creek, the small community of Mackeys looks out on the sound from the old Mackeys Ferry Landing. From 1733 until 1938, when a vehicular bridge was built across Albemarle Sound, Mackeys Ferry operated continuously, serving as the primary means of transportation for freight and passengers across the 14-mile-wide sound.

Historical marker for Mackeys Ferry

A post office established the community as Mackeys Ferry in 1856. In 1910, three years before the name was shortened to Mackeys, the Norfolk and Southern Railroad built a rail bridge across the sound near the ferry landing. Prior to that time, trains were ferried across the sound. Originally, the ferry carried only two railway cars, but in 1886, the railroad company introduced the *John W. Garrett*, a 265-foot-long barge, which carried up to thirty-three railway freight cars at a time.

Retrace your route 1 mile west on N.C. 308 to the junction with S.R. 1301. Turn south on S.R. 1301 for the 3.2-mile drive to the venerable lumber town of Roper. Turn left, or east, onto U.S. 64 Business and drive 6 blocks through the town.

With a population of approximately eight hundred, Roper serves as the trade center for the vast rural areas between Plymouth and Columbia. Lining its streets are a variety of handsome, two-story, century-old frame dwellings. These stately houses blend into a commercial district that displays an interesting array of late-nineteenth- and early-twentieth-century buildings.

At first glance, Roper appears to be a tired old village—little more than a small trade center in the midst of farms and swamplands. Yet despite its modest appearance, this town was the site of the birth of the oldest industry in North Carolina.

Near the close of the seventeenth century, Captain Thomas Blount, a blacksmith and ship's carpenter from Chowan County, settled on the eastern banks of Kendricks Creek. He subsequently bought Cabin Ridge Plantation, on which present-day Roper stands. In 1702, Blount dammed the creek and built the first sawmill in the region. After he died in 1706, his

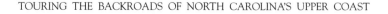

TOURING THE BACKROADS OF NORTH CAROLINA'S UPPER COAST

widow married Colonel Thomas Lee, who continued to operate the business. In time, the mill and the settlement that grew up around it came to be known as Lees Mills.

Over the years, Washington County's greatest natural resource was exported from the mill. Massive quantities of pine, cypress, juniper, oak, ash, hickory, and gum were sawed into lumber and shipped to distant markets. In 1889, John L. Roper, a giant in the lumber industry, purchased the mill and gave the town its present name. Milling operations were continued by Roper until 1921. With the cessation of mill activities, an industry that had operated for 219 years came to an end.

During the colonial era, several large, important plantations were located near and along Kendricks Creek near Roper. A state historical marker in the heart of the town calls attention to Buncombe Hall, one of the most prominent of the plantations.

In 1766, Edward Buncombe came to the area from the West Indies to inspect the 1,025 acres of land he had inherited from his uncle. Two years later, Buncombe returned to take up residence in the mansion he had authorized to be constructed in his absence. Buncombe Hall was originally an enormous two-story frame building with three cellars. Subsequently, a wing was added, giving the structure an L shape. When completed, the elegant house contained fifty-six rooms.

At the outbreak of the Revolutionary War, Buncombe was appointed colonel of the Fifth North Carolina Regiment. At Buncombe Hall, he equipped and trained—at his own expense—the soldiers he recruited from the surrounding countryside. Buncombe died a prisoner of war in Philadelphia in 1779, when he reportedly bled to death after he reopened battle wounds during a sleepwalking episode. Buncombe County, North Carolina, was named in his honor.

Following Buncombe's death, his famous estate fell into disrepair. By 1878, all that remained of Buncombe Hall was the naked framework of the dining room and some kitchen walls. When the Norfolk and Southern Railroad laid its tracks to Roper, the last remnants of the house were destroyed. Today, the only evidence of the once-elegant palace is a depression marking the site of the kitchen cellar.

Edward Buncombe's mansion lay along some of the deepest waters of

Kendricks Creek. Ships landed near the house at Buncombe Landing. Tradition has it that the dark waters below the landing are unusually deep—so deep that they have no bottom.

The site of dark waters became known as Guinea Hole because of an incident that supposedly occurred before Buncombe built his mansion. A vessel from the West Indies loaded with slaves called at Buncombe Landing. Among the crew was a young man who had spent time on a Guinea slave trader. He noticed that some of the men handling the cargo were natives of Guinea. Deciding to play a joke on the Africans, the young man informed them that he had recently been in their country. Filled with excitement, the cargo handlers began asking questions about their homeland. He answered their inquiries with whatever response came to mind.

The Africans, satisfied with their informant's credibility, requested that he point out the direction to Guinea. Whether he meant to continue the joke or to indicate their home was on the other side of the sea, the prankster pointed over the side of the ship into the black waters. Tragically, the Africans believed their new "friend" meant that the waters contained a secret passage to their homeland. After probing the waters with a pole, they grew convinced that they had been let in on an amazing secret. On a dark night that followed, the Africans sneaked down to the landing. There, they loaded themselves with weights to speed their journey. Into the murky water they jumped, never to be seen again.

Turn right, or southeast, off U.S. 64 Business onto S.R. 1126 for an 11.7-mile drive through the beautiful, fertile farmland and forests of the East Dismal Swamp.

Much of the wilderness that earned this once-vast morass its various names—such as the Great Eastern Dismal Swamp and the Great Alligator Dismal Swamp—has been drained by a complex of canals. Ten miles south of the current route lies one of the few remaining untamed portions of the swamp: Pungo National Wildlife Refuge. Encompassing 12,230 acres in Washington and Hyde counties, the refuge has as its centerpiece Pungo Lake, an expansive 2,700-acre bay lake. Surrounding the lake is a veritable jungle that is the domain of the black bear, bobcat, cougar, and mink. Unfortunately, there is no road access to the lake.

Pungo National Wildlife Refuge is part of the expansive Pocosin Lakes

National Wildlife Refuge, established in 1990 after the Richard King Mellon Foundation and the Conservation Fund donated ninety-three thousand acres of land in the southern Albemarle area to the United States Fish and Wildlife Service. Purchased at a cost of $8 million, the vast tract was the largest gift of its kind ever made to the federal government. Much of the land was once owned by First Colony Farms, a giant corporate farming enterprise backed by German and Japanese investors. When the farming operation went bankrupt, attempts by Japanese investors to buy the land for peat mining were thwarted by the Environmental Defense Fund.

At the junction of S.R. 1126 and S.R. 1164, turn right, or south, onto S.R. 1164. After 1.7 miles, the road merges into S.R. 1165. Proceed east on S.R. 1165 for 2.2 miles as it crosses Mountain Canal and Thirty Foot Canal, two of the ancient drainage canals connected to Lake Phelps, to the south. To reach the lake, turn right, or south, off S.R. 1165 onto S.R. 1160. It is 0.6 mile to Pettigrew State Park and Somerset Place State Historic Site.

The largest of all of the parks in the state system, Pettigrew State Park contains approximately 17,500 acres, including the 16,500 acres of majestic Lake Phelps. Visitor facilities are located among the 349 acres at the current stop on the northeastern shore of the lake. An additional tract of 500 undeveloped acres on the southern shore completes the park holdings.

Most prominent among the visitor attractions is Somerset Place State Historic Site. The story behind the entire state park centers around two aristocratic families of the eighteenth and nineteenth centuries whose names are etched in North Carolina history: the Collins family and the Pettigrew family.

Somerset Place was the domain of the Josiah Collins family. In 1774, Collins emigrated from England to Edenton, where he became a successful merchant. In the 1750s, he joined a group of influential North Carolinians—including William Richardson Davie, the father of the University of North Carolina—in an unsuccessful attempt to drain Lake Phelps and farm its fertile bed.

Undaunted by the failure of the project, Collins joined with two other Edenton businessmen to purchase a hundred thousand acres adjoining Lake Phelps in 1785. Instead of draining the lake, the Lake Company, as the new

venture was known, set about constructing canals to drain the nearby swamps. The canals allowed the businessmen to harvest prodigious quantities of crops from the once-useless swamps and to cut virgin stands of timber from the dense forest. A 6-mile canal connected the lake with the Scuppernong River, thereby providing commercial access to Albemarle Sound.

Blessed with great prosperity, Collins constructed a plantation house on the northeastern shore of the lake in 1804. An avenue of trees was planted to grace the approach to the house. By 1816, Collins had purchased the interests of his partners. He chose to name his ever-growing plantation Somerset, after the county of his birth.

Josiah Collins, Jr., inherited his father's massive empire in 1819. A visitor who called at Somerset the following year described it as "the finest river plantation in America" and noted that the land compared favorably with the banks of the Nile.

In 1835, after receiving his education at Yale and a Connecticut law school, Josiah Collins III returned to the plantation to take charge of the family agricultural empire. In the same year, he completed, enlarged, and lavishly furnished the fourteen-room mansion now standing in the state park. Because of his unusual business acumen, the plantation grew to become one of the largest and most prosperous in North Carolina.

In North Carolina history, only four planters held more than three hundred slaves. Josiah Collins III was one of the four; on the eve of the Civil War, he owned 328 slaves. Since the summer of 1986, descendants of 21 slave families who lived and worked on the plantation have returned to preserve their heritage.

The Civil War was the beginning of the end for the great plantation. In 1939, the state acquired title to the old mansion and the surrounding 16,628 acres, including Lake Phelps, for development as a state park. Additional parcels were acquired in 1947, 1952, 1961, 1963, and 1986.

Located on an eight-acre parcel within the confines of the park, Somerset Place was officially dedicated as a state historic site in 1939. Today, visitors get an immediate taste of the grandeur of the great estate as they approach it along the avenue of ancient oak and cypress trees planted centuries ago by the Collins family.

Of the twenty outbuildings that once dotted the mansion grounds, the kitchen, kitchen storehouse, icehouse, and smokehouse are still standing, along with the structure called Colony House. While the mansion was under construction, Josiah Collins and his family resided in Colony House. Afterwards, it served as a residence for Collins's sons and their teachers and as a guesthouse. Today, it serves as the visitor center. Plantation slave records are available at the visitor center for genealogical research.

Listed on the National Register of Historic Places, the proud manor house features three sets of double gallery porches. Its interesting mixture of Federal and Greek Revival details makes it one of the finest surviving coastal plantation houses in the United States. Built from hand-hewn heart cypress grown on the plantation, the white three-story structure rests on a brick foundation.

On the interior, windows stretch from floor to ceiling. Brick fireplaces adorn every room. Graceful stairways lead to upstairs living quarters and a "cooling room," where bodies of the dead were kept awaiting burial. One first-floor room is decorated with original furnishings, while the other rooms contain early Federal-style furnishings. Visitors can become acquainted with the house and grounds on a house tour conducted by park guides.

The well-maintained grounds feature beautiful English gardens. On the large front lawn, there remains a circular planting of chestnut oak trees that shaded mothers while their children played more than two centuries ago. White wooden fences and the Somerset Canal provide pleasant boundaries for the mansion grounds.

Pettigrew State Park bears the name of the second distinguished family that made its home on the shores of Lake Phelps. Adjoining the Somerset estate are the former plantation lands of the Pettigrew family. In 1779, the Reverend Charles Pettigrew acquired a parcel of a hundred acres on the eastern shore of Lake Phelps, at the western edge of Tyrrell County. On this tract, Pettigrew began his famous plantation, Bonarva, meaning "Good Lands." Ten years later, he took up residence on his modest farm, and in 1796, he built Belgrade, the plantation house.

To make his operation efficient, Charles Pettigrew ran his plantation like a feudal manor. Even though he probably never owned more than forty slaves at any one time, Pettigrew augmented his slave labor by hiring local artisans. By the time he died in 1807, Charles Pettigrew had established a model plantation.

Just as Josiah Collins was blessed with intelligent, capable heirs, so was Charles Pettigrew. His son, Ebenezer, not only continued the success of Bonarva, but purchased an additional six hundred acres from the Collins plantation as well. In 1844, he designed and built another plantation house, Magnolia. Quite bizarre in design and appearance, Magnolia was a two-story frame structure with close-set windows encircling the top floor. Unusual "shed-roofed" wings surrounded the main floor. At one time, medieval gargoyles were attached to the eaves.

Ebenezer Pettigrew achieved political prominence in eastern North Carolina. He was the only Tyrrell County resident ever elected to the United States Congress. As owner of the Belgrade and Magnolia plantations, Ebenezer made them rivals of Somerset in productive acreage and profits.

Like its neighbors at Somerset, the Pettigrew family was forced to abandon its holdings at the outbreak of the Civil War. Attempts to rejuvenate the beleaguered plantations after the war failed. During the 1930s, much of the acreage was included in the 10,635-acre Scuppernong Farms project—a futile attempt by the federal Farm Security Administration to provide farms for unemployed Depression-era farmers. Although Scuppernong Farms was short-lived, the program brought public roads to Lake Phelps. By 1953, all of the original Pettigrew homes were gone. A few bricks are all that remain of the structures today.

The offices for Pettigrew State Park are located near the entry gate. Ample parking spaces are adjacent to the headquarters building. Near the parking lot, a picnic ground, enclosed by a split-rail fence and covered by a canopy of ancient cypress, gum, and sycamore trees, is equipped with two dozen tables and several playing fields. Two campgrounds, one of which is located near the former site of Bonarva, offer a variety of camping facilities.

Headquarters of
Pettigrew State Park

Hiking is one of best ways to enjoy the flora and fauna of the park.

On the nature trail known as the Carriage Trail, hikers can walk a portion of the original route traveled by Collins family carriages between Somerset Place and Bonarva. From the trailhead at the parking lot, the first section of trail is 1.6 miles in length. It proceeds east past the family campground and Somerset Place at the 0.4-mile mark. Beyond the old Collins mansion, the trail winds past Bonarva and through a sweet-gum forest to Bee Tree Canal. At the canal overlook, an elevated wooden platform offers a spectacular view of Lake Phelps.

Between Bonarva and Bee Tree Canal, a side trail approximately 1 mile in length leads to the Pettigrew Cemetery. Among the graves in this ancient burial ground is that of Confederate general James Johnston Pettigrew, the son of Ebenezer Pettigrew. Considered by many historians and scholars as perhaps the most brilliant man ever born in North Carolina, Johnston Pettigrew was born and grew up on the family plantation on the lakeshore. In 1847, following an unsurpassed academic career at the University of North Carolina at Chapel Hill, he was handpicked by President James Knox Polk to be a professor at the Naval Observatory in Washington, D.C. Subsequently, Pettigrew achieved fame as an author and attorney. In General George Pickett's charge on July 3, 1863, Pettigrew led North Carolina troops to the high-water mark of the Confederacy at Gettysburg. Ten days later, he was killed while serving as part of the rear guard of the massive Confederate retreat from Pennsylvania.

The second section of the Carriage Trail leads northwest from the parking lot along a wide, grassy trail that snakes through ancient stands of bald cypress, gum, poplar, and sycamore. This 2.7-mile segment also affords several good views of the lake. It terminates near Moccasin Canal, where a three-hundred-foot boardwalk overlook was completed in 1988.

Of the great variety of plant life in the park, most impressive are the magnificent trees. Josiah Collins III once observed an ancient cypress five feet in diameter four feet above the ground. On the sawed end of a cypress log, Collins counted more than eight hundred rings. Although visitors are not likely to see specimens of the kind Collins noted in 1838, the park does present a grand display of large, beautiful trees. Some bald cypresses measure ten feet at their bases. At least five state champion trees—among them black gum, pawpaw, sugarberry, shagbark hickory, and devil's walking stick—can be seen on the annual tree walk presented by park rangers.

Animal life in the park is diverse and abundant. On summer evenings, the air is filled with a cacophony of amphibian sounds. A wide variety of snakes, poisonous and nonpoisonous, are present. In addition to the large assortment of water birds and shorebirds that frequent Lake Phelps, a number of interesting raptors are present. Bald eagles continue to increase in number every year. And although visitors rarely see them, mammals abound in the wilderness, pocosins, and forests of the park. Here is one of the last domains of the black bear. Hikers are sometimes able to see white-tailed deer, rabbits, squirrels, opossums, gray foxes, and bobcats. Nearer the lake, mink, muskrats, raccoons, and river otters can be observed.

Although Pettigrew State Park is the largest state park in North Carolina, more than 90 percent of its area is covered by water—Lake Phelps. Measuring 6 miles wide by 8 miles long, the second-largest natural lake in the state has always been something of an enigma.

Lake Phelps is located only 12 miles from Albemarle Sound, yet white settlers lived within 10 miles of it for many years without even knowing of its existence. Few explorers were daring enough to venture more than a mile or two into the dense, forbidding swamp of the South Albemarle.

Finally, in 1755, a band of men went into this great wilderness in search of game or farmland after observing deer run into the swamp. A day or so into the expedition, all but three of the explorers lost their courage and turned back. As the hardy trio made its way deep into the jungle, one of the men, Benjamin Tarkington, climbed a tree to scout a route. From his vantage point, Tarkington spied the great body of water that none of his race had ever seen. He cried out his amazing discovery to his companions on the ground. Before Tarkington could descend the tree, Josiah Phelps raced to the lake. There, he fell on his face, drinking of the fresh water. Accordingly, the body of water came to be known as Lake Phelps, instead of Lake Tarkington.

This shallow, round lake is located in the center of a saucerlike basin encircled by a ridge twelve to fourteen feet above sea level. Situated like a teacup on the saucer, the lake rests on a plateau higher than the surrounding countryside. Thus, no creeks, streams, or rivers flow into or feed it. Apparently, its clear, but tinged, water comes from springs and rainfall.

Since the 1980s, the lake has been receding. When the mansion was built at Somerset Place, it stood close to the lakeshore. From the wide porches, the Collins family and its guests enjoyed a beautiful view of the sparkling lake. Today, the waters are much farther from the house, and vegetation completely obstructs the view.

In 1985, the lake level was lowered when millions of gallons of water were pumped to fight devastating wildfires that scorched ninety thousand acres of peat bogs, brush, and timber in Washington, Tyrrell, and Hyde counties. Although the lake has not recovered, there has been one distinct benefit of the lower water level. Since 1985, the lake bed has yielded more than thirty Indian dugout canoes and dozens of other ancient Indian artifacts. Prior to these discoveries at Lake Phelps, the oldest dugout canoe in North Carolina had been found on the Lumber River. That canoe was estimated to be almost 1,100 years old. However, one of the canoes pulled from the sand and muck of Phelps has been carbon-dated to 4,380 years, making it the second-oldest canoe found in the country, and older than the great pyramids of Giza.

Lake Phelps

Four of the canoes range from thirty to thirty-seven feet in length. They represent the longest dugout boats ever discovered east of the Mississippi. Fortunately, the water in Lake Phelps has a wood-preserving quality about it, and as a result, most of the recovered canoes are remarkably well preserved. Near the lake, a small information center displays some of the canoes pulled from the lake bed.

Like Lake Mattamuskeet, its sister lake in nearby Hyde County, Lake Phelps is more than thirty-eight thousand years old. In contrast to the Hyde County lake, Phelps is deep enough to allow boating. Every summer, it is dotted with boats of all kinds—fishing boats, powerboats, sailboats, canoes, and rowboats. Near its southeastern end, the lake reaches its maximum depth of twelve feet. Near the center, the depth is seven feet.

A gravel road leads from the park office past a picnic ground to an eastern roadbed which dead-ends at the lake. Facilities located here include two boat ramps and two small piers.

From the park, proceed north on S.R. 1160 for 4.5 miles to the intersection with S.R. 1142. Turn northwest onto S.R. 1142 and drive 2 miles to downtown Creswell.

Located on the edge of the Scuppernong Swamp, this small farming village of fewer than five hundred residents features an interesting group of nineteenth-century dwellings built in the Greek Revival and Victorian styles by local carpenters. Its commercial district is lined with late-nineteenth- and early-twentieth-century store buildings.

Creswell took root in 1826, when the village was born as Cool Spring. Incorporated in 1874 as Cresville (in honor of the postmaster general of the United States), the town officially adopted its present name in 1885.

Retrace your route on S.R. 1142 for 0.5 mile to the intersection with S.R. 1159. Turn northeast onto S.R. 1159 and drive 0.5 mile to S.R. 1158. At

St. David's Chapel

TOURING THE BACKROADS OF NORTH CAROLINA'S UPPER COAST

this intersection stands one of the most historic churches of the South Albemarle. St. David's Chapel, listed on the National Register of Historic Places, was constructed in 1803 by the Reverend Charles Pettigrew at his own expense to serve the needs of his nearby plantation, Belgrade.

Pettigrew was the first bishop-elect of the Protestant Episcopal Church in North Carolina. Instrumental in founding the University of North Carolina, Pettigrew sat on its first board of trustees. State historical markers have been erected on nearby U.S. 64 to honor the Reverend Pettigrew and his grandson, General James Johnston Pettigrew.

In 1857, the church was enlarged into the form of a cross after a design by Richard Upjohn. At that time, its name was changed from Pettigrew's Chapel to St. David's Chapel. All of the existing interior furnishings are hand-carved. A memorial window honors the Reverend Pettigrew.

Turn left off S.R. 1159 onto S.R. 1158, drive 0.2 mile, and turn east onto U.S. 64. After 1.3 miles, U.S. 64 passes into Tyrrell (pronounced TEER-rul) County.

Although it is one of the ten oldest counties in the state, Tyrrell is also the least populated and one of the most economically deprived. For many years, wide bodies of water on the north (Albemarle Sound) and east (the Alligator River), the lack of highways from the west, and the forbidding swamps and wilderness to the south combined to make Tyrrell County one of the most isolated places in the entire state. Within this century, the great sound and river have been bridged, U.S. 64 has linked the county with the east and west, and N.C. 94 has connected the county's southern end with its northern end. Nevertheless, to most outsiders, Tyrrell remains cloaked in a cape of obscurity.

This longstanding anonymity comes from a variety of factors that are apparent on the 7.1-mile drive from the county line to Columbia, the county seat. A small population base of fewer than five thousand people—fewer people lived in the county in 1990 than in 1850—the lack of an urban center, the sparse historical attractions and tourist accommodations, and an almost total absence of industry combine to discourage lengthy visits.

But more than any other factor, geography has kept Tyrrell an unknown frontier. U.S. 64 traverses the county in its northern quadrant. To the south and throughout most of the county lie thousands upon thousands of acres

Tyrrell County Courthouse

The Scuppernong River at Columbia

of wilderness, such as the Big Savannah, the East Dismal Swamp, and Hollow Ground Swamp. Practically all of the county's terrain is flat and poorly drained, ranging in elevation from sea level to no more than nineteen feet. Ironically, some of the highest spots are found in swamps in the southwestern part of the county and on bluffs overlooking Albemarle Sound.

Tyrrell has been blessed with two magnificent rivers: the Alligator and the Scuppernong. The Scuppernong, the smaller of the two, is one of the most majestic rivers in coastal North Carolina. It rises in eastern Washington County in the East Dismal Swamp and flows into Tyrrell County. Turning north, the river widens dramatically at Columbia and empties into Albemarle Sound just northwest of the county seat.

The beautiful river can most easily be seen in Columbia, where it serves as a picturesque gateway for motorists approaching town from the west on U.S. 64. Its black waters are bounded by banks lined with splendid cypress trees laden with gray Spanish moss.

Park your car at the scenic waterside park on the eastern side of the bridge in Columbia. A walkway leads along the shore of the river and under the bridge to the waterfront.

Despite its length of only 22 miles, the Scuppernong River has left its mark on North Carolina history. While in the service of Sir Walter Raleigh's captains, Amadas and Barlowe, explorers discovered luscious grapes growing along the river, believed to be the birthplace of the famous scuppernong grape. These early explorers are thought to have taken clippings of the grapes back to Roanoke Island, from which grew the now-famous Mother Vineyard.

County tradition has it that the local Alexander brothers "discovered" the grapes in the eighteenth century. Senator Nathaniel Macon sent two bottles of scuppernong wine to Thomas Jefferson at Monticello in 1819. Jefferson described the wine as "the best in America."

As the seat of government and the county "metropolis," Columbia, with a population of less than a thousand, must wear many hats. For the past two centuries, this settlement in the wilderness has been the service and trading center for the entire county.

As white men began to arrive in the region, the area now encompassed by Columbia was the domain of King Blount, an important Tuscarora chief who befriended the new settlers. Columbia began in the eighteenth century from a trading center known as Shallop's Landing. In 1791, the town was laid out on the eastern banks of the river.

Because of the nearly total devastation suffered by the town during the Civil War, Columbia experienced a recovery that was slower than that of most tidewater towns. At the close of the nineteenth century, it appeared to be a hastily thrown together frontier town. In 1908, the railroad reached town, bringing a sense of modernity. By the time the Scuppernong River was bridged in the 1920s, Columbia boasted three hotels and one of the largest general stores in all of coastal North Carolina.

Today, only one of the hotels, The Columbia, survives. It stands abandoned near the waterfront. Most of the buildings in the business district are two-story brick structures dating from the early part of the twentieth century. At the corner of Main and Broad streets, the Tyrrell County Courthouse sits on a site deeded to the county in 1800. Erected in 1903, the Italianate structure is listed on the National Register of Historic Places.

After you have enjoyed the waterside park, return to your car and drive east on U.S. 64 as it passes through the Big Savannah on a 4.9-mile run to the junction with S.R. 1229. Turn north on S.R. 1229 and proceed 2 miles to the crossroads settlement of Newfoundland, located at the head of Alligator Creek. At Newfoundland, turn left on S.R. 1221 and proceed north

2 miles to the junction with S.R. 1209. Turn right, or east, on S.R. 1209; the road terminates at Fort Landing after 3.7 miles.

Located near the mouth of Alligator Creek, this tiny fishing village is thought to be the oldest settlement in Tyrrell County. Fort Landing began around 1700, when a small group of men made their way up the Alligator River in search of land. They chose to seek shelter at the first creek on the river. Despite the presence of Indians in the area, the adventurers decided to settle there. To protect themselves, they constructed a log stockade. Several hundred feet from the present shoreline, logs from the old fort are still visible at low tide.

Until the nearby Alligator River was bridged in 1961, the river ferry landing was located at Fort Landing.

Retrace your route to Newfoundland and turn left, or east, on S.R. 1229. After 3.2 miles, turn left, or east, on U.S. 64 at the farming and grazing community of Alligator. For the next 6.3 miles, the highway passes through the wilderness of the Big Savannah.

Suddenly, the drainage canals filled with the black waters of the nearby swamps give way to a vast body of water. Visitors to coastal North Carolina are awed by the sight that greets them as they reach the Alligator River, on the Tyrrell County–Dare County line. Spanning this wild, beautiful river is one of the longest bridges in the state. For almost as far as the eye can see, the Lindsay Warren Bridge stretches into the horizon like a ribbon of concrete and steel.

Rising in Hyde County, the Alligator River flows east and north to the Hyde County–Tyrrell County line, then flows along the entire length of Tyrrell County until it empties into Albemarle Sound. The route of the Intracoastal Waterway follows the river for much of its length.

Why the Alligator River is so named is not known for certain. Some contend that it was named because of alligators found in its waters. However, it is doubtful that the water ever supported a quantity of alligators that would have led locals or geographers to name the river after them. A more logical reason is apparent from a study of a North Carolina map: the river is shaped much like the reptile.

Regardless of the origin of its name, the river and its shoreline are about as wild as the animal. Mariners who are daring enough to enter some of the

The Lindsay Warren Bridge across the Alligator River

TOURING THE BACKROADS OF NORTH CAROLINA'S UPPER COAST

creeks feeding into the river are treated to some of the most isolated, unspoiled scenery along the entire North Carolina coast.

Before 1931, there was no vehicular access across the mighty river. In that year, Captain Thomas Baum of Nags Head began a private toll-ferry service on the river. From 1933 to 1943, the state subsidized the ferry operation, finally making it toll-free in 1942. After Baum's death, the state took over complete operation of the ferry service.

Completed in late 1961, almost a half-year ahead of schedule, the 2.8-mile bridge ended the long delays endured for so many years by tourists in their trek to the Outer Banks. Truly an engineering marvel, the bridge is twenty-three feet off the water at its highest point. Prestressed concrete piles, some of which were driven into the muck of the river bottom as deep as ninety-four feet, support the bridge.

As they cross the Alligator River and enter mainland Dare County, many motorists consider the 12.5-mile stretch through this largely undeveloped area of bogs and forestland as the last leg of their trip to the Outer Banks. From the highway, travelers see little more than mile after mile of roadside drainage canals, and beyond them, nothing more than an apparently impenetrable wilderness.

Mainland Dare is attached to Hyde County along a portion of its southern boundary. Were it not for this land connection, this great peninsula would be an island. Three bodies of water—the Alligator River, Albemarle Sound, and Pamlico Sound—comprise the western, northern, and southern boundaries of the peninsula. As is the case with most of its interior, the peninsula shoreline is wild and virtually undeveloped.

Of the few farming and fishing communities in mainland Dare, the first to greet motorists on the east side of the river is East Lake. Turn left, or north, off U.S. 64 onto S.R. 1153 approximately 0.5 mile east of the end of the bridge. East Lake lies on the river shore 0.2 mile from the intersection.

Because of its peace and solitude, East Lake has long inspired outsiders to construct fishing camps along the nearby waterways, to which they return annually. No more than a few hundred people call this old community home on a permanent basis. Widely spread along the highway and the dirt roads leading into the wilderness of the Alligator Dismal Swamp, the community was settled about 1790.

East Lake is the home of the vessel known in North Carolina coastal waters as the "shad boat." A local fisherman named Creef designed the prototype many years ago. He crafted a round-bottomed vessel with a square stern, a sharp-pointed bow, and a shallow keel. Constructed of naturally curved cypress knees from the Alligator River and juniper from nearby swamps, the boats patterned after his model ranged from twenty-three to twenty-six feet long. Creef designed the boat to use extra sails and employed sandbags as ballast, as they could be shifted when the sails were tacked. Before engine-powered fishing boats, Creef's invention was the standard for shad fishermen in Pamlico Sound and neighboring waters.

Return to U.S. 64 and continue east. One building of historical importance lies on the north side of the road after approximately 2.7 miles. East Lake Methodist Church is a beautiful frame structure erected in 1887. At the time the church was constructed, and for many years afterward, East Lake included three communities: the Lake neighborhood, the Twiford neighborhood, and Buffalo City.

Just past East Lake Methodist Church, turn right, or south, onto the unpaved S.R. 1103. This isolated 2.2-mile stretch of road will take you on a

A remnant of Buffalo City

TOURING THE BACKROADS OF NORTH CAROLINA'S UPPER COAST

visit into the dim past of Dare County. Near the terminus of this dusty trail, on the north bank of Milltail Creek, stood what was once the largest community in the entire county. But for nearly forty years, Buffalo City has been a ghost town.

As with many places on the North Carolina coast, a controversy exists over the origin of Buffalo City's name. There are some people who contend that the community was named for area Confederate renegades, or "Buffaloes," as they were called. However, the settlement was most likely named for Buffalo, New York. Just before the turn of the century, Northern timber interests sent hordes of lumbermen from New York to set up a lumber camp in the untamed wilderness of the Alligator River region. From this initial camp, the Dare Lumber Company emerged.

Buffalo City, the company town, sprang up almost overnight. It soon sported a hotel, a boardinghouse, stores, houses, a pulp mill, a blacksmith shop, and a machine shop. A railroad for tiny steam locomotives reached deep into the jungle. Ultimately, 100 miles of track were laid.

At its zenith, more than six hundred people were employed at the Buffalo City Pulp Mill. The population of the settlement grew to more than a thousand. Showboats made their way up Milltail Creek to entertain the community. The population dropped to no more than a hundred by 1940, although milling operations continued until 1950. Once the mill closed, the few remaining inhabitants moved away, leaving the once-thriving settlement to the elements of nature. Over the past few decades, the rattlesnake-infested forest has swallowed up Buffalo City.

Today, a careful search of the forest floor will reveal remnants of old buildings and railroad tracks. Twenty-five miles to the east, old oceanfront cottages along the Nags Head strand are the most tangible evidence of the once-great lumber town of mainland Dare. Juniper shingles, the hallmark of the old company, were used to cover many of the old cottages.

Milltail Creek, a tributary of the Alligator River, rises in the wilderness of central Dare County. Reaching maximum depths of forty feet, the creek has an average depth of fifteen to twenty feet more than 15 miles upstream. Bordering this waterway are lands that are about as wild and as isolated from civilization as any in the United States. Here are stretches of ground the feet of white men have never touched.

The area at the southern end of S.R. 1103 serves as an access area for the Alligator River National Wildlife Refuge. There is a canoe and kayak trail on Milltail Creek. Several wooden overlooks provide panoramic views of the creek.

It was along the banks of the snakelike creek that the hardy lumbermen hacked out Buffalo City. Miles upstream, near the point where the creek ends in a swampy morass, a settlement known as Beechland existed prior to the Civil War.

Although its name likely came from the profusion of beech trees in the area, the origin and much of the history of Beechland are shrouded in mystery. At some indeterminate time in the antebellum period, approximately two hundred white residents and their slaves worked plantations encompassing more than five hundred acres in the middle of this remote wilderness. From the surrounding forests, the residents of Beechland produced shingles and floated them down Milltail Creek, where they were loaded onto ships on the Alligator River for shipment to the West Indies. To facilitate a trade route out of this isolated area, a 7-mile bridge of logs was constructed to Long Shoals Bay and a 2-mile canal was dug to Milltail Creek.

A cholera epidemic brought to the region by foreign traders decimated the Beechland population in the years immediately preceding the Civil War. About the time Buffalo City was being settled, the last permanent residents of its upstream neighbor were moving out.

Around 1956, the West Virginia Pulp and Paper Company, the owner of thousands of acres in the area, undertook to build some logging roads and drainage canals at the former site of Beechland. In the course of the canal construction, the heavy machinery dug into a large mound. When workers examined the earth scooped from the mound, they made a startling discovery. Not only had the equipment operator dredged up an assortment of Indian artifacts, including arrowheads and pottery, but he had also disturbed a burial ground. The excavation produced several coffins of solid cypress construction.

Upon examination of the coffins, the workers found them to resemble two dugout canoes placed on top of each other. Even more bewildering were inscriptions and carvings on the tops of the coffins. A Latin cross, the symbol of Christianity, had been chiseled deep into the wood. Carved below the cross were the letters *INRI*. This inscription was most likely an abbreviation of *Jesus Nazarenus, Rex Judaeorum*, the same inscription as on the cross of Jesus Christ. Despite the bizarre discovery of coffins with what were probably Elizabethan-era English carvings buried in a mound of Indian artifacts, the workers were directed to cover the graves.

No one knows who the first white residents of Beechland were or when they settled along Milltail Creek. Thus, the origin of the wooden coffins remains a mystery. Local tradition holds that the survivors of the Lost Colony were the original settlers of Beechland. There is historical evidence from which some have concluded that the claim is more than coastal folklore. That John White and the Roanoke colonists had formulated a plan to move inland if threatened has been well documented.

Old-timers around East Lake still remember a tribe of fair-haired, blue-eyed Indians in the Beechland area. Strangely enough, these Indians with Caucasian features carried names identical to some of those listed on the roll of the Roanoke colony. Deep within the recesses of the inaccessible swamp, miles away from the nearest road, lived Indians bearing names such as John White, Michael Bishop, John Bright, Thomas Coleman, Henry Paine, and John Gibbs.

After Beechland was abandoned, at least two old cemeteries were reclaimed by the forest and its population of wildcats, black bears, and rattlesnakes. Today, the site of Beechland is leased to the federal government as part of a military bombing range. Unfortunately, these activities may ultimately destroy any remaining graves that might hold clues to English America's oldest mystery.

Return to U.S. 64 and continue east on a 7.7-mile drive to where the road merges with U.S. 264. This route passes through the wilderness of the Alligator River National Wildlife Refuge. Located in Dare, Hyde, and Tyrrell counties, this sprawling refuge covers 41,600 acres of wetland habitat. Most of the northern portion of Dare has been swallowed up by the refuge. Within its bounds are some of North Carolina's best examples of non-riverine swamp forests, pocosins, and salt marshes.

Of particular importance in the refuge are the swamp forests bordering the Alligator River and the tributary black-water creeks. These are considered the best surviving examples of the swamp forests that were once prevalent throughout North Carolina pocosins. Dominated by cypress, Atlantic white cedar, and loblolly pine, the shoreline forest in the refuge has no rival on the mid-Atlantic coast in terms of extent, size, age of trees, and tree quality.

Several kinds of animals seldom seen in North Carolina live within the confines of the refuge. Some American alligators are known to live in the area; in fact, this is northernmost reach of the reptile. The refuge is also believed to be one of the black bear's last strongholds in the state.

Of all the animals that make their home in the wilderness preserve, the red wolf has drawn the most interest. Red wolf crossing signs have been erected along U.S. 64 through the refuge.

When eight red wolves were released in the Dare County wilderness in 1987, there were only seventy-five members of this endangered species left in the country. Despite a number of problems with the federal project overseeing the effort, officials hope the red wolf population in the refuge will survive and multiply.

Tourists hurrying to and from Roanoke Island on U.S. 64/264 often pass through the northeastern quarter of mainland Dare without visiting the old villages of Manns Harbor and Mashoes. Both are ancient fishing communities which have been bypassed by changing times and highways to the Outer Banks.

Manns Harbor is located 1.6 miles east of the junction of U.S. 64 and U.S. 264. To visit the historic waterfront on Croatan Sound, turn east on Old Ferry Dock Road and drive to the end of the road. Wooden fish houses of many sizes and descriptions line the docks, making it evident that the chief livelihood of Manns Harbor residents comes from the nearby waters. A large fleet of fishing and pleasure boats is based here. Before Croatan Sound was bridged, the ferry to Roanoke Island was based here.

Manns Harbor lies almost ten feet above sea level. As a result, it is not subject to the high salt tides that are common on much of the mainland Dare shoreline. Its three hundred–plus inhabitants are able to cultivate beautiful gardens in the rich, sandy loam.

The community traces its history to an Algonquin village located on the site at the time Raleigh's expeditions were attempting to colonize nearby Roanoke Island. White settlers are first known to have come to Manns Harbor in the early eighteenth century.

The weathered buildings of Manns Harbor

Early residents called their village Croatan. This name traces its roots to the long-established legend that the survivors of the Lost Colony of Roanoke took refuge in this portion of mainland Dare County.

Before he departed for England to obtain supplies for the Roanoke colonists in August 1587, Governor John White devised a signal with those he left behind, through which he might know the new site of the colony in the event it was forced to relocate during his absence. The name of the new location was to be carved on a conspicuous tree or post at the Roanoke settlement. When White was finally able to return to the North Carolina coast in 1590, he found the settlement abandoned. On a tree near the entrance to the overgrown fort at the site was carved the word CROATOAN. Unfortunately, White was unable to search the mainland for the colonists, and their fate remains a mystery today. (For more information on the Lost Colony, see The Roanoke Island Tour, page 147.)

The marshlands of Mashoes

Manns Harbor first made its appearance on a map in the 1730s. That name apparently came from an early settler named Mann who migrated to the area from Rhode Island.

Return to U.S. 64/264 and continue 0.3 mile to the junction with S.R. 1113. Turn north on S.R. 1113 for a winding 5.7-mile drive to the village of Mashoes, located on the remote northeastern tip of mainland Dare. This route provides an excellent opportunity to view the Dare County pocosin—a vast, boggy wilderness of stunted pines, wax myrtle, evergreen shrubs, and grasses which actually floats on masses of peat.

Several theories exist as to the origin of the name Mashoes.

An Indian village named Mashawatoc is shown on the Virginia shore on the John White map of 1585.

A legend holds that one evening, a young woman from the area was boarding a boat with her husband to attend a church service. In the process of stepping onto the boat, she dropped her shoes into the sound. The disheartened lady reportedly screamed, "Muh shoes! Muh shoes!" thereby giving the village its name.

A more logical theory comes from the eighteenth century. Frenchman

Peter Michieux and his wife and child shipwrecked on a nearby beach in 1738. When the unfortunate fellow gained consciousness, he discovered that his wife and child were dead. After burying them on the beach, Michieux fabricated a raft from the broken ship. He sailed across Croatan Sound and settled on the Dare mainland at the present site of Mashoes. His spirit broken, the heartsick man lived there for twenty years as a hermit. He chronicled his tragedy by carving the story on a board.

Michieux died one day while sitting against a cypress tree. His skeleton and the account he had carved were found years later by settlers who migrated to the area. They decided to name the community in honor of the hermit—or so the theory goes.

During the latter portion of the nineteenth century, Mashoes was a commercial fishing center. Large quantities of fish were brought by sailboat to the packing houses and fish camps that lined the waterfront. Steamers hauled the processed fish to Elizabeth City.

In 1891, the village had a post office, long since closed. The road from Manns Harbor was constructed through the swamp in the 1940s. Prior to that time, Mashoes was accessible only by water.

Retrace your route from Mashoes to U.S. 64/264. The tour ends on the western shore of Croatan Sound.

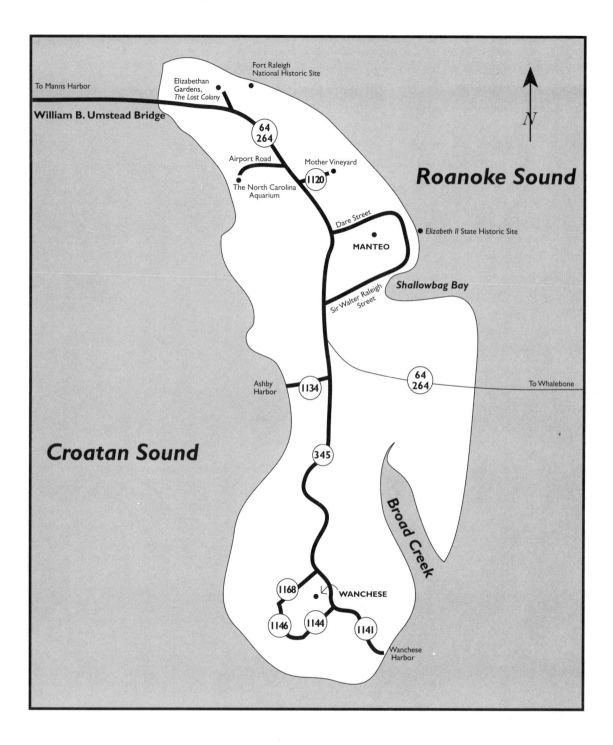

The Roanoke Island Tour

This tour begins at the northern end of Roanoke Island and proceeds to Fort Raleigh National Historic Site. It then curves south to Manteo, located on Shallowbag Bay near the middle of the island, before heading to the busy fishing village of Wanchese, at the south end of the island.

Among the highlights of the tour are Fort Raleigh National Historic Site, the story of the Lost Colony of Roanoke, a tale of ghosts of the Lost Colony, the Elizabethan Gardens, a branch of the North Carolina Aquarium, Mother Vineyard, historic downtown Manteo, the *Elizabeth II*, and the Wanchese waterfront.

Total mileage: approximately 19 miles.

This tour begins on U.S. 64/264 at the eastern end of the William B. Umstead Bridge on Roanoke Island.

When considered in the totality of the American experience, no place in the nation has more historic significance than Roanoke Island. Tucked neatly between the Outer Banks and the mainland, the hourglass-shaped island was the birthplace of English America. Though the efforts of Sir Walter Raleigh to plant a permanent English colony on Roanoke Island in the 1580s failed, his dreams and the bravery and resolve of the Roanoke colonists set the stage for the Jamestown colony of 1607 and the emergence of British America.

Approximately 11 miles long and 2.3 miles wide, the island is flanked on the north and south, respectively, by Albemarle and Pamlico sounds. Two smaller sounds, Croatan and Roanoke, lie off the west and east shores, respectively.

A rest area operated by the state is located at Weir Point on the south side of the highway approximately 0.3 mile east of the William B. Umstead Bridge. It offers a good spot from which to view Croatan Sound and the long bridge that spans it. Park in the parking lot and walk to the sound shore.

Mainland Dare County and Roanoke Island are separated by this wide,

William B. Umstead Bridge across Croatan Sound

deep lagoon connecting Albemarle Sound with Pamlico Sound. Both of Croatan Sound's shores are virtually undeveloped. During colonial times, the sound was a wide marsh with a single shallow ditch running through it. At the beginning of the nineteenth century, the drainage of the rivers of the Albemarle region was diverted into this area, creating the deep body of water known today as Croatan Sound.

Prior to 1957, access across Croatan Sound was limited to boat. In the spring of that year, the state replaced the ferry with the existing 3-mile bridge. On an average day, two thousand vehicles use the span, which has a high middle arch to allow water traffic to pass.

Before you leave the rest area, be sure to note the cluster of state historical markers located near the parking lot.

One of the familiar metal signs introduces Roanoke Island as the site of the first English settlements in the New World.

Other signs call attention to Forts Huger and Blanchard, two of the Confederate forts erected to defend Roanoke Island in the early days of the Civil War.

In their attempts to defend the island, Confederate engineers faced a serious dilemma because of the unusual geography of Roanoke. The northern end (the current tour stop) boasted high, stable terrain, but the southern end, which would be first exposed to Union attack, was low and marshy. To further complicate matters, a long string of islands in Croatan Sound, known as the Roanoke Marshes, extended from the lower end of the island to the mainland. Recognizing the problems inherent in lowland construction, the Southern defenders decided that the battle for the island would be fought from a chain of forts on the higher ground to the north.

The Confederates constructed a quartet of earthwork forts on the northern half of the island. Fort Huger, the largest, was armed with a twelve-gun emplacement. It was located at Weir Point near the current tour stop. About two hundred yards south of Huger was Fort Blanchard, a four-gun fortification. Set back from the shore about 1.5 miles southwest of modern Manteo, Fort Bartow mounted eight guns. Nearby, a nameless two-gun battery on the south side of Shallowbag Bay protected the channel between the island and Nags Head. At the midpoint of the island, the Confederates erected the three-gun Fort Russell on a natural causeway where the landscape changed into almost impenetrable swamp. Directly across Croatan Sound from Roanoke Island, a mainland battery mounted on an old canal barge was called Fort Forrest.

Also near the parking lot, a large historical marker encased in brick commemorates the Naval Battle of Roanoke Island.

Despite the Southern attempts to fortify the island and the efforts of the small, outmanned North Carolina Navy—better known as the "Mosquito Fleet"—General Ambrose Burnside moved his massive Union fleet into Croatan Sound on February 7, 1862. A day later, his landing force of 7,500 men was wading through the island swamps to do battle with 2,400 Confederate troops on the island. During the short battle, some 60 soldiers were killed and 272 were wounded. Realizing that the situation was hopeless, Colonel H. M. Shaw of the Eighth North Carolina sent forth the white flag of surrender. For the duration of the war, Roanoke Island remained under Union control, and as a consequence, the United States Army held much of northeastern North Carolina in its grasp.

Weir Point on Croatan Sound

You will see state historical markers for Fort Bartow, the Confederate channel obstructions, and the Battle of Roanoke Island later on the tour on U.S. 64/264 and N.C. 345. Unfortunately, few of the earthworks from the forts have survived.

There is yet one other state historical marker at the parking area that is of special interest. It calls attention to Reginald A. Fessenden, a special agent for the United States Weather Bureau and former member of Thomas Edison's staff. In 1901, Fessenden arrived in Manteo to conduct experiments that set the stage for his most famous achievements: the first radio broadcast in history and the first two-way transatlantic radio transmission.

Fessenden, one of history's greatest radio pioneers, set up shop on the northwestern side of the island near what is now the approach to the William B. Umstead Bridge. He experimented with wireless telegraphy, the forerunner of radio, by transmitting messages among a fifty-foot tower at Weir Point and two other towers, one to the south at Cape Hatteras and one to the north at Cape Henry, Virginia.

Before he shut down operations in Dare County, Fessenden transmitted musical notes and voices among his towers. He and his wife, Helen, lived in a hotel in Manteo during their time on the island. Helen Fessenden later authored her husband's biography, *Fessenden, Builder of Tomorrows*, which contains excerpts of letters written by the scientist in Manteo. (For more information on Reginald Fessenden and the days of radio pioneering in coastal North Carolina, see The Cape Hatteras Tour, page 201.)

From the rest area, drive east on U.S. 64/264. Miles of beautiful crape myrtles, planted for the celebration of America's four hundredth anniversary in 1984, grace the roadway leading to Manteo and serve as an invitation to sample the natural beauty of the island, much of which remains undisturbed.

A Union soldier, digging for artifacts near the site of Fort Raleigh during the Civil War, failed to appreciate the beauty of the island when he wrote about the Lost Colonists, "How they ever found it or why they chose it as an abiding place, I cannot imagine. It is easier to account for the fact that the colony was abandoned." Almost a century and a half after his questionable observations, trees standing when Virginia Dare was born in 1587 still grow on the heavily forested island.

America's first publicist, Arthur Barlowe, provided a glowing account of Roanoke on his first visit in 1584: "One [island] is sixteen miles long, at which we were, finding it to be a most pleasant and fertile ground, replenished with goodly cedars and divers other sweet woods, full of currants, of flax and many other notable commodities."

Barlowe's description of the island ultimately led Englishmen to settle Roanoke and to sample its goodness. In the four centuries since, the island has yielded to modern man's designs without sacrificing the allure of Barlowe's day.

To see the portion of the island where Barlowe and his compatriots chose to locate the first English colony in America, turn north at the entrance to Fort Raleigh National Historic Site, located approximately 1 mile east of the bridge.

Just as the Roanoke colonists of 1587 disappeared into history, so has the exact site of their settlement on the island. Despite sophisticated efforts by archaeologists, no one has located the place on the northern tip of the island where the Lost Colonists lived until their disappearance. Most experts believe that the site is now underwater, having eroded into the sound. Nevertheless, there has never been any serious dispute concerning the

Monument at Fort Raleigh National Historic Site

TOURING THE BACKROADS OF NORTH CAROLINA'S UPPER COAST

general location of the colonists' habitation. Consequently, North Carolinians and their countrymen have taken steps to preserve the birthplace of British America. These ventures culminated in the establishment of Fort Raleigh National Historic Site on April 4, 1941.

The entrance road ends at the spacious parking lot for the trio of adjacent historic attractions—Fort Raleigh National Historic Site, *The Lost Colony* outdoor drama, and the Elizabethan Gardens—all of which are related to the Roanoke colonists of the sixteenth century. Park here and begin by stopping at the visitor center.

Managed by the National Park Service, Fort Raleigh National Historic Site covers 144 acres. Located adjacent to the park headquarters is the Lindsay Warren Visitor Center. Inside the center, visitors are treated to a short orientation film, displays of artifacts from the site, and exhibits on Elizabethan life. From Memorial Day to Labor Day, the center offers various programs and activities, including talks by park interpreters.

From the visitor center, walk the short trail that leads to the partially restored fort. This shaded route covers the very ground where, more than four hundred years ago, British men and women lived and died while sowing the seeds for Anglo-America.

On July 4, 1584, English sea captains Philip Amadas and Arthur Barlowe, sailing for Sir Walter Raleigh, first entered the sounds of North Carolina in search of a suitable site for a permanent English colony in America. Upon their arrival, they went ashore to claim present-day North Carolina for Queen Elizabeth.

During this scouting expedition, Amadas and Barlowe developed amiable relations with the Indians of the North Carolina coast. When the time came for the return trip to England in late summer, the friendly Indians consented to having two of their number, Manteo and Wanchese, make the ocean crossing. The memory of these two Indians lives on today in the names of the two towns on the island.

As a result of the glowing accounts prepared by his explorers, Raleigh, with the blessings of the queen, outfitted an expedition to colonize the island selected by the scouts: Roanoke Island. In late July 1585, a well-equipped fleet carrying six hundred men, commanded by Raleigh's cousin, Sir Richard Grenville, arrived at the island. The first order of business was constructing a fort: Fort Raleigh. The fort on the grounds today was reconstructed much in the manner that the original was built in 1585. Archaeologists dug out the original moat and piled the dirt inward to build a parapet. To prevent erosion, grass was planted on the earthworks. The resulting fort is square, with pointed bastions on two sides and an octagonal base.

No contemporary drawing or written description of the fort of 1585 is known to exist, but the reconstructed fort on Roanoke Island resembles the fortification erected by Ralph Lane, the military governor of the Roanoke colony, in Puerto Rico prior to his arrival on the North Carolina coast. Both forts measure seventy feet across and feature appendages for gun mounts.

Visitors to Fort Raleigh are often shocked by its diminutive size. However, it most likely contained only one building, because colonists did not live in the fort. Instead, they lived in dwellings built close enough to the fort that the inhabitants could hurriedly find protection in time of danger.

In late August 1585, Grenville and his fleet set sail from Roanoke Island to England, leaving behind Governor Lane and 106 soldiers to man the colony and to explore the surrounding territory.

The following spring, Lane and his half-starved colonists waited in desperation for the promised relief fleet. Just as hope was about gone, the

Site believed to be spot where Raleigh's colonists first came ashore on Roanoke Island

TOURING THE BACKROADS OF NORTH CAROLINA'S UPPER COAST

massive thirty-vessel fleet of Sir Francis Drake stopped to check on the colony while on its way home after a successful cruise against Spanish shipping in the Caribbean. Drake supplied the colonists and offered them a ship from his fleet. A week later, a terrible storm lashed Roanoke Island and scattered Drake's offshore fleet.

On June 18, 1586, Lane gave orders for the colonists to sail to England with Drake. So hasty was the departure that three of Lane's men—on an expedition at the time—were left behind because there was no time to search for them. Ironically, the three unfortunate souls gained the dubious distinction of being the first "Lost Colonists of Roanoke."

Had Lane known that one of Raleigh's supply ships—operating in advance of the main relief expedition headed by Grenville—would appear on the horizon just two days later, the first English colony in America might have survived.

Lane had been gone only two weeks when Grenville arrived at Roanoke Island with four hundred men. After searching for the colonists, he found only the hanged bodies of an Englishman and an Indian at the deserted fort.

When Grenville set sail for England, he left behind just fifteen men to fight for survival against the overwhelming odds that had already bested a much larger group.

Despite the disappointing turn of events, Sir Walter Raleigh remained undaunted. He began formulating plans for a third colonization attempt. As he had done in the past, Raleigh assembled a competent group to carry forth his expedition of 1587. Although Grenville and Lane were now involved in other pursuits, there were other men with previous experience in Virginia. Foremost among them was John White, who was named governor of the new colony.

Experiences from the expeditions of 1584, 1585, and 1586 had taught Raleigh that Roanoke Island, devoid of a protected harbor and deepwater access, was not a suitable site for the colony. Instead, when the new group of colonists sailed in the spring of 1587, its destination was Chesapeake Bay. For the first time, women and children were allowed to make the voyage.

Of the 150 men who originally signed on as colonists, only 91 actually sailed from Plymouth, England, on May 8, 1587. White appointed 12 of them as his assistants. One of the aides was his son-in-law, Ananias Dare. Eleanor, Ananias Dare's wife and John White's daughter, was pregnant when the voyage began. She was one of 14 married women to make the crossing. Additionally, there were 9 children and 3 single women aboard the trio of ships.

Trail marker at Fort Raleigh National Historic Site

After a harrowing transatlantic journey of six weeks, White and his colonists arrived at Roanoke Island on July 22 to locate the fifteen men left behind by Grenville. They found no trace of the men save the skeleton of one unfortunate individual. Moreover, the fort had been razed. John White's despair turned to misery when his Portuguese pilot, Simon Ferdinando—the mariner who had navigated each of Raleigh's expeditions—refused to transport the colony farther.

For a fourth consecutive summer, an English colony was planted on Roanoke Island. Houses were repaired, but the time for planting a crop had passed. Members of the colony implored White to return to England to obtain supplies. Reluctantly acceding to their wishes, White set sail from Roanoke Island on Sunday, August 27. Just nine days earlier, his daughter had given birth to a daughter, Virginia Dare—the first child born of English parentage in the New World.

Upon his return to England, John White was dismayed to learn that his country was at war with Spain. The exigencies of war prevented him from returning to Roanoke Island until 1590.

White reached the site of the colony on August 17, one day before his granddaughter's third birthday. Darkness had fallen by the time the boats reached Roanoke Island. In the stillness of the night, trumpets blared and the would-be rescuers sang "familiar English tunes of Songs and called to them friendly," according to White. His party roused none of the colonists, but instead discovered a tree on which the letters *CRO* were carved. The men pressed onward to the spot where the houses of the colonists had stood. All of the structures had been taken down, but the fort, although overgrown, was standing. On a big tree to the right of the entrance to the fort, five feet from the ground, was carved the legend *CROATOAN*.

Prior to his 1587 departure for England, the governor had made it his final order of business to arrange a signal through which he might know the new site of the colony, in the event that it was forced to relocate during his absence. The name of the place was to be carved on a conspicuous tree or post at the Roanoke settlement, and in the event the move was occasioned by Indian or Spanish attack or other danger, a distress signal in the form of a Maltese cross was to be carved over the name.

White knew Croatan as the home of Manteo and the Indians friendly to the colonists. He was relieved that the prearranged distress symbol was not found on any tree. However, none of the colonists was found by the time White had to leave the island. He was never able to return to resume the search.

And so it was with the Lost Colony of Roanoke. Human history is full of ironies. One of the greatest of these is that the United States, perhaps the most stable, predictable nation in the history of the world, began with a mystery that remains unsolved more than four hundred years later. At some unknown date in the three-year span from August 27, 1587, to August 15, 1590, approximately 117 English men, women, and children vanished from Roanoke Island with scarcely a trace. Ever since John White found the settlement at Roanoke Island deserted, scholars and amateur historians alike have tried in vain to conclusively answer the question, What happened to the Lost Colony of Roanoke?

In 1778, nearly two hundred years after the colony vanished, island residents were well aware of the location of Fort Raleigh. They were happy to show visitors the stump of the live oak on which the letters CRO had been carved.

George H. Throop, a tutor working at Nags Head during the summer of 1849, was drawn to the site. He noted that "the remains of the fort, glass globes containing quicksilver and hermetically sealed and other relics occasionally discovered there, give rise to a thousand conjectures destined never to be solved."

Over the years, countless theories have been put forward to solve the baffling conundrum. Some of the most popular are that the colonists drowned at sea bound for England in a homemade ship; that they were killed by Spaniards or Indians; that the colony settled at Cedar Island rather than Roanoke Island; that it moved north; that it moved west to Beechland in mainland Dare County; that some of the colonists fled to Georgia; that the colony moved to Croatan (Hatteras Island); that it moved to the Pamlico River–Neuse River area; that it moved to Occoneechee in Orange County, North Carolina; that the colonists moved to the mountains of western North Carolina and eastern Tennessee; and that they moved to the Green Swamp or the Lumber River region in southeastern North Carolina.

There are varying amounts of plausible evidence in support of the different theories. Newspaper stories bearing headlines such as "The Mystery of Sir Walter Raleigh's Famous Lost Colony Solved At Last" have been published around the nation. But the grim truth is that no one is any closer to determining the fate of the colonists than was Governor White when he searched the island in 1590.

Colorful ghost stories and legends have been handed down to explain many of the fascinating mysteries of coastal North Carolina. But unlike most of these fanciful tales, one "true life" adventure with apparitions of the Lost Colony of Roanoke borders on the edge of reality.

This chilling event occurred in 1919. Tucker Lee, a lifelong resident of the tiny coastal village of Grandy and a World War I pilot, did not allow a near-fatal airplane crash during the war to dampen his love of flying. When he returned home to Currituck County after the war, his interest turned to the ten-thousand-pound prize offered by an English newspaper to the first aviator to make a nonstop flight across the Atlantic.

Tucker vowed to claim the prize. At his father's blacksmith shop, he spent his spare time refurbishing an old biplane. To make sure that his craft was capable of making the crossing, he decided to test it on a course which would take him over a portion of the Atlantic, then over the vast Pamlico Sound, and finally over Albemarle Sound. On a cold January morning in 1919, Tucker took his restored plane up for the major test. Initially, the craft performed flawlessly, but problems developed after he turned it toward Pamlico Sound. Smoke began to pour from the burning engine.

Tucker refused to panic, even though the smoke made it almost impossible for him to look for a landing site. Suddenly, the plane impacted some trees, turned over twice, and came to rest still in the trees. Fearing that it might explode, Tucker jumped twenty feet to the ground.

Rendered unconscious by the jump, he awoke in the evening. Pain shot through his head and chest. Finding it impossible to sit up, he closed his eyes as he lay on the ground. The next thing he saw was a young woman looking down upon him with a smile. She had sad eyes, fair skin, and blond hair. In a British accent, she asked him how he felt. In obvious pain, Tucker told her his name.

The mysterious woman identified herself as Victoria. She told Tucker that her husband wanted to speak to him but was busy looking for Tucker's ship. The pilot related the story of his engine fire and crash in the treetops.

Victoria did not understand what he was talking about. She asked him if he had brought supplies. Tucker did not understand. Before he could question Victoria further, her attention was drawn by a crying child.

As he rested on the ground, Tucker noticed that his wounds had been cleaned and that a crude splint fashioned from a tree branch had been applied to his broken leg. He pondered Victoria's question about supplies. Even though it was dark, he could see well enough to ascertain that he was on a beach at the edge of a forest. Near him were various bundles lined up on the shore. Besides Victoria and the small child, there was a sickly woman lying on the beach. From the light of the campfire, Tucker could see Victoria's unusual attire: a long, dirty, brown dress, a ragged white blouse, and a fur wrap. Her feet were wrapped in pelts reminiscent of the dress Tucker had seen in a book about the early settlement of America.

The pain in his head was relentless. Tucker assumed he was having a hallucination. But the characters were so real, so alive. Three men clad in a manner similar to Victoria approached along the bank. One of them hugged Victoria and informed her that no ship had been found. According to the men, they had no alternative but to attempt to reach "the continent" on their raft. These out-of-place, out-of-time people decided to take Tucker with them, even though Victoria considered his statements the ramblings of a delirious man.

Tucker listened intently and watched what was going on. Suddenly, he had an unnerving thought: perhaps he had crashed on Roanoke Island. But it was as if he had hit a time warp and awakened among the settlers of John White's colony of 1587. As he struggled to understand the situation, his injuries and the bizarre events of the day took their toll on him. He fainted.

Tucker was awakened the following morning by an old man dressed in a twentieth-century suit who asked him if he were alive. Nodding that he was, Tucker managed to tell the man about his crash. Bewildered by the story, the man asked where the plane was. With the man's assistance, Tucker sat up so he could locate the wreckage. He was relieved that his pain had subsided, but he was mystified by his location. Instead of being on Roanoke Island, he was on a mainland beach 3 miles across the sound from the island.

The man disbelieved Tucker's story that his aircraft had hit treetops and flipped. There were no trees in the area, only bare beach and sand dunes extending in both directions. But regardless of what had happened, Tucker needed immediate medical attention, so the man loaded him in his buggy and took him to a physician at nearby Buffalo City.

During the next few weeks of convalescence, Tucker attempted to sort through his ordeal. Family and friends tried to convince him that he had swum ashore after crashing in the water. Yet Tucker could vividly see in his mind the treetops that his aircraft had clipped and the strangers who had helped him.

Haunted by the eerie events surrounding the crash, Tucker was determined to find some answers. He prevailed upon a friend to allow him to use his sailboat to sail around Roanoke Island on a search for his plane.

After spending almost an entire day in a fruitless search, Tucker finally located the wreckage amid the trees in a remote part of the island. His discovery confirmed what he had suspected since the crash. The people he had seen on that cold January night were members of the Lost Colony of Roanoke, or at least their ghosts. He had survived the crash only because they had transported him across the sound to the open mainland beach, where he could be easily spotted. Otherwise, he would have died from exposure at the isolated crash site.

If you're in the mood for a brief walk, follow the Thomas Hariot Nature Trail as it loops 0.3 mile from the restored Fort Raleigh to Roanoke Sound, passing through a heavily wooded area adjacent to Waterside Theatre. Thomas Hariot was a highly respected scientist and mathematician and a member of Sir Walter Raleigh's expedition of 1585. Interpretive signs about the plant life that Hariot found on his visit to the North Carolina coast are located along the trail. For example, one marker bears Hariot's words: "There is a herb which is sowed in part by itself and is called by the inhabitants Uppowoc. . . . The Spaniards generally call it Tobacco."

Return to the visitor center and walk the marked trails to Waterside Theatre. It is most fitting that the nation's first symphonic outdoor drama, *The Lost Colony*, took root on the very shore where the United States took its first breath. Yet in a strange twist of irony, this spectacular theatrical production about the joys, the trials, and the struggle for survival of the short-lived Roanoke colony remains the longest continuous-running outdoor drama in America.

Except for five years during World War II, when the coast was blacked out, the play has been presented at Waterside Theatre every summer since 1937. Paul Green, the North Carolina–born literary giant, wrote the play, which blends drama, dance, music, and history into a theatrical masterpiece. The Pulitzer Prize–winning author and playwright began work on the play in 1936 in response to a request by the Roanoke Island Historical Association that he compose a pageant for the celebration of the 350th birthday of Virginia Dare.

The lights flooded the stage for the first time at eight-fifteen on the evening of July 4, 1937—353 years to the day after Amadas and Barlowe first entered North Carolina. Some twenty-five hundred spectators sat spellbound as they witnessed the birth of the symphonic outdoor drama.

Two events a month later gave the drama a high profile. In its August 15 issue, the *New York Times* offered a complimentary review of *The Lost Colony*. Then, three days later, on Virginia Dare Day, President Franklin D. Roosevelt came to Roanoke Island, where he witnessed the drama from his car at the rear of the theater.

Since the premiere performance, nearly three million people, including Vice President Hubert Humphrey and Lady Bird Johnson, have witnessed the spectacle under the stars at Waterside Theatre. Presented in two acts with a total of eleven scenes, the drama offers a unique theatrical look at the four-hundred-year-old mystery. More than a hundred performing artists and stage technicians bring the story to life every evening except Sundays from mid-June until late August.

Of the numerous stars who have had roles in the drama, the most famous is Andy Griffith, a native North Carolinian who maintains a permanent home on Roanoke Island. After his graduation from the University of North Carolina in 1947, Griffith was a player in *The Lost Colony* for five consecutive seasons. During his last few seasons, he was cast as Sir Walter Raleigh.

Of all Griffith's experiences as a player in the Roanoke Island drama,

Waterside Theatre

TOURING THE BACKROADS OF NORTH CAROLINA'S UPPER COAST

perhaps the most embarrassing took place in front of an audience but away from the theater. Griffith and a fellow cast member rented a sailboat at Wanchese one Saturday in August and sailed it around the island to Manteo. About noon, they reached the drawbridge and blew their whistle for the bridge tender to allow them to pass. By the time the bridge was opened, cars were backed up and the sailboat was becalmed. Neither Griffith nor his friend was a boater, and their best efforts caused the boat to go round and round in circles. Irate motorists screamed and honked their horns. Finally, the embarrassed sailors managed to get their boat through the bridge. As they passed, a man on the bridge asked, "Who are those fools?" As fate would have it, the director of *The Lost Colony* happened to be one of the stranded motorists. He responded, "That's Sir Walter Raleigh and Governor White making their last voyage!"

Waterside Theatre

Virtually every seat in the semicircular bowl at Waterside Theatre offers an excellent view of the color and pageantry of the court of Queen Elizabeth, the grace of the Indian dancers, the comedy of Old Tom, the christening of Virginia Dare, and the terror of Indian attacks. Many theatergoers carry insect repellant, as mosquitoes are a constant menace during the warm summer evenings.

Despite the unpredictable weather of the Outer Banks, *The Lost Colony* has averaged only two rainouts per season over its fifty-plus years.

From the theater, return to the parking lot, then walk to the Elizabethan Gardens, a living memorial to the brave colonists who came to Roanoke Island between 1585 and 1587. Conceived and developed as a project of the Garden Club of North Carolina, Inc., in 1951, this special garden is maintained as an authentic example of a sixteenth-century Elizabethan pleasure garden.

Since the gardens were first opened to the public, constant efforts have been made to improve and enhance the beauty of the site. Approximately two acres have been developed into formal gardens, and the remaining eight acres have been left in their natural state so as to represent the terrain first encountered by the sixteenth-century colonists.

Visitors are immediately impressed by the magnificent, ivy-covered Great Gate, which once adorned the French Embassy in Washington, D.C. The perforated wall enclosing the gardens was built of handmade bricks salvaged

Virginia Dare statue, Elizabethan Gardens

from all over North Carolina, from old structures ranging from churches to tobacco flues.

Self-guided tours begin at the hexagonal Gate House Reception Center. Inside, you will find Elizabethan furniture, drawings by John White, and portraits of Queen Elizabeth and Sir Walter Raleigh. The portrait of Raleigh—an excellent copy of the original, which hangs in the National Portrait Gallery in London—is encased in a hand-carved wooden frame with gold leaf, dating from around 1629. Framed in antique ebony, the oil portrait of Queen Elizabeth dates from 1592.

Leaving the Gate House, you will be greeted by the pleasant fragrance of herbs. A walkway leads to the centerpiece of the entire garden: the Sunken Garden. Here, an ancient fountain and pool are surrounded by statuary and enclosed by rows of hedges. The fountain was the gift of John Hay Whitley, the former United States ambassador to Great Britain. Whitley and his wife also contributed a fine assortment of antique marble statuary dating back to Elizabethan England.

Throughout the garden, spectacular pieces of statuary attract history lovers. The most intriguing piece in the garden is the figure of the adult Virginia Dare carved from Carrera marble. Displayed atop a special pedestal, the full-bosomed figure rises from a bath in the surf, clad only in a fishnet and accompanied by a swan. Playwright Paul Green, the man who donated

Bust of Paul Green, Waterside Theatre

the statue, selected the spot where it stands—at the end of a leafy avenue of oak trees. When asked how he came to choose the site, Green responded, "I have a feeling this is where she played as a young girl."

But the Virginia Dare statue and the other pieces of statuary do not alone make the gardens the national showplace they have become. Indeed, it is the spectacular mixture of flowers, shrubs, hedges, trees, and other plants that has earned the site its distinction as the natural beauty spot of the Outer Banks. Each year, more than seventy thousand persons enjoy the majestic showplace, which was selected as the most outstanding garden-club project in the United States in 1961.

Although the grounds are open all year, the hours of operation vary according to the season.

Return to the parking lot and retrace your route to the entrance of Fort Raleigh National Historic Site.

After experiencing all the historic attractions at Fort Raleigh, many visitors find themselves pondering the significance of the events played out on this ground over four hundred years ago. The success of the colonial ventures on the island in the 1580s cannot be judged according to their brevity or the myriad problems with which they were plagued. Rather, their value lies in the lessons learned, the information gained, and the new ground broken by the brave men and women who ventured forth from their native country to settle a promising, yet unknown, land. Many people continue to feel that Roanoke Island, and not Jamestown, was the birthplace of British America. From 1584 to 1587, some forty English ships called here and more than a thousand English subjects landed.

Each of the Roanoke voyages was blessed with talented journalists and artists.

Thomas Hariot began writing his treatise, *A Briefe and True Report of the New Found Land of Virginia*, while still on Roanoke Island. Not only was it the first book written in and about North Carolina, but it was also the first English treatise published about the New World. Only eight copies of Hariot's book are known to exist today.

Complementing Hariot's journalistic skills were the artistic abilities of John White. White drew the first accurate maps of the Atlantic coast of North America. His beautiful watercolors of North American flora and fauna, now preserved in the British Museum, are regarded as the finest of the period. Reproductions of White's art were included in the Latin, French, and German editions of Hariot's book.

In addition to the literary and artistic works that grew from the Roanoke colonies, the English people got their first tastes of various new crops and products—such as tobacco—from the ships returning from North Carolina. They were introduced to the American Indian when Manteo and Wanchese were transported across the Atlantic.

In late 1991, Ivor Noel Hume, the retired senior archaeologist for Colonial Williamsburg, found evidence of America's first science center while working at Fort Raleigh National Historic Site. Historians and archaeologists are now convinced that in 1585, Thomas Hariot and Joachim Gans established this initial laboratory on Roanoke Island.

Finally, it should be noted that the British traditions now deeply interwoven into the fabric of American life were first imported at Roanoke Island. When Manteo was baptized on Sunday, August 13, 1587, history recorded the first Protestant religious service in the New World. Five days later, British America boasted its first birth, that of Virginia Dare. These milestones cannot be minimized. As a consequence of the foundations laid by the Roanoke colonists, most Americans today speak English as their first language, rather than Spanish, French, or German.

Return to the highway entrance to Fort Raleigh National Historic Site, turn left onto U.S. 64/264, drive 0.9 mile, and turn right on Airport Road. Follow the signs on the 1.3-mile drive to the North Carolina Aquarium at Roanoke Island.

Located adjacent to Dare County Regional Airport, this facility is the northernmost of the three coastal laboratories operated by the state for marine research and education. Each year, increasing numbers of visitors make their way here to take advantage of a wide variety of interesting exhibits, displays, lectures, workshops, films, and other programs related to the complex natural environment of Dare County and the surrounding region.

Young and old alike are attracted to the twenty aquariums filled with native fish and sea creatures. These lighted tanks stand out like shining jewels along a long, darkened hallway. Two large tanks are used as gallery exhibits. The Red Drum Gallery showcases trophy-size fish. Also known as the channel bass, the red drum is the official state fish of North Carolina. In the expanded Grandy-White Shark Gallery, visitors may enjoy a closeup look at North Carolina sharks swimming about a three-thousand-gallon tank.

Other exhibits detail the human and natural history of the area. These include a display on the North Carolina alligator and an exhibit about the Pea Island Lifesaving Station, the only all-black lifesaving station in United States history.

Admission to the three state aquariums was free until 1994, when the state legislature imposed nominal fees in order to generate additional funds for the operation of the centers.

Monument to Pea Island Lifesaving Station

Retrace your route to U.S. 64/264 and continue south for 1.1 miles. Turn left onto Mother Vineyard Road (S.R. 1120) and follow it as it curves toward Roanoke Sound. Tucked deep within this fashionable neighborhood on the outskirts of Manteo is a grapevine which may be a living remnant of the Lost Colony of Roanoke. Long known as Mother Vineyard, the ancient scuppernong vine on the shores of the sound is believed to be the oldest cultivated grapevine in the United States.

Few tourists see Mother Vineyard, because it is off the well-beaten path. The gnarled and twisted vine, with its broad canopy of leaves, covers a half-acre on private property approximately three hundred feet on the left after the sharp turn of the road at the sound.

Researchers agree that the massive plant was set out and cared for by intelligent planters, but there is widespread disagreement as to when it was planted and who planted it. When Abraham Baum was an eight-year-old boy growing up on Roanoke Island in 1750, he recalled that the grapevine was "big and old." Most experts concur that the vine is at least four hundred years old. As a result, there has long been speculation that it may have been brought to Roanoke Island by the expeditions of Sir Walter Raleigh. However, botanists are now in agreement that the scuppernong vine and its white fruit are native to North Carolina.

Mother Vineyard

Thus, the vine, consisting of five gnarled trunks twisted around each other, with a combined circumference of thirteen feet, must have grown from seedlings planted and cultivated by Raleigh's colonists or the local Indians. Without question, Roanoke Island was covered with wild grapes at the arrival of the English explorers in 1584. There is evidence that the Indians knew how to make wine from grapes at the time Raleigh's colonists reached the island. Consequently, Mother Vineyard may predate the European settlers by a century or more.

In the first half of the nineteenth century, Mother Vineyard was the base of operations for America's first vine growers. Off and on from 1835 to 1950, "Mother Vineyard Scuppernong, the Original American Wine," was produced from ten thousand vines growing in and around the mother vine. Though the winery no longer operates on Roanoke Island, Mother Vineyard Scuppernong is still produced by a company in Petersburg, Virginia. Grocers in Dare County carry the product, which is described as a pink, sweet wine similar to white port.

Follow Mother Vineyard Road to where it intersects Scuppernong Road (S.R. 1166). Turn onto Scuppernong Road, which merges with Swain Drive near U.S. 64/264. Turn south onto U.S. 64/264. Near this intersection, a mileage sign on the east shoulder of U.S. 64/264 reads, "Murphy 543 miles." This sign was erected to honor that time-honored North Carolina travel slogan, "From Murphy to Manteo."

Drive south on U.S. 64/264 approximately 0.5 mile to the intersection with Ananias Dare Street in Manteo.

Motorists en route to the Outer Banks from the west often see no more of Manteo than the motels, restaurants, and shopping facilities along U.S. 64/264. Similarly, vacationers from points north who make their way across Roanoke Sound to attend *The Lost Colony* often bypass "downtown" Manteo. Sadly, these tourists miss the charm and quaintness that lie just beyond the federal highway. Streets bearing names like Devon, Ananias Dare, Budleigh, Sir Walter Raleigh, Agona, and Fernando hint at the Elizabethan style of downtown Manteo on Shallowbag Bay.

Most of the old commercial structures in the heart of Manteo have been refurbished to resemble Tudor England. A modern $5-million condominium-retail complex highlights the revitalized waterfront area. A bridge at the foot of Ananias Dare Street crosses Shallowbag Bay to Ice Plant Island, the site of the Elizabeth II State Historic Site.

Turn east off U.S. 64/264 onto Ananias Dare Street as it makes its way 5 blocks to the waterfront.

En route, you will see Mount Olivet Methodist Church on the

northeastern corner of Ananias Dare and Essex streets. This is one of the oldest surviving churches in Dare County. Completed in 1889, the beautiful white frame structure has been modified and enlarged several times during the past century, yet it retains much of its original nineteenth-century charm. Particularly beautiful are the unique stained-glass windows, which contain some of the original glass.

Continue on Ananias Dare Street. Near the intersection with Queen Elizabeth Street, park in the on-street spaces or in the public parking area near the waterfront. The brick and masonry columns at the parking-lot entrance honor the Roanoke colonies.

At the foot of Ananias Dare Street stands the Cora Daniels Basnight Bridge, a graceful wooden vehicular and pedestrian bridge built for the celebration of America's four hundredth birthday. It was named in honor of the beloved Manteo resident who for decades played the role of the Indian maiden Agona in *The Lost Colony*.

Walk across the bridge to the Elizabeth II State Historic Site.

As the host of the celebration of America's quadricentennial, Manteo received a permanent tangible benefit: a state historic site. The centerpiece of the site is the *Elizabeth II*, an exact replica of an Elizabethan sailing vessel. Built solely with private funds raised by America's Four Hundredth

Anniversary Committee, the three-masted, sixty-nine-foot vessel was presented to the state on July 13, 1984.

Except for brief visits to other North Carolina ports and a 1990 voyage to Virginia for an appearance as the *Santa Maria* in a National Park Service documentary on the voyages of Columbus, the ship has remained at its berth on the Manteo waterfront.

No plans survive for the vessels involved in the Roanoke voyages, so the *Elizabeth II* was constructed to be a representative sixteenth-century sailing ship. It was named for the *Elizabeth*, a fifty-ton ship in the seven-ship fleet of 1585.

A visitor center at the state historic site offers wall murals and exhibits that explain the reasons for European exploration of the New World. Life-size dioramas offer a view of the life of the colonists on Roanoke Island. Archaeologists' finds and reproductions of John White's drawings are on display. Admission to the visitor center is free, but a nominal fee is charged for guided tours of the ship.

Located in a building adjacent to the visitor center, the Outer Banks History Center is a repository of more than twenty-five thousand books, a thousand periodicals, forty-five hundred official documents of the Coast Guard and its predecessor, the Lifesaving Service, and a wide variety of maps, photographs, and audio and video recordings. Open to the public, the facility is a treasure trove of information about the North Carolina coast. It was established in 1988 largely through the efforts of coastal author and historian

David Stick. The collection of North Carolina history at the center is among the best anywhere in the world.

From Ice Plant Island, the panorama of the Manteo waterfront unfolds before the visitor. Downtown Manteo began receiving its badly needed facelift in 1966.

The town had its beginnings almost a century earlier, during Reconstruction. In 1870, Roanoke Island, which had up to that time belonged to Tyrrell County, was made part of Dare County, created by the legislature from portions of Currituck, Hyde, and Tyrrell counties. When the commissioners of the new county got together for the first time on April 4, 1870, they chose to meet at Shallowbag Bay, in deference to the picturesque body of water that continues to grace the Manteo waterfront. At the time, there were only a few houses in the settlement.

When a wooden courthouse was erected in 1873 to replace the temporary structure that preceded it, the county seat was still known as Shallowbag Bay. Federal postal officials then stepped in to give the community a new name, as they did for many communities along the North Carolina coast. On October 2, 1873, a post office was established here under the name of Manteo. Residents of the growing settlement liked the name and found it to be a fitting tribute to the friendly Indian who protected the first white settlers on the island.

Return to the Manteo waterfront via the bridge and walk along the boardwalk. A public pier and gazebo provide an outstanding view of Shallowbag Bay and the colorful pleasure craft that dock at Manteo. Federal engineers worked from 1909 to 1910 to create this harbor by dredging the bay. The two modern buildings towering over the harbor house an inn, shops, and condominiums.

Washington Creef Park (Bicentennial Park) is located on the south end of the waterfront at the foot of Agona Street, near the pier and gazebo. On this site stood the first electrical plant in Dare County. Constructed around 1914, it generated electricity by means of the motor and light plant taken from the luxury liner *Leviathan*.

One monument—the Revolutionary War Memorial Cross—stands in the park. It was constructed from the cornerstone of the old Manteo High School.

Revolutionary War Memorial Cross

When you have finished exploring the waterfront, walk back to Queen Elizabeth Street on the sidewalk adjacent to the waterfront shopping and condominium complex. Proceed 1 block to the Dare County Courthouse, located in the heart of town at the corner of Queen Elizabeth and Budleigh streets.

Despite its relative youth as a coastal city, Manteo has a dozen or more buildings of historic importance. Chief among these is the courthouse, a brick Italianate structure erected in 1904. Ironically, the courthouse was built to be a fireproof building, but it sustained significant hurricane damage in 1933. Even though subsequent renovations and additions have modified the exterior, the chimneys, portico, and cupola are original.

Continue your walk with a visit to Essex Square, located adjacent to the courthouse on Sir Walter Raleigh Street. Manteo's first elementary school was once located here, as was the Bank of Manteo. This bank held the distinction as being one of just five banks in the country to close only one day—the mandatory "Banking Holiday"—during the Great Depression.

With the approach of the America's quadricentennial celebration, the final phase of the restoration of Manteo began in the late 1970s. Native son John Wilson IV returned home to spearhead the project after making his mark as a big-city architect and urban planner. Beginning in 1977, Wilson worked his architectural magic on the cluster of Tudor-style retail shops and apartments that is Essex Square. At age twenty-nine, Wilson was elected mayor of Manteo. During his tenure, he planned many of the projects that beautified the business district. While most of his plans were still on paper, he earned a National Trust Award for his efforts.

Ye Olde Pioneer Theater

From Essex Square, turn right onto Old Tom Street, an alley connecting Sir Walter Raleigh and Budleigh streets. From the end of Old Tom Street, Ye Olde Pioneer Theater is visible on the opposite side of Budleigh. This three-hundred-seat theater is the only movie house on the island, but more important, it is the oldest single-family-operated theater in the country. George Creef began the operation in 1918 in his boatyard. The business was moved into the current theater building around 1934. Creef's grandson now runs the theater.

Turn right off Old Tom Street onto Budleigh Street, walk 1 block, and return to where you parked your car. Drive east on Queen Elizabeth Street for 2 blocks and turn right on Agona Street. After 1 block, turn left onto Fernando Street, where the Asa Jones House stands as one of the oldest homes in Manteo. Some portions of the structure date from 1860. An additional story was added to the frame dwelling by John Wilson IV, a descendant of the original owner.

At the junction of Fernando and Uppowoc streets, turn right onto Uppowoc. Drive 2 blocks to the corner of Sir Walter Raleigh Street to see the Theodore S. Meekins House, a magnificent example of the Queen Anne style.

Constructed before 1900, the house was originally the home of the Meekins family, who fled Hatteras Island after a terrible hurricane. Designed by Theodore S. Meekins from a picture his wife had seen in a Sears-Roebuck catalog, the house features a wraparound porch, shingled gables, and a rounded corner tower with a conical roof. Meekins is also credited with building the famed Chicamacomico Lifesaving Station on Hatteras Island. The Theodore S. Meekins House is listed on the National Register of Historic Places.

Turn left onto Sir Walter Raleigh Street and drive 1 block to the intersection with U.S. 64/264. Turn south.

On the left side of the highway stands the Island Gallery and Christmas Shop, a shopping facility that has become a legend in coastal North Carolina. In 1967, the proprietor, former New York actor and *Lost Colony* performer Edward Green, opened this wonderland of stores, housed in seven

The Manteo waterfront

multilevel buildings nestled under live oaks and tall pines. Its thirty-four rooms are furnished with antiques and stocked with more than fifty thousand different items from more than thirty-five countries. Glistening Christmas ornaments by the thousands are showcased in a room filled with thirty or more Christmas trees.

Continue in your original direction on U.S. 64/264. Near the geographic center of the island, U.S. 64/264 turns sharply east toward the Outer Banks, while N.C. 345 makes its way to the south end of the island. Turn south onto N.C 345 and proceed 1 mile to the junction with Skyco Road (S.R. 1134). Turn right on Skyco Road and proceed approximately 0.7 mile to its terminus near the Croatan Sound shore. Here is the site of Ashby (or Ashbee) Harbor, a sound-side port that achieved a degree of commercial prominence after the Civil War.

It was here that General Ambrose Burnside landed the Union expeditionary force that captured Roanoke Island in 1862. At the time, the community had only a few houses, one of which was used as a hospital by the Federal army.

Thirty years later, Ashby Harbor emerged as a vibrant trading center. Much of the island's commerce with the outside world in the late nineteenth and early twentieth centuries passed through this harbor.

In 1892, postal officials selected Skiko as the name for the new post office established at Ashby Harbor. It was so named for the son of an Indian chief once held hostage by Ralph Lane's men. By the turn of the century, Skyco, as the name was then spelled, had emerged as an important port for the steamers of the Old Dominion Steamship Line.

Skyco succumbed to the mainland railroad and the upriver movement of the shad industry in the second decade of the twentieth century. In 1913, the post office was closed, and the village became a virtual ghost town. Now, its once-busy waterfront is marked by rotting pilings, reminders of the heyday of this early hub of island commerce.

Retrace your route to N.C. 345 and turn right. After 2.4 miles, you will reach the junction with S.R. 1168 (Old Wharf Road) at Wanchese, the old village on the southern end of the island. Turn right onto S.R. 1168 and drive 1.3 miles to the intersection with S.R. 1146. Turn left onto S.R. 1146 and drive 0.7 mile, then turn left on S.R. 1181 and proceed 0.8 mile to the

Skyco

intersection with S.R. 1144. Turn right onto S.R. 1144 and proceed 0.6 mile to N.C. 345. Scattered about these village roads are the homes of the two thousand persons who call this unincorporated fishing village home. This pleasant drive along the village lanes reveals abundant evidence that local residents earn their living from the same source as their forebearers a century earlier. Boats, fishing nets, old anchors, and related fishing and boating paraphernalia decorate the yards of the 1920s-style frame homes.

Wanchese

While this salty fishing community is not postcard pretty, it offers a true-life portrait of a bustling fishing community. Indeed, not every vista in Wanchese is a panorama of beauty. Worn, dilapidated piers extend into roadside "skeeter ditches"—canals dredged many years ago to control mosquito infestations. Nowhere does Wanchese attempt to hide the fact that it is a working village.

In the years just after the Civil War, the two settlements at either end of the island were known as "the Upper End" and "the Lower End," rather than Manteo and Wanchese. It was not until a post office was established here on June 14, 1886, that "the Lower End" gave way to Wanchese.

Turn right on N.C. 345 and proceed 0.8 mile to the end of the road at Wanchese Harbor on Mill Landing. Here is the center of village activity and the highlight of any visit to the southern end of Roanoke Island. Fish houses and busy wharves crowd the quarter-mile of sound front known to locals as Mill Landing.

As the home port of the largest commercial fishing fleet on the northern Pamlico Sound, this harbor is crowded with fishing boats by midafternoon. Every year, more than 21 million pounds of fish are unloaded from the fleet. Crates of fresh seafood are stacked on the docks and in the fish houses, where visitors can inspect the daily bounty and purchase as much as they please. Seafood not sold dockside is packed in ice and shipped to Northern markets.

Adjacent to the harbor is the North Carolina Seafood Industrial Park. Established by the state legislature in the 1970s with an aim of making Wanchese one of the major seafood processing and distribution centers on the Atlantic coast, the sixty-nine-acre complex has enjoyed limited success, due to the shoaling problems at nearby Oregon Inlet.

The tour ends here, at the southern end of historic Roanoke Island.

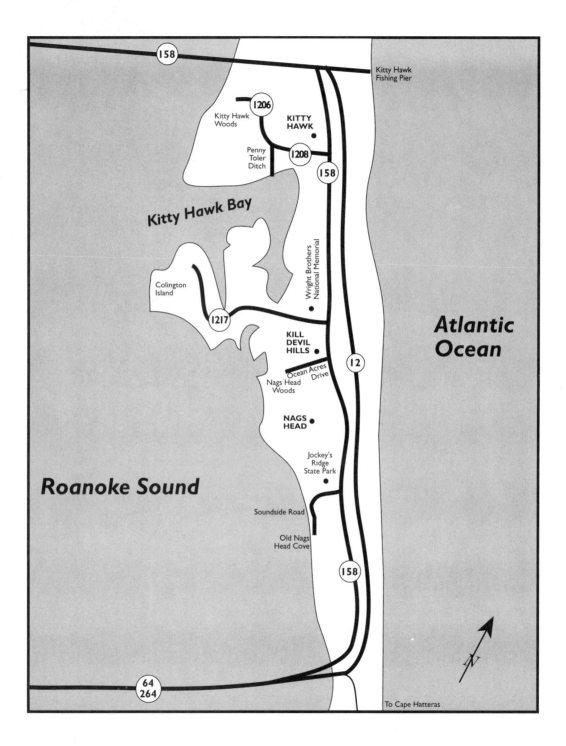

158

Kitty Hawk
Fishing Pier

1206

Kitty Hawk
Woods

**KITTY
HAWK**

Penny
Toler
Ditch

1208

158

Kitty Hawk Bay

Wright Brothers
National Memorial

Colington
Island

1217

**Atlantic
Ocean**

**KILL
DEVIL
HILLS**

12

Ocean Acres
Drive

Nags Head
Woods

**NAGS
HEAD**

Roanoke Sound

Jockey's
Ridge
State Park

Soundside Road

Old Nags
Head Cove

158

N

64
264

To Cape Hatteras

The Heart of
the Outer Banks Tour

This tour begins on U.S. 158 in Nags Head and makes its way north on the bypass to Jockey's Ridge, Colington Island, Kill Devil Hills, and Kitty Hawk. It then loops back to where it began on N.C. 12, which runs along the strand.

Among the highlights of the tour are Jockey's Ridge State Park, Nags Head Woods, Wright Brothers National Memorial, the sites of three shipwrecks in the Graveyard of the Atlantic, and the Unpainted Aristocracy of Nags Head.

Total mileage: approximately 49 miles.

This tour begins at Milepost 16.5, at the intersection of U.S. 64/264, U.S. 158, and N.C. 12 in southern Nags Head. Proceed north on U.S. 158 as the highway runs through the fabled beach resorts of Nags Head, Kill Devil Hills, and Kitty Hawk—an area long known as the heart of the Outer Banks. To the east and often within sight of U.S. 158, N.C. 12 runs a parallel route along the strand to Kitty Hawk.

Throughout the entire nation, there are few places more synonymous with resort living than Nags Head. Indeed, no place names in North Carolina have more nationwide recognition than Nags Head, Kill Devil Hills, and Kitty Hawk.

As the granddaddy of North Carolina's coastal resorts, Nags Head enjoys a reputation that transcends state and national boundaries. Because of its location at the intersection of the major highways servicing the Outer Banks, the resort town serves as the northern gateway to Cape Hatteras National Seashore and the southern gateway to the booming beach towns in Dare and Currituck counties. Most traffic reaches the Outer Banks from the west at Nags Head via U.S. 64, the state's longest highway. From Murphy to the Atlantic at Nags Head, the highway stretches 549 miles.

On the drive north on U.S. 158, you will notice small signs posted every mile; they are posted on N.C. 12 as well. For many years, these signs—from

Milepost 1 on U.S. 158 in Kitty Hawk to Milepost 21 on S.R. 1243 in southern Nags Head, at the boundary of Cape Hatteras National Seashore—have served as reference points for landmarks, businesses, and homes.

Over the past several decades, the multilane U.S. 158, originally designed as a bypass, has become the true business avenue of the three beach resorts. Upscale restaurants, fast-food outlets, movie theaters, supermarkets, countless shopping centers, water slides and amusements parks, real-estate offices, residential subdivisions, and rows of resort homes line the very road designed to avoid the busy areas on the beach road. Outer Banks Mall, located on the west side of U.S. 158 at Milepost 14.5, is representative of the commercial development that is now rampant along the highway.

Much of the laid-back lifestyle and romantic maritime charm that have lured generation after generation to this famous stretch of strand is fast fading away. As the outside world has marched into the modern era, so has this resort area, but at a less rapid pace.

No longer do hardy lifesavers man picturesque lifesaving stations located every 7 miles along the nearby strand. Modern advances in navigation have robbed the Graveyard of the Atlantic of its killer instinct, making shipwrecks in the offshore waters a rarity rather than a common occurrence.

Many weathered beach cottages that survived the pounding of wind and surf for decades have given way to condominiums and time-share resorts. Winding, sandy lanes connecting the villages have been replaced by a network of paved highways and streets that are often snarled with traffic at the peak of the summer season.

Indeed, the Nags Head–Kill Devil Hills–Kitty Hawk area is not the same place it was in the 1950s, or even the 1960s and 1970s. But time and change have not completely stripped the old resort of its quaint charm. There are still backroads which yield a glimpse of the days of old, before fast-food restaurants and hotels and motels invaded the island landscape.

Turn left off U.S. 158 onto Soundside Road 0.1 mile north of Milepost 13. This narrow, winding lane is bordered on the north by, and at times covered with the sands of, Jockey's Ridge and the other towering dunes that have long been landmarks on the island. After 0.5 mile, the road veers sharply south for 0.7 mile along the shore of Roanoke Sound. Clustered along this ancient path are the remnants of old Nags Head village. Of special interest are the classic Outer Banks homes, some constructed more than a century ago. A few of the oldest are set upon pilings in the sound.

It was here that the state's first coastal resort was born in the 1830s, as a result of the malaria that plagued tidewater plantations. Each summer, swamps, marshes, and other low-lying land surrounding the plantations gave off a vapor, or miasma. Planters and their families and slaves often died from fever, which they believed was induced by the miasmas. In their search for a cure, doctors concluded that the miasmas came from decomposing animal and vegetable matter in the swamps. Doctors reasoned that regular breathing of salt air and bathing in salt water prevented the dread disease. They therefore recommended that the planters summer near the shoreline.

Francis Nixon, a planter from Perquimans County, was apparently the first person to take the advice of the physicians. He scouted various parts of the Outer Banks in the early 1830s in hopes of finding a place to erect a summer residence. Nixon was awed by the mighty sand dunes upon his approach to Nags Head. Once ashore, he walked beyond Jockey's Ridge and the marshy dunes to find a maritime forest and the few houses of the hermits, shipwreck victims, and farmers who inhabited the area. Although Nixon was originally interested in purchasing only a few acres, he bought two hundred acres on Roanoke Sound for the sum of one hundred dollars.

Once their summer home was completed, Nixon and his family welcomed friends and neighbors to Nags Head after the crops were harvested in July. It did not take long for affluent mainlanders to discover that the Nags Head area offered not only an escape from the miasmas, but also an unspoiled playground of sun, sand, and water. Around the tall dunes near the sound, a resort community sprang up. All of the early houses were constructed above the water on pilings. A sound-side pier stretched far into the water, because shallow conditions forced the packet steamers from Albemarle Sound to anchor nearly a half-mile from shore. Scows and flats were then used to transport passengers and freight to the pier.

In less than a decade, the resort was so popular that demand for accommodations was greater than supply. To meet the need for a lodging and entertainment facility, Malachi Russell constructed a two-hundred-room hotel in the center of the growing resort community in 1838.

From the outset, the hotel suffered from poor management. Following several changes of ownership, A. J. Batemen of Edenton purchased the hotel in the winter of 1849–50. Batemen quickly perceived that the hotel's lack of success resulted from the "difficulty of reaching." To alleviate the problem, he arranged for a steamer to make regular weekend runs to Nags Head from southeastern Virginia. An advertising campaign was launched to attract out-of-state visitors. Batemen also made a concerted effort to improve the hotel by adding forty rooms, nightly band music, and a horse-drawn tram that took guests to a bathhouse on the beach.

When a writer from *Harper's New Monthly Magazine* arrived at Nags Head in 1860, the hotel was as large as any at the present-day resort. The atmosphere at the hotel was described in glowing terms by *Harper's*: "Fashion and frolic hold revel as though that remorseless leveler, old ocean, did not daily threaten a revolution. We found the celebrated band in full squeak, and a few couples threading the mazy under the influence of the same. . . . Among the two or three hundred guests was a full share of female loveliness."

Happy times at Nags Head were brought to a screeching halt by the Civil War. Brigadier General Henry A. Wise, the commander of the Confederate defenses on nearby Roanoke Island, established his headquarters at the hotel at Nags Head in January 1862. After Union forces captured Roanoke Island a month later, Wise and his lieutenants retreated up the Outer Banks. To prevent the hotel from falling into enemy hands, Wise ordered it torched.

In 1867, the hotel was rebuilt, but it soon succumbed to the shifting sands of Hotel Hill, a large, unstable sand dune. A subsequent hotel operated on the sound until it burned in 1900. In 1923, Nags Head became the first of the three resort communities to incorporate, but the lack of bridges across the sound continued to deter growth.

Retrace your route to U.S. 158 and proceed north as the highway passes awesome Jockey's Ridge. Nowhere does the cliche "You can't miss it" seem more appropriate. No visitor to Nags Head can possibly miss Jockey's Ridge, and no one who climbs or even sees this, the largest natural sand dune on the Atlantic and Gulf coasts, ever forgets it.

Rising high above the flat barrier-island landscape, Jockey's Ridge and its half-dozen or so sister dunes stand out like sand piles meant for the children of giants. In reality, the massive mountains of sand are similar to the

Jockey's Ridge

barkhans, or marching dunes, of northern Africa. Geologists consider the dunes prime examples of the formation called a medano—a huge, asymmetrical, shifting hill of sand which lacks vegetation.

Although all of the prominent sand dunes at Nags Head are spectacular, the most magnificent is Jockey's Ridge. Actually, Jockey's Ridge is two large dunes, the lower one parallel to the highway, the higher one in the background. Wind and storms cause constant changes in the height of the dunes. At its maximum, the higher dune towers almost 140 feet above sea level. At other times, it measures almost 30 feet shorter.

From the highway, Jockey's Ridge looms as a mini-Sahara. Its color changes from white to beige to yellow depending on the time of day, the amount of sunlight, and the amount of moisture. Swirling winds constantly redecorate the dune with myriad intricate patterns. At the peak of summer, temperatures on its surface reach upwards of 150 degrees Fahrenheit.

Jockey's Ridge can best be examined and explored at Jockey's Ridge State Park. Turn left off U.S. 158 onto Carolista Drive at the entrance to the state park, near Milepost 12. After 0.3 mile, turn south off Carolista Drive into the parking area on the north side of the dune. Visitor facilities located near the parking lot include restrooms and picnic shelters with tables and grills. Natural-history programs and activities are offered by park rangers during the summer season.

Persons of all ages and walks of life find it difficult to resist a trek to the peak of the big dune. Most casual hikers find that it takes approximately an hour to walk to the top of the dune and return to the parking lot.

The bird's-eye view from the summit is one of the real pleasures of a visit to the Outer Banks. To the east, the Atlantic Ocean seems endless. To the west lie placid Roanoke Sound and, beyond, Roanoke Island. The sister dunes dominate the view to the south. On the north, the birthplace of powered flight looms on the horizon.

Not only does the peak provide a matchless panorama of the landscape and seascape, but it also offers a closeup view of the exciting sport of hang gliding. In the early 1970s, Jockey's Ridge was the site of the revival of hang gliding, an activity developed in the late nineteenth century by Otto Lilienthal, a German. Since its rebirth at Nags Head, hang gliding has become an international sport. It is a rare occasion when one or more world-class hang-glider pilots cannot be found here. After all, most of the sport's biggest names earned their wings at Nags Head, and many return to Jockey's Ridge every May for the annual Hang Gliding Spectacular, the oldest continuous hang-gliding competition in the country.

Most of the hang-gliding activity originates at Kitty Hawk Kites, housed in a large complex just across U.S. 158 from Jockey's Ridge. Professional instructors provide gliding lessons to novices and to experienced pilots who want to hone their skills. Billed as the largest school of its kind in the world, Kitty Hawk Kites has trained most of the hundred thousand daredevils who have attempted flight at Nags Head aboard the brightly colored gliders, constructed of Mylar and aluminum tubing.

Were it not for the hand of man, Jockey's Ridge might be no taller than the other significant sand dunes along the Outer Banks. Scientists believe that all of these natural dunes were created from sand washed and blown ashore by hurricanes and coastal storms. However, Jockey's Ridge grew to its current stature as a result of the early settlers on the Outer Banks, who destroyed the natural cover by cutting it and by allowing their stock to overgraze. As the vegetation disappeared, the wind shifted the exposed sand and piled it onto the great "walking dunes" of Nags Head. As they began a steady migration to the southwest, the growing dunes swallowed up houses and the few remaining trees in the area.

Local tradition holds that Jockey's Ridge acquired its name long ago, when it was used as a natural grandstand for a racetrack in the flats just southwest of the dunes, where Banker ponies were raced.

Perhaps the earliest reference to the imposing dune was contained in a land grant to John Campbell in 1753. In that document, it was referred to as Jockey's Hill. A symbol on the Mouzon map of 1775 indicates the existence of the dune, though it does not offer a name for it. Some of the other eighteenth-century maps of the Outer Banks show the surname Jackey or Jacock in the vicinity of the dune. Cartographers of that time customarily included the names of landowners on their maps and charts. Consequently, the dune may have been named for the Jackey family. In fact, it was shown as Jackey Ridge on some maps until 1953.

By 1851, Jockey's Ridge was already a popular tourist attraction. A Norfolk newspaper editor printed the legend that "the lady who may accompany you to its summit if not already a wife will shortly become yours." Engagement Hill, the sixty-eight-foot dune just south of Jockey's Ridge, carried a similar legend.

Nearby, the Seven Sisters, a contiguous line of seven dunes measuring up to seventy feet in height, also became a historic landmark in the first half of the nineteenth century. When Francis Nixon established a "health spa" on his 250 acres at Nags Head in 1832, he brought seven sisters—all from slave families—afflicted with disease. As time passed, the seven sand hills located near this experiment in communal health care became known as the Seven Sisters, a name still in common use today.

As Nags Head and environs grew into a world-renowned resort in the twentieth century, so grew the popularity of Jockey's Ridge. Though explosive commercial and residential development began to unfold around the dune after World War II, tourists and residents alike appeared to take it for granted that Jockey's Ridge would always be there.

In 1973, however, plans were announced for the construction of a multi-unit housing complex and golf course at Jockey's Ridge. Although the sprawling sand dune would soon thereafter be included in the National Registry of Natural Landmarks, that designation would offer no legal protection against development. It appeared that Jockey's Ridge was set for extinction.

No one seemed willing to oppose the development plans until Carolista Fletcher Baum physically placed herself between a bulldozer and the dune on a beautiful summer morning in 1973. Baum, the granddaughter of novelist Inglis Fletcher, had spent every summer of her life on the Outer Banks. She had a deep appreciation for the natural beauty of the area. Her determination was such that she remained in the path of the bulldozer until the operator shut it down.

Baum subsequently spearheaded a public campaign that, in 1975, led the North Carolina legislature to appropriate $420,000 for the purchase of a 60-acre tract near the dune for the establishment of a state park. Since that time, additional parcels have been purchased by the state, and a 100-acre tract was donated by the Nature Conservancy. Today, the state park encompasses 385 acres of dunes, forest, and wetlands.

Each year, more than 650,000 visitors come to the park, making it the second-most-visited park in the state system. For park patrons who are not disposed to climb Jockey's Ridge, a 1.5-mile self-guided nature trail with fourteen stations leads around the dune through the many plant environments in the park. Near the trailhead at the parking lot, thickets of wax myrtle, bayberry, red cedar, live oak, and red bay abound. At the base of the dune, small patches of American beach grass grow. To the west of the dune lies a small shrub forest of southern red oak, sweet gum, hickory, and loblolly pine. Beyond the shrub forest, the trail leads to brackish marshes on Roanoke Sound. Cattails and freshwater plants thrive in the upper marsh before giving way to black needle brush and cordgrass nearer the open water.

Return to U.S. 158 and continue north. Between Mileposts 10 and 9, the glut of fast-food restaurants has earned this stretch of highway the dubious nickname "French Fry Row."

A random survey of automobile license plates on U.S. 158 on any summer day may lead you to question whether this legendary resort area is really in North Carolina. Plates from Virginia, Pennsylvania, and Ohio outnumber those from the Tar Heel State on a regular basis during the summer vacation season. The proximity to the Virginia metropolitan center of Norfolk–Newport News and the crowded conditions of the coastal resorts of the mid-Atlantic have made the Nags Head area a prime vacation spot for millions of people to the north. Conversely, many North Carolinians choose to summer at the state's coastal resorts south of Cape Hatteras. This is not from lack of affection for the famed resorts of Dare County, but due to the great distance that separate the resorts from the majority of Tar Heel residents. Each of the ten largest cities in North Carolina lies more than 200 miles away.

At Milepost 10, Nags Head gives way to Kill Devil Hills. Other than a city-limits sign announcing the change in municipalities, the highway scenery varies little from one town to the other.

As to the names of the sister resorts, no one is exactly sure about their origin.

At least six legends have evolved concerning the origin of Nags Head. Of these explanations, the most enduring is the salty tale of land pirates based on the beach at Nags Head who unscrupulously used a horse, or nag, to lure ships to the deadly shoals just offshore. A lantern was supposedly placed around the horse's neck, and the horse was then driven up and down the beach to create the illusion of a ship riding at anchor in a sheltered harbor. Sea captains weary from navigating the Graveyard of the Atlantic sometimes saw the light as a welcome haven. After heading for shore, the ships would run aground, providing the land pirates with the opportunity to plunder. Although there is debate as to the merits of the legend, the United States Congress passed a law in 1825 whereby it became a felony to show a light with the intention of confusing ships at sea into "danger or distress or shipwreck."

Up the beach, confusion invariably arises as to whether the correct name is Kill Devil Hills or Kill Devil Hill. Both are correct. Kill Devil Hills is the name of the incorporated village, while Kill Devil Hill is the name of the tall, stabilized dune upon which rests the monument to the Wright brothers.

Old Nags Head

The earliest settlers knew the area by its Indian name of Rowspock, or Roesepock. However, on the Price map of 1808, the name shown for the large dune is Kill Devil Hill.

As with Nags Head, a number of legends exist to explain the unusual name. By far the most popular story involves William Byrd of Virginia. In 1728, Byrd supposedly described the rum consumed in the area in vivid terms, saying, "That thar rum is powerful enough to kill the devil."

Several other legends involve tales of the devil.

One story says that a ship carrying powerful rum from New England wrecked on the beach at Kill Devil Hills. Men assigned to guard the cargo reported that large quantities were disappearing under mysterious circumstances at night. Alarmed by the bizarre happenings, the guards enlisted the services of a local man known as Devil Ike to protect the valuable cargo. While at his post, Devil Ike solved the mystery: he saw another local man tie a rope around the cargo and attempt to pull it away by horse. He chased the thief off but decided not to tell the authorities about his neighbor. Rather, Devil Ike related that it was the devil who had been pilfering the cargo and that he had killed the demon.

Another tale involves a local resident who made a pact with the devil. In exchange for the man's soul, the devil was willing to pay a bag of gold. Arrangements were made for the exchange to take place at a set time on top of Kill Devil Hill. A day prior to the rendezvous, the local man secretly made his way to the top of the mountain of sand, where he laboriously dug a hole to the bottom of the dune. When the meeting took place, the crafty man coaxed the devil into the deep hole and covered him with sand.

Most likely, the name came from the killdeer, or killdee, a shorebird that was once common in the area. Over the years, the name evolved from Kill-deer Hill to Kill Devil Hill.

Motorists traveling along the heavily commercialized highway in Kill Devil Hills are often astonished to learn that a pristine maritime forest lies just west of U.S. 158.

At Milepost 9.7, turn left onto Ocean Acres Drive and proceed 1.2 miles west into Nags Head Woods. As the road nears this majestic forest, it climbs high, wooded sand dunes. The nature preserve's entrance sign, located near the point where the pavement ends, introduces visitors to the last exten-sive maritime forest north of Cape Hatteras. Although the Nags Head Woods Ecological Preserve is private property, it is open to the public. Guests are required to register at the visitor exhibit center, located near the end of Ocean Acres Drive. Interpretive programs and scheduled nature walks are offered at the center.

Two trails loop from the center through portions of the preserve. Inside the woods, the hustle and bustle of the nearby resorts seems a world away. A cool canopy of giant oak, maple, and hickory trees gives the impression of a mountain forest, rather than one less than a mile from the Atlantic Ocean. Amidst the visual splendor of moss-draped hardwoods, the stillness is broken only by the splash of a turtle or the call of a bird. In the distance, the crash of the Atlantic surf can be heard.

Sandwiched between two great sand dunes—Jockey's Ridge on the south and Run Hill on the north—the preserve encompasses fourteen hundred acres of forest, relict dunes, freshwater ponds, pine hummocks, and marshes. Described as the most ecologically diverse maritime forest on the east coast of the United States, the tract was designated a National Natural Land-mark by the Department of the Interior in 1974.

Among the trees growing on the ancient dunes in the forest are Southern red oak, beech, loblolly pine, black gum, and pignut. The second-largest holly tree in existence thrives here. Scattered throughout the forest are thirty-five interdunal freshwater ponds. They vary in size from a few feet in diame-ter to one exceptional pond covering 125 acres, located a mile south of

Wright Brothers National Memorial. Local legend has it that this enormous pond has no bottom.

Tidal creeks flowing from the forest into the marshes on the western edge of the preserve serve as the spawning ground for commercially valuable seafood. Canoe trips on the creeks are available during the summer months.

More than a thousand years ago, the forest provided shelter for the Algonquin Indians who fished and camped in the area. In 1524, the European explorer Giovanni da Verrazano was so captivated by the beauty of the magnificent forest that he named it Arcadia. Growing within the preserve are some live oaks that were in existence at the time of Verrazano's visit.

In the middle of the eighteenth century, two families, the Baums and the Tillets, built their homes in this spectacular wooded area on the shore of Roanoke Sound. Gradually, more than forty families joined them. A church and a school were constructed. Over time, these early settlers abandoned their community in the forest to move closer to the beach. Their homes decayed as the wooded area returned to its natural state. Today, visitors can venture from the sandy road leading into the woods to examine the ruins of a few deserted homesteads, as well as several ancient family graveyards containing tombstones with almost illegible markings.

After the community was abandoned, incursions into the woods were very rare until the 1970s. Suddenly, developers began to eye the pristine land as a prime spot for development. Sensing that the nation was about to lose something that it could never replace, the Dunes of Dare Garden Club stepped forward to bring the plight of Nags Head Woods before the state and nation. In 1978, as one of its first projects, the fledgling North Carolina Nature Conservancy put forth its best efforts to raise funds to buy a portion of the forest. Since then, subsequent purchases and donations have protected all of Nags Head Woods, save a few small, scattered parcels.

Retrace your route on Ocean Acres Drive to U.S. 158. Turn left on U.S. 158 and proceed north to the intersection with Ocean Bay Boulevard (S.R. 1217) at Milepost 8.5. Turn left onto Ocean Bay Boulevard in the shadow of Kill Devil Hill, surmounted by the monument to the Wright brothers. The road becomes Colington Road. After 1.3 miles, you will pass over Colington Creek onto Little Colington Island, the first of two Roanoke Sound islands named Colington.

This is another place that seems incongruous with the nearby resort development. Here, the hotels and shopping centers of Kill Devil Hills give way to the modest frame homes of fishermen, to fishing boats docked in picturesque creeks whose waters reflect the beautiful sunsets on the sound, to stacks of crab pots at docks and in yards, and to sturdy live oaks laced with Spanish moss.

Big Colington Island

Another 0.7 mile will bring you to Big Colington Island, which lies just west of Little Colington Island. Although Big Colington is more than twice as large as Little Colington, and has a far bigger population, it exhibits many of the features of its sister island.

Colington Road curves along the eastern shore of the island for 0.8 mile until it ends at the forks of Kitty Hawk Bay Drive and Colington Drive. Turn north on Colington Drive and proceed 0.7 mile to the north end of the island, overlooking Kitty Hawk Bay.

Although most of the oldest structures on the island date from the early twentieth century, Big Colington was the site of one of the first English settlements on the Outer Banks.

After the disappearance of the Lost Colony on nearby Roanoke Island, almost seventy-five years passed before a permanent settlement appeared on the barrier islands just across Roanoke Sound. King Charles II opened the

door for settlement in 1663, when he granted the Carolina territory to the eight Lords Proprietors. One of their number was Sir John Colleton (1608–1666), who, ironically, may never have visited the province.

In any case, on September 8, 1663, Colleton received the very first land grant issued in Carolina and in the southern third of the present United States. Through the grant, he obtained title to Carlile Island. Named for Christopher Carleill, the stepson of one of Sir Francis Drake's lieutenants, it was shown as Carlile Island on the Ogilby map of 1671. Colleton's first order of business after assuming control of the island, which measured 2 miles wide and 2 miles long, was to rename it after himself. Over time, the spelling of the island changed from Colleton to Collitons to Colington.

Anxious to implement his plan for turning his holdings into a prosperous enterprise, Colleton appointed John Whittie to establish a plantation on the island in the winter of 1664–65. Soon, the first settlers were constructing homes and outbuildings, clearing land, and planting corn and other crops. Tobacco farming and grape cultivation were subsequently introduced to the island, and a winery followed. Several years later, two additional Lords Proprietors entered into a whale-oil venture on Colleton to take advantage of the many whales that washed ashore on the nearby strand.

Big Colington Island

Despite the initial success enjoyed by the plantation, it was doomed to failure. A series of hurricanes brought the project to an end ten years after it was started. Although there is little documented history for the island in the fifty years that followed, it is almost certain that it has been continuously inhabited since that first agricultural project.

About 1750, slave labor was used to extend the meandering creek which ran about halfway through the island. By 1769, the combination creek and canal had been extended from Kitty Hawk Bay on the north to Buzzard Bay on the south, thereby creating two distinct islands: Great (or Big) Colington and Little Colington.

Before leaving Big Colington, take time to enjoy the beauty of Kitty Hawk Bay.

In his *History of North Carolina*, written in 1709, John Lawson described a superstition about the bay that was maintained by residents of Colington Island. They swore to Lawson that the apparition of Sir Walter Raleigh's rescue ship often appeared on Kitty Hawk Bay. Historians have long speculated that Kitty Hawk Bay was the Trinitie Harbor used as a safe harbor for the ships of the Raleigh expeditions. Long after the time of Lawson, Colington natives continued to report sightings of the phantom ship.

Retrace your route to U.S. 158, turn left, and proceed north to the entrance to Wright Brothers National Memorial at Milepost 8. Turn west at the entrance gate and proceed to the parking lot adjacent to the visitor center.

On December 17, 1903, a cold, blustery day, the wind-swept landscape of Kill Devil Hills was the site of one of the crowning achievements of human history: powered flight. An imposing sixty-foot monument atop Kill Devil Hill looks down over the spot where two brothers from Dayton, Ohio, accomplished a feat that man had dreamed of for centuries. This magnificent granite shaft is the centerpiece of a 431-acre memorial park administered by the National Park Service since 1933. It is one of the most popular tourist attractions on the Outer Banks north of Cape Hatteras.

Most of the half-million visitors who come to the park each year begin their tour at the visitor center. Displays and exhibits tell the well-chronicled story of how Orville and Wilbur Wright changed the course of human history through their experiments at this site during four successive years at the turn of the century. Replicas of their 1902 glider and the *Flyer*, the aircraft that made the famous first flight, have a prominent place in the visitor center. When it was constructed in 1903, the *Flyer* cost a thousand dollars; its reproduction carried a price tag of half a million in 1963. The original aircraft is on display at the National Air and Space Museum, part of the Smithsonian Institution.

A blowup of the photograph of the first flight is featured in the center. This magnificent photograph gives visitors a visual taste of the dramatic moment. At 10:37 A.M. on December 17, 1903, Orville started the machine forward into the wind. Wilbur ran alongside, holding the wing to balance the craft on the track. Suddenly, after a forty-foot run, the plane lifted slowly off the ground. Over the next twelve seconds, it darted up and down because of the irregularity of the air and handling problems, but it stayed in the air. Orville safely landed the craft 120 feet from its takeoff point. The two young men from Dayton, neither of whom graduated from high school, had conquered flight.

The story behind the famous photograph is filled with irony. Due to their foresight and their previous experience as newspapermen, the Wright brothers made sure that the red-letter event was captured on film. Just before the flight, they set up their camera and gave John T. Daniels, a crew member of the Kill Devil Hills Lifesaving Station and one of the five witnesses on hand, instructions to photograph the event. Daniels, who had never seen a camera prior to that day, took a perfect photograph—one of the most recognizable pictures in American history.

The two wooden structures located a short walk from the center were built by the National Park Service as a reconstruction of the 1903 camp of the Wright brothers. One of the buildings represents the hangar for the *Flyer*, while the other is a furnished replica of their combination workshop and living quarters. Adjacent to the camp buildings is the first-flight area— the field where the events of December 17, 1903, unfolded. A large granite boulder rests on the exact spot where the first flight left the ground, and numbered markers indicate the distance of each of the four flights that day.

From the historic field, visitors can walk to Kill Devil Hill, or they can reach the dune by a roadway from the visitor center parking lot. Ascending the hill is a physically exerting experience, particularly on a hot, humid

First-flight air field

summer day. Nevertheless, the reward at the top is deemed worth the effort by most park patrons. The monument is as beautiful a piece of architecture on close examination as it is from a distance. Its outer walls are adorned with wings in bas-relief. Inscribed in the granite is a fitting tribute to the Wrights: "In commemoration of the conquest of the air by the brothers Wilbur and Orville Wright, conceived by Genius, Achieved by Dauntless Resolution and Unconquerable Faith."

Before Congress adjourned in 1927, it passed a bill sponsored by Congressman Lindsay Warren of North Carolina and Senator Hiram Bingham of Connecticut authorizing the erection of the monument on Kill Devil Hill. Some thirty-five designs were subsequently submitted to Frank B. Cheatham, the quartermaster general of the United States. A jury provided by the American Institute of Architects selected the design of New York architects Robert P. Rogers and Alfred E. Poor.

On the first annual observance of First Flight Day, held December 17, 1928, Secretary of War Dwight D. Davis laid the cornerstone, and Orville Wright sealed materials relating to the first flight in a box and placed it in the stone. (Wilbur had died in 1912.) During the impressive ceremonies, the ever-modest Orville turned to Congressman Warren and remarked, "I wonder if the whole thing isn't a mistake. Fifty years from now might be soon enough to determine if this monument should be built. To do it now seems like an imposition on the taxpayers."

After Kill Devil Hill, a migrating sand dune, was stabilized, work began on the monument. A concrete foundation was sunk thirty-five feet into the center of the hill. Above the foundation, yet extending twelve feet into the sand, a star-shaped base was constructed of durex blocks. On top of the base, the shaft was built by encasing a sixty-foot-tall concrete core with North Carolina granite. Each of the granite blocks was cut at the quarry—the pink in Salisbury and the white in Granite Quarry—to fit its proper place in the shaft.

Because the monument was also designed to serve as a lighthouse, a beacon was installed atop the shaft. Shortly after it was lit, the beacon, visible for 30 miles on a clear night, became a source of confusion for mariners, who sometimes mistook it for the nearby lighthouses at Corolla and Bodie Island. Consequently, the bright light on top of the shaft was extinguished.

At impressive ceremonies on November 12, 1932, the monument was dedicated before a large crowd. Orville Wright was again an honored guest. His remarks contained praise for the people of Kitty Hawk who had befriended the brothers during their stays on the Outer Banks. He recalled the part the locals had played in the achievement of 1903: they had provided lodging, sewn fabric for the aircraft wings, and provided encouragement and assistance while the rest of the world ignored the brothers.

Until the early 1960s, the monument was used as the visitor center for the park. However, the ever-increasing number of park patrons put undue stress on the stairs leading to the observation platform at the top of the shaft. Once the existing visitor center was completed, the interior of the shaft was closed to the public.

Massive, beautifully crafted doors lead to the inside of the shaft. If visitors could venture through the doors, sculpted with scenes of man's efforts at flight, they would first find the magnificent memorial room of pink granite. A circular stairway leads to a map room and its stainless-steel table, on which is engraved a map charting all the notable flights in the first twenty-five years of aviation. From the map room, the stairway ascends to the

Wright Brothers National Memorial

observation platform, where visitors enjoyed spectacular views of the surrounding countryside in times past.

The life-size bronze busts of Wilbur and Orville Wright on stone pedestals outside the monument are replacements for the originals, which were erected at the memorial site in 1960. Vandals damaged the originals in 1985, and thieves made off with them in 1988. Through the generosity of the First Flight Society, funds were raised to cast four new busts, two of which are now held in reserve inside the pylon.

At night, floodlights make the monument a breathtaking vision of splendor that can be seen as far north as Duck.

On the night of July 20, 1969, when Neil A. Armstrong became the first man to set foot on the moon, a large crowd gathered at the visitor center to watch the event within eyesight of the lighted monument. As the time for Armstrong's famous steps neared, Outer Banks publicist Aycock Brown left the visitor center with radio in hand and walked to a place where he could photograph the moon above the monument at the exact moment Armstrong stepped down the ladder of the lunar lander. His photo became one of the most publicized of the history-making event. Appropriately, when astronauts Armstrong and Buzz Aldrin landed on the moon, they carried with them a piece of fabric from the *Flyer*.

A three-thousand-foot asphalt airstrip is located in the woods northwest of the monument. It is used extensively during the Wright Brothers Fly-In, held each spring. In July, the National Park Service sponsors the annual Wright Kite Festival on the grounds of the memorial. Designed to honor the brothers' beginnings as kite builders, the festival features competitive events and workshops and lectures by kite experts. And continuing the time-honored tradition started in 1928, the First Flight Society and the National Park Service celebrate December 17 as First Flight Day at the memorial every year. Among the giants of aviation who have spoken at past observances are John Glenn, Chuck Yeager, and Igor Sikorsky.

A nominal fee is charged for admission to the memorial site.

Return to U.S. 158 and proceed north. At Milepost 5.2, you will enter the corporate limits of Kitty Hawk.

Since the first white settlers made their way to the area, Kitty Hawk has been known by many names. While the legends surrounding the origin of the name are not as romantic or whimsical as those for Nags Head and Kill Devil Hills, they are nonetheless interesting. Two are related to the Indians living in the area at the time of white settlement.

According to one theory, the Indians referred to the wildfowl hunting season as "killy honker" or "killy honk." Over time, the name changed to Killy Hawk and then ultimately to Kitty Hawk.

On maps prepared for the Lords Proprietors in the first half of the eighteenth century, the Indian name Chickehauk is shown for the place now occupied by Kitty Hawk. Although there are no remains of it today, an Indian settlement once existed in the area. Local Indians used the word *hauk* to imitate the honking sound made by the geese inhabiting the nearby sound and marshes. Old deeds make references to Kitty-hauk.

Finally, there is some merit to the theory that says the name is derived from the mosquito hawks that once plagued the area during the summer season. From the name Skeeter Hawk emerged the existing place name.

While driving past the sprawling commercial development along U.S. 158 in Kitty Hawk, you may find it difficult to imagine that at the time Roanoke Sound was bridged in 1928, the 7-mile stretch between the Coast Guard Station at Kill Devil Hills and Kitty Hawk was a virtual wasteland. The road connecting Nags Head to Kitty Hawk was nothing more than a sandy path, often impassable in foul weather. Virtually all of the residents of Kitty Hawk lived in a forested sound-side village tucked neatly away from the ocean strand.

Much of that old village remains on the west side of U.S. 158. At Milepost 4.8, turn left onto S.R. 1206 (Kitty Hawk Road). Along this route, you will pass through a beautiful, shaded landscape laced with glistening creeks and canals. Century-old frame homes, much like the one in which the Wright brothers stayed, line the roadside.

After 0.5 mile on S.R. 1206, turn left on More Shore Road (S.R. 1216). Located on the right a few hundred feet down More Shore Road is a replica of the first memorial to the Wright brothers established in the United States.

Before plans were unveiled to erect the tall shaft for the brothers at Kill Devil Hill, the citizens of Kitty Hawk village, through contributions of not less than a nickel and not more than a quarter, erected a seven-foot needle-shaped monument to the Wrights. It designates the location where

Site where the Wright brothers began construction of their first full-size glider

the brothers began work on their first full-size glider, along a narrow dirt road that was the only road in the village. An image of the Wright glider is engraved above the following inscription: "On this spot on Sept. 17, 1900, Wilbur Wright began assembly of the Wright Brothers First Experimental glider which led to man's conquest of the air. Erected by citizens of Kitty Hawk, N.C. 1928."

The original monument suffered fire damage and began to deteriorate over the years. In the late 1980s, a replica of the monument was placed on the current site, and the original was moved to the lobby of Kitty Hawk's municipal building, where it remains.

Return to S.R. 1206, turn left, and continue west 0.3 mile to Kitty Hawk Methodist Church. Inside this church is a unique cross crafted from pieces of area history. Presented in 1968, the large wooden cross was constructed from the weathered timber salvaged from two notable shipwrecks in the Graveyard of the Atlantic. The patibulum, or crossbar, came from the timbers of the famous ghost ship *Carroll A. Deering*, which foundered on Diamond Shoals on January 31, 1921. When coast guardsmen reached the ship, they found the captain's and crew's quarters in order. In the dining room, the would-be rescuers were startled to discover a dinner table displaying a complete meal which had not been touched. Yet, no living thing was found on board–save a large, friendly gray cat. To this day, the fate of the human passengers of the *Carroll A. Deering* remains a mystery.

The stipe, or upright part of the cross, was handcrafted from the wood of the Italian bark *Nuova Ottavia*. On the night of March 1, 1876, the ship wrecked on the beach near the village of Corolla.

Continue on S.R. 1206 through Kitty Hawk village. After approximately 1.3 miles, you will reach an intersection with S.R. 1207. Turn around here and retrace your route to U.S. 158. Proceed north on U.S. 158 to the intersection with N.C. 12 (Virginia Dare Trail) at Milepost 1.5. Turn right onto N.C. 12. Just as this strand road begins to curve south, park at the Kitty Hawk Fishing Pier, the northernmost of the five ocean fishing piers in the area.

Of the many anecdotes told about the old piers, the most interesting concerns the one at Kitty Hawk. One Sunday morning in May 1964, Walter Royal Davis, an Elizabeth City native who earned a fortune in Texas oil, left his vacation home at Southern Shores in search of a bottle of Orange Crush. Upon stopping at the Kitty Hawk Fishing Pier, he learned that the soft drink was not served there. His apparent dismay led the unwary proprietor to suggest that Davis buy the pier if he did not like its beverage offerings. Davis promptly pulled out his checkbook, issued a $96,000 check to purchase the pier, and instructed the employees to stock Orange Crush.

On the drive "down the beach" on N.C. 12, you will see the old mingled with the new. Cottages in various states of repair, family motels, multistory hotels, fishing piers, convenience stores, restaurants, gift shops, art galleries, and miniature golf courses are wedged into the precious real estate on each side of the 19-mile road.

On the 3.5-mile drive through Kitty Hawk, you will note that the strand is lined primarily with aging beach cottages and some independent motels. Erosion is evident here, and the tired old beach resort lacks the visual appeal of Kill Devil Hills and Nags Head.

In its heyday, the United States Lifesaving Service had more lifesaving stations on the North Carolina coast than on the coast of any other state. Two of the historic shake-shingled structures survive on the strand at Kitty Hawk and Kill Devil Hills.

On the west side of the road at Milepost 4.5, the Black Pelican Oceanfront Cafe is housed in the old Kitty Hawk Lifesaving Station (Lifesaving Station No. 6). It was from this building that the Wright brothers telegraphed their father in Ohio with news of their successful flights in December 1903.

At Kill Devil Hills, the small, single-story motels of Kitty Hawk are replaced by modern multistory hotels. Indeed, after completing the drive on N.C. 12 from Kitty Hawk to Nags Head, few motorists are surprised to learn that the trio of resort beaches has more hotel and motel rooms than any other coastal resort in the state.

On the strand side of the highway at Milepost 9, the Kill Devil Hills Coast Guard Station—the second station on this site—has been converted into a private residence. Adjacent to the station stands the original boathouse.

Two large ships went down at almost the same spot approximately 1 mile north of the station in the late 1920s.

On Sunday, December 4, 1927, the crewmen of the stations at Kill Devil

Hills, Nags Head, and Kitty Hawk joined forces to save twenty-four people from the *Kyzikes*, a 2,627-ton, 227-foot Greek steamer. Most of the wreck now lies underwater. Its bow is almost fully covered with sand, but the stern, a wrecked mass of decking, pipes, cable, and machinery, juts upward. At low tide, one small section of the stern can be seen above the surface.

Parallel to and touching the *Kyzikes* is the wreckage of the 265-foot, 1,504-ton Swedish steamer *Carl Gerhard*. In the darkness of the night of September 23, 1929, the skipper of the ship was hopelessly lost. At the moment the steamer plowed into the wreckage of the *Kyzikes* and the outer reef at Kill Devil Hills, the captain believed he was 50 miles at sea. Four Coast Guard crews rescued a woman, the twenty crewmen on board, two dogs, and a cat from the wreck. The battered and rusty hull of the *Carl Gerhard* lies in fifteen feet of water less that two hundred feet off the beach at Kill Devil Hills. At low tide, fishermen use her decks for footing.

Historical marker for the USS Huron

Of the shipwrecks off the shore of this resort area, none is more famous than that of the USS *Huron*. A state historical marker at Milepost 11.5 chronicles the wreck of the *Huron*, one of the deadliest mishaps in maritime history. Constructed in 1874, the 541-ton barkentine-rigged screw steamer was considered one of the finest warships of the United States Navy. Its 143-man crew was the pride of America's sailing forces. After putting forth from Hampton Roads, Virginia, on November 24, 1877, on a scientific expedition to the West Indies, the *Huron* veered too close to the Nags Head shoreline just after midnight and began coming apart in cold, violent seas.

In this disaster, the Graveyard of the Atlantic claimed not only one of the great warships of the time, but ninety-eight of the finest officers and men of the United States Navy as well. News of the senseless loss of life stunned people throughout the nation. American citizens were angered that Congress had been so shortsighted as to man the lifesaving stations for only three months of the year. Soon afterward, federal funds were appropriated to keep the stations open nine months every year.

The *Huron's* remains lie two hundred yards north of the Nags Head Fishing Pier in twenty feet of water approximately two hundred yards offshore. When the sea is calm, portions of the wreck are visible from the beach. Over the years, the wreck has been a popular spot for divers, who have

stripped it of many artifacts, including a pistol, cannonballs, rifle parts, coins, and a porthole.

Since the ship went down, rumors have persisted that there were twenty thousand dollars in gold on board at the time of the mishap. After the wreck, the United States Navy salvaged the site, but there is no record whether the gold was ever recovered. Divers have noted that the area where the paymaster's safe was supposedly located has been blown away by explosives.

In a ceremony held at Nags Head on November 24, 1991, a plot in the Graveyard in the Atlantic bearing the remains of the *Huron* became the state's first Historic Shipwreck Preserve. Initiated by the North Carolina Division of Cultural Resources, the program seeks to give the state more control over wrecks and to aid in their preservation. Federal, state, and local officials participated in the dedication of the underwater museum, which was scheduled for the 114th anniversary of the loss of the ship.

An exhibit located in a gazebo at the beach access area at the intersection of N.C. 12 and Bladen Street gives an account of the wreck.

One mile south of the marker for the wreck of the *Huron*, N.C. 12 and U.S. 158 almost kiss each other within sight of Jockey's Ridge. Arguably the most famous part of the Nags Head oceanfront is the mile-long stretch just south of the close approach of the highways. Located on the ocean side of the road, the long row of handsome cypress-shingled beach cottages is

Saint Andrews By-The-Sea Episcopal Church

collectively known as the Nags Head Cottage District. These old vacation homes are reminders of a time when the area was an isolated summer resort. Planters, merchants, and professionals from the Albemarle region built these rambling summer homes in the years from the Civil War to World War II. Time and salt air have combined to color the shingle exteriors a rich gray-brown. Because of their age and beauty, Jonathan Daniels, North Carolina author and former editor of the *Raleigh News and Observer*, named this select group of cottages "the Unpainted Aristocracy."

Because of its historic significance, this select group of beach cottages is listed on the National Register of Historic Places. Embodied in these great old ladies of the Nags Head oceanfront is a unique architectural style dictated by the fierce weather of the Outer Banks. S. J. Twine (1874-1973), an architect from Elizabeth City, has been credited with developing the style. From the second decade of the century through the 1940s, Twine designed, built, and remodeled the stately cottages on the Nags Head strand by incorporating the time-tested features of beach houses that had survived countless Atlantic storms.

These spacious one-and-a-half-story structures tower high above the pounding surf on pilings. Broad porches that offer sanctuary from the blazing sun and an ideal spot to take advantage of cool ocean breezes sweep around two, three, and four sides of the houses. The wooden shutters afford protection from violent winds; hinged at the top, they are propped open with sticks in summertime to ventilate the interior. Full dormers punctuate the front and rear slopes of the gabled roofs. Some of the older cottages contain adjoining kitchen wings and servants' quarters linked to the main structure by breezeways.

S. J. Twine spent many summers in Nags Head, not only designing and building the Unpainted Aristocracy, but also enjoying vacations. In 1915, he used his talents to construct one of the most famous pieces of architecture on the Outer Banks: Saint Andrews By-The-Sea Episcopal Church.

This picturesque frame building is located on the west side of N.C. 12 at Milepost 13.3, near the south end of the Nags Head Cottage District. It was dedicated on Sunday, August 6, 1916.

For many years prior to that time, the tiny Episcopal congregation had been forced to worship in various cottages along the oceanfront. All Saints'

Church, built in 1847, was the predecessor of Saint Andrews. It fell victim to the Union occupation of the area during the Civil War. Federal troops demolished the sound-side church and used the lumber to construct housing for runaway slaves on Roanoke Island.

Some years after the war, the Reverend L. L. Williams of Elizabeth City led an effort to gain recompense from the federal government for the destruction. Following a lengthy delay, Congress appropriated the sum of seven hundred dollars to the trustees of the Diocese of East Carolina in settlement of the claim. Matching funds were collected from residents of Nags Head and vacationers. John Lowe, the owner of the old Nags Head Hotel, donated two lots in the vicinity of the original church, on which Saint Andrews was subsequently erected.

After the highway was built through Nags Head, the congregation decided in 1937 to move the church building to its present site, just across the highway. When the church was moved, Mrs. Virgilia Brent of Nixonton presented the bell that once hung in All Saints' Church at Nags Head. Cast in West Troy, New York, in 1853, the bell had found its way to a Pasquotank County farm after the destruction of the old church building.

Of special interest in the sanctuary is the unique altar cross. It was constructed of live oak from a tree at Fort Raleigh.

At Milepost 16.5 in southern Nags Head, near the point where N.C. 12 curves west to intersect the other major highways serving the Outer Banks, Jennette's Fishing Pier has long been a popular gathering spot. Built in 1939, it is not only the oldest ocean fishing pier in the area, but at a thousand feet, it is also the longest.

If you would like to take a brief side trip, turn off N.C. 12 onto S.R. 1243 near the pier for a 4.7-mile drive to Milepost 21 at the edge of Cape Hatteras National Seashore. This route features an assemblage of modern beach cottages.

This tour ends 0.2 mile west of Jennette's Fishing Pier at Whalebone Inlet, at the intersection of N.C. 12, U.S. 158, and U.S. 64/264.

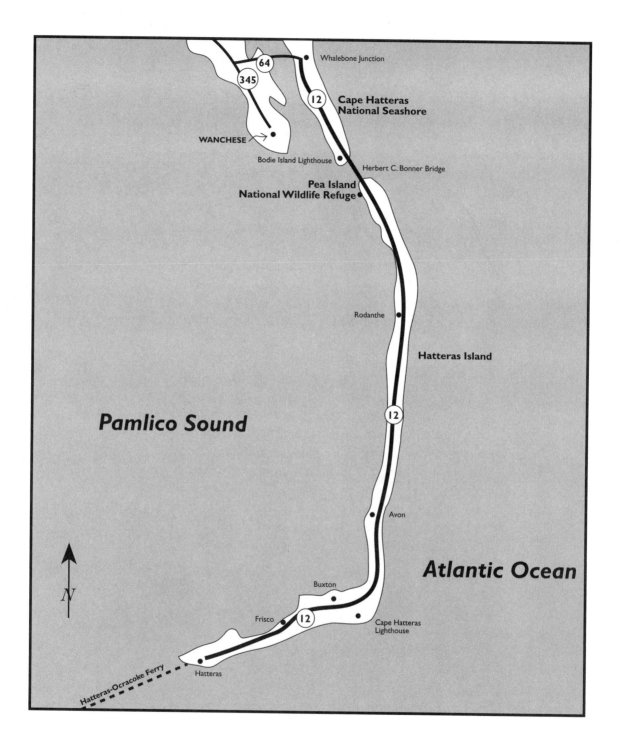

64

345

WANCHESE

Whalebone Junction

12 Cape Hatteras
    National Seashore

Bodie Island Lighthouse

Herbert C. Bonner Bridge

Pea Island
National Wildlife Refuge

Rodanthe

Hatteras Island

12

Pamlico Sound

Avon

Atlantic Ocean

Buxton

N

Frisco 12

Cape Hatteras
Lighthouse

Hatteras

Hatteras-Ocracoke Ferry

The Cape
Hatteras Tour

This tour begins at the entrance to Cape Hatteras National Seashore and follows N.C. 12 south down Bodie Island, across the majestic Oregon Inlet, and down Hatteras Island. After visiting the villages of Rodanthe, Waves, Salvo, Avon, Buxton, Frisco, and Hatteras, it ends at the Hatteras-Ocracoke Ferry landing at the southern end of Hatteras Island.

Among the highlights of the tour are Cape Hatteras National Seashore, the Bodie Island Lighthouse, the Herbert C. Bonner Bridge, Pea Island National Wildlife Refuge, the Chicamacomico Lifesaving Station, the celebration of Old Christmas at Rodanthe, Buxton Woods, and the Cape Hatteras Lighthouse.

Total mileage: approximately 71 miles.

This tour begins on N.C. 12 at Whalebone Junction in Nags Head. Long regarded as the crossroads of the Outer Banks, Whalebone Junction was named for the whalebone deposited in front of a service station located where the crude roads and sand trails of the 1930s formed an intersection. Now, Whalebone Junction is the place where N.C. 12, U.S. 64/264, and U.S. 158 meet.

Although there are no visible reminders today, Roanoke Inlet, the principal waterway for the Roanoke colonists in the sixteenth century, was located near Whalebone Junction. It has been closed for almost two hundred years.

Proceed south on N.C. 12 as it passes the entrance signs for Cape Hatteras National Seashore. On the east side of the road, you will notice cottages along a 4-mile stretch of beach. This oceanfront strip was retained in private ownership when Cape Hatteras National Seashore was established. On the other side of the road, the scenery is a wilderness of shrub thickets and green vegetation.

Although it is the granddaddy of all national seashores, the Cape Hatteras park has lost none of its popularity. For more than forty years, this 70-mile oceanfront recreational area has introduced millions of visitors to the breathtaking natural vistas and the historic significance of the North Carolina coast. Annual attendance is now in excess of 2.2 million visitors.

The Cape Hatteras Tour

The federal government could not have found a better place than the Outer Banks of North Carolina for its first national seashore. Encompassing more than 30,318 acres of ocean and sound beaches, dunes, and marshland on Bodie, Hatteras, and Ocracoke islands, Cape Hatteras National Seashore preserves the most extensive stretch of undeveloped seashore on the Atlantic coast of the United States.

From the national seashore entrance at Whalebone Junction to Oregon Inlet almost 9.5 miles to the south, N.C. 12 makes its way down Bodie (pronounced Body) Island. Bodie Island is separated from Hatteras Island by Oregon Inlet. Wild and uninhabited like much of Hatteras, Bodie has changed in size, shape, and location over the centuries by virtue of the numerous inlets which have opened and closed. In reality, it is no longer an island, because the inlet to the north has long been closed.

First mentioned by John Lawson in his narratives of 1700, Bodie is a place name of unknown origin. It most likely came from a family that arrived among the first settlers in the area. Another theory suggests that the name came from an early Virginia practice whereby a unit of land was referred to as a "body" of land. At any rate, cartographers of the early eighteenth century showed the present name on their maps.

Never heavily populated, Bodie has been used primarily as a site for lighthouses and lifesaving stations. Prior to its inclusion in the national seashore, several gun clubs operated on the island to take advantage of the large population of waterfowl in the area.

Three key recreational areas of the national seashore are located at Bodie. To see the first of them, turn into the parking area for Coquina Beach, located 5.5 miles south of Whalebone Junction on the ocean side of N.C. 12.

Regarded as one of the safest swimming beaches in an area plagued by severe undertow and sudden underwater drop-offs, Coquina Beach takes its name from the tiny, brightly colored seashells which delight beachcombers who visit the site. Bathhouses, showers, restrooms, and picnic tables are provided here, and a wide variety of historical and natural programs and activities is offered by the National Park Service. The beach is protected by lifeguards during the summer season.

Adjacent to the Coquina Beach parking lot is the preserved shipwreck of the *Laura A. Barnes*.

There was a time not so many years ago when a leisurely stroll along almost any beach in the national seashore would uncover the remains of ships that could not escape the shoals of the treacherous offshore waters. Those days are gone. Shipwrecks have become rare occurrences, and the shifting sands and ceaseless tides have taken their toll on the wrecks deposited on these shores many years ago.

The wreck of the **Laura A. Barnes**

Still, visitors who come to Cape Hatteras National Seashore to see the graves of some of the ships that have given the area much of its fame usually do not leave disappointed. A wreck long buried under the sands is occasionally uncovered by a storm, only to be hidden again by the next high tide. The chance of discovering a "new" wreck is remote for the park visitor on a given visit. Nonetheless, at least five wrecks have been visible from the beaches of the national seashore for a number of years.

Of the visible shipwrecks in the park, the largest and most accessible is the *Laura A. Barnes*. This four-masted schooner ran aground 4.5 miles south of Whalebone Junction in the midnight darkness of June 1, 1921, while en route to South Carolina from New York. In order to prevent the Atlantic from finishing the job it started fifty years earlier, the National Park Service removed the ribs of the wreck to the present site.

Deep in the waters off Coquina Beach lies one of the most historic wrecks of World War II. Just after midnight on the bright, clear, starlit night of April 14, 1942, the USS *Roper*, a World War I–class destroyer, was patrolling the ocean waters in search of enemy vessels. While still within sight of the beam from the Bodie Island Lighthouse, the *Roper* discovered the *U-85* running on the surface. A direct hit from the destroyer's three-inch guns sent the German submarine to the ocean floor a hundred feet below. Thus, the first U-boat kill recorded by the United States Navy during World War II took place in North Carolina waters.

Return to N.C. 12. On the west side of the highway opposite Coquina Beach stands the Bodie Island Lighthouse. Turn west at the sign directing you down a 1.1-mile winding drive to the lighthouse.

Of the three historic lighthouses within the confines of the national seashore, the Bodie Island Lighthouse attracts the fewest professional artists and photographers. Yet the imposing 163-foot brick tower is by no means lacking in aesthetic qualities. Rather, its imposing stature on the flat, barrier-island landscape and its graceful lines serve to make it a welcome landmark at the northern entrance to the national seashore.

Although the existing tower was completed in 1872, it is the third lighthouse to stand on Bodie Island.

A survey of the Atlantic coast in 1837 disclosed an urgent need for a navigational light along the isolated 35-mile stretch north of Cape Hatteras. Construction delays prevented completion of the original lighthouse—a squat, circular, fifty-four-foot brick structure—until 1847. Because of an unstable foundation, the lighthouse soon began to lean toward the sea, much like a nineteenth-century Leaning Tower of Pisa. Efforts by the federal government to straighten the tower failed in 1850. Eight years later, Congress appropriated twenty-five thousand dollars to erect a new lighthouse.

Built on sturdy piles, the new eighty-foot structure cast its beam 15 miles out to sea. However, the improved tower was destined to stand less than three years. After the fall of Hatteras Island to Union forces in August 1861, Confederate forces were determined to darken the lighthouses along the Outer Banks. In 1862, a band of Confederate soldiers made its way to the lighthouse, stacked explosives inside, and blew it up.

Bodie Island Lighthouse

By the time the federal government decided to rebuild the lighthouse after the war, Oregon Inlet had migrated south to within four hundred yards of the ruins of the old light. A fifteen-acre site north of the inlet was purchased from the former keeper of the antebellum lighthouse. Constructed at a cost of $140,000, the third and present Bodie Island Lighthouse was patterned after the Cape Lookout Lighthouse. The construction foreman, a veteran of the nearby Cape Hatteras Lighthouse project, constructed the sturdy Bodie Island tower from materials left over at Cape Hatteras.

Equipped with a first-order Fresnel lens that made the light visible 19 miles at sea, the lighthouse was illuminated on October 1, 1872. Less than a month later, a flock of geese crashed into the lantern, causing extensive damage to the lens. Repairs were quickly effected, and the lens is still used today.

To distinguish it in daylight from the other lighthouses on the Outer Banks, the graceful Bodie Island tower was painted with horizontal black and white stripes.

Today, the lighthouse complex serves as an eye-appealing introductory attraction to the national seashore. A paved parking lot adjacent to the

TOURING THE BACKROADS OF NORTH CAROLINA'S UPPER COAST

National Park Service visitor center provides ample parking. Located in a two-story frame dwelling constructed in 1872 as the keeper's quarters, the visitor center serves as a museum, an information station, and a bookstore.

Within a stone's throw of the old white house stands the conical tower, which now projects a 160,000-candlepower beam. The fully automated lighthouse is maintained by the Coast Guard. In order to allow the public to climb the tower, the National Park Service has considered an extensive restoration of its interior. Unfortunately, funds have not been made available for the project, so the lighthouse remains off-limits to visitors. Nevertheless, the surrounding grounds afford a spectacular view of the light and an excellent opportunity for photographs.

Visitors may also avail themselves of a short nature trail behind the lighthouse. This route winds around a scenic pond and broad marshes inhabited by a variety of shorebirds and adorned by an abundance of plants including yaupon, wax myrtle, bayberry, and cattails.

The entire lighthouse complex is listed on the National Register of Historic Places.

After you have seen the lighthouse, return to N.C. 12 and continue south. It is 2 miles to Oregon Inlet Campground and Oregon Inlet Fishing Center, the remaining two recreational facilities provided by the National Park Service on Bodie Island.

Located on the oceanfront, the campground, one of five in the national seashore, is the only place to stay on Bodie Island. Open from April to October, it offers 120 primitive campsites, restrooms, drinking water, cold showers, and picnic facilities.

Nearby on the sound side of N.C. 12, Oregon Inlet Fishing Center is one of the best and most complete fishing and pleasure-boating facilities on the North Carolina coast. This marina and sportfishing complex is operated by concessionaires regulated by the National Park Service. Known as the "Billfish Capital of the World," the facility often welcomes boats back to port with fish weighing five hundred to six hundred pounds each.

Just west of the marina stands the modern Oregon Inlet Coast Guard Station. Completed in 1990 to replace an old station on the southern side of the inlet, the structure was designed to reflect the historic architecture of the lifesaving stations built up and down the Outer Banks more than a century ago.

One of the most magnificent sights of the North Carolina coast awaits you just south of the marina, near the end of Bodie Island. Linking Bodie Island and Hatteras Island, the Herbert C. Bonner Bridge looks much as it did when it opened to traffic in November 1963. Its majestic, serpentine lines make the 3.5-mile-long span one of the most beautiful man-made structures in the state.

However, since Saturday, May 2, 1964, when Herbert C. Bonner, longtime United States congressman and friend of coastal North Carolina, spoke to the crowd of two thousand people assembled for the dedication of the bridge named in his honor, the structure has required the attention of state highway officials to prevent it from falling into the constantly migrating Oregon Inlet.

State highway engineers estimate that barring a natural or man-made catastrophe, the Herbert C. Bonner Bridge will be nearing the end of its life span by the turn of the century. Consequently, various proposals are being formulated for the day when the bridge is no longer serviceable. Current cost estimates for a replacement bridge reach as much as $53 million, more than thirteen times the original cost of the 1962–63 project.

Alternatives to a replacement bridge are also being considered. Engineers have investigated the feasibility of a tunnel. However, not only would such a project carry a prohibitive price tag of $235 million, but it would also pose enormous environmental problems. Many environmentalists and coastal geologists argue that the only logical solution is to allow the aging bridge to collapse without the construction of a replacement. Future access across the inlet would be by ferry or hovercraft. But because vehicle space on ferries is limited, rapid hurricane evacuation of Hatteras Island would be impossible without a bridge. Moreover, twelve ferries would cost $10 million more than a replacement bridge.

The Herbert C. Bonner Bridge across Oregon Inlet

On October 26, 1990, a storm-tossed dredge smashed into the great structure, leaving a gaping 370-foot hole in the middle of the span. Countless tourists and the five thousand residents of Hatteras Island found themselves stranded until the state could put an emergency ferry system into operation. Repairs cost $5.5 million and took three and a half months to complete.

From the crest of the bridge, you will enjoy a spectacular view of Oregon Inlet.

No waterway on the North Carolina coast has generated as much controversy over the past three decades as Oregon Inlet. Since a savage hurricane opened the inlet on September 7, 1846, it has been one of the most dynamic inlets on the Atlantic coast. Over the past century and a half, it has migrated almost 3 miles to the south. As the only ocean artery for fishing and other commercial traffic for the entire Albemarle Sound–Roanoke River area, and as a primary outlet for much of the traffic from Pamlico Sound, Oregon Inlet continues to be of vital importance to the coastal economy.

The inlet took its name from the side-wheeler *Oregon*, the first ship that passed through it, albeit by accident. Finding himself caught in a ferocious storm while making his way up the Atlantic coast from Bermuda, the captain of the *Oregon* decided to beach his vessel along the North Carolina coast. In the process, he inadvertently navigated through the inlet and into Pamlico Sound.

After the inlet opened, coastal engineers predicted that it would soon close. Instead, it began to widen into one of the major inlets on the coast.

To protect the waterway and the Outer Banks from enemy attack, Confederates built Fort Oregon on the south side of the inlet in the early stages of the Civil War. The steady migration of the inlet over the past century has resulted in the complete erosion of the site of the fort, as well as the site of the original Bodie Island Lighthouse and the Bodie Island Lifesaving Station of 1874.

At the conclusion of World War I, there was still no public access across the inlet from Bodie Island to Hatteras Island. In 1924, Captain Jack Nelson of Colington Island initiated a short-lived ferry service by towing cars on a small barge behind his fishing boat. He gave up after only a few months of operation. Toby Tillett of Wanchese began a similar service a year later. After a quarter-century of service, Tillett sold the ferry operation to the state, which ran it until the inlet was bridged thirteen years later.

When you reach the south end of the bridge, drive to the parking area on the ocean side. Here, a 244,000-ton, nine-foot-tall jetty stretches nearly a half-mile on the north side of Hatteras Island. Completed in early 1991 at a cost of $13.5 million, the jetty project was the culmination of decades of statewide and national debate over possible ways to stabilize the shifting shoreline and navigation channel of Oregon Inlet. Although the jury is still out on the ultimate success of the jetty, it appears to be working.

From the parking area, drive south on N.C. 12 for approximately 0.4 mile. Turn left on S.R. 1257 and proceed 0.3 mile to the end of the road at the old Oregon Inlet Coast Guard Station. Although this structure is still maintained by the Coast Guard, it was abandoned in December 1988 after shoaling and erosion rendered the boat basin at the facility useless. At the time, it was the oldest active lifesaving station on the North Carolina coast. Listed on the National Register of Historic Places, the structure with its tower and dormered roof was constructed in 1897.

Return to N.C. 12 and head south.

The famed Outer Banks of North Carolina stretch 175 miles in a long, semicircular arc from the Virginia line southward to Bogue Banks. Strategically situated in the middle of this gentle arc is Hatteras Island, a slender, 56-mile-long barrier island shaped like a bent check mark. Hatteras Island juts farther into the Atlantic than any other land body on the North Carolina coast.

From the southern end of the Bonner Bridge, N.C. 12 begins its long run down the slender barrier island that is Hatteras. Were it not for this heavily traveled roadway, built and maintained at great expense by the state, the

The old Oregon Inlet
Coast Guard Station

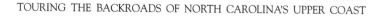

TOURING THE BACKROADS OF NORTH CAROLINA'S UPPER COAST

people of Hatteras Island would not only be isolated from the outside world, but also from each other. N.C. 12 is the only major artery on the island, and as such, it brings vital supplies and services to the residents clustered in the seven tiny villages along its route, as well as to the millions of tourists who spend some $92 million annually in the national seashore.

Island residents steadfastly maintain that this lifeline to the mainland must be preserved at all costs, and the state has acknowledged its obligation to keep the road open until such time as erosion renders Hatteras no longer habitable. But the state's commitment to the constant maintenance of the highway comes at a high price. Erosion and storm overwash annually chew up and cover large portions of the road, rendering it temporarily impassable and cutting the island in two.

Some Hatteras residents have proposed that the state save N.C. 12 by constructing a causeway similar to that linking the Florida Keys. Environmental concerns and a cost projected at $7 million per mile make the proposal unfeasible. On the other hand, a recent study conducted by state highway officials estimates that a sand renourishment project to save the highway would cost $37 million. While the options are debated, the state patches and rebuilds where necessary.

For the first 14 miles of the Hatteras highway, you will see little evidence of human habitation, past or present. To the east lies the vast Atlantic, hidden in most places by massive dunes covered by sea oats. On the west, picturesque sand barrens and marshlands stretch to Pamlico Sound.

Some travelers, anxious to get an early peek at the sea, are tempted to pull off and park on the sandy shoulders of the highway for a short hike to the top of the dunes overlooking the isolated beaches and the sea. However, motorists are well advised to park only in the paved turnoffs, because the sandy shoulders are an inescapable sand trap for most vehicles. Observation platforms and walkways to the beach have been constructed near the turnoffs to keep pedestrian traffic off the fragile dunes.

Located between Oregon Inlet and the village of Rodanthe along a 13.5-mile stretch of Hatteras Island, Pea Island National Wildlife Refuge is a park within a park. Its strategic location on one of the great migratory flyways of America makes Pea Island one of the most popular spots in the nation for bird watchers.

Some 6,700 acres of beaches, dunes, salt marshes, low sand ridges, and freshwater ponds on the northern end of Hatteras and 25,700 acres in adjacent Pamlico Sound were set aside by the federal government on April 12, 1938, as a haven for migratory waterfowl.

Pea Island National Wildlife Refuge

Pea Island is actually a misnomer, because the former 8-mile-long island ceased to be an island in 1945, when New Inlet, which once separated it from Hatteras Island, was closed by a series of storms. From N.C. 12, you can still see the ruins of old wooden bridges that crossed the inlet in the 1930s. The name of the island is thought to have come from the profusion of wild peas that once grew in the area.

Until Oregon Inlet was bridged, the refuge attracted only a few thousand visitors annually. At present, more than a million people come here every year. The sanctuary serves as a wintering ground for ducks, snow geese, swans, and shorebirds. More than 350 species of birds can be observed within the confines of the refuge in the course of a year. Managed and administered by the United States Fish and Wildlife Service, the refuge offers facilities that give naturalists an opportunity to enjoy its bird population.

Approximately 3 miles south of the Herbert C. Bonner Bridge, you will reach the first of the three freshwater impoundments in the refuge. Here, at the north end of North Pond, observation platforms provide breathtaking views of the island, the sound, the ocean, and the bird population.

Continue 1.5 miles south on N.C. 12 to the turnout for the Pea Island Comfort Station, located on the sound side of the highway. Near the parking lot is the trailhead for a self-guided 4-mile nature trail that winds its way along the dikes and around the pond.

Just across the highway from the comfort station, a boardwalk leads to an observation platform overlooking the beach and the ocean. At low tide, the black boiler of the Federal transport *Oriental* is often visible. On the beach nearby, the wooden remains of two unidentified ships are sometimes uncovered by the elements.

Continue south on N.C. 12. It is less than a mile to South Pond, which also offers observation platforms.

Although fishing is not permitted in the ponds and marshes, surf fishing and crabbing are allowed in the refuge. Shutterbugs can use photo blinds to take spectacular shots of the waterfowl and other birds that frequent the planted feeding areas throughout the sanctuary.

During the fall months, snow geese and brant arrive from the Arctic, while Canada geese and black ducks arrive from the Maritime Provinces and Hudson Bay. Among the many wading birds found in summer are glassy ibis, snowy and common egrets, and a variety of herons including great blue, green, Louisiana, and little blue. Pea Island is one of the few places in the United States where the rare peregrine falcon, bald eagle, osprey, and pelican are found every year. On occasion, birds from the West Coast, Europe, and other places have been sighted.

In the spring of 1970, the greatest migratory bird movement ever recorded on the North Atlantic coast occurred at Pea Island. Over a three-day period, ornithologists observed more than twenty-five thousand seabirds—and perhaps as many as two or three times that number—pass over Hatteras Island.

Continue 2 miles south to the refuge headquarters. Here, personnel offer tours, talks, demonstrations, and information. Eight paved parking turnouts have been constructed along the highway to provide access for bird watchers.

If you would like to see what is left of the Pea Island Coast Guard Station, walk east from the refuge headquarters and cross the highway and the dunes beyond. The remnants of the station's foundation are visible at the surf line.

From 1878 to 1947, the Pea Island Coast Guard Station and its crewmen achieved a record of heroism and service equalled by few other stations in the nation.

Ironically, the station was mired in controversy. An official inquiry concerning the response of Lifesaving Station No. 177 at Pea Island to a shipwreck on a stormy night in 1879 resulted in the dismissal of the white members of the mixed-race crew. Captain Richard Etheridge, a black man, was subsequently placed in command of the outpost, and a crew of eight black men was assigned to him.

On December 31, 1880, the Pea Island facility was destroyed by fire. Captain Etheridge and his crew barely escaped with their lives. Years later, one of the discredited white crewmen confessed on his deathbed that he had started the fire.

Captain Etheridge acquired a reputation as a tough but respected drillmaster. His attention to duty and discipline became legendary. From 1879 to 1915, ten vessels with a total of six hundred passengers went down off Pea Island, but only three people were lost.

Etheridge died in 1900. His grave is located outside the front door of the North Carolina Aquarium at Manteo on lands once owned by his family. The six station keepers who succeeded him were also black. In fact, for sixty-eight years from the time Captain Etheridge took command of the station, Pea Island was the only all-black Coast Guard station in the nation.

In 1991, the Coast Guard held special ceremonies at the aquarium to dedicate a memorial to the black lifesavers of Pea Island. The late author Alex Haley served as a speaker. A bronze plaque on the four-foot marker honors "the crews of Pea Island who risked their lives and endured hardships so that others might live."

Continue south on N.C. 12. The route down the uninhabited northern quarter of Hatteras Island yields few clues to the human history of the island. When the first European explorers stepped ashore on Hatteras Island in the sixteenth century, they found the island to be the domain of the Hatteras Indians, the southernmost tribe of Algonquin Indians in North Carolina. Anthropologists believe that these Indians first came to the area between the years 500 and 1000 A.D.

Conventional wisdom is that the Hatteras tribe built several villages or camps on the island to use as a base for hunting, fishing, and gardening activities. Although the tribe was never large—boasting perhaps sixteen hundred people at its height—its numbers began a steady decline following the arrival of white settlers. European diseases, wars with other tribes, and the loss of traditional hunting and fishing grounds to the new settlers decimated the tribe. In 1701, there were only eighty surviving tribe members, confined to one village.

Undoubtedly, the scant white population on Hatteras before 1700 was an unusual mixture of whalers, runaways, stockmen, shipwreck victims, and small landowners, all eking out an existence among the wooded hummocks on the sound side of the island. Thereafter, most of the immigrants to Hatteras were second-generation Englishmen who made their way from Tidewater Virginia in search of less-crowded territory. Today, many of the old families on the island trace their roots to these settlers from Virginia. Their names continue to dominate the Hatteras populace: Midgett, Burrus, Mann, Baum, Tillett, Etheridge, Twiford, and Gray.

When the American colonies united to achieve independence from Great Britain, Hatteras Island boasted a small but stable population. With the closure of Hatteras Inlet prior to 1770, Hatteras and Ocracoke islands were one. Accordingly, island residents played a vital role in supplying the American war effort through trade at Ocracoke Inlet.

On the eve of the Civil War, there were twelve hundred people living on the island, a hundred of whom were slaves. Most of the residents were scattered in small communities, located at the same sites of the modern enclaves within the national seashore. Following the capture of the two Confederate forts guarding Hatteras Inlet on August 28, 1861, Hatteras Island fell under Union control, and remained that way for the duration of the war. Many islanders took the oath of allegiance to the United States and assisted the occupation forces.

So loyal to the Union were the local people that on Monday, November 18, 1861, a convention was held on Hatteras Island, with the result that "a provisional or temporary Government for this Commonwealth was instituted at Hatteras. . . . More than half the counties of the state were represented as delegates and authorized proxies." Delegates adopted ordinances declaring vacant all state offices and pronouncing void the secession of North Carolina from the United States. Named as provisional governor of North Carolina was the Reverend Marble Nash Taylor, a Methodist minister.

Subsequently, an election was held by loyalists to choose a United States congressman from the Hatteras District. Charles Henry Foster won the contest, but he was never allowed to take a seat in the House of Representatives. Following the denial of Foster's credentials, the loyalist government on Hatteras Island made little news.

In 1870, the whole of Hatteras Island was transferred from Hyde County to the newly formed Dare County. Its inclusion in a new political subdivision did little to bring the island into the mainstream of North Carolina life. Miles of water and sand continued to separate island residents from their county seat and the mainland. Hatteras Island entered the twentieth century in a state of isolation, little changed since its settlement. There were no bridges to the other islands or the mainland. Storms often rendered the unpaved roads impassable. Commercial development was unheard of, as the homogeneous population maintained its unique speech, customs, and folk heritage.

By the early part of the twentieth century, the dense maritime forests that once covered much of Hatteras Island had been decimated, save for small wooded areas near Frisco and Buxton. Relentless winds blew sand about the barrier island, threatening to turn the landscape into a desert. The few trees that had survived the woodman's ax were engulfed, smothered, and killed by huge piles of sand.

No part of the nation suffered more from the woes of the Great Depression than Hatteras Island. The wind-swept island offered little promise for its residents, scattered up and down the banks in small sound-side settlements.

But amid the economic misery, the seeds were sown for the future vitality of the island. It was aboard a barge temporarily grounded on a shoal in Currituck Sound on December 17, 1928, that the idea for America's first national seashore was born. Among the scores of dignitaries on the stranded vessel were President-elect Franklin D. Roosevelt, Congressman Lindsay Warren, Governor Angus McLean of North Carolina, and Orville Wright. They had come to Dare County to lay the cornerstone of Wright Brothers National Memorial at Kill Devil Hill. While stranded in the middle of the sound, Congressman Warren and Governor McLean, inspired by the recent establishment of Great Smoky Mountains National Park 500 miles away, took hold of the idea of a national seashore park on the North Carolina coast. Roosevelt was receptive to the proposal, but the Great Depression continued to rob the nation of much of its energy and resources.

Adopted Outer Banker Frank Stick kept the dream alive through a series of newspaper articles beginning in 1933. Stick and others sold the Public Works Administration on a conservation project that resulted in the construction of a continuous line of frontal dunes on Hatteras, Bodie, and Ocracoke islands. By the eve of World War II, a well-vegetated barrier dune ranging in height from fifteen to twenty-five feet stretched down the Outer Banks. Much of this barrier dune remains along the present tour route.

Through state, federal, and private land donations and acquisitions, the national seashore became a reality with its formal dedication on April 24, 1958. America's first national seashore enjoyed almost immediate popularity. From the new park, the nation has learned valuable lessons in coastal preservation. It has been the mold from which nine other national seashores have been shaped.

To assuage the hostile feelings of islanders threatened with the loss of their homes, the eight village enclaves and surrounding lands were excluded from the national seashore.

Approximately 6 miles south of the refuge headquarters, you will reach Rodanthe (pronounced Ro-DAN-thee), the northernmost village on the island. One of the largest of the island enclaves, it offers an ever-expanding variety of amenities, including motels, campgrounds, rental houses, restaurants, and gift shops.

Rodanthe holds the distinction of being the easternmost point in North Carolina. It is located on the northern reaches of the historic settlement known as Chicamacomico. Derived from an Indian word, Chicamacomico was spelled many ways by the early white settlers.

While the Union army was camped in the fledgling community during the Civil War, one Northern soldier recorded an interesting account of the local people: "There are queer folks in this region; they make their living by fishing, gathering oysters, 'wrecking,' and piloting. Most of them were born here, never saw any other locality, and all are happy. There are women

Chicamacomico Lifesaving Station

here who never wore shoes. The people seldom see money, indeed, they have no use for it."

On November 6, 1874, a post office was established at Chicamacomico, but postal officials in Washington, D.C., decided that the community should be known by the name Rodanthe instead of its original, hard-to-spell name. By that time, three distinct communities had grown up in the Chicamacomico area: North Rodanthe, Clarks (or Clarksville), and South Rodanthe. They became Rodanthe, Waves, and Salvo.

Be sure to stop at the most recognizable landmark in Rodanthe, located in the heart of the village on the ocean side of N.C. 12. Constructed in 1874 as one of the first seven stations built by the United States Lifesaving Service on the Outer Banks, the Chicamacomico Lifesaving Station subsequently became one of the most famous stations in the history of American lifesaving. It was the first of ten stations on Hatteras Island. For a period of eighty years, its courageous lifesavers effected some of the most miraculous rescues in the annals of the Lifesaving Service. In 1930, six Chicamacomico lifesavers were awarded Congressional Grand Crosses of the American Cross of Honor for "unusual and extraordinary heroism to the maximum degree." Only eleven of these prestigious medals have ever been awarded.

Following the closure of the station in 1954, its buildings suffered from years of neglect, until residents of the island and other Outer Bankers joined forces in 1976 in an effort to salvage the site. A nonprofit organization, the Chicamacomico Historical Association, was created to spearhead the project. Following the acquisition of the property, restoration funds were obtained from federal and private grants and individual contributions. Under the watchful eyes of the National Park Service and the North Carolina Division of Archives and History, the station is gradually being restored to its past glory. In June 1984, the complex was opened on a limited basis for the first time. As additional money has become available, further repairs have been effected, including the station's first coat of white paint since 1939.

Visitors to the site, who number in excess of ten thousand annually, see the most complete collection of buildings at any of the surviving lifesaving stations, active or inactive, on the North Carolina coast. Listed on the National Register of Historic Places, the complex features two buildings of enormous historical importance. The older of the two, the original station, was converted to a boathouse when the newer, more spacious station was erected in 1911. The older station, a one-story frame structure covered with board and batten, originally stood on the beach. It was later moved to its present location several hundred feet east of the 1911 station.

A picket fence encloses the grounds of the 1911 building, which is typical of the structures built by the Lifesaving Service in the early part of the twentieth century. Among the other buildings located on the grounds are several storage buildings, a kitchen, three water tanks, and a cistern.

Admission to the complex is free. Exhibits covering the history of Outer Banks lifesaving are located in the main building. From mid-June to early September, the National Park Service conducts a lifesaving drill at the site on a weekly basis.

Of the many Hatteras families that served with distinction at the Chicamacomico station and the other lifesaving stations up and down the island, one stands out above all the others: Midgett. In fact, no other surname is more prominent on Hatteras Island. From one end of the island to the other, the name appears on mailboxes and businesses. In the annals of the United States Coast Guard and its predecessor, the United States Lifesaving Service, no family has been more honored than the Midgetts of Hatteras Island.

No one knows when the first Midgett came ashore at Hatteras, but at the time of the first national census in 1790, there were more Midgetts then people of any other family name on the island. As the young nation grew and prospered, so did the Midgetts of Hatteras Island. They lived by the sea, earned their livelihood from it, and always maintained a deep, abiding respect for it.

When the United States Lifesaving Service was established, the jobs it provided seemed tailor-made for the Midgetts. Over the past century, more than 150 members of the family have selected careers as lifesavers. Coast Guard records are filled with accounts of the Midgetts' courage, self-sacrifice, and heroism in the dangerous waters off Hatteras. Seven members of the family have won the nation's highest lifesaving award, the Gold Lifesaving Medal.

On July 2, 1992, the Coast Guard honored the family with a Midgett Day observance at the state port facilities in Morehead City. The highlight of the day came when a gleaming, new 378-foot cutter, appropriately named the *Midgett*, arrived at the port.

A marker erected by the North Carolina Division of Archives and History in front of the Chicamacomico Lifesaving Station commemorates the gallant rescue of crew members of the tanker *Mirlo* on August 16, 1918, by Captain John Allen Midgett, Jr., and the men of the station. In one of the most heroic episodes in lifesaving history, forty-two survivors were pulled from the flaming waters of the Atlantic after their ship hit a mine laid by the German submarine *U-117*.

In addition to the lifesaving museum, other reminders of Rodanthe's maritime heritage are found throughout the village. Several small cemeteries along the lanes of the village contain the graves of drowned sailors from many times and places. On the sound side, the old harbor and channel now used by the picturesque local fishing fleet was constructed for the Coast Guard in 1936–37.

Continue south from the lifesaving station. It is approximately 0.3 mile to the Hatteras Island Fishing Pier, visible from the highway. You may want to stop just north of the pier, where the steel wreck of the *LST. No. 471* can be seen at low tide. This military landing craft beached here on February 5, 1948, while being towed to Charleston, South Carolina.

The people of Rodanthe have always been characterized by an independent spirit. That spirit is best evidenced by the annual celebration of Olde Christmas, one of the most colorful traditions of the Outer Banks. No one can pinpoint the exact year when islanders first began the custom, but the unusual celebration is believed to have started not long after King George ordered England and her colonies to change from the Julian to the Gregorian calendar in 1752. Outer Bankers protested the loss of eleven days and decided to continue the celebration of Christmas on the old day, January 6.

In the bygone days of the celebration, village residents awoke and left their homes to fall in line behind musicians. By noon, the long procession reached the center of the village, where a sumptuous holiday feast was enjoyed by all. Following the banquet, visits were paid to the sick and feeble of the village.

Over the years, much of the original meaning behind the tradition has been lost, but widespread television and newspaper coverage has made it as popular as ever. Now observed on the Saturday after January 6, the raucous party has little resemblance to the celebration of the eighteenth century.

However, one colorful part of the tradition endures to this day: the appearance of Old Buck. According to Outer Banks legend, Old Buck was a magnificent bull first spotted standing on the beach at Rodanthe after swimming ashore from a shipwreck. He became a familiar figure on the island, owned by no one but friend to all. While wandering one day in Trent Woods down the beach, Old Buck was killed by a hunter.

Olde Christmas is still celebrated in Rodanthe.

To honor the special bull, the islanders have made replicas of his head for use at Olde Christmas. Originally, Old Buck made his appearance affixed to a pole, but now men dress in a cow's hide and hold horns and a bull's head in front of them. Village children look upon Old Buck much as mainland children do Santa Claus—with reverence and anticipation. For the people of Rodanthe, the appearance of Old Buck preserves the spirit of Olde Christmas for another year. Legend has it that after the celebration, Old Buck once again takes on his original appearance and runs down the beach to Trent Woods, where he remains hidden for twelve months.

Continue south on N.C. 12. Located 2 miles south of Rodanthe, the village of Waves stands in stark contrast to its neighbor to the north. It is much smaller and exhibits far less commercial development. Its former name, South Rodanthe, was abandoned by postal officials when the village post office was opened in 1939. There seems to be no explanation for the present name, other than a vague reference to the nearby ocean.

Proceed 2 miles south to Salvo, the third of the three communities that once made up Chicamacomico. Clarks, the original name of the village, did not appear on any chart or map when Union warships made their way up the sound in 1861. The naval commander ordered his men to "give it a salvo" from their guns, and Salvo was accordingly entered on maritime charts. By the time a post office was established in the village in 1901, the Civil War name had been perpetuated on maps. Thus, the village retained its unusual Civil War legacy.

Much like Waves, Salvo is small in population, containing only several hundred residents. Until a destructive fire in October 1992, its most-photographed building was a tiny, eight-by-twelve-foot post office. When the United States Postal Service conducted a 1989 survey of post offices based on size, local population, number of boxes, and number of delivery-route stops, the Salvo facility tied with Birds Landing, California, and Ochapee, Florida, as the smallest post offices in the nation. A plaque on the building acclaimed this unusual distinction, and stamp collectors the world over made it a point to stop by the post office while visiting the island.

Continue south from Salvo. On the sound side of N.C. 12 just south of the village, a National Park Service campground is the last visitor amenity on the northern half of the island. Beyond the campground, the highway begins a scenic 13-mile run along an uninhabited portion of the island. This section of the route provides a refreshing respite from human development and a majestic panorama of dunes, shrubbery, thickets, and the sound.

Four miles south of Salvo, Ramp 28 provides access to the strand, where another of the shipwrecks in the park can often be seen. In August 1933, the four-masted schooner G. A. *Kohler* ran aground here with a load of timber.

It is approximately 4.5 miles on N.C. 12 from the wreck of the G. A. *Kohler* to Little Kinnakeet, the southernmost of the seven original lifesaving stations on the Outer Banks. The original board and batten building, built around 1874, and a larger station with an observation tower, built around 1904, stand on the west side of the highway, abandoned relics of the time when shipwrecks were a common occurrence on this stretch of the North Carolina coast. Listed on the National Register of Historic Places, the complex will be restored and converted to a visitor center by the National Park Service when funds become available.

Continue on N.C. 12. It is 4.5 miles from the old lifesaving station to Avon, formerly known as Kinnakeet. In recent years, this has become one of the fastest-growing villages on the island.

From the sound-side shore of Avon, you can gaze across the expansive, seemingly endless Pamlico Sound. It is here that the sound is at its widest point. Giovanni da Verrazano was probably near this spot when he proclaimed the sound to be a sea. Indeed, so vast are Pamlico Sound's waters that even the modern mariner senses that he is at open sea when both the eastern and western shores are no longer visible.

On the map, the immense lagoon resembles a giant inverted comma. From Hatteras Island, it stretches 30 miles to the west until it gently kisses the mainland. Its 80-mile length extends from the foot of Croatan Sound at

Oregon Inlet south to the tip of Portsmouth Island, at the northern entrance of Core Sound. Covering more than 1,700 square miles, Pamlico Sound is the largest sound on the East Coast. It is more than three times the size of the famed Puget Sound on the West Coast. Although the sound appears limitless, it is relatively shallow, with depths ranging from eight to twenty-one feet.

Pamlico Sound was the site of the sinking of the only state ferry vessel ever to go down. When the *Governor Scott* sank in the sound during stormy weather in March 1962, the converted navy landing craft had been retired from active ferry service and was being used as a workboat for the ferry system. No hands were lost in the mishap, and the vessel was later refloated and returned to service.

The Corps of Engineers dug a sound-side harbor at Avon in 1946. Before that date, the sound was filled with freight houses on stilts. Large boats could dock at the houses to pick up freshly caught fish and seafood. The new harbor eliminated the need for the houses, and they have since vanished from the picturesque sound front.

On the Avon oceanfront, the Avon Fishing Pier is the second of the Hatteras Island fishing piers licensed by the National Park Service.

South of Avon, the island becomes extremely low and narrow until it bends to the southwest near the village of Buxton. It is along this dangerous stretch of Hatteras Island that N.C. 12 takes its worst beating during storms.

In conjunction with the establishment of the national seashore, the state of North Carolina completed a monumental, six-year project whereby N.C. 12 was paved from one end of the island to the other in 1953. More than 2,274,160 gallons of asphalt and 129,922 cubic yards of sand were used to surface the 71 miles of roadway. When the mighty Ash Wednesday Storm slapped the Outer Banks on March 7, 1962, the island was cut completely in two by the surging ocean. A 200-foot-wide inlet opened from ocean to sound along the current tour route, forcing the state to scramble to fill the chasm before the damage was irreparable.

It is approximately 3 miles from Avon to Canadian Hole, a body of water on the sound side of the island. Located near the site of the former inlet, Canadian Hole attracts large numbers of windsurfers. A sign at the parking area calls attention to this spot, which continues to grow in popularity.

South of Canadian Hole, you will notice a state historical marker commemorating Reginald Fessenden, one of the radio pioneers who worked in North Carolina. In the first decade of the twentieth century, Hatteras Island played a vital role in the development of wireless telegraphy and modern radio.

In 1902, at a mast tower constructed at Kings Point, Fessenden sent the first musical notes ever relayed by radio waves. The transmission was received at Fessenden's tower on the northern end of Roanoke Island. (For more information on Reginald Fessenden, see The Roanoke Island Tour, page 147.)

Another radio pioneer also visited this area. In 1901, Guglielmo Marconi gained worldwide fame for his successful transatlantic transmission of a wireless telegraphic signal. Three years later, the fifty-seven-year-old Marconi came to Hatteras Island to inspect the tower constructed by his company, the Marconi Wireless Telegraph Company. During his short stay on the North Carolina coast, the Italian inventor lived aboard a yacht anchored well out in Pamlico Sound. His 157-foot-tall antenna near Cape Point was the first in his worldwide network of such towers. Soon after Marconi departed, the tower became the first commercial wireless station in the Western Hemisphere.

Business was so brisk and the demand for "marconigrams" so great that the station at Hatteras soon operated around the clock. It was during the night shift of April 10, 1912, that the station received one of the most famous distress signals of all time. Richard Dailey, the twenty-one-year-old grandson of Captain Benjamin Dailey—the first winner of the Congressional Medal of Honor for lifesaving on the Outer Banks—was on duty at the wireless operation. Suddenly, he received a startling distress signal from a sinking ship more than 2,000 miles away in the Atlantic.

Just days before, Dailey had read with interest news accounts detailing the beginning of the maiden voyage of the "unsinkable" HMS *Titanic*. Much to his consternation, the plea for assistance received at Hatteras on the night of April 10 came from the great ocean liner after a towering iceberg had ripped a gaping hole in its hull. Dailey reduced the signal to writing and relayed it to Norfolk on his ground-line telegraph instrument. Little did he know that he had received the first news the world had of the impending disaster in the cold waters off Newfoundland.

A hurricane toppled the tall wooden tower on Hatteras Island in 1916. It was replaced with masts from a wrecked schooner, which were in turn replaced with steel towers in the early 1920s. The towers were removed three decades later. Today, nothing remains of the station.

Continue on N.C. 12 toward Buxton, located approximately 3 miles beyond Canadian Hole. Buxton is perhaps the easiest of the Hatteras Island enclaves to identify, thanks to the towering Cape Hatteras Lighthouse, which can be seen for miles in all directions.

But the majestic lighthouse is not the only attraction for visitors who make their way to this beautiful village. Just west of the lighthouse lies a high, heavily forested area that extends some 8 miles to the south. Known alternately as Buxton Woods, Cape Hatteras Woods, and Hatteras Woods, this forest is the most extensive maritime forest on the North Carolina coast. It covers approximately three thousand acres at the widest part of the island. Its ridges feature a canopy of loblolly pine, live oak, and laurel oak and an understory of dogwood and red cedar.

A battle for the preservation of the forest is presently being waged. While more than half of the acreage is owned by the National Park Service, the state of North Carolina, and the Cape Hatteras Water Authority, the remainder is privately owned.

Visitors can sample the splendor of the forest on Buxton Woods Natural Trail. To reach the trail, turn left onto the entrance road to the lighthouse complex in the heart of the village. This short, scenic drive affords vistas of coastal fauna and a beautiful pond that often casts a reflection of the lighthouse. At the end of the road, turn west, away from the lighthouse, and proceed 0.3 mile to the trail parking lot.

Three-quarters of a mile in length, the trail climbs over low sand dunes and ridges, passes scenic freshwater marshes, and enters a world of wildflowers, magnificent trees, and mixed shrubbery of yaupon, bayberry, and gallberry.

Markers along the trail identify the role of each natural element in the fragile ecosystem on the island. Of particular interest is the semitropical vegetation which grows in the forest as a result of its proximity to the Gulf Stream. *Sabal minor* palmettos thrive here at the northernmost point of their range, and grapefruit and other citrus trees grow to maturity and bear fruit annually.

Picnic tables and charcoal grills are located at the end of the trail.

Although this nature trail is the best of its kind on the Outer Banks, hikers are cautioned to beware of the cottonmouth snakes that are often found on it. These fat-bodied reptiles are easily identified by their dull colors of brown, yellow, and gray.

From Buxton Woods Nature Trail, proceed 1 mile south to the end of the road to reach Cape Point Campground and Cape Point Beach. These facilities are provided by the National Park Service to afford access to Cape Point, the tip of famed Cape Hatteras. From the parking lot at Cape Point Beach, a boardwalk leads over the dunes to the beach. It is a difficult hike of 1.2 miles over soft sand and water-covered portions of the strand to Cape Point. En route, the remains of the 102-foot, three-masted schooner *Altoona* are sometimes visible.

When compared to her sister capes to the south—Lookout and Fear—Cape Hatteras has a rather tame name. But beachcombers gazing into the Atlantic from Cape Point see an ocean that is anything but tame. From their vantage point, they can witness the spectacular head-on collision of tall whitecaps that sends salt spray and frothy spume more than a hundred feet into the air. It is here that the two great ocean currents—the cold Labrador Current from the Arctic and the warm Gulf Stream from the tropics—clash to create an agitated, tempestuous sea. Indeed, the observer at Cape Point has a ringside seat at one of the most infamous ocean areas in the world: the Graveyard of the Atlantic.

Underneath these treacherous waters lies the submerged tail of Cape Hatteras. This sandy finger of death, known as Diamond Shoals, extends more than 9 miles out to sea and is some 25 miles in length. Ironically, from the time of the earliest European explorers, navigators have deliberately sailed into the Hatteras deathtrap. They have done so not from a lack of respect for, or fear of, the hazardous waters and shoals—indeed, most of the sailors who have survived harrowing journeys around the cape have left the area with a sense of awe—but rather from a lack of choice. Historically, a curious interplay of currents, winds, geography, and economic considerations has forced north-south sailing traffic along the Atlantic coast straight into the clutches of Diamond Shoals.

It is little wonder, then, that throughout America's maritime history, Cape Hatteras has seen the largest concentration of shipwrecks on the Atlantic coast. The seas and sands of the North Carolina coast will never disclose just how many ships have been claimed by Diamond Shoals, but historical research has conclusively proved the loss of more than two thousand vessels in the Graveyard of the Atlantic. Innumerable others have vanished without a trace and found their final resting places here.

It was none other than the nation's first and youngest secretary of the treasury, Alexander Hamilton, who coined the name Graveyard of the Atlantic. As a fifteen-year-old boy, Hamilton survived a harrowing voyage around Cape Hatteras—a traumatic journey he would never forget. Eighteen years later, as the second-ranking member of President George Washington's cabinet, he worked diligently to reduce the danger to mariners off the North Carolina coast. It was at this time that Hamilton conceived the enduring name for the area and put it in writing for the first time.

Before the tour leaves Cape Point, it is worth noting a few intriguing quirks of North Carolina geography to lend some sense of the extreme eastern orientation of the cape. The closest point of land to the island of

Bermuda is Cape Hatteras. Within the confines of the state of North Carolina, the sun rises a half-hour earlier at the cape than it does in the mountain town of Murphy. But on a more ominous note, this eastern orientation makes Hatteras Island, and more particularly the cape, the most hurricane-prone area in North Carolina.

Return to the parking lot for Cape Point Beach, then drive north on the access road to the parking lot at the Cape Hatteras Lighthouse.

Of the 850 lighthouses now standing in the United States, none is more imposing, more resplendent, more beautiful, or more photographed than the Cape Hatteras Lighthouse. Few motorists on N.C. 12 can ever forget their breathless reaction at the first glimpse of America's tallest lighthouse. For more than 190 years, the existing brick structure and its predecessor have stood guard over the Graveyard of the Atlantic.

Like the 450 other American lighthouses that remain in active service, the Cape Hatteras Lighthouse is no longer essential to safe passage. Because of computerized navigation and advanced technology, the Cape Hatteras Lighthouse and the other towers have gone the way of the streetcar, the ocean liner, the fireplace, and the oil lamp—things more valued for their beauty than their utility.

Cape Hatteras Lighthouse

Although mariners are no longer forced to rely on the Cape Hatteras Lighthouse to warn them of Diamond Shoals, it remains a national treasure of inestimable value. Sailors continue to hold the lighthouse in awe. They welcome its friendly beam in the dark shipping lanes of the Atlantic. For those who are not mariners, the magnificent tower keeps their romance with the sea burning brightly. It offers to all Americans a sweet taste of their priceless maritime heritage. Those who have admired the strength and grace of the tower concur with George Bernard Shaw, who once called lighthouses "society's most altruistic invention." Indeed, the stately tower at Cape Hatteras is the epitome of the American lighthouse.

Alexander Hamilton not only gave the Graveyard of the Atlantic its name, he also initiated the effort that led to the construction of the first lighthouse at Cape Hatteras. Through his leadership, on April 7, 1789, the first United States Congress passed its ninth bill, whereby the process for the construction of lighthouses by the federal government was begun.

Construction of the drab, brown, octagonal sandstone tower at Cape

Hatteras was completed in 1803. But no sooner had the new lighthouse, which rose 112 feet above the sea, been put into service than it was besieged by a variety of problems. Mariners constantly complained about the quality of the light produced by the tower. One United States Navy officer declared the Cape Hatteras Lighthouse to be not only "the most important light on the entire east coast," but also "the worst in the world."

Following constant attempts to improve the lighthouse as a navigational aid, federal authorities decided to replace it after the Civil War. Because erosion had been a lingering problem at the original lighthouse, a new site was secured six hundred feet to the north and fifteen hundred feet from the high-tide line. The new tower was designed to be the sister of the newly built, much-admired Cape Lookout tower, with one significant difference: it would be thirty feet taller than Lookout, because the light at Hatteras had to be visible beyond Diamond Shoals.

When the final cost of the new lighthouse was calculated, the price tag of $150,000 was more than twice the original congressional appropriation. Although it most likely took place in December 1870, the exact date of the lighting of the new lighthouse has been lost to history.

When the great Charleston earthquake of 1886 struck on August 31 at 9:50 P.M., the initial shock rocked most of the eastern seaboard. At Cape Hatteras, the lighthouse shook and trembled for almost fifteen seconds. Several significant aftershocks, shorter in duration, followed at ten-minute intervals, but the ever-faithful beacon continued flashing throughout the entire event.

In 1934, when the tower was electrified, there was little joy, because the days of the lighthouse appeared to be numbered. As early as December 1933, leading newspapers in the state, including the *Charlotte Observer* and the *Raleigh News and Observer*, had carried grim headlines such as "Hatteras Light, Tallest On U.S. Coast, To Be Replaced" and "Hatteras Light Yields To Seas." Severe erosion finally forced the federal government to make a long-expected decision official: the Cape Hatteras Lighthouse was to be abandoned.

In May 1936, the lighthouse keeper had the unpleasant duty of supervising the formal "lights out" ceremony at Cape Hatteras. Most Americans believed that the picturesque lighthouse had seen its last glory—the era was over.

Few people, either locals or outsiders, could be found who liked the unsightly, skeletal steel tower constructed to take the place of the spectacular lighthouse. Resembling a fire observation tower, the awkward-looking 160-foot structure with spider legs was erected on a sand hill in Buxton Woods well back from the ocean. From 1936 to 1950, its three red blinking lights were a sad substitute for the bright white beam of the old tower.

By the end of World War II, the ocean had retreated more than three hundred yards eastward and was no longer a threat to the abandoned lighthouse. Three years later, when workers began restoring the tower, the ocean at high tide was more than a thousand feet from the tower. In 1950, after a year-long project of repairing the damage done by vandals and the coastal elements, the Cape Hatteras Lighthouse once again began flashing its friendly signal to mariners every seven and a half seconds.

A quarter-century later, the effects of erosion were evident. Only 600 feet separated the lighthouse from the waters of the Atlantic. At the same time, the surf pounded just 175 feet from the remaining foundation of the old lighthouse.

Two years later, waves were breaking at the ruins. A blizzard in March 1980 swept all of the remnants into the sea.

With the ocean only 150 feet away, the successor to the old light looked to be next. National Park Service officials were dismayed to find themselves without national or state funds. As the sea pounded within 70 feet of the foundation in October 1980, workers frantically dumped thousands of pounds of broken rubble to create a temporary wall.

At the height of the emergency, the lighthouse received help from a man who had stepped forward twenty years earlier to save the USS *North Carolina* from the scrap heap. Linville businessman Hugh Morton spearheaded the formation of the Save the Cape Hatteras Lighthouse Committee. Money raised by the committee funded erosion-control measures that bought time while the National Park Service debated a number of proposals to save the lighthouse.

In 1989, the National Park Service formally announced that the lighthouse would be moved five hundred feet back from the present site in one piece, at a cost of approximately $9 million. However, no date has been set for the relocation, and no money has been appropriated for the project.

Admirers of the lighthouse fear that inaction by the National Park Service signals its intention to allow the sea to claim the structure.

While the waiting and watching go on, the 208-foot-tall lighthouse stands as resplendent as ever, thanks to an extensive restoration project. The work was necessitated after a 1984 inspection revealed two severe cracks running the length of the lighthouse, as well as other severe structural defects. Although the cause of the cracks was not determined, it has been speculated that they were caused by the earthquake of 1886.

In 1993, for the first time since 1984, the interior of the lighthouse was opened to the public. Sightseers can now climb the 268 steps of the spiral wrought-iron staircase to the top of America's tallest lighthouse, where the tower balcony offers a windy but panoramic view of the cape, the island, and Pamlico Sound. From its rock-solid base to its lantern room, which casts a beam that has been observed as far as 51 miles at sea, the spiral-striped, 3,469-ton Cape Hatteras Lighthouse remains a beloved symbol of man's continuing struggle against the sea.

Visitor Center at Cape Hatteras Lighthouse

In the shadow of the lighthouse, the old double keepers' quarters, constructed in 1854 to house two keepers and their families, serves as the visitor center. Inside the center is a museum with exhibits detailing the history of the lighthouse, the Civil War on the Outer Banks, and the United States Lifesaving Service. Park rangers are on duty to provide information and schedules for special programs, activities, and presentations offered in the lighthouse area.

Surfing is extremely popular on the beach near the lighthouse. In fact, the beach at Buxton is known as the hot spot for surfing on the Atlantic coast. The world-class conditions attract surfers from all over the country.

Return to N.C. 12 from the lighthouse parking lot and continue through Buxton. When the post office came to Buxton in 1873, the community was known as The Cape. Nine years later, the name was changed to Buxton in honor of the English town of the same name. Before they arrive on the island, many first-time visitors logically expect that the famous lighthouse stands in the village of Hatteras, rather than in Buxton.

As Hatteras Island veers sharply to the southwest at Buxton, N.C. 12 hugs the sound side. Unlike most parts of the island, the final third is well forested. This forested area is called Cape Hatteras Woods.

It is approximately 5 miles from Buxton to Billy Mitchell Airfield, the principal airfield on Hatteras Island. The airfield is located on the east side of N.C. 12 adjacent to the National Park Service campground serving the Frisco area.

This site was the venue for the first successful demonstration of a new method of warfare, designed to be waged with the magnificent invention successfully tested twenty years earlier at Kill Devil Hill by the Wright brothers.

On September 5, 1923, Brigadier General Billy Mitchell dispatched a squadron of eight United States Army airplanes from Frisco to a point near Diamond Shoals. There, the pilots unloaded thirteen 1,100-pound bombs on two obsolete American battleships, the USS *Virginia* and the USS *New Jersey*. Today, these two ships remain on the ocean floor where they settled after the bombardment.

Despite the lessons learned from this display of air power, General Mitchell was unable to convince the army of the importance of his contribution to modern warfare. He was later court-martialed. Mitchell died in retirement in 1936. Just five years after his death, he was vindicated in a tragic manner when Japanese aircraft unleashed their devastating attack on Pearl Harbor. A state historical marker honoring General Mitchell stands nearby on N.C. 12.

Historical marker honoring Billy Mitchell

Traveling the access road to the airport, you will see many of the imposing dunes found in this area. Two dunes—High Point of the Hills and Frisco Dune—tower more than thirty-five feet above the flat landscape. Many other landmark dunes have been leveled by erosion, wind, and development.

It is approximately 1.5 miles from the airfield to the Frisco Fishing Pier, located on the southern side of the village of Frisco. This is the third of the National Park Service concession piers in the national seashore. Adjacent to the pier, the National Park Service has provided the Frisco Day Use Area for easy public access to the ocean beach.

Nestled at the western edge of Cape Hatteras Woods, the tree-shaded, picturesque village of Frisco has one of the largest permanent populations on the island, boasting five hundred residents. This community was originally known as Trent, but postal officials changed the name on January 31, 1892, to avoid confusion with another coastal village of the same name. The new name was suggested by the community's first postmaster, who had settled on Hatteras after surviving a shipwreck. His fondness for San Francisco never waned, as evidenced by the name of the island village.

Continue south on N.C. 12. Located on the east side of the highway approximately 0.2 mile south of the Frisco Fishing Pier, the former Creeds Hill Lifesaving Station has been converted into a private residence.

It is approximately 1.9 miles from the old lifesaving station to Hatteras village, the glistening outpost on the northern shore of Hatteras Inlet. One of the oldest settlements on the island, the village has grown to be the most populous—nearly a thousand people call it home. Hatteras is the self-proclaimed fishing capital of the island. Four sizable full-service marinas offer charter-boat trips to the nearby waters of the Gulf Stream, Hatteras Inlet, and Pamlico Sound.

Bridges cross winding creeks and scenic marshes as N.C. 12 makes its way through the historic village to Hatteras Inlet. There are no records as to when the community actually started, but it was already a vital place in 1858, when the first post office on the Outer Banks north of Ocracoke was established here.

Former Creeds Hill Lifesaving Station

Well into the twentieth century, village natives spoke with broad Devonshire accents. Many of the old families are descended from shipwrecked English settlers. They reside in the old houses that give the village much of its beauty and charm. Their accents have gradually faded as the isolation once enjoyed, and endured, by the village has come to an end.

Hatteras is either the first or the last of the villages encountered by tourists on their visit to the island. Its geographic location has led to the development of a significant tourist industry. In quantity and variety, the lodgings, restaurants, shops, and service facilities in Hatteras are rivaled only by those at Buxton.

In the heart of the village, the two-story frame building that housed the United States Weather Bureau in the last quarter of the nineteenth century stands behind the Burrus Supermarket, itself a nineteenth-century establishment.

Follow N.C. 12 to where it ends its long run down the island at the Hatteras-Ocracoke Ferry landing. Nearby is the Hatteras Inlet Coast Guard Station. From the landing on the southern tip of the island, state-operated

Hatteras Inlet

vessels carry more than 264,000 vehicles and more than half a million passengers across Hatteras Inlet between Hatteras and Ocracoke islands each year. This route is one of the oldest on the Outer Banks, dating back to April 1953, when Frazier Peele began transportation of vehicles across the inlet on a wooden boat. Since that time, the demand for ferry service has increased to the point that it is not unusual during the height of the summer season to see more than three hundred hot drivers waiting in line to catch one of the free ferries that make the forty-minute crossings from early in the morning until late at night.

From the parking lot at the ferry landing, you can enjoy a magnificent view of Hatteras Inlet. Born of the same fury that created its sister inlet to the north, Hatteras Inlet quickly took on commercial importance. Redding D. Quigley, an Ocracoke mariner, piloted the first commercial vessel, the schooner *Asher C. Havens*, through the inlet on February 5, 1847. Fourteen years later, in late August 1861, Union military forces achieved their first military victory of the Civil War at the inlet.

A state historical marker near the ferry landing is virtually the only evidence of the fall of Fort Hatteras and Fort Clark. These forts were completed by the Confederacy in mid-June 1861 to protect the inlet. Hatteras, the principal, but weaker, of the two installations, was erected approximately 0.1 mile from the inlet to command the waterway. It stood 2 miles southwest of the ferry landing. Clark, the smaller of the two, was built approximately 0.8 mile east of Hatteras and closer to the ocean.

When the forts capitulated, newspapers in the North brought the joyful tidings to their readers, who were in dire need of good news. In announcing the first Northern victory of the war, a New York newspaper suggested that the news "contributes to the cheerful feeling that prevails by encouraging hope that the tide of victory is now turned from the rebels to Union arms." A brisk walk down the beach from the ferry landing reveals few, if any, remains of the old earthworks.

A site adjacent to the ferry landing will be the future home of the Graveyard of the Atlantic Museum, which will detail the history of shipwrecks on the Outer Banks and encourage their preservation. Of particular interest will be exhibits concerning, and artifacts from, the most famous ship claimed by the Graveyard: the USS *Monitor*. After resting 220 feet below the ocean surface in an unknown location for more than 110 years, the famed Civil War ironclad was discovered by a Duke University scientist in 1973.

The museum at Hatteras Inlet will anchor the southern end of the NOAA's proposed *Monitor* trail, a variety of regional exhibits detailing the vessel's design, construction, and battle with the CSS *Merrimac*.

The tour ends here, at the southern tip of Hatteras Island.

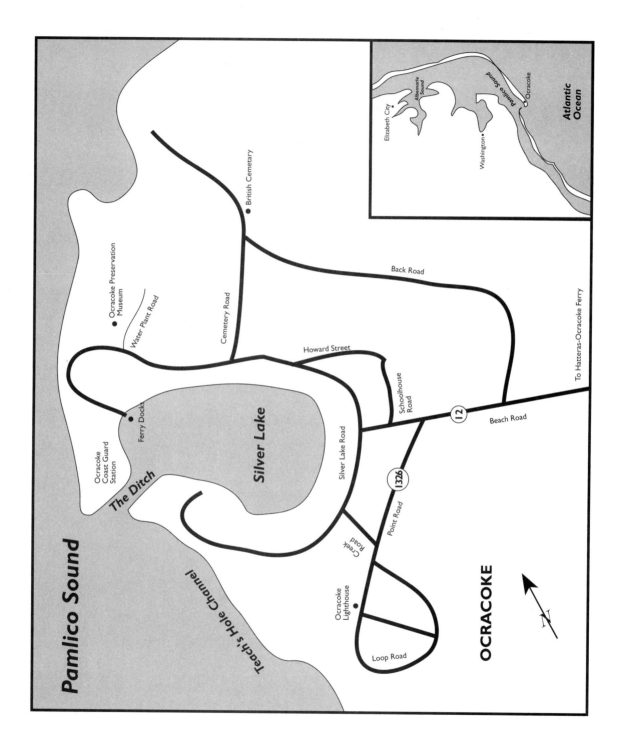

The Ocracoke Tour

This tour begins at the Hatteras-Ocracoke Ferry landing on the northern end of Ocracoke Island and proceeds south down N.C. 12 to Ocracoke village, near the southern end of the island. It ends at Ocracoke Island's other ferry landing, located on Silver Lake.

Among the highlights of the tour are the southernmost portion of Cape Hatteras National Seashore, the Ocracoke ponies, a walking tour of the historic village of Ocracoke, lovely Silver Lake, the British Cemetery, the Ocracoke Lighthouse, and the story of the demise of Blackbeard.

Total mileage: approximately 14 miles.

This tour begins at the Hatteras-Ocracoke Ferry landing on the northern end of Ocracoke Island. Proceed south down the island on N.C. 12.

The name Ocracoke refers to a number of different things: an island, an inlet, a village, a state of mind. Ocracoke Island is a barrier island on the southern end of Cape Hatteras National Seashore. Approximately 16 miles long, the island ranges from 0.5 mile to 2 miles in width and is bounded by the Atlantic, Pamlico Sound, Hatteras Inlet, and Ocracoke Inlet. As one of the three inlets along the Outer Banks which have been open continuously since 1585, Ocracoke Inlet was the route of much of North Carolina's oceangoing trade before the Revolutionary War. Located at the southwestern tip of the island is Ocracoke village, one of the most picturesque places in the world. It is the only populated place on the island in private ownership.

For many people who travel the North Carolina coast, the word *Ocracoke* refers to the state of mind that comes from the truly unique charm of the island and the quaint village there. Although other populated islands on the coast, such as Bald Head, are accessible only by boat, their development was the result of intentional design in the years since World War II. On the other hand, Ocracoke has been inhabited by descendants of European settlers for more than two and three-quarter centuries. Due to its isolation, it has remained the most unspoiled settlement on the North

Carolina coast. A visit to the island not only offers a walk back into history, but also provides perhaps the best escape from the "outside" world in all of coastal North Carolina.

The southern route of N.C. 12 from the ferry landing to the village offers a pleasant drive through an area free of any development and provides visitors with a taste of the island's charm—its unspoiled natural state. Of the 5,535 acres which make up Ocracoke Island, only the 775 acres in and around the village fall outside the domain of Cape Hatteras National Seashore. Since the national seashore became a reality, 85 percent of the island, including the entire beachfront, has been preserved for public use.

On the northern side of the highway, gnarled and stunted pine, juniper, and oak appear sporadically on the landscape of sand flats and small, meandering tidal creeks. On the ocean side of the road, much of the dune line is artificial, and unless the line has been temporarily broken by a storm, you will get no view of the ocean along the entire drive. Very low in elevation, the island is subject to extensive overwash. As a result, the state continues to face difficulties in maintaining N.C. 12.

There are several natural dunes towering twenty feet or more on the drive to the village. Near the ferry landing, you will encounter the first of the high dunes, the twenty-three-foot Styron Hills.

Ocracoke-Hatteras ferry landing

Visitor Center for Cape Hatteras National Seashore, located on Ocracoke Island

Visitors are welcome to take advantage of the entire stretch of spectacular island beaches. Because of the undeveloped nature of Ocracoke Island, the sands are enjoyed by beachcombers, shell collectors, fishermen, and sunbathers. Swimming is allowed, but extreme caution should be exercised, because dangerous undertows and riptides are common. For safer swimming, a protected beach is provided by the National Park Service about 2 miles northeast of the village.

Exactly when the first Europeans set foot on the island is uncertain, because it is not known whether Giovanni da Verrazano's party landed at Ocracoke in the first quarter of the sixteenth century. It is known that the ships transporting Raleigh's first colonists in 1585 made a landing at Ocracoke Inlet. There, Sir Richard Grenville's flagship, *Tiger*, grounded on the bar at the inlet. While the ship was being refloated, Grenville, Ralph Lane, and some of the three hundred troops on the expedition explored Ocracoke Island.

From this initial exploration, a map of the island was drawn in 1585. Apparently, Ocracoke was only 8 miles long at that time. Narratives by Raleigh's early explorers indicate that the island was not inhabited by Indians. The small Woccon, or Wacocon, tribe lived on the mainland opposite the island, and it is presumed that the island took its name from these Indians, since it was known as Wocokon in the sixteenth century. Thereafter, a wide variety of spellings were used. On various maps and in various publications, the name has appeared as Wacocon, Wococan, Waccock, Okok, Okerecocke, Okerecock, Occacock, Ocacock, and Ocracok, until its final evolution into Ocracoke in 1782.

A number of possible origins of the present spelling exist. Probably the most plausible is that it is an Anglicized corruption of the Algonquin word *waxkahikawi*, meaning "fort." Through years of mispronunciation and misspelling, the name evolved. Although not as plausible, a local legend claims that Blackbeard gave the island its name when, impatiently waiting for the break of day to do battle, he reportedly cursed, "O cry cock!" Still another legend maintains that Blackbeard gave the island its name by yelling the phrase after he had dropped anchor in the inlet and become disturbed because of the stillness about him.

Though it is likely that the first settlers on the island spilled over from

Hatteras Island in the early part of the eighteenth century, the first recorded settlers were sea pilots. With increasing numbers of ships using Ocracoke Inlet, the colonial assembly passed "an Act for Settling and Maintaining Pilots at Roanoke and Ocacock Inlett" in 1715. The village that grew from this legislation was the forerunner of the present island village, one of the oldest settlements on the Outer Banks.

As early as 1730, old Hatteras Inlet began closing, and sometime during the 1750s, it closed completely. As a result, Ocracoke Island temporarily passed from existence, as it was connected by land to Hatteras Island. Not until 1846, when the present Hatteras Inlet opened, did the Ocracoke Island of today take its form.

Together with Portsmouth, its twin port town just across Ocracoke Inlet, Ocracoke became known as the port of Beacon Island Roads prior to the Revolution. When America began to fight for independence, the treacherous shoals off Ocracoke prevented large British warships from effectively closing the port at Ocracoke Inlet, thereby allowing many of the supplies that fed and equipped George Washington's army to pass through the inlet.

In the decade before the Civil War, the golden age of the port of Ocracoke drew to a close. At that time, the white population was 536, with an additional 100 or more slaves living on the island. As commercial traffic through the inlet waned, Ocracoke began to attract some tourists and vacationers. In 1855, a group of businessmen built the Ocracoke Hotel, which stood on the island until a fire in 1900. A summer ferry ran irregularly from New Bern and Washington, North Carolina, to Ocracoke during the pre–Civil War years.

To protect Ocracoke Inlet, Confederate authorities erected a fort near Ocracoke on Beacon Island, a small island in Pamlico Sound. Named for the two large beacons which had earlier been placed there for use by pilots, the island was the site of an earlier fort built by the federal government in 1794–95. From 1799 to 1939, Beacon Island was listed on government records as Beacon Island Military Reservation. Alternately known as Beacon Island Fort, Fort Morgan, and Fort Ocracoke, the installation was abandoned by Southern forces in August 1861 after the fall of the forts on Hatteras Island. Thereafter, Ocracoke Island was occupied by Federal troops for the duration of the war and was spared the bloodshed of the conflict.

After the war, Beacon Island was used for sheep grazing and as a fishing and hunting camp. In 1938, ownership of the twenty-four-acre island passed out of the government's hands for the first time since the eighteenth century, when it was sold to a group of North Carolina businessmen for use as a hunting preserve. For many years thereafter, Beacon Island was the smallest island shown on the highway maps issued by the state.

Until the late 1930s, Ocracoke Island remained one of the most isolated populated places on the entire Atlantic coast. Most of the island's residents remained clustered in the village of old weathered houses, where there was no electricity, no paved roads, no bridges, no regular ferry service, and no telephones (although the Coast Guard provided radiotelephone facilities in emergencies).

Changes began to occur when a native Ocracoker, Stanley Wahab, came home after making good on the mainland. Wahab soon became known as "Mr. Ocracoke" because of the improvements he made on the island. Due in large part to his efforts, electricity finally came to the island in 1938. He constructed numerous modern conveniences on the island, including an ice plant, a hotel, a movie house, resort houses, and a cafe.

From the time Cape Hatteras National Seashore was first proposed in 1933, some Ocracoke residents opposed the inclusion of their island in the park. Ultimately, the opposition subsided, and the island, save the small village, was spared from future development by its inclusion in the national seashore.

But creation of the national seashore did not automatically make Ocracoke accessible to the outside world. Until 1957, there was no paved road from Hatteras Inlet to the village, nor was there any regular ferry service. Soon after the state paved the island road and established ferry routes, the first modern motel on the island was completed. Since that time, a significant tourist industry has supplemented the traditional maritime economy of the village.

Without question, the favorite stop on the drive down the island is the Ocracoke pony pen, located on the sound side of the island 6.2 miles south of the ferry landing. No family on Ocracoke can trace its roots on the island as far back as can the famous ponies. Long a tourist attraction on the island, the pony population has been significantly diminished by the National Park Service.

Ocracoke ponies

Although the ancestors of the ponies roamed the island long before the first permanent settlers arrived, their origin has long been the subject of dispute.

One theory is that these horses were introduced to the island by early Spanish explorers in the sixteenth century. Evidence garnered from scientific tests on the ponies indicates that they descended from Spanish mustangs. During the 1970s, the Spanish Mustang Society examined each of the ponies in the herd. Not only did the examinations reveal that the animals had the same bone alignments as Spanish mustangs, but also the same general shape, size, posture, color, and habits. Some authorities have deemed the Ocracoke ponies the purest herd of Spanish mustangs in the entire world.

An alternative explanation says that the ponies came ashore after one of Sir Walter Raleigh's ships ran aground at Ocracoke Inlet during Sir Richard Grenville's expedition in 1585. That the ponies are Spanish mustangs is easily explained under this theory, since it is known that before Grenville proceeded toward the North Carolina coast, he purchased a brace of horses in the West Indies, which at that time were under Spanish control.

Regardless of their origin, these magnificent horses had free run of the island until the National Park Service took control. At one time, their number was estimated at over a thousand. As a result of the large pony population that existed after World War I, annual roundups were held until 1960. After the road to the village was paved, fences were erected along N.C. 12 to protect the animals and motorists. In the 1950s, ponies could often be seen roaming the streets of the village. During that time, the only mounted Boy Scout troop in the United States was located at Ocracoke.

When the National Park Service assumed control of the lands where the ponies had roamed, fed, and thrived for centuries, the animals were penned. Suddenly, their numbers began to dwindle. Under National Park Service supervision, the herd of animals that had survived in the harsh natural environment for at least 225 years withered to just nine ponies.

Now, the herd numbers about two dozen ponies. They are maintained in a two-hundred-acre enclosure on the northwestern side of the highway. The sound-side pens provide the only chance for island visitors to get a glimpse of one of Ocracoke's oldest tourist attractions. Signs direct motorists to a viewing platform, where the National Park Service has erected a plaque detailing the theories of the origin of the ponies. Unfortunately, the ponies often graze far away from the platform. If you don't have binoculars, they may appear as colored specks on the horizon.

Even though the herd is substantially smaller than it was in its natural state, it remains one of the most-photographed and most-viewed groups of horses in the country. Larger in size than Shetland ponies, the russet-colored Ocracoke ponies do not reach the size of regular horses. While they were free to fend for themselves on the island, these hardy animals subsisted on sea oats and marsh grass. Since fresh drinking water has always been in limited supply on Ocracoke, the ponies were forced to locate water in a most amazing way. A group of the animals would gather in a circle and paw broad, shallow water holes. To drink, they would then lie prone on the sand.

Continue south from the pony pen. Scrag Cedar Hills, the tallest dunes on the island, tower twenty-seven feet above the ocean approximately 0.5 mile beyond the pen. A mile farther down the road rises The Knoll, almost twenty-two feet high.

Along the remainder of the drive to Ocracoke village, the readily apparent sand flats are as much as a mile in width. Some of these great barrier plains are the result of frequent overwash. However, the condition

Isolated stretch of N.C. 12 leading to Ocracoke village

of this landscape is due mainly to defoliant used by the military during World War II to thin the vegetation. Not only did the chemical agent produce the desired result, but it also acted to the detriment of certain animals on the island.

According to local legend, the defoliant completely decimated the frog population on Ocracoke. After the war, an Ocracoke woman originally from Hatteras Island returned to her native island, where she collected a pair of frogs and put them in a shoebox. As soon as she got back to Ocracoke, she released them in her garden, thereby reintroducing frogs to the island.

Approximately 5 miles from The Knoll, and less than 0.5 mile before the limits of Ocracoke village, follow the road sign directing you to Ramp 70, located on the ocean side of N.C. 12. A parking lot is provided for this lifeguard-protected beach area. Nearby is the Ocracoke airstrip. Five miles south of this spot is Oregon Inlet; travel down the long, isolated stretch of beach to the southern end of the island is limited to walkers and those with four-wheel-drive vehicles.

From Ramp 70, return to N.C. 12 and proceed into the village. N.C. 12 terminates at Silver Lake near the ferry landing in Ocracoke village. Park in the public parking area near the end of the road.

Ever since tourists have been coming to the only populated place on the island, one truism about the village has held fast: You either like it or hate it. Few people who come to this tiny village, located on the sound side of the island about three-quarters of the way down its length, deny that it has a unique charm. Described by admirers as the most picturesque village on the East Coast, Ocracoke can attribute much of its charm to its isolation and lack of commercialism. No other community on America's shoreline has the character of this village.

With the Atlantic Ocean as its front yard, the enormous Pamlico Sound as its backyard, Ocracoke Inlet as its side yard, and Silver Lake as its yard ornamentation, the village continues to pay homage to the water that has sustained its people from earliest times. Now, more than six hundred thousand tourists pour into the tiny village every year.

To accommodate this massive influx, the village has yielded to some changes in recent times. Visitors who return to the island after an absence of a decade or more are stunned by what they see. Rising above the profile

Ocracoke village

TOURING THE BACKROADS OF NORTH CAROLINA'S UPPER COAST

of Silver Lake are several multistory hotels. The village once had only a couple of general stores, but shopping opportunities increased significantly during the 1980s. That same decade, cable television was introduced to the village, and Hyde County opened a jail facility here.

Begin your 3.2-mile walking tour of the tidy village clustered around Silver Lake at one of the most prominent structures on the lake, the National Park Service visitor center, located in a building near the ferry landing. Completed in 1980, the center is a storehouse of information about the island. A schedule of the extensive program of nature walks, village tours, beach hikes, lectures on local history, and other activities provided by the park rangers is available here.

Ocracoke Museum and Visitor Center

A museum at the center features exhibits on the famous ponies, piracy, shells, and other local history. The center also serves as the registration office for boaters using the nearby Silver Lake Marina, operated by the National Park Service.

From the center, walk south across the road to the marina and the ferry landing.

Nothing in the village adds more to its postcard beauty than Silver Lake. Rimmed by the village, this sheltered harbor remains the focal point of Ocracoke. Situated on the shores of the 0.4-mile-wide harbor are motels, homes, the National Park Service visitor center, the ferry landing, a Coast Guard station, and numerous docks and piers. A pleasant afternoon can be spent on the docks taking in all the activities here. Fishermen go about their duties as boats of all sizes and shapes make their way in and out of the harbor.

Local residents refer to Silver Lake as "the Creek," a reference to its old name of Cockle Creek. The lake is connected to Pamlico Sound by a water thoroughfare commonly known as "the Ditch." Many island fishermen use the Ditch to get their boats to the sound.

It was this water course that inspired an old rivalry on the island. Persons residing north of Cockle Creek were referred to as "Pointers," while those across the ditch were "Creekers."

Until 1931, Cockle Creek was nothing more than a tidal creek. Then, because of the strategic importance of the island, the creek was dredged to a depth of fourteen feet to form Silver Lake. Shallows and marshland adjacent to the creek were filled with sand from the dredging.

TOURING THE BACKROADS OF NORTH CAROLINA'S UPPER COAST

Construction of a United States Navy section base at the undeveloped Silver Lake harbor began in June 1942. Three deepwater piers and numerous facilities were built as part of the base at the present site of the National Park Service facilities. Silver Lake was dredged and deepened for use by military craft. For the first time, some roads in the village were paved to provide access to ammunition dumps. A number of these concrete roads are still in use today.

Across the road from the ferry landing on Silver Lake stands the Ocracoke Coast Guard Station, constructed in 1938 to replace a turn-of-the-century facility. At one time, there was a second station on the other end of the island at Hatteras Inlet. Built in 1883, that station was abandoned long ago, and the only evidence at its former site are some rotting pilings.

Ocracoke Coast Guard Station

Looking east from the ferry landing, you can see the gable-roofed Berkley Center Country Inn. This magnificent nine-room inn was known as Berkley Manor when it was built in the 1950s by one of the village's most famous citizens of the twentieth century: Sam Jones. Originally from Swan Quarter, on the Hyde County mainland, Jones went to Norfolk early in life. There, he acquired a fortune as a principal figure of the Berkley Machine Works and Foundry. When Jones retired to his native county, he built six houses on Ocracoke, including Berkley Manor, which is known for its well-kept lawn and its interior of beautifully carved woodwork.

Overlooking Silver Lake is another of Jones's splendid structures: Sam Jones Castle. Both Berkley Manor and the castle are imposing wooden buildings that feature towers offering a spectacular view of the sea. Romantics have compared the Sam Jones Castle to the home in *The House of the Seven Gables*. It is located close to the lighthouse at the former site of the Union headquarters during the Civil War. The headquarters were razed when the castle was constructed.

Walk south from the ferry landing alongside N.C. 12 on the eastern shore of Silver Lake. After approximately 0.3 mile, about midway on the eastern shore, turn left onto Cemetery Road, a shaded road leading to the British Cemetery, one of the most visited places in the village. For those who know the bittersweet story behind the cemetery, the place leaves a lasting impression.

Berkley Center Country Inn

Just as the United States was caught off-guard when the Japanese attacked the Pacific fleet at Pearl Harbor in December 1941, the nation was totally unprepared for the deadly pack of U-boats unleashed by Adolf Hitler upon the Atlantic coast in January 1942. Cruising under the name "Operation Drum Roll," the U-boats exacted a heavy toll against shipping off the North Carolina coast during the first six months of 1942.

Early that year, the United States made a desperate plea to Great Britain for help against the U-boat menace. Responding to the request, the British government agreed to provide the United States Navy with a small fleet of twenty-four antisubmarine trawlers. These former fishing ships had been refitted by the British to defend the waters of the North Atlantic.

During the first weeks of February 1942, the trawlers and their crews of British sailors sailed for the United States. One of the ships in the flotilla was the HMS *Bedfordshire*, a 1935-vintage commercial fishing trawler. Stretching 170 feet in length, she was only one-fourth the size of a destroyer.

Silver Lake

After a short stay at the Brooklyn Navy Yard in late March 1942, the *Bedfordshire*, working out of a base at Morehead City, was assigned to protect the North Carolina coast. Unfortunately, the appalling death toll had continued to mount while America waited for the British ships to arrive. The grim task of identifying the dead bodies that washed up almost daily along the Outer Banks during the Nazi onslaught fell to Aycock Brown, a man from the North Carolina mountains who had adopted the North Carolina coast as his home. Working for naval intelligence, Brown identified the bodies of four British sailors in the surf at Nags Head in April 1942. At the request of his superior officer, he attempted to locate some British flags in order to give the sailors a proper burial.

Upon learning that the *Bedfordshire* was in port at Morehead City, Brown called upon the ship in late April in his quest for flags. At the ship, he was greeted by its second officer, a twenty-eight-year-old British lieutenant, Thomas Cunningham. Brown was graciously welcomed aboard, and Cunningham provided him with six new Union Jacks, two more than were needed at the time. While chatting with the bearded British officer, Brown learned that the lieutenant had been married just over a year; earlier that day, both Cunningham and the ship's commander had received word informing them of their impending fatherhood in October.

In early May 1942, the *Bedfordshire* refueled for the last time at Morehead City. On the night of May 11, the ship was patrolling off Cape Lookout when, at approximately eleven-thirty, *U-558* spotted her. After two torpedoes missed the trawler, the third struck squarely amidships, and the *Bedfordshire* plunged bow first to the bottom of the Atlantic.

On the morning of May 14, a young Coast Guardsman on patrol on the beaches of Ocracoke discovered two bodies in the surf. They were transported to the village, and Aycock Brown was flown in from Cherry Point to identify the remains. The minute the tarpaulin covering the bodies was removed, Brown was aghast, as he recognized one of the bodies as that of Lieutenant Cunningham. Papers found on the other body revealed him to be Seaman Stanley Craig, the telegrapher from the *Bedfordshire*.

Despite the shortage of wood on the island during the war, Ocracoke residents used two "sink boxes"—floating duck blinds—to fashion coffins for the British seamen. A local family graciously donated land near its cemetery for the burial of the bodies. There was not a resident minister on the island, so a Methodist layman conducted a simple memorial service, at which the men were laid to rest at a spot close to the sea that had claimed their lives. Draped over the homemade coffins were the two extra Union Jacks from the *Bedfordshire* that Lieutenant Cunningham had provided Aycock Brown.

A week after Cunningham and Craig were buried, a Coast Guard patrol boat spotted two badly decomposed bodies in the waters off Ocracoke. Even though the bodies were clad in the same dark blue turtleneck sweaters worn by Cunningham and Craig, Aycock Brown was not able to make positive identification.

Burial space remained in the plot where Cunningham and Craig had been laid to rest. Wood for coffins again posed a problem, but village residents came through once more, and the unknown seamen were buried beside their countrymen.

Brush was cleared from the grave site at the direction of the commander of the Ocracoke Navy Base in October 1943. At that time, a white picket fence was erected around the graves. The crude wooden crosses that had marked the graves were replaced with stone markers donated by the contractor assigned to construct the navy base. Attached to these new markers were bronze identification plates.

For a time after the war, the little cemetery deteriorated due to irregular maintenance, because no one had authority over it. Local citizens, civic organizations, and patriotic individuals sporadically cleaned the plots of weeds and placed flowers and wreaths on the graves. Then, on the afternoon of July 2, 1969, a detail of five British seamen arrived at Ocracoke village in a station wagon driven by a United States Navy sailor. They had driven from Norfolk, where their ship, the aircraft carrier HMS *Eagle*, was docked. After learning of the cemetery at Ocracoke, the skipper of the *Eagle* had asked for volunteers to spruce up the graves. At the cemetery, the five men replaced the worn fence posts with British wood carried on their ship.

The granite markers on the graves were provided in the 1970s by the British War Memorial Commission to replace the old white stone markers. During America's bicentennial celebration in 1976, the cemetery site was purchased by the state of North Carolina and deeded to Great Britain. Fittingly, the white picket fence surrounding the cemetery bears a brass plaque with the immortal words of Rupert Brooke: "If I should die, think only this of me; That there's some corner of a foreign field, That is forever England."

In the mid-1980s, the Coast Guard station at Ocracoke assumed responsibility for the upkeep of the site. Every week, the grass is mowed. Each year, the picket fence is painted and a new flag erected.

Few visitors leave the beautiful little cemetery without being awed by its simple grandeur. In 1963, a tourist from Louisville visited the cemetery, where she read the names of Lieutenant Cunningham and Seaman Craig. Although neither name meant anything to her at the time, Mrs. Robert Probst later told her mother, Mrs. Frank Rycroft of Teaneck, New Jersey, about the graves. Mrs. Rycroft then refreshed her daughter's memory of the time in 1942 when the younger woman was eighteen years old and living in the family home in New Jersey. It was at that time that the *Bedfordshire* docked in New York. During its call, several of the crew stayed in the Rycroft home. One of the crew members left his dog tags on the bathroom door. Upon discovering them, the Rycrofts called the Brooklyn Navy Yard, where they delivered the dog tags to their smiling owner, Seaman Stanley Craig of the *Bedfordshire*.

Several years ago, a Morehead City dive-shop owner discovered the wreck of the *Bedfordshire*. It lies in a hundred feet of water approximately 36 miles

The British Cemetery

from Beaufort Inlet. Divers report that the wreckage is strewn across the ocean bottom—mute testimony to its utter destruction by the torpedo.

It was only a few weeks after the trawler went down, however, that the most important part of its wreckage was discovered. Aycock Brown was walking on a dock in the mainland village of Atlantic when he spotted a white board approximately fifteen feet long lying on the dock. Black letters on the board spelled *BEDFORDSHIRE*. Brown learned that it had washed ashore near the old Coast Guard station on Core Banks.

Continue a short distance past the British Cemetery to the Wahab Cemetery, typical of many of the overgrown family burial plots found near some of the village homes. This cemetery contains the graves of many old Ocracoke families. Shaded by a giant water oak, the Wahab Cemetery has an interesting old gravestone which erroneously shows that the deceased died before he was born.

From the cemeteries, retrace your route to Silver Lake, turn left, and walk along the waterfront. At the post office, turn south onto Howard Street.

Howard Street is the most historic avenue in Ocracoke. Shaded by cedars and majestic water oaks adorned with Spanish moss, it is lined with some of the oldest houses in the village. Most are neat white clapboard structures surrounded by picket fences. They are characteristic of the old seacoast design: a simple two-story boxlike shape with an angled roof, a front porch on one side, and a perpendicular addition on the other. One interesting feature common to many of these houses is the sturdy foundation of shipwreck timbers of heart pine or heart cedar.

You will notice large cisterns in the yards of these houses—relics of a time not so long ago when Ocracokers depended on rainwater as their only source of fresh water. Water was fed into the cisterns from rooftop downspouts that can still be seen hanging from some of the houses.

Howard Street is named for William Howard, to whom the island was sold in 1759. From this man descended the Howard family that has lived on the island ever since. Some members of the family claim that their ancestor was the same William Howard who was Blackbeard's quartermaster at a young age.

After 0.2 mile, Howard Street ends at Schoolhouse Road. Turn left onto Schoolhouse Road. Near the junction of the two streets is Ocracoke United

Howard Street

Methodist Church. Inside this church with its white pews is a cross memorializing James Baugham Gaskill, a native son of Ocracoke. It has often been written that truth is stranger than fiction. Jim Gaskill's real-life story, with more twists of fate than are found in the best novels, unfolded during the early days of World War II.

Born in the village just after World War I, Gaskill spent his childhood and teenage years at the Pamlico Inn, operated by his parents as one of the island's earliest tourist facilities. After his mother died in 1940, he did as many Ocracokers have done throughout the island's history: he went to sea. Young Gaskill was only twenty-two years old when America's Pacific fleet was annihilated at Pearl Harbor. By early 1942, he had attained the rank of second mate in the United States Merchant Marine.

During the Nazi U-boat assaults on shipping along the North Carolina coast, the *Caribsea* was one of the vessels transporting freight between New York and the Caribbean. When she left Cuba en route to Norfolk in early

March 1942, the 251-foot freighter was transporting a valuable load of manganese and balsa wood. On board was Second Mate Jim Gaskill.

On the night of March 11, the *Caribsea* was nearing the "Torpedo Junction" of the North Carolina coast when it encountered a storm. On the 8:00 P.M.-to-midnight watch stood Gaskill. It was his custom to be on the bridge when the beacon of the Ocracoke Lighthouse greeted his ship as it passed his home.

By the time he was relieved, his strength was drained by the strain of keeping a constant vigil for U-boats on a night of poor visibility. Leaving his post, he passed through the door of the bridge, over which hung eight picture frames containing the licenses of the officers of the ship.

Ocracoke United Methodist Church

Jim had hardly put his weary head on his pillow when the *U-152* caught sight of the *Caribsea*. In an instant, the submarine fired two torpedoes from her bow tubes with deadly accuracy. They tore into the starboard side of the ship at almost the same time. There was no opportunity for lifeboats to be launched, because the *Caribsea* was on the floor of the Atlantic three minutes after the torpedo attack. Miraculously, seven of the twenty-eight men on board survived the sinking, but Jim Gaskill was not one of them.

Residents of Ocracoke were by this time accustomed to finding wreckage on the island shore from the almost daily U-boat kills. Ironically, two unusual pieces of wreckage from the *Caribsea* found their way to Ocracoke.

On the ocean side of the island, the only officer's license frame to withstand the attack was found. That framed license belonged to James Baugham Gaskill. Family members on the island decided that the frame should be used to memorialize Jim. A portion of the frame and other pieces of wreckage from Gaskill's doomed ship were used to craft a cross atop a pedestal. An engraved plaque placed on the pedestal bears the following message: "In memory of Capt. James B. Gaskill, July 2, 1919–March 11, 1942. This cross constructed from salvage from the ship upon which Capt. Gaskill lost his life." Today, the cross is displayed on the altar of Ocracoke United Methodist Church.

About the same time that Jim's framed license was found on the beach, a piece of wreckage floated up to the dock of the Pamlico Inn, where Jim had grown up. Almost unbelievably, the name plate of the *Caribsea*, measuring

Grave marker of James B. Gaskill

only eighteen inches by five feet, had survived the torpedo blast, had floated on the ocean through Ocracoke Inlet and into Pamlico Sound, and had come to rest at Gaskill's boyhood home. Some people say that it was Gaskill's cousin who found the nameplate. The nameplate is now on public display at the National Park Service visitor center in the village.

Although the body of Jim Gaskill was never found, the legend holds that he came home when the two bizarre pieces of wreckage were found at Ocracoke. A grave marker bearing his name can be seen today in a very special place: in the shadow of the Ocracoke Lighthouse, the light Jim always looked for as his ship passed home.

Just east of the church stands Ocracoke School, the lone school in the village. With a total enrollment from kindergarten through twelfth grade of only ninety to a hundred students, the tiny school remains the smallest in all of North Carolina. Its largest graduating class has been thirteen.

After visiting the church and the schoolhouse, walk 0.1 mile west on Schoolhouse Road, cross N.C. 12, and proceed 0.4 mile west on S.R. 1326 to the lighthouse.

For more than 150 years, the most prominent landmark on Ocracoke Island has been this striking white tower. Since 1823, the seventy-six-foot conical lighthouse has guided mariners along the treacherous coast. Unlike most of North Carolina's famed lighthouses, which are all-brick structures, the exterior of the Ocracoke Lighthouse is covered in masonry. It has sported its neat whitewashed appearance since it was first constructed. The cost of construction, including the keeper's dwelling, was $11,359.35.

Extensive repairs were made to the tower in 1868, and a second story was added to the keeper's dwelling in 1887.

As part of the nation's desperate attempt to stem the tide of the U-boat terror of 1942, a red lamp was used to "cover the beam" in an attempt to confuse the submarines.

After World War II, the lighthouse underwent a major renovation. The old wooden stairs were replaced with a spiral stairway made of steel, and the keeper's dwelling was remodeled for use by officers at the Ocracoke Coast Guard Station. Lighthouse keepers lived in the dwelling until 1946, when the light was fully automated.

For as long as tourists have been coming to Ocracoke, the squat, white tower has stood above the beautiful village. Paintings and photographs of the lighthouse can be seen on walls all around the world. While famous North Carolinian Josephus Daniels served as United States ambassador to Mexico, an Aycock Brown photograph of the venerable light was proudly displayed on the wall of the American embassy in Mexico City.

Located in the heart of the village, the lighthouse stands about 0.75 mile from the sound. It is listed on the National Register of Historic Places.

Since World War II, the light has been closed to the public. On occasion, however, a National Park Service ranger opens the door at the five-foot-thick base to allow the public to admire the unusual construction of the light—the interior wall is straight, while the exterior wall slopes inward from the base to the top. This phenomenon resulted from laying fewer and fewer courses of brick as the tower rose.

Ocracoke Lighthouse

At present, the lighthouse is equipped with an 8,000-candlepower fixed white light, visible up to 14 miles at sea. Through automation, the light burns from late afternoon to early morning. A white picket fence encloses the entire lighthouse complex. A turnoff for parking is provided near the light.

As one of America's great historic lighthouses, the Ocracoke Lighthouse can claim many superlatives. It is the oldest operational lighthouse in North Carolina and the second oldest in the United States. It is also the shortest navigational light on the Atlantic coast.

Continue west 0.25 mile from the lighthouse to the point where the road loops on the forested western end of the village. Springers Point lies less than 0.4 mile to the south, across private property. There, the shore of the sound faces a navigable channel called Teach's Hole, once the home harbor of Edward Teach, better known as Blackbeard.

Although Ocracoke has a national reputation as a place to get away from it all, the island's greatest claim to fame is an event that occurred more than 275 years ago. For most of 1718, the fiercest and most infamous pirate in American history used the channel that bears his name as his base of operations.

Blackbeard's reign of terror on coastal shipping, as well as the sympathy he received from some colonial officials in North Carolina, caused residents of the colony to turn to Governor Alexander Spotswood of Virginia for help. In November 1718, two small sloops manned by fifty-four crewmen from two British warships set sail from the James River to Ocracoke. Lieutenant Robert Maynard commanded the expedition, which reached its destination on the night of November 21. Because of darkness, Maynard decided to wait until high tide the next morning to attack Blackbeard's famous ship, *Adventure*.

When Maynard sought out the pirate, he found the *Adventure* in its customary hiding place, Teach's Hole. As the two vessels from Virginia approached the pirate ship, Blackbeard reportedly greeted Lieutenant Maynard, "Damn you for villains, who are you?" The British officer promptly hoisted the ensign of the Royal Navy, after which Blackbeard's heavily armed ship fired a broadside which killed a number of Maynard's men, including the commander of the smaller sloop.

With the smaller of his two vessels disabled, and fearing another broadside, Maynard ordered all of his men below. As Maynard's sloop drifted near the pirate ship, Blackbeard saw that only Maynard and his helmsman were on the deck. When the ships made contact, Blackbeard ordered his men to toss "grenados"—homemade grenades made of bottles filled with gunpowder and iron shrapnel—onto the deck of the sloop. As the grenades exploded, Blackbeard led his men onto the British ship. Maynard's men then charged to the deck from below, and a bloodbath ensued.

Blackbeard and Maynard squared off against each other, firing their pistols almost simultaneously. Maynard's aim was true, and Blackbeard suffered a wound. Undaunted, the fierce pirate drew his cutlass and dueled with Maynard until the lieutenant's weapon broke. As Maynard attempted to fire his pistol to ward off his attacker, one of the British crewmen came to his rescue by slashing deep into Blackbeard's neck with his sword. Bleeding profusely from the neck wound and the gunshot, Blackbeard fought on amid bodies of the dead and wounded who had fallen earlier in the fray. As blood dripped from the deck of the sloop, the nearby waters were tinted red.

Blackbeard seemed indefatigable as he withstood wound after wound. It was not until he had suffered an assortment of twenty-three cuts, gashes, slits, and gunshots that he fell forward onto the deck. His fellow pirates jumped overboard, but they were quickly captured.

As proof of his great feat, Maynard severed Blackbeard's head. Local legend holds that the headless corpse swam around the sloop seven times after it was pushed overboard. Maynard displayed the head from the bowsprit as he sailed up the Pamlico River to Bath.

Blackbeard was not only the best-known buccaneer of the golden age of piracy, but also one of the most successful. What, then, happened to the vast loot that he captured during his reign of terror on the high seas? Some historians have speculated that because of Blackbeard's lavish lifestyle and his penchant for free spending, he may have left no riches. As for the whereabouts of his treasure, Blackbeard said shortly before his death that nobody but he and the devil knew. Nevertheless, since the pirate's death, treasure hunters have searched for it up and down the Atlantic coast from New England to Florida, as well as in the Caribbean. So strong were the rumors of treasure buried on the central coast of Georgia that an island there was named and is still known as Blackbeard Island. The only known treasure which probably belonged to Blackbeard was found on an island off the coast of New Hampshire in the early part of the nineteenth century and during World War II.

During a significant portion of his short career in piracy, Blackbeard called the North Carolina coast home. It would therefore stand to reason that if he buried treasure, he would have stashed some in his home colony. Numerous stories and legends have been told of a number of hiding spots in North Carolina.

At Plum Point, just south of Bath on Back Creek in Beaufort County, treasure was buried at some time in the past. In the 1920s, a startling discovery was made there in the vicinity of the former site of one of Blackbeard's homes. A vault of crude design revealed rust marks outlining the spot where a large chest had been implanted in the walls of brick. Who took the chest, when it was discovered, and what it contained are unknown. Yet residents of the Bath area maintain that the contents of the chest were a portion of Blackbeard's treasure.

Another incident fueled the belief that his treasure was hidden in the environs of Bath. While plowing a field years ago, a farmer near the ancient village unearthed numerous gold and silver coins that were very old and foreign in origin.

Blackbeard is alleged to have had a sister who lived near the present-day town of Grimesland, located on the Tar River about 10 miles east of

Greenville. It is debatable as to whether the woman was even related to the pirate, but it is known that Blackbeard visited her at her farm on a regular basis. At the farm, an ancient cypress tree with roots extending into the river stood above all nearby trees. Known as "Old Table Top," the tree served as a lookout station from which Blackbeard's men could monitor activity on the Tar River. Excitement grew in 1933, when a man excavated a riverbank close to the site of the old tree and found a small iron pot containing old silver coins that could have been buried by Blackbeard. However, no further discoveries are known to have been made on the river.

A number of spots along either side of the Chowan River are reputed to be sites of the buried treasure of Blackbeard. Blounts Creek, Catherine Creek, and Bennetts Creek are sites mentioned in local legend. Oral tradition maintains that Blackbeard and his crew threw a large chest overboard and into the river at the mouth of Spikes Creek in Gates County.

One of the most interesting spots where Blackbeard is said to have buried his treasure was the place he met his demise: Teach's Hole. Numerous individuals and groups have searched the island near where the pirate often holed up while his ships were tarred and caulked. No treasure discovery has ever been reported at Teach's Hole. (For further information on Blackbeard, see The Great Dismal Swamp Tour, page 55, The Northern Pamlico River Tour, page 291-94, and The Southern Pamlico River Tour, page 329-30.)

Return to the lighthouse and continue east along S.R. 1326. Near the intersection with N.C. 12 stands the most historic of all the visitor facilities in the village. The Island Inn and Dining Room is the oldest building on Ocracoke currently used for public lodging. In 1901, the Odd Fellows built the original part of the current complex, its three-story center section. For a time, the first floor was used as the island's public school. Many of Ocracoke's senior citizens attended school here.

Turn north off S.R. 1326 onto N.C. 12 and proceed along the shore of Silver Lake. Along this route, it is often possible to see one of the most colorful wildflowers on the North Carolina coast. Better known as the Joe Bell, the gaillardia is a hardy daisylike plant that exhibits its beauty close to the shore. It maintains its bloom—a golden center rimmed by red petals—from April until December.

How the flower came to be known as the Joe Bell is explained in a bitter-sweet legend from Ocracoke. To the distinguished Bell family from nearby mainland Washington was born a son named Joe. After Joe grew to man-hood, he brought great concern to his family when he fell in love with a young lady who did not meet their standards. In order to put a damper on the romance, the family sent Joe Bell to Europe on business. Upon his return to North Carolina, Joe was dismayed to discover that his true love had married another in his absence.

Heartbroken, Joe had no desire to remain in Washington, where his former sweetheart lived with her husband. After searching for a place of solitude, the jilted young man settled at Ocracoke. Joe quickly gained favor with the local residents. Respected by islanders because of his education and business experience, he was asked to serve as the local magistrate. Despite his attempts to do a good job, Joe failed miserably. Accordingly, he withdrew from the mainstream of island life, but he never lost the respect and affection of the residents of Ocracoke. They often saw him along the sandy island roads with bunches of gaillardias. To take care of Joe, the islanders left baskets of food at his door. When they returned for their baskets, Joe had filled them with gaillardias.

The love affair between Joe and the people of Ocracoke ended one day when he was found dead in his fishing boat. Inside the craft, around his body, were the beautiful red-and-yellow flowers which today carry his name.

Over the years, artists, writers, and people simply attempting to get away from the dog-eat-dog world have been attracted to Ocracoke for the same reason Joe Bell sought refuge here: isolation. Throughout its history, Ocracoke has served as North Carolina's busiest port, as a World War II naval base, and as an integral part of the first national seashore. Yet despite its enduring importance to North Carolina and the nation, the island has refused to yield the isolation which has long been its hallmark. In fact, walking the shaded route through the village along the rim of the lake reinforces the sense of isolation that pervades the place.

One of many creeks on Ocracoke Island

As amazing as it may seem, the little village of Ocracoke, despite being unincorporated, is the most populous town in all of Hyde County. Since 1836, the mainland town of Swan Quarter has remained the seat of Hyde County government, which has only served to accentuate Ocracoke's isolation.

In the 1950s, before most island residents owned automobiles, Ocracokers who had to do business in the county seat were faced with a terrific dilemma. For example, if an islander found it necessary to go to the courthouse in Swan Quarter, he first caught the mailboat to the mainland town of Atlantic, in northeastern Carteret County. But since there was no bus service at Atlantic, the Ocracoker had to hire a taxi or hitch rides to Beaufort, the county seat of Carteret County, some 30 miles to the south. Bus service between Beaufort and New Bern, a distance of 38 miles, was available. From New Bern, the county seat of Craven County, the Ocracoker took a 35-mile bus trip to Washington, the county seat of Beaufort County. From Washington, a final bus ride of 50 miles put the islander in Swan Quarter. In the process, he had passed through the county seats of three other counties before he reached his own.

It is approximately 0.5 mile on N.C. 12 from S.R. 1326 to the ferry landing, on the northern shore of Silver Lake.

For most visitors to Ocracoke, the means of access is one of the three state-operated ferries serving the island.

One ferry runs from the village of Hatteras, near the southern end of

Hatteras Island, to the northern end of Ocracoke Island, where this tour began.

The other two ferries depart from Silver Lake.

The older of these two routes is the Ocracoke–Cedar Island run, which began as a private operation from the mainland town of Atlantic in 1960. The first ferry on this route, the *Sea Level*, was a gift to the people of North Carolina from the Taylor brothers of the mainland town of Sealevel. On February 9, 1961, the North Carolina Highway Commission purchased the ferry, and the state operation began on May 1, 1961. Three years later, the Cedar Island landing was completed, and a second daily crossing was added. Because of the popularity of this crossing, reservations—which may be made thirty days in advance—are almost essential during the summer season. It takes approximately two hours and fifteen minutes to cross Pamlico Sound. During the crossing, passengers lose sight of land entirely, and it is easy to believe that the ferry is on the open seas.

In 1977, the North Carolina General Assembly enacted legislation to institute the second ferry route from Silver Lake. This resulted from an outcry by Ocracoke residents for a more direct route to their county seat. The crossing time to Swan Quarter is two and a half hours.

Fares are charged for both ferry routes from Silver Lake.

The tour ends here, at the ferry landing.

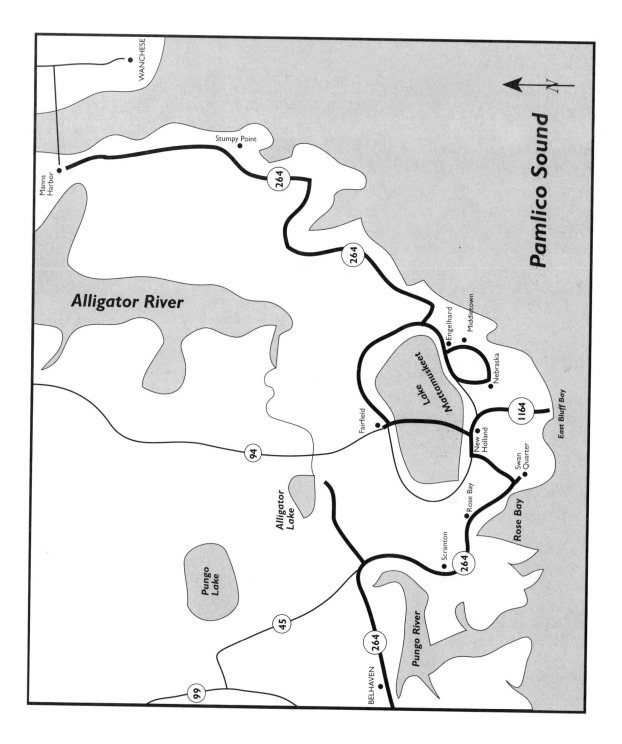

The Pamlico Sound Tour

This tour begins just west of the Dare County fishing village of Manns Harbor and runs south to Stumpy Point, then crosses into Hyde County and visits Engelhard and the tiny sound-side villages of Middletown, and Nebraska. Next, it skirts a portion of Lake Mattamuskeet to reach Fairfield, then crosses the lake on a causeway to New Holland. It visits Swan Quarter and skirts a portion of Alligator Lake before ending at Belhaven, located on the Intracoastal Waterway in Beaufort County.

Among the highlights of the tour are the great farming experiment at Lake Mattamuskeet, Providence United Methodist Church in Swan Quarter, Swan Quarter National Wildlife Refuge, the story of John Maynard Smith and his airplane, the River Forest Manor, and the Belhaven Memorial Museum.

Total mileage: approximately 134 miles.

This tour begins at the intersection of U.S. 264 and U.S. 64 approximately 2 miles west of the mainland Dare County village of Manns Harbor. Proceed south on U.S. 264 for the drive through the desolate wilderness of Alligator River National Wildlife Refuge to the small sound-side community of Stumpy Point.

On either side of the roadway are canals which hold the dark, reflective waters of the nearby swamps. On the west side, the jungle and thickets stretch to the Alligator River and beyond—a wide swath of more than 20 miles without a single human inhabitant. Several miles beyond the forbidding wilderness on the east side of the road lie Croatan and Pamlico sounds. Near the sound shore are the Roanoke Marshes, an extensive marshy area stretching almost 6 miles in length.

Stumpy Point, a picturesque old fishing village, is the only outpost in the wilderness area bordering U.S. 264 along its 38-mile run from Manns Harbor to Engelhard. To reach Stumpy Point, turn east off U.S. 264 onto S.R. 1100 after 12.5 miles and follow S.R. 1100 for 2.3 miles into the heart of the community.

Majestically situated on a peninsula that extends into Pamlico Sound and Stumpy Point Bay, the village features a beautiful working waterfront. Stumpy Point Bay has an almost round shape, giving a hint that it was a lake in times past. On the Moseley map of 1733, it appears as Stumpy Point Lake. Gradually, erosion opened the lake into the sound. Today, the bay provides an excellent harbor for the sizable commercial fleet that docks here.

Exactly when the crescent-shaped village was settled is not known. Although Stumpy Point was first shown on the John Lawson map of 1709, there is no evidence that the village or even a settlement was located here at the time. Most likely, the reference was to the point of land. An established local tradition claims that Stumpy Point received its name from Indians who observed a large number of stumps protruding from the shoreline.

Stumpy Point Bay

It is likely that Stumpy Point was settled in the eighteenth century by people from Roanoke Island and the Outer Banks. Soon after the village took root, its upper and lower ends acquired distinct place names which remain in use today: Tadmore and Drain Point.

Prior to the Civil War, the economy of Stumpy Point was dominated by farming. Planters cleared the fertile land on the fringes of the Great Alligator Swamp. Through a remarkable engineering feat, they constructed an intricate network of canals that transformed the surrounding swamp into profitable farmlands. Some of these ancient canals are in evidence today.

Following the war, fishing gradually supplanted agriculture as the primary means of livelihood in the community. By the end of the nineteenth century, the village had become an important center for shad fishing. Stumpy Point shad were highly sought-after in New York and distant markets—so much so that by 1920, the village was known as the "Shad Capital of the World."

Over the past two centuries, residents of Stumpy Point have interwoven the traditions of the Outer Banks with their own lore and legends. For many years, the villagers celebrated Olde Christmas on January 6, a custom brought across the sound from Hatteras Island. (For more information on Olde Christmas, see The Cape Hatteras Tour, page 218–19.) And some Stumpy Pointers claim even today that a light seen over the Little Dismal Swamp is Teach's Light. This eerie light is said to be guarding one of Blackbeard's treasures.

Retrace your route on S.R. 1100 to U.S. 264 and continue south.

In 1950, the United States Army Corps of Engineers dredged a channel through the bay which allows boats to dock at the Stumpy Point fish houses adjacent to U.S. 264. Most highway travelers see only this small portion of the village of three hundred inhabitants.

As you proceed U.S. 264, the wilderness will again engulf both sides of the road. Since the mid-1980s, the area surrounding Stumpy Point has been in the middle of a controversy over the United States Navy's plans to expand its Dare County bombing range. The tour route passes near the boundary of the range, which covers more than fifty thousand acres of wilderness. Each year in July, the navy holds an open house at the range. The public can use the occasion to watch bombers carry out practice missions on outdated pieces of military equipment. Range personnel are on hand to answer questions.

Until 1926, Stumpy Point was virtually inaccessible except by water. In that year, a road was constructed by Dare County through the swamps to Engelhard. Construction funds were borrowed from the Metropolitan Life Insurance Company, which had acquired much of the area wilderness from the failed Dare Lumber Company. To repay the loan, the county raised taxes on the extensive holdings of the insurance company.

It is 26 miles from Stumpy Point to Engelhard. About halfway into the route, the highway crosses into mainland Hyde County. Although blessed with magnificent water resources, mainland Hyde is devoid of resorts. As one of the least populated counties in North Carolina, Hyde has no town with more than several hundred permanent residents.

From the county line south to Engelhard, U.S. 264 passes through 12 miles of almost uninhabited land alternating between swamps and pocosins, forests, and low savannas.

The village of Engelhard appears as the highway makes a close approach to Pamlico Sound. Located at the head of Far Creek, this charming nineteenth-century community is separated from the sound by the creek and marshland. Adding to its salty flavor are a number of canals punctuating the landscape. For more than a century, the sea and sound have provided the primary source of income for Engelhard residents.

Continue on U.S. 264 west from Engelhard. Most of the population of mainland Hyde County is found along the 30-mile run to Scranton. Along the highway west and south of Engelhard are a number of interesting structures that date from the nineteenth century, including more than a dozen picturesque churches and farmhouses.

Approximately 2.4 miles southwest of Engelhard stands Wynne's Folly, an unusual house built by Richard Wynne of Philadelphia. Its extremely large windows gave the house its name.

Proceed 1 mile south on U.S. 264 to the tiny crossroads community of Amity. Two historic church buildings are located in the village near the junction of U.S. 264 and S.R. 1107.

On the northwestern side of the highway is Amity Methodist Church, built around 1852.

Nearby stands Saint George's Episcopal Church, constructed in 1874. The adjacent cemetery contains an interesting grave. A marker at the plot is the exact size of a coffin, but it bears no inscription. Buried in the grave is A. L. Creedle, who died in 1884 at the age of thirty-five. His coffin was buried vertically at his request. Creedle was ill for a long period prior to his death, and one of his last wishes was that he be buried standing up because he had grown "tired of lying down for such a long time."

Turn left, or east, on S.R. 1107 and drive 1.5 miles to Middletown, a pretty little village at the head of Middletown Creek, which flows to Pamlico Sound. Incorporated in 1787, this fishing community is one of the oldest settlements in Hyde County.

At the Middletown waterfront, turn southwest onto S.R. 1110 and drive 3.8 miles to the village of Nebraska. Along this route, the vast fields of corn lend the impression that you are indeed traveling in the Midwest, rather than in coastal North Carolina.

Although Nebraska is 2 miles inland from the sound, it was once a prosperous port. Indeed, at one time, the small town was the only water outlet for the agricultural products of eastern Hyde County. A winding 2.5-mile canal once used by commercial boats still connects the town with Wyesocking Bay, on the sound. Most likely named for the Kansas-Nebraska Act of 1854, Nebraska was incorporated the following year.

Approximately 0.9 mile west of Nebraska, turn right, or north, off S.R. 1110 onto S.R. 1116. It is 1.2 miles to Lake Landing. Situated near the southeastern shore of Lake Mattamuskeet, this small village has never regained the importance it enjoyed as the county seat more than 150 years

All roads lead to Middletown.

ago. Located in the village is the building which housed Hyde County's old private academy, the forerunner of the public-school system in the county.

At Lake Landing, turn right, or northeast, off S.R. 1116 onto U.S. 264. On the east side of U.S. 264 just north of Lake Landing stands one of the most intriguing structures in coastal North Carolina.

The Octagon House

Known as the Ink Bottle House or the Octagon House, this unusual house was constructed around 1840. Dr. William Sparrow decided to build the house after his previous home was destroyed by a hurricane. He believed that its eight-sided design would provide protection against powerful winds. With the exception of the windows and doors, no posts were used in its construction. Instead, the home was constructed of overlapping timbers, much like a rail fence. Cypress shingles now cover the exterior. A huge octagonal chimney runs through the center of the structure and opens into fireplaces in the four rooms. In recent years, a joint effort of state and local agencies has restored the house, which is listed on the National Register of Historic Places.

Follow U.S. 264 as it passes back through Amity on a 4.2-mile run to the junction with S.R. 1311. Turn northwest onto S.R. 1311 for a semicircular drive along the eastern and northern shores of Lake Mattamuskeet.

This scenic drive through the fertile agricultural lands of Hyde County crosses a number of drainage canals, some of which were constructed in antebellum times, when the county was known as "the Granary of North Carolina." The road closely hugs the lakeshore, yielding glimpses of the largest natural lake in North Carolina.

After 13.8 miles on S.R. 1311, you will reach the junction with N.C. 94 on the north shore of the lake. Turn north onto N.C. 94 and drive 0.5 mile to the handsome village of Fairfield.

Besides the tiny community of Ponzer, far to the west on the Pungo River, Fairfield is the only populated place in the northern half of mainland Hyde County. Incorporated in 1885, this coastal farming community has been little touched by the changes that have come to the North Carolina coast since World War II. It is said to have received its name from the "fair fields" of crops in the nearby reclaimed swampland.

A canal linking the village with the Alligator River to the north was forged by slave labor prior to the Civil War. Well into the twentieth century, steamer traffic from Elizabeth City continued to use the canal to call on Fairfield. After the Alligator River cut of the Intracoastal Waterway rendered the canal obsolete by steering water traffic away from the town, Fairfield settled down to its agricultural way of life.

A number of structures in the town are of historic and architectural interest.

Located on the western side of N.C. 94 near the downtown crossroads, Fairfield United Methodist Church is virtually unaltered from when it was constructed in 1877. Original furnishings embellish its interior. Outside, a beautiful three-tiered belfry highlights the handsome appearance of this Gothic Revival building.

Two frame commercial buildings dating from the nineteenth century are the main features of Fairfield's commercial district, located on the north side of S.R. 1305 near its junction with N.C. 94—the downtown crossroads.

If you have time to explore, these streets offer several exquisite nineteenth-

Lake Mattamuskeet

TOURING THE BACKROADS OF NORTH CAROLINA'S UPPER COAST

century residences, appealing reminders of a more prosperous time in Fairfield's past.

Turn around and head south on N.C. 94. Just south of the village, N.C. 94 crosses Lake Mattamuskeet via a causeway. This pleasant 6.1-mile drive offers the best view of the lake from an automobile. Yet only from the air is it possible to comprehend the vast size of the state's largest natural lake. Stretching more than 18 miles in length and 6 miles in width, the lake covers 40,000 acres. The water level is subject to great fluctuation. Ironically, the expansive lake is extremely shallow. Its average depth is only 2.5 feet and its maximum depth 5 feet.

Fairfield United Methodist Church

Beautiful cypress trees and freshwater wetlands rim the shoreline. Numerous canals, some of which were dug by slave labor, radiate from all sides of the lake into the Hyde County countryside. They continue to drain water from the lake to irrigate nearby farmlands.

Strict regulations now govern drainage into the lake. When the United States Fish and Wildlife Service took control of the lake in 1974, the surrounding farmlands were made part of a lake drainage district. Today, only those lands, most of which have been farmed for generations, are allowed drainage into the lake.

Lake Mattamuskeet is thought by many to be one of the Carolina bay lakes. Deriving their name from the area of their greatest concentration and from the place where they were first studied, the Carolina bays number more than half a million lakes along the Atlantic seaboard from New Jersey to Florida. These peat-filled swamps range in size from four acres to thousands of acres.

Scientists have never been able to agree on Lake Mattamuskeet's origin. There is no question, however, as to the origin of its name. It came from the Algonquin Indians, who hunted the lake area long before the arrival of white explorers. In their language, the word *mattamuskeet* meant "dry dust."

The Indians fostered a legend concerning the formation of the lake.

Long, long ago, the Indians inhabiting the area now covered by the lake were blessed with an abundance of game, fish, fruits, and vegetables until an extreme drought came. Suddenly, the animals died of thirst or ran away in search of water. Streams and creeks where the Indians had once fished dried up. Fields that once yielded maize and other crops in copious quantities were parched.

As the drought lingered for several years, the Indians grew desperate for food, some of their number dying of starvation. As a last resort, the survivors built a great ceremonial bonfire to appease the rain gods. To the dismay of the Indians, the gods were outraged. Fanned by strong winds, the fire spread into the nearby forests. For a year, the conflagration raged.

Once again, the Indians attempted to appease the gods. When they selected their finest young brave to be offered as a human sacrifice, a beautiful Indian maiden interceded on his behalf. Kneeling at a sacrificial altar, she prayed to the Great Spirit to save the brave and her perishing people.

After her invocation, a star fell to the earth, and rain soon followed. Days and days of rain quenched the fire. Great holes burned in the earth by the fire were filled, forming a great inland sea. Once again, large birds floated on the limpid waters teeming with fish. Deer, bear, and other game took up residence along the lakeshore. Fields flourished with crops.

Even though the Indian legend has no basis in fact, some scientists have theorized that the lake may have been born of fire. Evidence supporting this theory has come from the shallow bottom—ancient charred tree trunks have been pulled from Mattamuskeet. Because the local landscape is characterized by peaty soil which burns for months at a time, scientists adhering to the fire theory argue that the lake was formed by a great fire which burned deep into the soil.

On the other hand, there are some scientists who believe that the lake formed naturally in a juniper swamp.

When you reach the southern side of the lake, turn left, or east, off N.C. 94 onto U.S. 264 and drive 2.3 miles to New Holland. Located near the midpoint of the south shore, this community bears mute testimony to the great project for which it was headquarters more than a half-century ago.

When Thomas Pollock explored the area around Lake Mattamuskeet in 1713, he described the terrain as being "about 100 miles in length and of considerable breadth, all in a manner of lakes, quagmires, and cane swamps . . . one of the greatest deserts in the world." Pollock would never have believed that almost exactly two centuries later, the lake bed and surrounding areas would for a short time be the scene of an agricultural miracle that attracted experts from around the globe.

Although nothing came from a pre–Civil War proposal by the state to drain the enormous, saucer-shaped lake, the idea would not die. Because of the lake's location, those interested in the project realized that any attempt to drain it would be replete with problems. The open waters of Pamlico Sound are 8 miles away, and more than 25 miles separate the lake from the Atlantic. Despite its inland location, the lake is three feet below sea level, and it had no natural outlet.

In 1913, a stock company was formed to empty the lake in order to gain access to the fertile, silty bed. Shortly after the company purchased the lake bottom, it began to go by the name New Holland Farms, Inc. It was so named because the conditions at Mattamuskeet reminded corporate officials of the water and dikes of Holland.

To successfully drain the lake, the largest pumping station ever constructed in the world up to that time was completed on the southern shore in 1915. Four batteries containing four huge pumps each gave the plant the capacity to pump 1,250,000 gallons of water per minute. An extensive system of canals had to be constructed to remove the vast amount of water in the lake and to keep it drained. Some of the main channels were fifty to seventy-five feet wide. From the station, an 8-mile outfall carried the lake water to the sound. Had all the canals of the project been extended in a straight line, they would have been twice the distance from Lake Mattamuskeet to New York City.

Notwithstanding the complexity of the drainage system, the project was doomed to failure.

Another company succeeded New Holland Farms, Inc., but it was unable to resurrect the project. It was then that August Hecksher, a New York multimillionaire and real-estate developer, entered the picture. Hecksher was the man who would determine the lake's future for decades to come. Immediately after acquiring the lake in 1925, he showed his determination to bring the drainage and agricultural enterprise to fruition.

Even though he was in his late seventies when he purchased the lake sight unseen, Hecksher had the means to attain success. He employed Harlan P. Kelsey, a renowned Boston landscape gardener, to draw plans for a new town on the southern shore of the lake. New Holland, as the town was called, was designed with a Dutch motif. Almost overnight, the thirty-acre town sported homes, offices, warehouses, machine shops, a steam plant, an electric plant, and a post office. One of the buildings had an elevator. The centerpiece of the new town was a beautiful twenty-three-room hotel which maintained the Dutch motif down to its silverware.

Twenty-five miles of roads, beautifully adorned with silver maples, were laid out in and around the village. Hyde County's first and only railroad—the New Holland, Higginsport, and Mount Vernon—was constructed to link the town with the Norfolk Southern Railway. Over this 35-mile railway, the bounty from the agricultural project was transported to market.

By 1928, the lake was completely drained.

Hecksher then visited the site for the first time. He elected to engage the outstanding scientific talent of the day to tackle his great agricultural experiment. After an initial limited operation during the 1928 growing season, the yields were nothing short of phenomenal.

In 1929 and the two years that followed, the farming operation was expanded, with outstanding results. On the rich grounds once covered by the lake, between five hundred and six hundred laborers tilled the soil. Here was the largest farm in the eastern United States and one of the largest in the entire world. A number of noted agricultural experts called the reclaimed land the richest in the world. At the height of the operation, fifty-one tractors equipped with headlights were kept busy twelve hours each day. Two crops were harvested annually on the same ground. Only during the months of January and February did the fields lie fallow.

In the spring of 1932, the plantings became more diversified. Almost thirteen thousand acres of a wide variety of crops were being readied for harvest later that summer when the skies opened. Suddenly, in the midst of the deluge, the great pumps failed. Water overflowed the canals and poured into the former lake basin. Ironically, the crops growing in the lake bed were the best in the history of the farm. As water gradually reclaimed the fields, knee-deep mud made it impossible to operate harvesting machinery.

August Hecksher was an astute businessman. He realized that the great experiment, on which $17 million had been expended, was ended. Accordingly, on March 1, 1933, all work ceased. Slowly, Lake Mattamuskeet came

into being once again. Water covered much of the town site, the roads, and the railway.

A year later, the federal government purchased approximately fifty thousand acres of the lake and the surrounding land for a waterfowl sanctuary, and the village of New Holland was relocated to its current site on higher ground.

At New Holland, turn north off U.S. 264 onto S.R. 1330 and drive 0.6 mile to the southern shore of the lake. At the end of the road stands a great ghost of the past. The once-proud pumping station and its tall smokestack stand in silence, symbols of man's failure to best Lake Mattamuskeet.

After the drainage venture failed, the pumping station served as a hunting lodge until 1974. Standing watch over the building and the lake is the 128-foot smokestack, erected in 1926. It was subsequently converted into an observation tower for use by patrons of the lodge.

From a distance, the complex still presents an awe-inspiring sight. However, years of abandonment to the elements have taken their toll.

The tall, slender observation tower resembles a weather-beaten lighthouse. Its circular bands of white and green paint have faded to the extent that they are hardly distinguishable. The spiral staircase installed when the structure was converted to an observation tower has long been closed to visitors.

The administrative offices of Lake Mattamuskeet National Wildlife Refuge were housed in the old pumping station until a new headquarters facility was constructed several years ago. Now, the old building is padlocked and is used for storage.

Inside the once-famous building, there are reminders of its glory days as a hunting lodge. A large ballroom with a two-story ceiling dominated the center of the building. This room hosted many festive occasions, such as weddings and high-school proms. Its walls are lined with built-in closets, interrupted only by a six-foot-wide fireplace. From the ballroom, stairs lead to a lower room highlighted by six double doors with glass panels and arched tops. From that room, lodge guests and visitors could look out onto the pool of water at the intersection of the various drainage canals and the one canal connected directly to the lake.

Outside is a plaque installed at the plant in 1915. It was meant to be a memorial to the people who worked to turn the dream into reality. By a twist of fate, it is now more like an epitaph for the giant, tomblike building and the entire project. Emblazoned on the plaque is the following inscription: "This plant is dedicated to the spirit of co-operation which has here transformed a great lake into dry land and so created a new and fertile principality for the use and possession of man."

Efforts are under way to raise funds to renovate the facility, listed on the National Register of Historic Places, for use as a museum. Although it remains closed to the public, visitors to the wildlife refuge are allowed to picnic on the grounds and hike the nearby trails.

Since 1934, Lake Mattamuskeet and the surrounding marsh and croplands have made up Lake Mattamuskeet National Wildlife Refuge. Encompassing fifty thousand acres, the refuge has an international reputation as a wintering grounds for thousands of waterfowl. Nearly twenty thousand Canada geese and sixty thousand ducks of various kinds seek the protection of the refuge each winter. Almost 20 percent of the entire North American population of these beautiful birds spend their autumns on the lake. In all, more than a hundred thousand waterfowl can be found on the lake on any given day during the height of the season.

Large numbers of birds have been wintering at Mattamuskeet for centuries. Since the lake refilled and the refuge was established, bird-watching has attracted many enthusiasts to the area. In February 1940, watchers spotted an immense flock of mixed blackbirds flying between Washington and Belhaven en route to the refuge. Taking more than twenty minutes to pass, and stretching 7 miles, the flock was conservatively estimated to contain 184,000 birds.

Approximately two hundred different species of birds, including eighty species of nesting birds, have been sighted in the area. Some endangered species, including the bald eagle, have been successfully introduced at the refuge. In late 1985, during the Audubon Society's annual Christmas bird count at the lake, an extremely rare tropical kingbird was sighted. Prior to that time, this robin-sized bird, with its brilliant yellow breast, green back, and brown wings, had never been seen in North Carolina.

Some sixty-six thousand people visit the refuge annually. Duck hunting is allowed on a limited basis. Numerous blinds have been constructed, including an unusual blind for handicapped hunters. Fishing is allowed in the lake and canals. The waters teem with bream, largemouth and striped bass, catfish, carp, and spot. The dry land surrounding the marshy shoreline is the habitat of varying populations of deer, black bear, and bobcats. Hunters and fishermen must comply with all federal and state regulations.

Retrace your route to U.S. 264 at New Holland. Drive directly across U.S. 264; the road becomes S.R. 1164. Proceed south on the unpaved S.R. 1164 toward East Bluff Bay on Pamlico Sound. This route runs parallel to the drainage canal constructed to connect the lake to the sound.

Five miles into the drive, you will enter Gull Rock Game Land. Managed by the North Carolina Wildlife Resources Commission, this extensive preserve provides visitors with an excellent cross section of the various wetland habitats in the county: brackish marshes, low and high pocosins, pond pine woodlands, and hardwood flats. Small populations of black bear and American alligator are found here. Although the preserve covers 18,856 acres, camping is allowed in designated areas only.

Approximately 3 miles after entering Gull Rock Game Land, you will reach the end of S.R. 1164, where you can enjoy a magnificent view of the vast expanse of Pamlico Sound. From this spot, the closest point of land across the sound is Portsmouth Island.

Retrace your route to U.S. 264. Turn left, or west, and follow U.S. 264

for 8.5 miles to its junction with S.R. 1129. Turn south onto S.R. 1129 and proceed 1.1 miles to Swan Quarter.

A visit to Swan Quarter is a trip into the past. Old drainage canals line the streets of this fishing village, which has been the seat of Hyde County government for more than 150 years. The only Civil War skirmish in the county occurred just outside Swan Quarter. On March 4, 1863, New York troops were ambushed by Confederate forces.

Your first stop in the village is Providence United Methodist Church, located on the right at the corner of N.C. 1129 and N.C. 1131. This church rests on a site that has made it one of the most fabled churches in all of coastal North Carolina. The handsome brick structure is descended from a frame structure that was literally moved to the spot by a flood more than a century ago.

In 1873, area Methodists resolved to build a house of worship in the village. Because of the low elevation of the town, they sought high ground for their church. After months of fund-raising, they still did not have enough money to purchase land, so the building committee solicited Sam Sadler, a prosperous landowner, for the donation of a choice lot. Sadler was reluctant to part with a prime piece of real estate. His response was polite, but firm: "I can't help you. I have plans for that land."

To assuage the Methodists' discouragement, H. A. Hayes gave them a nice lot on a side street. Unfortunately, the lot was not much above sea level.

On Sunday, September 16, 1873, a modest wooden church set upon brick pilings was dedicated at the donated spot. A terrifying storm developed on the very night of the dedication. Violent winds destroyed local homes, and the heavy rains and high tides caused the town to be flooded. When the storm winds began to loosen their grip, the villagers still had to deal with the floodwater swirling in the streets.

Suddenly, the turbulent waters caused the new church to float off its pilings. As it began floating up the street, men tied ropes to the building in a vain attempt to halt its movement. Despite their efforts, the church careened off a general store and began to gain speed as it drifted toward the center of town. Unbelievably, at the very moment it reached the intersection with Main Street, the church veered sharply to the right. With men

Swan Quarter waterfront

still trying to stop the runaway building, it proceeded another 2 blocks until it reached what is now Church Street. As if it had a mind of its own, the building settled there on a spot of high ground—on the exact lot that the congregation had first selected.

As soon as the Hyde County Register of Deeds Office opened the next morning, the first person to come calling was Sam Sadler. He deeded the lot to the church at no cost. When asked about his sudden change of mind, Sadler responded, "I had plans for that land, but it appears God has His, too!" Ironically, the church was the only building that was actually moved by the floodwater.

Firmly convinced that God had moved the building to the site, the congregation named it Providence Methodist Church when it was rededicated. As church membership grew, the present brick building was constructed to accommodate the increased attendance, and the original building was sold to W. T. Berry, moved, and used as a barn. When Mr. and Mrs. Berry died, their children donated the venerable building to the church. It was moved back to the church site by conventional means and placed behind the brick building for use as a Sunday school.

Providence United Methodist Church

For many years, Swan Quarter has reigned as the commercial center of mainland Hyde. There are several interesting old commercial buildings on the village streets. Of particular architectural importance is the Hyde County Courthouse, located just beyond the church at the intersection of S.R. 1129 and N.C. 45/S.R. 1132. The building's remodeled Victorian appearance belies its age. Completed in 1850, the structure is one of the few surviving antebellum courthouses in North Carolina. It is listed on the National Register of Historic Places.

Near the courthouse, turn south onto S.R. 1136 to continue to the waterfront. The village's picturesque harbor overlooking Swan Quarter Bay is rimmed by fish and oyster houses. Fishing boats use the harbor as a base for operations in the nearby sound.

Many travelers would not have occasion to visit the village were it not for the state-operated Swan Quarter–Ocracoke Ferry. From the landing on the village waterfront, this ferry provides a shortcut for tourists who want to travel to Ocracoke without making the long trip down the Outer Banks. For the citizens of Hyde County, the ferry links Ocracoke with the seat of local government and the rest of the county.

Within sight of the harbor stands one of the oldest houses in mainland Hyde. Built in 1840, this ten-room structure served as a hospital during the Civil War.

Leaving Swan Quarter, retrace your route to the intersection of S.R. 1129 and N.C. 45/S.R. 1132 and turn left, or west, onto N.C. 45/S.R. 1132. It is 1.5 miles to U.S. 264. Turn west and drive 2.6 miles to the small community of Rose Bay.

Lying south and west of Swan Quarter and parallel to the current route is Swan Quarter National Wildlife Refuge. Established in 1932, the refuge contains 15,501 acres, encompassing island and water area in Pamlico Sound and mainland tracts south of the highway. Much of the mainland acreage is a wilderness dominated by loblolly pine. Near the shores of Juniper Bay, there is an 85-acre stand of old-growth bald cypress which hosts a great blue heron rookery. Along the Pamlico shoreline, the brackish marshes provide a habitat for many species of wildlife. In the adjacent waters, there are oyster beds.

Since the refuge was created, its primary mission has been to provide a wintering sanctuary for migratory waterfowl. Tens of thousands of ducks—including canvasbacks, redheads, and scaup—find their way to the area annually. Approximately nine thousand acres of the refuge are managed by the United States Fish and Wildlife Service as a wilderness area. Most of the remaining acreage is accessible to the public only by water. Off U.S. 264, a pier extends a thousand feet into Rose Bay, providing an opportunity to observe diving ducks and whistling swans.

At the northwestern edge of the refuge, U.S. 264 passes through the small community of Rose Bay, situated at the head of three bays: Rose Bay, Swan Quarter Bay, and Juniper Bay, collectively known as Cecils Harbor at one time. Of particular interest in the tiny village is Rose Bay Baptist Church, a handsome frame edifice constructed just after the Civil War.

Continue to Scranton, located 4.1 miles north of Rose Bay on the west side of the highway. Scranton stands as an outpost on the border of the vast, desolate wilderness and farmlands to the north and east. The waterfront is formed by Scranton Creek, a navigable creek which flows to the Pungo River on the west. Originally named Clark for the owner of a local lumbermill, the town took its present name from another lumbermill that was relocated here from Scranton, Pennsylvania. The Indian village Aquascogoc, shown on the John White map of 1585, was located in this vicinity.

There can be little doubt that the 12-mile drive along U.S. 264 from Swan Quarter to the Intracoastal Waterway near the Beaufort County line is one of the most beautiful on the coast. Tall, stately trees tower above both sides of the road. These magnificent trees provide an almost uninterrupted shade canopy for the entire stretch. When state highway officials proposed to cut about eight hundred of them for safety reasons, the Hyde County Historical Association and concerned citizens prevailed upon the state to spare the trees. To enhance the safety of the route, they placed reflective disks on metal posts along the roadside.

It is approximately 4.5 miles from Scranton to the Wilkinson Creek Bridge over the Intracoastal Waterway. Approximately 0.6 mile beyond the bridge, turn right, or north, off U.S. 264 onto S.R. 1302. After a drive of 0.6 mile, turn right, or northeast, onto S.R. 1303.

Follow S.R. 1303 on a scenic 9.9-mile drive through a vast, uninhabited expanse on the fringes of the Pantego Swamp. After 2.7 miles, the pavement ends. The remainder of the route parallels a network of drainage canals connected to Alligator Lake and the Pungo River. Approximately 5 miles into the route, the road circles around the southern end of Alligator Lake.

Although smaller in size than Lake Mattamuskeet, Alligator Lake is a sizable body of water. Almost 3.5 miles in diameter, it is known locally as New Lake. At its deepest point, it is six or seven feet deep. Drainage from nearby swamps fills the lake. A large portion of Alligator Lake is now a part of Pocosin Lakes National Wildlife Refuge.

S.R. 1303 ends on the upper half of the eastern shore of the lake, where the ancient settlement of New Lake was located.

Retrace your route to U.S. 264 and turn right, or west. The highway crosses the Pungo River after 3.8 miles. More inviting than its name suggests, the community of Leechville provides river access on the west side of the Pungo. Here, Hyde County gives way to Beaufort County.

West of Leechville, U.S. 264 traverses the southern fringes of the Pantego Swamp. Together, the Pantego Swamp, the Dismal Swamp—not to be confused with the Great Dismal Swamp, to the north—and the Great Swamp cover most of the northern quarter of Beaufort County.

Ancient cemetery at New Lake

Most people assume that the Wright brothers' machine was the first airplane ever constructed in North Carolina. However, fourteen years before the history-making flight in Dare County, an impoverished fourteen-year-old farm boy from the Pantego Swamp area may very well have built the first workable model airplane in North Carolina. There is no question that the teenager, John Maynard Smith, fabricated such an airplane in Beaufort County in 1889. President Grover Cleveland saw the machine.

Smith built his airplane by himself on his family's farm. He had little formal education and no scientific manuals or books about the theory of flight to guide him. When he completed his airplane, John Smith had never seen a picture of one. Holding the plane in his hands, Smith was fully convinced that he had built the first.

On Sundays, his neighbors came to the farm to see his amazing contraption.

It was four years after Smith built his airplane that a former neighbor, George Gaskins, saw it. As an official with the Philadelphia Navy Yard,

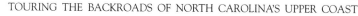

Gaskins was quick to recognize the enormous potential of Smith's brainchild. He tried to bring national attention to the airplane when he took it to Washington for an inspection by President Cleveland in the summer of 1893.

Even though the president of the United States was not impressed, he informed Gaskins that the federal government would be interested if Smith could build an airplane that could carry a man. Perhaps Grover Cleveland never fully appreciated the genius behind Smith's design. About his meeting with Gaskins, the President commented, "There is one fool in North Carolina, I know, who wants to put a propeller on the front of a ship, and any fool knows that if you put a propeller on the front of a ship, it would push the ship backwards."

Dejected, Gaskins returned to Beaufort County to inform Smith of his meeting with the nation's chief executive. He knew that no one in tidewater North Carolina was willing to put up the four hundred dollars necessary to build a full-scale airplane.

Frustration led Smith to put the airplane in his barn. Sometime after that, he showed it to a traveling salesman and other curiosity seekers who were passing through. One day, the airplane was stolen, and it was never recovered. For reasons known only to Smith, he never built another.

Smith lived out the rest of his life in relative anonymity in the Belhaven area as a worker in a barrel factory. He died on January 12, 1963, without fame or fortune.

U.S. 264 divides 5.4 miles west of Leechville. Drive into Belhaven on U.S. 264 Business.

Most visitors are surprised to learn that Belhaven is one of the youngest towns in Beaufort County. Settled in 1890 and incorporated in 1899, the town appears much as it did a century ago.

Ironically, Belhaven came into being as a result of the combined efforts of two men who fought as captains for the opposing armies in the Civil War.

Union cavalry officer John L. Roper envisioned the economic potential of the extensive forests of eastern North Carolina while stationed in the area during the war. By 1886, Roper's company, the John L. Roper Lumber Company, had leased vast tracts of timberland stretching from Washington County south to the Pungo River. To transport the lumber from the area, Roper chartered and built the Albemarle and Pantego Railroad.

Meanwhile, Dr. William J. Bullock was busy practicing medicine in Pantego, a small swamp-side town northwest of Belhaven. During the Civil War, Dr. Bullock had served as captain of Company A of the Fifty-fifth North Carolina Regiment of Confederate troops.

The two men met in 1887. The physician persuaded Roper to extend the railroad through the swamp to the Pungo River at Belhaven. It took two years to complete the railroad, which gave Roper access to Pamlico Sound.

Dr. Bullock dreamed of a town on the banks of the river. He went about establishing his new town by laying out streets and lots. Until 1891, the small settlement was known as Jack's Neck. In that year, the name was changed to Belle Port. Two years later, the name Belhaven was adopted.

Just before the turn of the century, a man who would prove to have a strong local influence for many years came to Belhaven. Railroad magnate John A. Wilkinson incorporated the Belhaven Lumber Company on January 30, 1899, when he opened a medium-sized lumber plant on the Belhaven waterfront. Other lumber companies followed suit, thereby making Belhaven one of the lumber centers of the state.

Wilkinson was also the man behind the River Forest Manor, whose Southern hospitality has made Belhaven known far and wide. This world-famous restaurant, hotel, and marina complex has graced the covers of, and been featured in, numerous travel guides and magazines.

To see the River Forest Manor, simply follow the signs when you reach downtown Belhaven. Located at 600 East Main Street in a quiet, shady setting along the banks of the Pungo, the majestic turn-of-the-century mansion was constructed by Wilkinson from 1899 to 1904. It was built on the site where the very first house in the Belhaven area was constructed in 1868. Eight years after the manor was completed, Wilkinson made a beautiful New Yorker his bride and brought her to Belhaven, where they lived for many years.

River Forest Manor

In 1947, Axon Smith, a Belhaven resident, purchased the estate. Smith had gained valuable experience in hotel management at The Drake and The Palmer House in Chicago. He started a popular buffet, which continues to enjoy widespread acclaim.

Today, luxurious yachts from distant ports tie up at the waterfront marina behind the mansion. The house itself is an opulent reminder of the grand lifestyle and wealth of John A. Wilkinson. Set amid beautifully landscaped grounds, it greets guests with a front porch surmounted by massive, two-story, white Ionic columns. Featuring beautiful oak paneling and ornate hand-carved Italian moldings, the spacious lobby is a visual delight.

All of the guest rooms are elegantly decorated with antiques. Each of the eleven fireplaces in the manor is adorned with a carved oak mantel. The windows sparkle from the cut glass which was leaded into them many years ago. Two of the original bathrooms were built so large that they included oversize tubs big enough for two.

When you have seen the River Forest Manor, retrace your route to where you turned off U.S. 264 Business. Turn south at this intersection and proceed 1 block to Front Street and the waterfront.

The name Belhaven means "beautiful harbor," and no town in coastal North Carolina is more accurately named. This enchanting river town has been blessed with a magnificent natural setting. Bounded on two sides by water—the Pungo River and Pantego Creek—Belhaven possesses a long, picturesque waterfront on the Intracoastal Waterway.

Downtown Belhaven

With a current population of approximately twenty-five hundred, the town has exhibited steady growth over the past several decades. It continues to attract growing numbers of yacht owners plying the Intracoastal Waterway. To meet the demands of this boat traffic, several large marinas have been constructed on the waterfront.

The town's sizable commercial district, located just off the waterfront, has shown little change since the early part of the twentieth century. Corner drugstores and one-of-a-kind hardware stores give the town a charm that is quickly being lost in America. Along its quiet, wooded residential streets are a number of charming homes, many of which are representative of the traditional "down East" style of coastal North Carolina.

Belhaven's third drawing card for tourists—in addition to the River Forest Manor and the Intracoastal Waterway—is located on the second floor of the old city hall on U.S. 264 Business (West Main Street) in the downtown area. With its blue-roofed, tilting bell tower looking out over the harbor, this red-brick building, listed on the National Register of Historic Places, is impossible to miss. Inside, you will have to ascend a flight of wooden stairs to reach the Belhaven Memorial Museum.

Perhaps the best one-word description of this museum is *indescribable*. After touring it, some visitors leave with the impression that they have just seen a miniature Smithsonian Institution. Others who come expecting well-organized displays and high-tech exhibits depart disappointed. However, those who are willing to tolerate the heat in a building without air conditioning, a room filled to the brim with thousands of trivial curiosities, and an atmosphere more akin to a country store than the British Museum of History will be rewarded with one of those unique experiences that make the North Carolina coast such a magical place.

An overview of the museum would be incomplete without a look at its origin. About 1940, in an effort to aid the Red Cross, Eva Blount Way opened her home, one of the oldest in Belhaven, for visitors to inspect the more than ten thousand curiosities she had collected over the previous fifty-five years.

Mrs. Way was not an eccentric pack rat. She simply could not bear to throw anything away. Her unusual assortment of oddities began with a button collection, which grew to include thirty thousand items. From buttons, she moved on to shells, books, magazines, newspapers, paintings, furniture,

Belhaven Memorial Museum

gourds, jewelry, farm tools, baskets, pottery, and military items. The collection eventually outgrew the Way house and expanded into the family barn.

When Mrs. Way died in 1962 at the age of ninety-three, her children donated a large number of the items to the town of Belhaven for use in a museum. Since 1965, these items have been on display in the old city hall building.

A complete list of the items in the museum would fill an entire book. Among the rocks and stones are some from Will Rogers's stable and the wall of Jericho. Many pieces of ordinary-looking metal have interesting origins. One piece is from a United States spacecraft found off the Bahamas. Another was salvaged from the battleship *Maine*. There is also a watch fob fashioned from the first transatlantic cable, laid from Havana to Liverpool in 1857.

A foot bone removed from a Prussian cavalryman in the honor guard of Kaiser Wilhelm is on display. A piece of slate came from the roof of the White House. The bucket with three holes in it came about as the result of a bear's bite.

Every object seems to have an intriguing story behind it. The common workshop drill on display was being used by a neighbor when he was electrocuted while standing barefoot in the rain.

There are other items that some visitors may find offensive. These include numerous preserved animals with a variety of deformities. Among the surgical remains taken from Mrs. Way's neighbors is an enormous tumor stored in a ten-gallon aquarium.

Of all the items exhibited, the two fleas dressed in formal wedding clothes attract the most interest. They stand on pins, the lady flea holding a parasol.

Regardless of personal taste or interest, the museum holds something for everyone. Admission is free, but donations are welcome.

The tour ends at the Belhaven Memorial Museum. From the museum, U.S. 264 leads to Washington, 30 miles to the west, while N.C. 92 leads to Bath, 17 miles to the south.

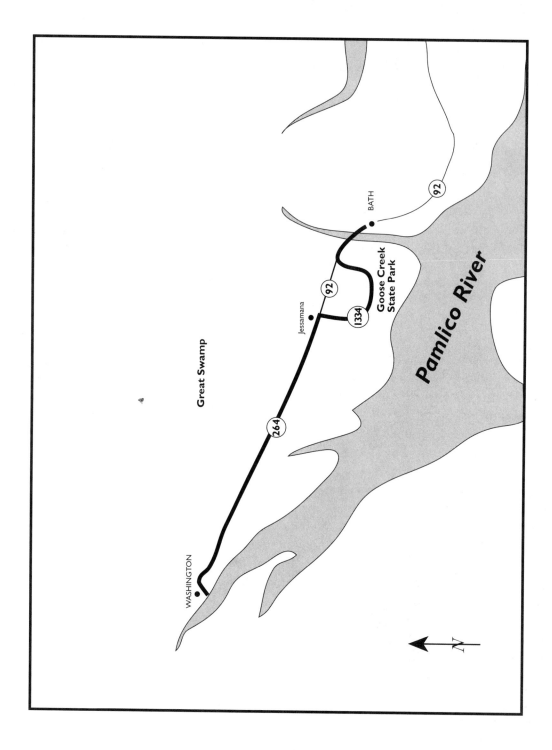

Great Swamp

WASHINGTON

264

Jessamana

92

1334

Goose Creek
State Park

BATH

92

Pamlico River

N

The Northern
Pamlico River Tour

This tour begins with a brief walk around Bath, the oldest town in North Carolina. From the picturesque village on the banks of Back and Bath creeks, it heads west to visit Goose Creek State Park, then continues to the nation's original Washington, where it concludes with another walking tour.

Among the highlights of the tour are Historic Bath State Historic Site, the story of Blackbeard, the story of the mysterious hoofprints, the historic river port of Washington, the story of the De Mille brothers, and the story of *The Showboat*.

Total mileage: approximately 24 miles.

This tour begins at the Historic Bath Visitor Center, located on N.C. 92 (Carteret Street) between Harding and Main streets in the heart of Bath, the oldest town in North Carolina.

Pretty as a picture postcard, the little town of Bath stands as a wonderfully preserved reminder of North Carolina's colonial era. It rests peacefully on the west bank of a peninsula formed by Bath and Back creeks. Most of its 250 or so residents make their living from the water and the land, just as the town's inhabitants have done for almost three centuries.

Bath's waterfront is now quiet and lazy, in sharp contrast to the port facilities that once welcomed governors, Blackbeard, John Lawson, and other famous figures in North Carolina history. The wilderness that surrounded Bath and made it a frontier town was long ago tamed. Now, this historic village lies in the midst of a farming area known for its production of tobacco, corn, and soybeans.

Because Bath's greatness lies in its past, visitors come to sample its storied history. Although no part of the village is without historic structures, the actual historic district encompasses the area bounded by King Street on the east, Bowen Avenue on the north, and Bath Creek on the south and west. Managed by the state of North Carolina since July 1, 1965, the Historic Bath State Historic Site is the centerpiece of the town's treasures of the past.

Bath waterfront

As with most of the early settlements along the North Carolina coast, geography played a vital role in the development of Bath. Because most of the tillable land in the upper Albemarle region had been claimed by the last decade of the seventeenth century, planters were attracted to the fertile lands along the Pamlico River to the south.

Once the shores of the river were settled, the influential planters of the Pamlico soon recognized the need for the development of a trade center in the area. They selected a parcel of high ground on the banks of Bath Creek about a mile north of the point where the creek enters the river. Not only was the site blessed with an excellent natural harbor, but it was also located far enough inland to offer some protection from the terrible hurricanes that raked the Outer Banks.

No copy of the original town plan is known to exist, but it is certain that Bath was laid out by John Lawson, surveyor general to the Crown. On March 8, 1705, Bath became the first incorporated town in North Carolina. Some historians have contended that Bath was named for the English town of the same name. However, it was most likely named for John Granville, the earl of Bath, one of the eight Lords Proprietors of the Carolina colony. In 1676, Governor Archdale created Bath County in the Pamlico area in honor of the earl of Bath.

Most visitors begin their tour of historic Bath at the visitor center on N.C. 92. There is ample public parking adjacent to the center. A free twenty-five-minute film shown at the center acquaints visitors with the history of Bath and the restoration project administered at the facility.

Because of its diminutive size, Bath is best toured by foot. From the parking lot at the visitor center, walk west on N.C. 92 to its intersection with Main Street, an ancient avenue filled with historic treasures. Near the parking lot, a large state historical marker with a map of the village details the long history of Bath.

At the time of its incorporation, Bath had only twelve houses. Yet despite its small size, the town took on commercial importance in the colony. In the early eighteenth century, the navigable inlets north of Cape Hatteras were shoaling up. But Ocracoke Inlet remained open, and it was easily reached from Bath by the Pamlico River and Pamlico Sound. Not surprisingly, Bath became the colony's first official port of entry in the second

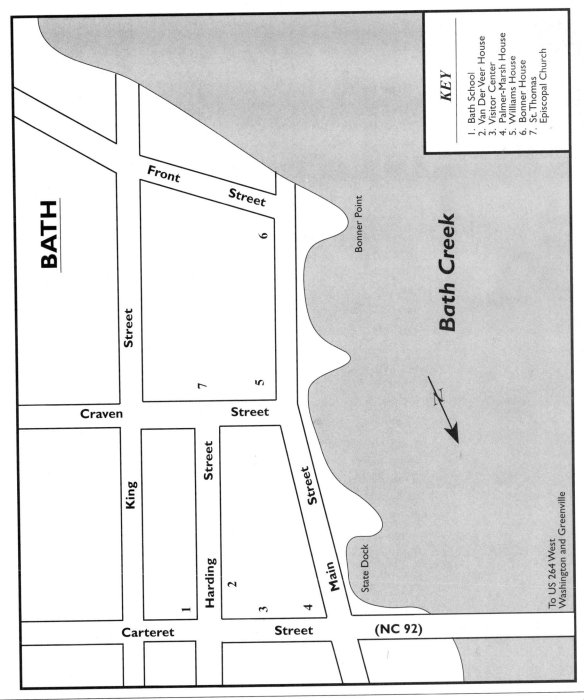

decade of the eighteenth century. Schooners and shallow-draught vessels from England made their way up Bath Creek to the bustling port.

At the traffic light, turn south onto Main Street, which parallels Bath Creek, where the masts of great sailing ships once towered above the waterfront.

Located on the east side of Main Street near its intersection with Carteret, the Palmer-Marsh House is the first of three restored houses owned by Historic Bath State Historic Site. This magnificent townhouse is one of the oldest houses in North Carolina. Not only is it the oldest authenticated house in Bath, but also the oldest dwelling owned by the state.

Michael Coutanche, a French merchant who settled in the colony in 1739, built the two-story structure around 1744. One of the town's commissioners, Coutanche constructed the dwelling on Bath's main thoroughfare in a way that allowed the room nearest the street to be used for business.

In February 1744 and again in April 1752, the colonial assembly met in this house. Colonel Robert Palmer, surveyor general of the colony and collector of the port of Bath, acquired the house in 1764. Following a succession of owners, Jonathan Marsh, a New England merchant and ship owner, purchased the house on June 10, 1802. For more than a century, the Marsh family owned the house.

Henry Ormond purchased the house in the early part of the twentieth century and converted it to a hotel that became the social center of Bath. Famous novelist Edna Ferber stayed in the house for several weeks in 1925 while she gathered material for her bestseller, *Showboat*. Her story later became a classic of the American stage and was also made into a popular movie. Ferber came to Bath to observe and talk with the crew and cast of the James Adams Floating Theatre, known as *The Showboat*. Launched in 1914 on a 128-foot-long barge in nearby Washington, the traveling theater was towed to communities along the North Carolina coast to provide a variety of entertainment to residents in remote areas.

Architecturally, the Palmer-Marsh House features a number of characteristics which were exceptional for the colonial period.

A massive double chimney on the eastern side of the house measures seventeen feet across and is four feet thick at the base. It is so massive that it has two small windows opening onto tile-floored closets between the upstairs and downstairs fireplaces.

Window glass was scarce and costly at the time the house was constructed. It thus exhibits an unusually large number of windows for a structure of its age.

A single timber fifty-four feet long runs the length of the house as its center beam.

As part of the restoration, the interior of the house has been tastefully decorated with contemporary antiques. Elsewhere on the grounds, the wellhouse and the smokehouse have been reconstructed.

Behind the house is the old family cemetery, containing graves dating back to the eighteenth century. Probably the most beautiful headstone is that of Mary Evans, the granddaughter of Michael Coutanche. According to the inscription on the marker, she died of a broken heart. The grave of Coutanche also lies in the cemetery.

Through the efforts of humorist Edmund Harding, local residents, and people from all over the state, the Beaufort County Historical Society acquired the Palmer-Marsh House on March 26, 1958. A year later, the North Carolina General Assembly created the Historic Bath Commission, from which emerged the Historic Bath State Historic Site.

In December 1989, a fire, apparently started by electrical wiring, caused extensive damage to the house. Although a quick response by the town's volunteer fire department prevented the flames from spreading beyond the roof and the attic, the house was closed for more than a year for repairs.

Public tours of the interior of this house and the two others owned by the historic site are available for a nominal fee at the visitor center.

A state historical marker describing the Palmer-Marsh House has been erected on the street nearby. This historical marker is one of a number of markers located on Main Street, silent reminders of a time when Bath was the center of political power in the colony. For much of the first half of the eighteenth century, the town served as the unofficial capital of North Carolina. In 1743, 1744, and 1752, the general assembly convened at Bath. However, in 1746, the upper house of the general assembly refused to pass a bill—approved earlier by the lower house—to make Bath the official capital of North Carolina. After that, the town was unable to retain its political clout.

One of the historical markers on Main Street calls attention to another reason for the importance of the town before the Revolutionary War: it was located on the post road, which extended from Portland, Maine, to Savannah, Georgia. Within the North Carolina colony, the road led from Edenton and the Albemarle settlements through a vast lowland wilderness. At the southern end of this great "desert," as the wilderness was called by the colonists, travelers found Bath a hospitable place. Inns and other lodging facilities thrived along the route, which connected Bath to New Bern.

As a result of this strategic location and its early political prominence, Bath was the site of many firsts in North Carolina history.

A historical marker on Main Street calls attention to the first public library in North Carolina. Just before the town was established, the St. Thomas Parish of Bath was formed as a result of the Vestry Act of North Carolina. This new parish subsequently received a collection of a thousand books through the efforts of the Reverend Dr. Thomas Bray, the founder and secretary of the Society for the Propagation of the Gospel. Covering a wide range of subjects, including history, science, literature, sports, and religion, the volumes were beautifully bound in gold-tooled leather. With these books, the first public library in North Carolina, and possibly the first in America, was opened at Bath in the early years of the eighteenth century. Only one of the original books is known to exist: *Application of the Church Catechism*, by Gilbert Towerson, printed in London in 1685.

As a complement to the first public library, the first free public school in the colony was also established at Bath.

Continue south on Main Street. Near the end of the street, the junction of Bath and Back Creeks is visible. Front Street curves off Main Street to the east, running parallel to Back Creek.

In 1708, while living in a house on Front Street overlooking the creeks, John Lawson wrote, "The mockingbirds often sit upon our chimney in summer, there being no fire in it, and sing the whole evening and most of the night." Now standing on the exact spot where Lawson's house once stood is the Bonner House, the second of the houses maintained by Historic Bath State Historic Site.

Built about 1830, the two-story frame structure is an excellent example of nineteenth-century North Carolina architecture. Noticeably absent from the exterior are shutters, which were considered unfashionable at the time. Several outbuildings dot the spacious grounds, which are surrounded by a handsome picket fence. On the interior, the house displays many of its original features, including small blown-glass windowpanes, wide-board pine floors, elegant Federal-style mantels, and chair rails. Original finger paint remains on the baseboard of the upstairs bedroom. Handsome nineteenth-century furnishings serve to enhance the decor.

Joseph Bonner, a prosperous naval-stores merchant and a descendant of the prominent Bonner family of Beaufort County, purchased this site. He and his wife loved the view it afforded of the waterfront. Not until the 1950s did the house leave the Bonner family.

A picnic area shaded by a canopy of majestic trees is located on the creek bank just across the street from the Bonner House. Here, visitors can gaze across to Plum Point at the junction of Bath and Back creeks. Near the point stood the house of perhaps the most infamous man to ever call North Carolina home. In the annals of American piracy, one name stands above all the rest. Blackbeard, by virtue of his fabulous success as a tyrant of the seas, his terrifying appearance, his proclivity toward cruelty, and an evil reputation unmatched by his peers, has throughout American history been synonymous with the word *pirate*.

Little is known about Blackbeard's origin. Even his name is subject to dispute. Some historians have contended that his real name was Edward Teach or Edward Thatch. But in the first book ever written about pirates, famous English author Daniel Defoe concluded that Blackbeard's name was Edward Drummond.

Whatever his name, Blackbeard embarked on a career as an honest sailor from his home of Bristol, England. From 1701 to 1713, he served his country during Queen Anne's War. Near the end of the war, he got his first taste of piracy, albeit legalized piracy, when he served on a privateer.

Blackbeard is known to have come to Bath as early as 1712. By that time, his infamy as the scourge of the Atlantic coast was widespread. He found the numerous coves and shallow inlets of the Outer Banks of North Carolina a perfect place to base his operations.

Two years after Blackbeard's arrival in Bath, Governor Charles Eden assumed office in North Carolina. Soon thereafter, rumors abounded in Bath that pirates prowling the Atlantic coast would not be bothered in North Carolina waters so long as they included Governor Eden in the division of their bounty.

During his tenure as governor, from 1714 to 1722, Charles Eden lived much of the time in Bath. His home, a fine plantation estate known as Thistleworth, was located on the west side of Bath Creek. Old bricks are all that remain of the estate. Across the creek from Eden's home was that of Blackbeard. Legends persist to this day that a subterranean passageway connected the two houses.

Even though the site of Blackbeard's house is accessible only by water, curiosity seekers and treasure hunters have visited it on many occasions since the death of the pirate. Numerous legends hold that Blackbeard buried gold nearby, but no treasure is known to have been found.

Around 1717, Blackbeard came "home" to Bath under the guise of a repentant man. Under the provisions of the recently enacted Act of Mercy, Governor Eden was only too happy to pardon Blackbeard. To demonstrate his intention to settle down to an honest life, Blackbeard married a girl of sixteen. Governor Eden was in attendance at the wedding. By some accounts, he actually performed the ceremony. The newlyweds took up residence in Bath. Unfortunately, Mrs. Teach had no idea that she was the pirate's fourteenth wife. Little did she know that her husband had other wives and homes at Elizabeth City, Edenton, Ocracoke, and Beaufort, among other places.

At his fine home in Bath, Blackbeard entertained wealthy planters and area notables. He apparently felt that he had been accepted into the upper social circles, for he boasted that he could be invited into any home in North Carolina.

Yet while outward appearances convinced most people that Blackbeard had turned over a new leaf, the pirate refused to mend his ways. His home was strategically located so as to allow him to keep track of the ships entering and leaving Bath harbor. There were secret passageways on either side of his elaborately carved banquet room. When an approaching vessel attracted Blackbeard's attention, he sent his men scurrying out of his cellar through a secret passageway to their waiting sloop. In the nearby waterways, they plundered a number of ships sighted in this manner.

Even during the lavish parties Blackbeard threw for neighboring planters, he could not resist the temptation to take what was not his. His rogues raided the homes of Blackbeard's unsuspecting guests as they were being wined and dined.

It was not long, however, before he grew tired of this small-time piracy. He was used to the good life—a style of living that required vast sums of money. To remedy the situation, Blackbeard recruited former members of his crew. His ship, the *Adventure*, was made seaworthy. When questioned about his plans, Blackbeard responded that he was going on a trading expedition.

Governor Eden looked the other way as Blackbeard resumed his pirating career. Eden reasoned that as long as the pirate brought his plunder back to North Carolina, local merchants could buy and sell it cheaply without British tax.

But citizens up and down the Atlantic coast, including North Carolinians, began complaining about the mayhem on the seas. During his final year of piracy, Blackbeard's cruises took him as far north as Philadelphia, where he and his crew walked the streets on a number of occasions. Finally, the mayor of Philadelphia issued a warrant for Blackbeard's arrest. Similar citizen outrage ultimately led to the demise of the pirate at Ocracoke.

Until recent years, the life of Blackbeard was dramatically portrayed at amphitheaters on the North Carolina coast. For a decade, *Blackbeard: Knight of the Black Flag* was presented as a summer outdoor drama in Bath. By the time it was canceled in 1987 due to financial difficulties, the drama, penned by playwright Stuart Aronson, had drawn more than seventy thousand spectators to the Bath Amphitheater on the waterfront. Ironically, Aronson's *Blackbeard's Revenge* ended a three-year run at Cape Carteret that same year.

A state historical marker for Edward Teach stands on Main Street. (For more information on Blackbeard, see The Great Dismal Swamp Tour, page 55, The Ocracoke Tour, pages 253–57, and The Southern Pamlico River Tour, pages 329–30.)

As they walk the quiet, lazy streets of Bath, many visitors are amazed that this sleepy little town was at one time the most important place in the colony. But while Bath was enjoying its place of prominence in colonial North Carolina, few improvements were being made to enhance its viability and ensure its growth. Other towns were established in the region while Bath rested on its laurels. Never large, the town had no more than thirty houses in the colonial period.

Some residents believed that Bath was relegated to being a backwater community because of a curse put on it by the famous religious reformer and preacher George Whitefield.

In the mid-eighteenth century, the post road brought many adventurers and travelers through town. As a settlement on the edge of a vast frontier, Bath gained a reputation for the merrymaking at its taverns. About the same time, America was undergoing a religious experience called the Great Awakening.

George Whitefield journeyed to Bath on four occasions during this period to bring his searing sermons to the people of the community. He preached about the evils of cursing, drinking, and dancing—vices he had observed in the local taverns. Dancing particularly raised his ire.

The English revivalist was a gifted speaker, but his fire-and-damnation messages fell on deaf ears in Bath. Locals were suspicious of him. They were alarmed because Whitefield invariably came to town with his coffin in his wagon. When questioned about this peculiar practice, the religious reformer had a simple response: he wanted to make sure that if he died, a coffin would be ready. Area residents were further infuriated when Whitefield insisted on sleeping in his coffin. The preacher reasoned that by so doing, he could avoid the sinful activities at the local public house.

His final visit to Bath came in 1765. When he arrived on that occasion, Whitefield was informed that he could no longer preach in town. In disgust, he returned to his wagon, where he removed his shoes and shook the dust of Bath off them. As he drove away for the last time, he is said to have muttered, "There's a place in the Bible that says if a place won't listen to The Word, you shake the dust of the town off your feet, and the town shall be cursed. I have put a curse on this town for a hundred years."

Whether it was Whitefield's curse or the geographical and political factors suggested by historians that led to Bath's loss of dominance, the resulting isolation has allowed the community to preserve the history of the special time when it was the preeminent town in all of North Carolina.

Retrace your route on Main Street to Craven Street. Turn right and proceed east on Craven to St. Thomas Episcopal Church, the oldest church in North Carolina. Visitors are welcome to enter the ancient edifice, which is Bath's most genuine link to the eighteenth century. It stands on a grassy knoll, separated from the street by a ballast-stone wall.

Construction began on the structure in 1734 on the same site as a previous church. Work on the building was not completed until 1762. Its two-foot-thick walls are cemented with lime from burned oyster shells and laid in Flemish bond. Though the building appears to be a simple rectangle, its walls are actually several feet out of square. Brick for the walls came from England. A hand-pegged wooden door with an arched brick pediment is the only opening on the front side of the church.

St. Thomas Episcopal Church

Inside, the original handmade straight-back pews are elevated on wooden platforms. The floor is covered with eight-inch-square red tiles. Slight traces of the decorations that once beautified the tiles—like dragons and flowers—are still visible. Although the tiles are now permanent, they were once set in sand to allow their removal. These tiles are silent reminders of the terrible Tuscarora massacre that took place in the Pamlico area in 1711. Lying under this ancient floor are the graves of settlers, placed there to avoid desecration by rampaging Indians.

Several interesting artifacts grace the interior of the church. A silver candelabra on the altar was a gift from King George II around 1740. A large silver chalice, a gift from the bishop of London, is two years older. On one side of the altar is a slate tablet placed there in 1765 as a memorial to Margaret Palmer, the wife of Colonel Robert Palmer, the collector of the port of Bath. The inscription on the tablet was quoted verbatim in Edna Ferber's *Showboat*. Perhaps the most treasured possession of the church is a Bible printed in 1703 and brought to America the following year. It was willed to the church in 1715.

In the churchyard, the Queen's Bell, cast in 1750 in London, is eighteen years older than the beloved Liberty Bell in Philadelphia. Its name is derived from the "Queen's Bounty," a fund established by Queen Anne for charitable purposes and the purchase of church furniture. The bell was recast in New York in 1872.

A state historical marker stands on Craven Street alongside the church.

Closely related to St. Thomas Episcopal Church is the Williams House, located adjacent to the church at the southeastern corner of Main and Craven streets. Also known as the Glebe House, this handsome two-story structure, constructed between 1827 and 1832, is likely the third house built on the property.

The Williams (Glebe) House

In 1846, Dr. John F. Tompkins and his bride moved into the house. A noted agricultural reformer, Dr. Tompkins later distinguished himself as publisher of the *Farmer's Journal* and founder of the North Carolina State Agricultural Society and the North Carolina State Fair. One of the historical markers on Main Street honors Tompkins.

Turn left, or north, off Craven Street onto Harding Street. Relocated to a lot on the west side of Harding Street, the Van Der Veer House is the third of the houses owned by Historic Bath State Historic Site. Although the house was constructed around 1790 by Ephraim Whitmore, its name comes from one of its subsequent owners, Jacob Van Der Veer, a prominent resident of Bath who founded the Bank of Washington in 1851.

Through the efforts of the Historic Bath Commission and the state, the frame gambrel-roofed house has been restored to its original appearance. Double-shouldered Flemish-bond chimneys at each end of the structure are its most distinctive features. The home is now open to visitors as a free museum chronicling the history of Bath.

Across Harding Street from the Van Der Veer House stands Bath School.

Beginning in 1925, this massive brick building housed students from kindergarten to twelfth grade. But in the autumn of 1988, the Bath High School Pirates played their last football game. The following year, a new consolidated high school opened for students from Bath and Belhaven. At the old school in Bath, an ancient ship's bell, rumored to have come from Blackbeard's ship, once summoned students to classes.

Old Bath School

Turn west off Harding Street onto N.C. 92 and return to your car at the Historic Bath Visitor Center. Drive west on N.C. 92. The bridge across Bath Creek provides a spectacular view of the historic waterfront.

Approximately 2.3 miles west of the bridge, turn left, or south, off N.C. 92 onto S.R. 1334. You will see a pull-off on the east shoulder of the road approximately 1 mile south of the intersection. In the woods nearby are the mysterious hoofprints that have captivated the interest of North Carolinians since the early nineteenth century.

These saucer-sized depressions in the earth have reportedly remained unchanged since they appeared almost two hundred years ago. That the same small indentations have existed for so long is remarkable. Yet even more bewildering is the fact that the holes have resisted all attempts to permanently eradicate or alter them. No plant life grows in the holes. Visitors to the site have tried their best to fill them with all sorts of debris. Children have deposited bits of trash there on their way to school, only to discover that the holes are clean at the end of the day.

Site of mysterious footprints

A thick carpet of pine needles completely surrounds the holes, but none of the needles ever finds a permanent resting place in the hoofprints.

Grain scattered about for chickens has fallen into the holes. The chickens collect the tasty morsels until they come to the hoofprints, at which time they refuse to peck into the earthen saucers.

At one time, the owner of the property decided to use the site for a pigpen. Like the chickens, the swine disdained any food which fell into the hoofprints. However, the hogs did reduce the hoofprints to a muddy quagmire. Amazingly, after the hogs were removed, the same strange depressions reappeared in the exact spot where they had been.

Scientists have investigated the hoofprints. A combined effort by the American Society for Psychical Research and Duke University used specially constructed equipment to take delicate measurements and to detect psychokinetic forces. In the process of the investigation, the team filled the depressions with trash and secured it with thread. While the scientists were away from the site, the material vanished from the hoofprints.

Throughout the years, a number of scientific theories have been espoused to explain the intriguing hoofprints. One theory suggests that they are vents for a subterranean pocket of water. Another speculates that the depressions are the result of salt veins.

Although the depressions do not really look like the prints of a horse's hooves, one of the most cherished legends of North Carolina says that is exactly what they are.

On Sunday morning, October 13, 1813, Jesse Elliott, a local horse-racing enthusiast, was preparing for a big race in Bath the following day. While local churches were holding worship services, the profane Elliott began drinking whiskey. Along the Bath waterfront, he encountered a stranger—some say he was named Buckingame—on a beautiful, shiny black horse. Pointing to Elliott's magnificent chestnut stallion, which was known to be superior to any local horse, the stranger taunted Jesse by betting a hundred dollars that the chestnut stallion could be beaten. Always willing to take on any challenger at any time, Elliott accepted the bet by replying, "I'll meet you at the track in an hour."

Jesse Elliott hurried home, where he downed two more glasses of liquor as he donned his riding boots. When his wife implored him not to violate the local prohibition against racing on the Sabbath, the possessed man cursed her and beat her. As he departed, his wife was heard to scream, "I hope you'll be sent to hell this very day!"

People coming home from church saw Elliott ride past.

Upon his arrival at the track, he noticed something different about the stranger. His ears and nose were pointed in a way that Elliott had not observed earlier. His dark, piercing eyes met Elliott's as the two men assumed their racing positions.

As the magnificent horses sped around the race course, Jesse was able to hold his own against the challenger. Goading his steed to run faster, Elliott proclaimed, "Take me in a winner or take me to hell!" Apparently, the words took hold of the horse, because Jesse soon found himself in the lead.

Yet the stranger did not appear to be worried about falling behind. Some observers said they even heard him give a soft laugh.

At the point where the track curved, Elliott's horse twisted its head and screamed in terror. There are those who believe the stallion looked back to see the devil riding the black horse. Regardless of what terrified the stallion, it screeched to a halt by digging its hooves into the soft ground. Jesse Elliott was thrown into a pine tree and killed instantly. Suddenly, the mysterious stranger and his horse vanished, never to be seen again. The black horse's hoofprints stopped in the road.

Continue southwest on S.R. 1334 for 3.9 miles to the entrance to Goose Creek State Park. Turn southeast onto the park road and follow it to its terminus near the picnic areas and swimming beach.

Situated about equidistant from Bath and Washington, this park is a visual treat for nature lovers. It encompasses 1,327 acres of brackish creeks and marshes, river swamp forests, and upland pine forests, all nestled in a beautiful setting on the shores of the Pamlico River.

Recreational area at Goose Creek State Park

The park yields few reminders of humans' imprint on the area. By maintaining the acreage in its natural state, North Carolina has preserved a portion of the unique Pamlico River shoreline. Because of the great abundance and variety of plants growing here, the Goose Creek area has been described as a "natural garden." Along the beautiful, sandy river beaches, magnificent live oaks are laden with Spanish moss. Wild rice growing in the adjacent marshes and wetlands attracts waterfowl, including herons, egrets, puddle ducks, and rails. Beyond the shoreline lies an evergreen shrub bog. Farther inland, the pocosin gives way to a forest of loblolly pines and hardwoods, where white-tailed deer, gray foxes, and bobcats live.

In addition to nature study, there are a variety of recreational opportunities in the park. The fishing in the river and creek is excellent. Boat access is available at Dinah's Landing on Goose Creek. Although there are no trailer hookups or fresh water for overnight visitors, camping is allowed. Hikers can use four trails that wind through the park. Both Live Oak Trail and Goose Creek Trail begin at the picnic area. Flatty Creek Trail, a side trail, leads to an observation tower. Some boardwalks have been constructed along the trails.

Leaving the park, turn left and drive 2.5 miles on S.R. 1334 to the

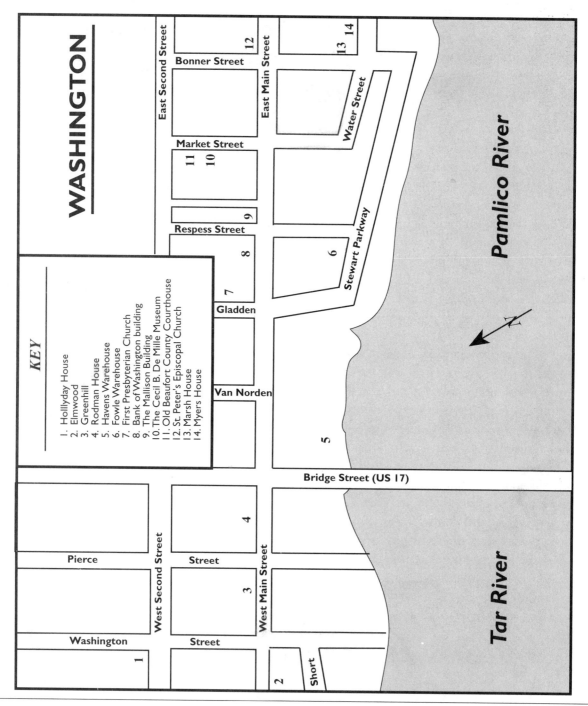

WASHINGTON

KEY

1. Hollyday House
2. Elmwood
3. Greenhill
4. Rodman House
5. Havens Warehouse
6. Fowle Warehouse
7. First Presbyterian Church
8. Bank of Washington building
9. The Mallison Building
10. The Cecil B. De Mille Museum
11. Old Beaufort County Courthouse
12. St. Peter's Episcopal Church
13. Marsh House
14. Myers House

Pamlico River

Tar River

East Second Street

Bonner Street

East Main Street

Water Street

Market Street

Respess Street

Stewart Parkway

Gladden

Van Norden

Bridge Street (US 17)

Pierce

West Second Street

Street

West Main Street

Washington

Street

Short

TOURING THE BACKROADS OF NORTH CAROLINA'S UPPER COAST

intersection with U.S. 264 at the community of Jessamana. Turn left, or west, onto U.S. 264 and proceed toward Washington. It is 8.6 miles to the intersection of U.S. 264 (West Fifth Street) and U.S. 17 (Bridge Street) in downtown Washington. Turn left, or south, on U.S. 17 and drive 4 blocks to the intersection with West Main Street. Turn left and park in the on-street spaces on West Main. Here begins a brief walking tour of historic downtown Washington.

Walk west to the Rodman House, located at 520 West Main. This dwelling, constructed in 1848, was once the home of two justices of the North Carolina Supreme Court. Before the house was constructed, a shipyard at the site was owned and operated by Hull Anderson, a free black who later emigrated to Liberia. Because much of Washington was burned during the Civil War, the Rodman House is one of the few surviving antebellum structures in the town's historic district.

Continue to Greenhill, located at 612 West Main Street. This structure was built in 1825. It was once the home of Edward Jenner Warren, the grandfather of native son Lindsay C. Warren, a multiterm United States congressman who championed issues of vital importance to coastal North Carolina in Washington, D.C.

Greenhill

In 1940, Lindsay Warren was acting majority leader of the House and was considered the top candidate to become Speaker of the House when he answered the call of President Franklin D. Roosevelt to serve as comptroller general of the United States. Among the accolades bestowed upon him was the title "Watchdog of Federal Spending." The visitor center at Fort Raleigh National Historic Site on Roanoke Island was named in his honor.

Warren's seat in Congress was filled by another Washington native, Herbert Covington Bonner. A close friend of every United States president from Roosevelt to Johnson, Bonner was a dynamic spokesman for coastal interests on a national level. To honor the service that he rendered his state and region, the people of North Carolina named the great bridge to Hatteras Island in his honor.

Turn south off West Main Street onto Washington Street and proceed to the end of the road to enjoy a view of the majestic waterfront. To the east looms the U.S. 17 bridge. At the point where the bridge crosses the river, the name of the river changes. West of the bridge, the river is the Tar, and east of the bridge, it becomes the Pamlico. From Person County in north-central North Carolina, the Tar flows southeast for 180 miles through the rich farmland of the northern Piedmont. It widens dramatically at Washington and completes its final 33-mile course to Pamlico Sound as the Pamlico River.

In the waters of the Tar just offshore from the current tour stop lies the wreck of the USS *Picket*, a Federal gunboat that served as the floating headquarters of General Ambrose Burnside during the Civil War. In the early-morning hours of September 6, 1862, the vessel exploded and went down, causing most of its crew to perish.

Return to West Main Street and continue west to Elmwood, located at 731 West Main. When it was constructed in 1820, this handsome structure stood at the end of West Main Street. In 1857, *Harper's Weekly* described the house as one of the most distinguished homes in the South.

Retrace your route to the intersection with Washington Street and turn left, or north, onto Washington. Near the northwestern corner of Washington and West Second streets stands the Hollyday House, at 706 West Second. Built at an unknown date during the antebellum period, the house is a reminder of the grim fighting and the conflagration that took place here during the Civil War. Federal forces used this building as a hospital.

Washington fell under Union occupation soon after the capitulation of New Bern in March 1862. A year later, a Confederate expeditionary force led by North Carolina general D. H. Hill laid siege to Washington, but the Southern troops were withdrawn in mid-April 1863 in anticipation of the Gettysburg campaign. Another year passed without incident.

Suddenly, Federal control of the town became tenuous at best in April 1864, when the news of Confederate general Robert F. Hoke's magnificent victory at nearby Plymouth spread throughout coastal North Carolina. In Washington, Union general I. N. Palmer realized that his garrison could not hold its position. A telegraph from General Grant authorized Palmer to abandon the town.

As Hoke's forces approached Washington, the evacuation was intensified. By April 27, the town was once again under siege. During the ensuing three days, Federal troops wreaked havoc throughout the town as they burned and looted. Official reports of the mayhem stated that the marauding Yankees "did not even respect the charitable institutions, but bursting open the doors of the Masonic and Odd Fellows lodges, pillaged them both and hawked about the streets the regalia and jewels." A board of investigation later concluded, "Government stores, cutlers' establishments, dwelling houses, private shops, and stables, suffered alike. Gangs of men patrolled the city breaking into houses and wantonly destroying such goods as they could not carry away."

When they finished sacking the city, the last of the fleeing Federal troops set fire to Washington in three places on the morning of April 30. Quickly, the holocaust spread from the warehouses on the waterfront to the northern limits of the town. Virtually half of Washington was reduced to ruins. The misery was heightened when, just after the arrival of the Confederates, an accidental fire fanned by high winds devastated much of the portion of the city that had not been incinerated by the fleeing Union army.

Continue 1 block north on Washington Street to West Third Street. Turn right, or east, onto West Third and proceed 2 blocks, then turn south onto Bridge Street. A state historical marker at the corner of Bridge and West Second streets chronicles the burning of Washington.

Following the devastating fire, the town was spared further conflict for the duration of the war, save for sporadic Federal raids and visits by gunboats. Yet the damage was done. Washington was a place of utter desolation and ruin. By the spring of 1864, hardly five hundred of the thirty-five hundred prewar inhabitants remained in the town. For those hardy souls who stayed, the city was only a shadow of its former self.

Hollywood, California, and its Walk of Stars are a long way from the current tour stop. Yet much of the early fame of Hollywood as the motion-picture capital of the world was due to the work of two brothers who spent much of their childhood at their paternal grandparents' home, which once stood on the nearby street corner.

William and Cecil B. De Mille were born into a family that had called Washington home since the early nineteenth century. In 1851, their grandparents received an elegant three-story brick house as a wedding gift. Henry Churchill De Mille, father of the famous brothers, was born in the mansion and grew up there. He subsequently achieved fame as a playwright who brought to the Broadway stage some of its most popular hits up to that time.

While Henry De Mille was earning plaudits for his work on Broadway, his son William was born at the mansion in Washington. William's younger brother, Cecil, was born while the family was vacationing in the Berkshires. Later, Henry De Mille moved his family to be near his work on Broadway. However, both boys spent extended periods in Washington.

William, following in his father's footsteps as a playwright, was the first of the brothers to achieve success. Even though he is best known today as the father of world-renowned choreographer Agnes De Mille, he wrote several stage hits.

When Cecil came to his elder brother with a proposal that William join him, Samuel Goldwyn, and others to form a company to make motion pictures, William was furious. He felt that Cecil was degrading the family name by entering into such a venture. Little did William realize that the proposed five-thousand-dollar investment would have been worth millions only a few years later.

Cecil B. De Mille quickly capitalized on his investment in the fledgling movie industry. Today, his name remains synonymous with filmmaking. Not only did he entice Hollywood's most glamorous and most talented stars to appear in his pictures, but he was also an innovator in the industry. He is credited with the production of the first color motion picture.

When he filmed *The Ten Commandments* in 1926, he assembled a cast of ten thousand actors. Nevertheless, that film became one of the biggest moneymakers of all time. He followed with the spectacular *The King of Kings*, a film which has been shown to more than a billion people in nearly every country of the world. When Cecil B. De Mille was questioned about his inspiration for *The King of Kings*, he said it came from his childhood days in the De Mille home in Washington. His place at the dining room table was directly across from a copy of Leonardo da Vinci's *Last Supper*, which hung on the wall above the mantel. Somehow, that painting became indelibly etched in his mind.

A state historical marker stands on nearby Market Street near the home owned by their father, where the boys lived as children.

Proceed south on Bridge Street for 1 block to its intersection with West Main Street. Turn east onto West Main. At the northwestern corner of West Main and Van Norden stands the Havens House. Constructed around 1820, this home was built to resemble West Indian–style houses that the Havenses, who were local shipping merchants, had admired on their trading journeys.

Located just across West Main Street on the waterfront is the Havens Warehouse, built around 1820. This historic structure, one of the few surviving buildings of its kind, is a link to Washington's distant past as a prosperous river port. From its founding in 1771 until the Civil War, Washington rivaled Wilmington as the chief port of North Carolina. Well into the nineteenth century, vessels sailing out of Washington carried on extensive trade with the West Indies. Chief among the exports were tar, pitch, turpentine, and other naval stores, which were stored in the Havens Warehouse and other warehouses that once stood nearby.

Continue 1 block on West Main, then turn south onto Stewart Parkway. Adjacent to the waterfront parking lot and fronting Respess Street is the Fowle Warehouse, constructed in 1825. Its basement and foundation, fabricated from ballast stones, attest to the maritime heritage of the historic waterfront.

The De Mille family plot, St. Peter's Episcopal Church

Fowle Warehouse

Washington waterfront, Stewart Parkway

Until the end of the War of 1812, the Blount family dominated the thriving port activities in the town. When the Fowle family subsequently arrived from New England, a healthy competition developed, and the great Blount and Fowle mercantile houses kept the wharves of the Washington waterfront teeming with activity.

A state historical marker on West Main Street stands near the site of the home of one of the Fowle descendants. Elected governor of North Carolina in 1889, Daniel G. Fowle is the only Washingtonian to serve as the state's chief executive.

From the parking lot, you will be treated to a panoramic view of the waters that have been vital to the economic viability of this town for more than two hundred years. In the early 1960s, the waterfront was nothing more than an eyesore of abandoned docks, wharves, and warehouses. Subsequent renovations by the city have resulted in a parklike setting landscaped with shade trees, walkways, and picnic tables. Harding Square, a public park just east of the waterfront parking lot, was dedicated to honor Edmund Harding, the local humorist who sparked initial interest in the restoration of historic Bath.

It was this waterfront that served as the berth for one of the most famous vessels in North Carolina history.

In Wilmington, the USS *North Carolina* proudly bears the title she received just after she was launched: *The Showboat*. Ironically, several decades before that great battleship slid down the ways of the Brooklyn Navy Yard, Washington, North Carolina, was the birthplace and home of the vessel known as the original *Showboat*.

Mr. and Mrs. James Adams, a former circus aerial team, came to Washington from Michigan in 1912. They employed Bill Chauncey to construct a large floating theater in the Farrow Shipyard at the foot of Bonner Street. By February 19, 1914, the boat was completed. Towed by a fifty-foot tug, the floating theater was equipped with more than five hundred seats on its main floor, with additional seats in the balcony.

Using their experience as circus performers and traveling vaudeville entertainers, the Adamses were able to produce comedies and other shows that made the boat a well-known attraction all along the Atlantic coast. At the time it was completed, the James Adams Floating Theatre was the only floating theater on the entire coast. After holding its premiere performance in Washington on February 14, 1914, the theater boat came back home every five years.

In the 1920s, the couple retired and turned the operation over to James Adams's sister and brother-in-law, Mr. and Mrs. Charles Hunter, two professional actors who had played the lead in many performances on the boat.

While the Hunters were operating the theater, Edna Ferber came to North Carolina to study the boat. It was one of the few times in her storied career that she was lured out of her New York apartment to actually experience the basis of one of her novels. After a four-day stay on board as a guest of the Hunters, Ferber began researching the legends and names of Beaufort County. Filled with inspiration, she hurried back to New York, where she completed her classic novel *Showboat*.

As the subsequent movie musical adapted from the novel gained popularity, Americans were singing "Old Man River." However, neither beautiful prose nor delightful songs could temper the rage of the people of Beaufort County when they learned that Ferber had set her book on the Mississippi while using names and experiences from the Pamlico.

The Showboat made its last call in the town of its birth in the late 1930s. At that time, there were only three showboats left in operation in the country. After the two boats operating on the Mississippi and Ohio rivers bowed out, *The Showboat* went it alone until it burned in the Savannah River in 1941.

From the parking lot, proceed east on Stewart Parkway to the junction with Water Street. Turn right, or east, onto Water Street. The second block of this street presents a handsome ensemble of late-eighteenth-century homes. At 210 Water Street, the Marsh House, built around 1795, has a cannonball lodged in its upper right facade, a reminder of the fierce fighting that took place here during the Civil War. This house and the Myers House at 214 Water Street, built around 1780, served as offices and quarters during the war. The Hyatt House, built around 1785, was constructed at 222 Water Street by an English sea captain. Its original Federal-style exterior has been substantially altered. A ghost is said to reside on the third floor.

The Hyatt House

Retrace your route west on Water Street and turn right, or north, on

Bonner Street. The town's historic district is bounded by Hickory and Third streets, the Pamlico, and Jacks Creek. Bonner Street, like most of the north-south streets in the historic district, is named for an important person in the early history of the city. James Bonner successfully petitioned the colonial assembly on November 30, 1771, to establish a town here, which soon came to be known as Washington.

Outsiders often refer to the town as "Little Washington," in deference to the nation's capital. But residents of the town on the Tar/Pamlico are quick to point out that the more appropriate name for their home is "the Original Washington." For as long as anyone can remember, the residents of this old river port have boasted that their town was the first anywhere named for General George Washington. Their claim has been challenged by other towns, particularly those in Virginia and Georgia.

To lay all such challenges to rest, the mayor of Washington, North Carolina, traveled to Washington, D.C., during the national capital's sesquicentennial celebration in July 1950. There, he joined the mayors of the nation's other Washingtons in various programs held during the anniversary festivities. When the North Carolina town put forth its assertion, half of the other towns represented cried foul, each claiming the honor. Congressman Herbert C. Bonner stepped forward to enter the fray. He cited the Post Office Department as the accrediting agency for the claim of the town in his congressional district. Indeed, records found in the postal archives confirmed that Washington, North Carolina, was the rightful owner of the honor. Further credence was given to the claim by the George Washington Bicentennial Commission when it concluded that of the 422 cities and towns in the United States named for George Washington, the town in North Carolina was the first.

Located at 101 Bonner Street, St. Peter's Episcopal Church is a beautiful, vine-covered, brick Gothic Revival building completed in 1868 to replace a wooden church built in 1822 and reduced to ashes in 1864 by the Civil War fire. As flames engulfed the original building, the extreme heat caused the church bell to toll its death knell until it fell from the bell tower.

Abram Allen, an elderly black member of the church, watched helplessly as the bronze bell melted in the inferno. After the fire, Allen pulled the metal of the bell from the ashes and carried it to his home for storage.

Once the war ended, he returned the metal so it could be sold to raise funds for the new church.

After 2 blocks, turn left, or west, off Bonner onto Second Street, then turn left, or south, onto Market Street after 1 block.

Constructed in 1786, the old Beaufort County Courthouse, located at the southwestern corner of Second and Market, is the most historic structure in old Washington. Listed on the National Register of Historic Places, it is one of the oldest public buildings in the United States. Now painted white, this square two-story structure with Georgian and Federal elements was constructed of brick laid in Flemish bond. Since it was retired from duty as a courthouse in the early 1970s, it has served as a public library and assembly hall.

Of particular interest at the old courthouse is the clock that graces the top of the building. No one really knows how old the clock is or how it ever got to Washington. Some historians believe that it was purchased for the town of Bath, where the Beaufort County Courthouse was slated for construction around the time of the American Revolution. The clock was shipped to Washington from Bath when the general assembly voted to move the county seat in 1785.

Each of the four faces of the clock is made of wood. In the 1960s, after

The old Beaufort County Courthouse

nearly two centuries of manual setting and maintenance, the clock was electrified. Ironically, once the electrification project was completed, the clock, which had lost less then two minutes in 150 years, began to lose time and ultimately quit running. Since the clock was returned to its original mode of operation, it has continued to tick on.

Continue to 124 North Market Street, where the old combination town hall and fire station has undergone renovation to serve as the Cecil B. De Mille Museum. The building was constructed in 1884.

Turn west off Market onto Main Street. Nearby on East Main Street stands a state historical marker honoring Susan Dimock, the first female physician in North Carolina. Dimock was born in Washington on April 24, 1847. She and a handful of other female physicians pioneered the entry of women into the medical profession in America. At the age of twenty-eight, she perished at sea when her ship went down off the English coast.

Several buildings of historic significance are located in the commercial district on West Main Street.

The Mallison Building was constructed at 162 West Main Street in 1872. Historians believe this Victorian structure was the first brick building constructed in Washington following the Civil War.

Located at 216 West Main Street, the former Bank of Washington is one

The former Bank of Washington

of the few commercial buildings in the state built in the monumental temple style. Listed on the National Register of Historic Places, it was constructed in 1852. Virtually fireproof, the venerable structure with its brick-lined roof has survived several fires that have ravaged much of the downtown area.

Turn right, or north, off West Main Street onto Gladden Street and walk 1 block to West Second Street to see First Presbyterian Church, located on the corner at 211 West Second.

Like the Episcopalians, the Presbyterians lost their church building to the Civil War fire of 1864. Before their 1823-vintage house of worship was destroyed, the members made a great sacrifice by donating their church bell to the Confederate cause. It was melted and used for bullets.

Soon after the dedication of the existing church building in 1867, the Presbyterian women began to collect scrap metal for a new church bell. Their efforts were rewarded, for by 1872, they had amassed a half-ton of metal, which was shipped north to be cast into a new bell. That bell was placed on board the *Catherine Johnson* for the return trip to Beaufort County. Off Hatteras, the ship was claimed by the Graveyard of the Atlantic. None of the ship's cargo was saved except the bell, which somehow made its way ashore. Today, the bell continues to hang in the majestic church.

The tour ends at First Presbyterian Church. West Main Street is 1 block south. Turn right onto West Main to return to your car.

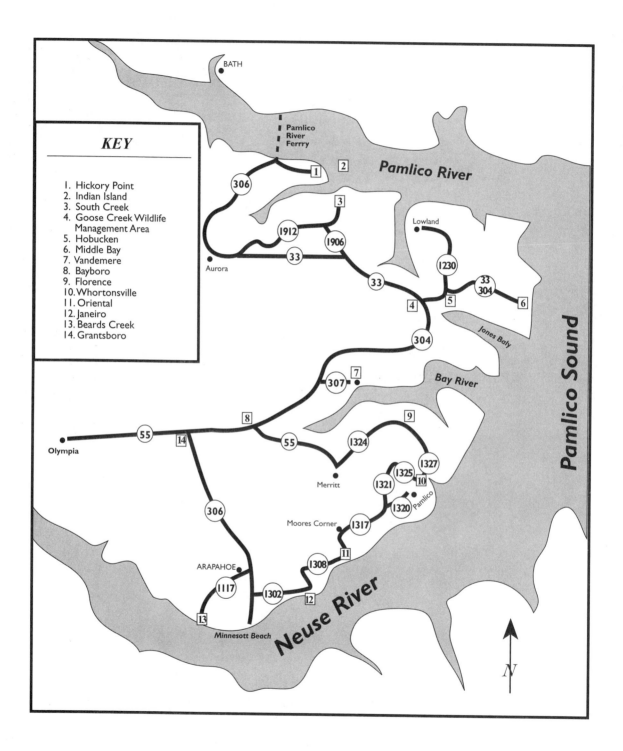

KEY

1. Hickory Point
2. Indian Island
3. South Creek
4. Goose Creek Wildlife Management Area
5. Hobucken
6. Middle Bay
7. Vandemere
8. Bayboro
9. Florence
10. Whortonsville
11. Oriental
12. Janeiro
13. Beards Creek
14. Grantsboro

BATH

Pamlico River Ferrry

Pamlico River

Lowland

Aurora

Jones Baly

Olympia

Bay River

Pamlico Sound

Merritt

Pamlico

Moores Corner

ARAPAHOE

Neuse River

Minnesott Beach

N

The Southern Pamlico River Tour

This tour begins at the shore of the Pamlico River and travels to the phosphate-mining town of Aurora. It then visits South Creek, the communities of Hobucken and Lowland on Goose Creek Island, Mesic, Cash Corner, Vandemere, Maribel, Bayboro, Stonewall, Whortonsville, and Pamlico. At the confluence of five large creeks and the Neuse River, it reaches the postcard-perfect sailing town of Oriental. The tour then travels to Janeiro, Cash Corner No. 2, Minnesott Beach, and Grantsboro before ending at Olympia.

Among the highlights of the tour are the story of Indian Island, the Aurora Fossil Museum, Goose Creek Wildlife Management Area, the Wise House near Pamlico, lovely Oriental, Teach's Oak, and the story of Wilkinson Point.

Total mileage: approximately 103 miles.

This tour begins on S.R. 1004 at the southern landing of the Pamlico River Ferry, located southeast of, and across the river from, historic Bath.

Operation of this toll-free ferry was instituted by the state in 1966 to provide economical transportation for employees of the area's phosphate-mining industry. Although the crossing time is only twenty-five minutes—among the shortest of the ferry routes on the North Carolina coast—the ferry across the Pamlico eliminates a 50-mile drive from Bayview on the northern shore to Aurora on the southern shore.

Proceed east from the ferry landing on S.R. 1004 for 3.5 miles to the end of the road at a place called Hickory Point. This scenic drive begins your tour of the large mainland peninsula in the central portion of the North Carolina coast, separated from the Outer Banks by the expansive Pamlico Sound and thus tucked neatly away from the treacherous shoals of the Graveyard of the Atlantic. Shared by Beaufort, Pamlico, and Craven counties, this historic region has been blessed with a long shoreline along Pamlico Sound and two of the most notable coastal rivers, the Pamlico and the Neuse.

At Hickory Point, you will enjoy a spectacular view of the Pamlico River—a river of history, beauty, and controversy.

Because of the numerous tributary creeks flowing into it from both shores, the 33-mile-long river has been said to resemble a monstrous creature with sprawling arms when viewed from the air. This magnificent waterway was first made known to Europeans by the Raleigh expeditions in the late sixteenth century. Arthur Barlowe explored the river, and John White marveled at the Native Americans living on its shores. A number of White's priceless watercolors of the Indians of the Pamlico area survive under lock and key in the British Museum.

After more than a quarter-century of phosphate mining on the southern shore of the Pamlico, environmental concerns over the health of the river continue to mount. Recent reports from the river are indeed alarming. For the first time in the memory of longtime residents, no crabs are to be found in the river. Scientists believe that its waters have been choked during the past several decades by nitrogen and phosphorous from industrial discharges, waste from sewer plants, and farmland runoff.

Unless the toxicity of the river can be reduced, the problem threatens catastrophic consequences for this important coastal resource. Environmentalists point out that the river has been a vital nursery for the marine life in both Pamlico and Albemarle sounds, which provide 75 percent of the shellfish harvested in the state.

Indian Island, a river island located 1.5 miles due east of Hickory Point, is an almost-forgotten historic landmark of the Pamlico region. At one time, the island contained more than two hundred acres, but over the centuries, the river has claimed much of its landscape. Now, it covers only fifty acres, measuring 1.1 miles long and 0.3 mile wide.

Archaeologists believe that Native Americans inhabited the Indian Island area as much as five thousand years ago, when it was not actually an island, but rather a long peninsula jutting into the river from its southern shore. Opposing currents from the Pamlico and South Creek gradually created the island about the time of Christ. A thousand years later, the Indians were cultivating large fields of tobacco, melons, corn, squash, and other vegetables on the island. John White visited the area in 1585. His drawing of the Secota village on the nearby mainland is regarded throughout the world as the most authentic reproduction of American Indian life in the last quarter of the sixteenth century.

If Indian Island were to reveal its secrets, it would yield some of the most fascinating tales in North Carolina history.

Here, the Tuscaroras gathered on the eve of their infamous massacre of white settlers in 1711.

Seven years later, the island may have hosted a visit by Blackbeard.

In January 1718, the pirate arrived in Bath aboard the *Queen Anne's Revenge*, a recently captured and converted French merchantman. Local residents had never seen a ship with such firepower—forty guns. After reaching the docks at the Bath waterfront in a dinghy, Blackbeard made his way to the only tavern in town, where he told his friend Governor Charles Eden of his recent success. Arrogantly, the pirate informed Eden, "The sea was good to us. The Spanish fools carried gold. Why not Indian Isle for this rare catch?" Quickly, the two men finalized plans to bury the treasure on Indian Island.

Ten months later, Blackbeard met his demise at Ocracoke.

Local residents claim that Blackbeard's ghost continues to roam Indian Island in search of his treasure. They say that the glow of his lantern can still be seen on clear, cold January nights.

People in the small community of South Creek on the southern shore of the Pamlico River have ancestors who either lived on or farmed Indian Island. After the last inhabitant of the island left, visitors used it as a picnic spot. Now, the fast-eroding island is almost forsaken, visited only by an occasional fisherman.

Retrace your route to the ferry landing and drive south on N.C. 306 for 7.1 miles to the Beaufort County town of Aurora.

Beaufort County is split in two by the Pamlico River, and there is no bridge spanning the river east of Washington. Historically, the southern half of Beaufort County has thus shared a kinship with Pamlico County.

The scenic drive to Aurora passes through the expansive Beacham Savanna, the fertile lands of which have long been claimed by agriculture.

Turn east off U.S. 306 onto Main Street in Aurora.

Although the phosphate-mining facilities that loom over the river at the ferry landing now dominate the news coming out of Aurora and the surrounding area, it has not always been so. Visitors to the handsome turn-of-the-century commercial district on Main Street are often surprised to learn that the large-scale mining operations did not begin until the early 1960s.

Continue 9 blocks to the terminus of Main Street on the waterfront.

Aurora rests peacefully on the banks of South Creek some 7 miles from Hickory Point, where the creek empties into the Pamlico River. This navigable waterway gives the town a pleasant maritime setting. Commercial fishing vessels can be seen along the South Creek waterfront, and several boat ramps provide recreational opportunities for boaters and fishermen.

Retrace your route 4 blocks along Main Street to Fourth Street. Several late-nineteenth- and early-twentieth-century buildings displaying rich cornices and window details enhance the charm of the downtown area. Particularly noteworthy are the structures on the north and south sides of Main Street near Fourth and Fifth streets.

Five years before the Civil War, the area now occupied by the town of Aurora was inhabited by free blacks and a few Indians. Their settlement was known as Betty Town, or Bettys Town, until 1856, when a Methodist minister named W. H. Cunningham and a few white settlers arrived.

A number of theories have been given for the Reverend Cunningham's decision to name the village Aurora. Some believe he so named it because it was new, fertile land in the east. Another story goes that the cleric found the area to be a dark, dismal place in need of light. Most likely, however, the town received its name from a former county newspaper, the *Aurora Borealis*.

The small town apparently grew rather quickly, because it was able to provide a full company of Confederate volunteers in 1861.

During the war years, local resident Michael M. Gray made a valuable contribution to the Confederate war effort. Ironically, Gray was a New Jersey native who came to the southern shore of the Pamlico River on the famous steamboat *Oregon* years before the war. He decided to make the area his new home and eventually became a zealous supporter of the Southern cause. To channel Gray's enthusiasm into worthwhile activity, Confederate authorities directed him to sink navigation buoys placed in the rivers and sounds by the Federal forces in control of the northern half of the North Carolina coast. Gray shot his gun from shore, only to discover that lead bullets could not penetrate the metal of the buoys. To remedy the situation, he invented the steel-jacketed bullet.

When the war ended, the people in the Aurora area returned to their agrarian lifestyle, shipping farm and timber products 7 miles up South Creek to its entry into the Pamlico River.

There was a time when Aurora was the potato capital of North Carolina, and most likely of the entire nation. Potato farming was introduced to Aurora when a German musician, Paul Lincke, purchased a farm near the village after the Civil War.

An enduring tale from the period when the tuber was king reveals the significance of the crop to the local economy. According to the account, a farmer requested to be excused from jury duty in order to tend his thousand acres of potatoes. Responding to the plea, the judge announced, "Excused. Anybody who'll plant a thousand acres in potatoes is too crazy to serve on a jury anyway."

Aurora town hall

In 1880, the town of Aurora was incorporated. By the turn of the century, nearly five hundred people lived within its corporate limits. Rail and water traffic linked the town with the outside world.

As potato production increased in Idaho, California, and New England during World War II, Aurora lost its position of prominence in the market.

Just as it seemed that the town was in an irreversible tailspin, the promise of a bright tomorrow came in 1964, when Texasgulf, Inc., announced plans to begin phosphate mining in the area. With the announcement came the prospect of dynamic growth for the town. Some observers predicted Aurora would experience a population explosion resulting in a city of fifty thousand residents. Much to the dismay of the natives, such high hopes have never borne fruit. Instead, the phosphate-mining operations have brought a variety of problems and continuing controversy to the Pamlico region.

It was in the early 1960s that scientists discovered one of the largest phosphate-bearing deposits in the world under the Pamlico River and its southern shore. Phosphate had by that time become a valuable commodity in agricultural fertilizer.

Texasgulf acquired a seven-hundred-acre tract on Lee Creek, a tributary of the Pamlico River, approximately 5 miles northwest of Aurora. In order to get to the phosphate rock resting a hundred feet under the sandy surface, open-pit strip mining was used. Once the grayish black material was brought to the surface, it was mixed with water and pumped to the processing plant a mile away. Gypsum, a waste by-product produced at the plant, was once stacked nearby in a sixty-foot-high pile that covered fifty acres.

Pollution problems related to the mining process surfaced in 1982. A series of air-quality violations at the plant resulted in significant fines being levied by the state in the 1980s.

In 1989, on the twenty-fifth anniversary of the opening of the facility at Aurora, Texasgulf announced that it would institute a new method of dry mining designed to restore land used in the mining process. Subsequent wastewater recycling systems have been implemented to reduce the amount of phosphate and fluoride discharged into the river.

Officials from the Smithsonian Institution have visited the phosphate mining pit near Aurora. They theorize that the ocean has covered the area countless times over the last 40 million years. From the depths of the pit, which reaches more than a hundred feet below sea level, numerous marine fossils up to 5 million years old have been recovered. Scientists believe that the mines in the Lee Creek area contain the richest deposits of invertebrate fossils on the Atlantic seaboard.

Because the bottom of the mining pit was several hundred feet below sea level at one time, the site is a paleontologist's delight. Almost every day, an estimated 84 million fossilized shark's teeth are brought forth from the pit. Among the rare treasures yielded by the mining operation are the tip of a walrus's tusk, a whole crab estimated to be more than 30 million years old, and the jaw of a sea cow, thought to be one of only three in the world. Numerous fossils from the Aurora site have been given to the Smithsonian.

These rich grounds have attracted fossil hunters from many parts of the nation. Because of the depth of the pit and the steepness of its walls, Texasgulf requires that all fossil hunters be escorted by a company employee, sign a release, and wear a safety helmet. Fossil hunting is permitted in the spring and fall.

Aurora Fossil Museum

For less adventurous visitors to Aurora, the Aurora Fossil Museum, located at the corner of Main and Fourth streets, provides a unique opportunity to gain an understanding of the phosphate-mining process and to learn about the fossils it has produced.

Fossils on display at the facility include enormous teeth from forty-foot-long sharks, backbones from gigantic whales, bones from birds extinct for millions of years, and skeletons of ancient dolphins that had necks.

Through murals, exhibits, and slide shows, the museum educates visitors about the unique geology of the coastal region. A simulated phosphate pit even allows them to view the mining process without going to the mine.

Admission is free. After touring the museum, visitors are welcome to search for specimens in a mound across the street.

From the museum, drive 1 block west on Main. Turn left, or south, on Fifth Street and proceed 4 blocks to N.C. 33. Turn left and travel east on N.C. 33.

Here begins an odyssey that leads to some of the most charming, quaint villages on the entire Atlantic coast. As the road winds its way into Pamlico County, these settlements appear as a semicircular cluster along Pamlico Sound. This tour provides an excellent look at the last vestiges of the uncommercialized coast in private ownership.

To reach South Creek, the first of the villages, follow N.C. 33 for 1.5 miles to the junction with S.R. 1912. Turn left, or east, onto S.R. 1912 and drive 4.8 miles, then turn left, or north, on S.R. 1910 for 0.7 mile.

Although the small village of South Creek lies in Beaufort County, it has close ties to the nearby sound-side villages in Pamlico County. Located on a peninsula formed by Bond and Muddy creeks at their entrance into the Pamlico River, this waterfront town was settled before 1794. In the early years of the nineteenth century, it was called Harold.

When the *Oregon* called at Harold in the middle part of the century, it became the first steamship to enter the Pamlico River and the creeks of the town. The locals were so impressed with the visiting steamer that they re-named the town Oregon. For a time, the ship was a lifeline for the town, since it carried the crops and natural resources exported from the Pamlico region and returned with much-needed merchandise.

Nothing remains of the great lumber empire that was established in the town just after the Civil War by a New Jersey soldier who had admired the dense forests while stationed in the area. The lumber operation flourished until the Great Depression.

When the town was incorporated in 1883, it was named Stanton. In 1925, the present name was adopted.

Boat ramps on the scenic waterfront give access to the creeks and the river.

Leave South Creek by retracing your route on S.R. 1910. Drive 0.1 mile west on S.R. 1912, then turn left, or south, onto S.R. 1906. A 1.9-mile drive on S.R. 1906 will bring you to an intersection with N.C. 33 at the small crossroads community of Campbell Creek. Turn east on N.C. 33. It is 6.7 miles to where N.C. 33 joins N.C. 304 at the Intracoastal Waterway. Here, the Waterway slices the northeastern neck of Pamlico County from the mainland. Goose Creek Island, as this neck is known, is the home of the two northernmost Pamlico County villages: Hobucken and Lowland.

Drive east onto the island across the Intracoastal Waterway (Goose Creek) via N.C. 33/N.C. 304.

When Pamlico County was created in 1872 from Beaufort and Craven counties, Goose Creek Island was not included in the new county. Two years later, this northern prong was added.

It is 1.4 miles from the bridge into Hobucken, the village that serves as a local boating, hunting, and fishing center. Although the picturesque town does not lie directly on the Intracoastal Waterway, access to the Waterway and Pamlico Sound is provided by Jones Bay, an arm of the sound. Marina facilities are located on the bay. The Coast Guard maintains a station on the waterfront.

An enormous mound of shells remains near Hobucken, evidence of the Indian habitation centuries before people of European descent came to the southern Pamlico shore.

Originally, Hobucken was known as Jones Bay. In 1880, Wiley Mayo, the first postmaster of Hobucken, prevailed upon the Post Office Department to rename the town for Hoboken, New Jersey, the destination of many shipments of Irish potatoes from Pamlico County.

Located 2 miles south of the Hobucken waterfront and separated from the mainland by the Intracoastal Waterway, Jones Island is the home of one of the premier hunting and fishing lodges on the Atlantic coast. In 1986, the exclusive Old South Rod and Gun Club began developing elaborate hunting facilities on the low-lying five-thousand-acre island. Although there are only fifteen hundred acres of high ground on the island, it offers 70 miles of shoreline. Its location in the heart of the Atlantic flyway makes Jones Island a favorite stopping place for ducks. Biologists believe that one of the largest herds of deer in the state thrives here. Access is by boat only.

Only the western portion of Goose Island is inhabited. Most of its eastern half is untamed wilderness dominated by extensive grass pampas and sedge marshes bordering Pamlico Sound. Due to the extensive marshland covering most of the eastern quarter of the island, it was not until well into the twentieth century that a road made its way across the island to the sound.

If you would like to take a brief side trip, turn east off N.C. 33/N.C. 304 onto the unpaved S.R. 1228. It is 2.2 miles from Hobucken to the sound near Ragged Point on Middle Bay. An undeveloped boat landing is located here. Attempts have been made to use this vast wilderness as a grazing area for cattle. Despite slow growth, the animals have been able to live in the wild through the winter without food or care from their owners.

Leaving Hobucken, turn north off N.C. 33/N.C. 304 onto S.R. 1229. It is 1.2 miles to the junction with S.R. 1230. Turn north on S.R. 1230 and drive 4.4 miles to Lowland, one of the most remote villages in all of coastal North Carolina. On the route from Hobucken to Lowland, water-filled drainage ditches line the roadway. Beyond these ditches is a desolate, forbidding wilderness.

Because of its remote setting, Lowland remains undiscovered by most coastal visitors. Nevertheless, until recent years, the village of seven hundred was the most populous town in Pamlico County. In 1856, it became the site of the first post office on Goose Creek Island.

Although the most concentrated portion of the widely scattered village

Lowland post office

does not border water, state-maintained roads radiate toward the bodies of water surrounding Lowland. To the south, S.R. 1236 leads 0.5 mile to Mill Seat Landing on Eastham Creek, a significant watercourse flowing into the Intracoastal Waterway. West of the village, S.R. 1232 terminates 1.6 miles from Lowland at Goose Creek. North of Lowland, S.R. 1233 terminates near Goose Creek's entry into the Pamlico River. On the northeast side of the village, S.R. 1234/S.R. 1235 leads 2.1 miles to Oyster Creek, a winding waterway which empties into the river near a small, uninhabited Pamlico River island known as Cedar Island. This proximity to the water allows many Lowland residents to earn their livelihood from fishing.

A close examination of the map of coastal North Carolina reveals that the Lowland-Hobucken area is located almost directly between the two favorite hangouts of Blackbeard: Ocracoke and Bath. Not surprisingly, then, there are tales that the pirate buried treasure on Goose Creek Island.

Geography may lend some credence to the story. In Blackbeard's day, the island was virtually inaccessible and very sparsely populated. It was the last bit of the mainland Blackbeard saw as he sailed out of the Pamlico River. Likewise, it was the first land he encountered as he made his way from Ocracoke across the sound en route to Bath.

Undoubtedly, Blackbeard found the numerous bays, creeks, coves, and inlets of Goose Creek Island to his liking. Not only could he take refuge here from severe weather, but he could also use the nooks and crannies of the island for his secret activities. Gold believed to have belonged to Blackbeard has been unearthed from time to time in the Lowland-Hobucken area.

Retrace your route from Lowland back to Hobucken and to the Intracoastal Waterway. Cross the Waterway and drive southwest on N.C. 304.

On N.C. 304, you will pass through the Goose Creek Wildlife Management Area. This game area, managed by the North Carolina Wildlife Resources Commission, is composed of 7,599 acres in Beaufort and Pamlico counties. Most of the acreage borders Goose Creek, primarily on its western shore. However, there is one significant chunk that is separated from the bulk of the preserve by the wilderness of the island. Located on the northeastern tip of Goose Creek Island on a sound-side bay called Mouse Harbor, this distant part of the wildlife area is accessible only by boat and ranks as one of the most remote parts of the coast.

Camping is permitted in designated areas only. Representative species in the Goose Creek Wildlife Management Area include fox, bear, deer, quail, and a variety of waterfowl and warm-water fish.

As the tour proceeds south from Goose Creek Island, N.C. 304 gradually bends toward the center of the county. As motorists make their way through the tiny villages along the route, they gain little perception of the jagged sound shoreline just to the east. Even the most detailed maps of the coast fail to give an accurate picture of the vast complex of rivers, bays, and creeks that gives the mainland coastline its irregular shape. Along the coast, the word *creek* does not mean a small stream or brook. Rather, it is considered to mean a navigable arm of a bay. By way of illustration, Mesic, located 3.3 miles south of the bridge over the Intracoastal Waterway, sits at the head of Bear Creek, a tributary of the Bay River.

Mesic, a fishing settlement of fewer than five hundred persons, was originally named Bear Creek. It was later renamed for S. R. Messick, a postmaster who served the community in the last quarter of the nineteenth century.

Mesic

While there is little to distinguish Mesic from the other small settlements in Pamlico County, the village does have one unusual claim to fame. One of its citizens may have directly contributed to the outcome of the Civil War. Many historians have theorized that if Robert E. Lee's most trusted lieutenant, Lieutenant General Thomas J. "Stonewall" Jackson, had not been shot down at Chancellorsville, the South may have faced a different fate later in the war. Private Rose of Mesic was one of the quartet of Confederate troops who mistakenly shot Jackson on the Virginia battlefield in May 1863.

Continue on N.C. 304. It is 4.5 miles from Mesic to Cash Corner. This community is one of two towns in the county by the same name. A second Cash Corner, known as Cash Corner No. 2, is located near the southern end of the county.

The current tour stop was settled about 1750 and was originally known as Hollyville—a name that still appears on some maps—for the profusion of holly trees that once grew here. It acquired its present name courtesy of

D. C. McCarter, a local merchant who reportedly sold his goods on a cash-only basis.

In Cash Corner, turn left, or east, off N.C. 304 onto N.C. 307. It is 1.3 miles to Vandemere, one of the leading seafood centers on the coast. Vandemere Creek, a tributary of the Bay River, provides a nice waterfront setting for the town. A public boat ramp offers water access. Fresh seafood is almost always available at the extensive commercial seafood docks. Vandemere's oysters are known far and wide as some of the most succulent on the North Carolina coast.

The town's name comes from the Dutch, meaning "from the sea." A former Union army surgeon who settled here with other Northerners after the Civil War gave the village its elegant name.

From 1872 to 1876, Vandemere served as the county seat of Pamlico County. Court was held in a local store.

Visitors who walk the streets of Vandemere can see the site of one of the first Indian villages encountered by Philip Amadas and Arthur Barlowe in July 1585. In his journal, Barlowe noted, "The 15th we came to Secotan and were well entertained there." Although there is no conclusive proof, archaeological evidence and locations traced from early North Carolina histories have led authorities to theorize that the village was located at the present site of Vandemere.

Foremost among the achievements of the Secotan tribe was the cultivation of the first flower garden in North America. Pomeiooc slaves were used to tend the flowers, shrubs, and trees planted in the garden. Its exact location has yet to be found.

Ever since the Indians vanished from the Vandemere area, innumerable pieces of pottery and other artifacts have been uncovered along the northern shore of the Bay River and its tributary creeks. Until the early part of the twentieth century, a forty-foot-high pile of oyster shells left by Indians stood near the seafood houses in Vandemere. Three Indian ovens, or "pitch kettles," found along Vandemere Creek have been preserved for archaeological study. Some of the streets in modern Vandemere can be traced back to ancient Indian trails.

Return to Cash Corner, turn left, or south, on N.C. 304, and drive 2.1 miles. Maribel, located at the junction of N.C. 304 and S.R. 1217, was

The Vandemere waterfront

named Shoofly when it was settled after the Civil War. Later, the postmaster gave the village its present name to honor his sweetheart in Georgia, a lady named Mary Belle.

The Bay River at Bayboro

Although Maribel is located on Chapel Creek, another of the numerous side waters of the Bay River, the lifestyle of its citizenry is dominated by agriculture, rather than fishing. Long ago, farmers discovered that the heavy muck in the area made excellent soil for growing cash crops such as potatoes, soybeans, and corn. This fertile ground extends for miles and miles north and south of the community. On the north, the Bay City Pocosin is 12 miles in width. Southwest of Maribel, the Light Ground Pocosin is smaller, measuring 4 miles by 5 miles.

Continue 4.5 miles to Bayboro, where N.C. 304 merges with N.C. 55. This pretty town of a thousand residents has been the seat of county government since it took the honor from Vandemere in 1876. It was named for the Bay River, which in turn was named for the bay trees and shrubs growing in the glades to the north. The Bay River lies entirely in Pamlico County. Though the road crosses the river within the corporate limits of the town, motorists gain little idea of the magnitude of the river at this point. Here, it is quite narrow, and navigation is extremely limited. East of Bayboro on its 16-mile route, the Bay River widens and becomes more useful to local residents. Much of its shoreline remains in a beautiful natural state. However, residential developments and cottages have begun to appear in recent years.

Over the past century, much of the growth and prosperity of Bayboro has resulted from its position as the seat of county government. A two-story frame building constructed in 1893 served as the courthouse until 1938, when the Works Progress Administration erected the existing Neoclassic brick facility on Main Street. A two-story annex completed in 1974 adjoins the western end of the courthouse. Inside the courthouse, visitors can tour the Pamlico County Historical Museum.

Follow N.C. 55 leaving Bayboro. Stonewall, located just to the southwest, is the sister city of the county seat. So closely joined are the towns that it is difficult to discern where one ends and the other begins. Numerous stately homes of architectural interest are located along the roadway.

The original settlers of Stonewall traced their roots to Somersetshire, England. They selected this site along the banks of the Bay River because it

Pamlico County Courthouse

provided a ready source of power to run the gristmills that served the farmers of Pamlico County.

Stonewall was incorporated as Jackson in 1857, so named to honor an owner of a local mill. After the Civil War, residents wanted to honor the memory of General Stonewall Jackson, but they were not satisfied that their town's name was identical to the last name of their fallen hero. Beginning in 1871, they insisted the town be known as Stonewall. A year later, the village served for a brief period as the first county seat of Pamlico County.

Continue approximately 3.9 miles on N.C. 55 to the small agricultural community of Merritt. Originally named Trent in honor of nearby Trent Creek, it was renamed in honor of General Wesley Merritt, a Union officer in the Civil War and a hero of the Spanish-American War.

At Merritt, turn left, or northeast, off N.C. 55 onto S.R. 1324. This portion of the tour runs parallel to the southern shore of the Bay River.

It is 6.5 miles to Florence, a town whose way of life has changed little over the decades. Settlers came to this old community in the eighteenth century to farm and to take advantage of the virgin timber.

Because of its location near Spring Creek, a significant tributary of the Bay River, the settlement was first known as Spring Creek. Its name was changed to Florence by the first postmaster in honor of his wife.

Turn right, or southeast, off S.R. 1324 onto S.R. 1325. It is 1.3 miles to the junction with S.R. 1327. Turn southeast onto S.R. 1327 and proceed 2.7 miles to Whortonsville (pronounced Hortonsville). Here, the tour closely approaches the sound, located just a short distance to the east.

This scenic village is strategically located on the water at the confluence of Broad and Brown creeks. Its small natural harbor is jammed with fishing boats, vivid proof of the maritime lifestyle of the local residents. Several seafood processing plants are situated on the waterfront, and homes more than a century old are sprinkled throughout the village. Originally named Bethel by settlers who arrived here in 1750, the town was renamed Whortonsville as a tribute to R. P. Horton, the first local postmaster.

The village of Pamlico is located only a short distance upstream from Whortonsville on the southern shore of Broad Creek. A boat trip between the two communities takes very little time. However, no bridge or ferry service links the two towns on the opposite shores of the waterway.

S.R. 1327 and S.R. 1325 intersect in the heart of Whortonsville. To avoid the 17.5-mile circle from Whortonsville via Merritt to Pamlico, proceed north on S.R. 1325 for 1.6 miles. Turn left onto S.R. 1321 and drive south 3.9 miles to the junction with S.R. 1320. This route cuts the distance between the two towns in half. The drive from Whortonsville to Pamlico will give you time to reflect on the travel difficulties coastal residents have endured for four centuries as a result of the unique geographic features of the region.

Turn east off S.R. 1321 onto S.R. 1320 and proceed 0.4 mile to the Wise House, the oldest house in the county and one of the oldest in the state. Majestically situated on a sweeping curve of Lower Broad Creek, the three-story house is privately owned and not open to the public. Its exterior can be seen from the road.

The Wise House was constructed around 1712 by Robert Burney and Joseph Fulcher. The two men came from England to join the wave of settlers flowing to the banks of the Neuse River and its tributaries in the first decade of the eighteenth century.

Burney and Fulcher constructed the house as a clubhouse and recreation hall for the growing number of pioneers in the region. The first-floor rooms were used as drawing rooms and dance halls. Boat races on Broad Creek entertained visitors. Horse "tournaments" were held on the straight stretch of road located near the house. To this day, local residents refer to this section of the highway as "Straight Stretch."

Approximately half the original home remains. Later additions are evident. Wooden pegs hold the older portions of the structure together. Heart-of-pine timbers and large, heavy windows provide evidence of the age of the dwelling. The long porches in the front and rear, the kitchen, and the servants' quarters date from the initial construction. Remains of the old slave quarters and an underground dungeon still exist as well.

On the interior, each of the first two floors has only two rooms, though very large. Four smaller rooms are on the third floor. A long, winding circular staircase gracefully connects the three floors.

The structure has been known as the Wise House since a family by that name acquired it earlier in this century. Records indicate that only five families have owned the house in its 275-year history.

No doubt, a house that has lasted through Indian uprisings, the Revolutionary War, and the Civil War harbors many memories. Probably the most interesting story about the house concerns the first governor of California, Peter H. Burnett (1807–1895). Some historians believe Burnett was born in the Wise House. In fact, local legend holds that between 1800 and 1850, the Burney, or Burnett, family took sole ownership of the house. After one of its sons met a violent, tragic death, the family decided to sell the house and plantation to move to California. Upon completion of the cross-country trip, one of the Burney/Burnett clan was said to have been elected the chief executive of California during the famous gold rush.

The fishing village of Pamlico is most likely the oldest settlement in the county. Records indicate that Hezekiah McColter settled the area in 1707. For the next century and a half, the growing settlement was known as Broad Creek. Joseph Dean of Fall River, Massachusetts, the first local postmaster, is credited with giving the town its present name.

From Pamlico, retrace S.R. 1320 to its junction with S.R. 1321. Turn south on S.R. 1321. After 0.4 mile, the road becomes S.R. 1317. Proceed 2.2 miles south on S.R. 1317 to the intersection with N.C. 55 at Moores Corner. Turn left, or south, onto N.C. 55. You will reach one of the very special places on the North Carolina coast after less than 2 miles.

A town located on a point of land formed by five large creeks and the Neuse River could only have been born of the water. And so it is with the charming town of Oriental. Morris Creek, Smith Creek, Kershaw Creek, and Greens Creek merge on the western side of town to form one of coastal North Carolina's finest harbors. A fifth creek, Whittaker Creek, provides a smaller harbor on the eastern side. On the southern side, the Neuse River and the Intracoastal Waterway provide a spectacular waterfront setting.

Located 30 miles from New Bern and 6 miles from the mouth of the Neuse River, this gateway to the Pamlico region is one of the popular stopovers for mariners plying the Intracoastal Waterway. The blessings of geography have helped make Oriental a major boating center in recent decades. So popular to pleasure boaters has this town become that it is now dubbed "the Sailing Capital of the East Coast."

But it has not always been so with Oriental. Prior to the 1960s, this was a tiny fishing and farming village on the verge of becoming a ghost town. Within the memory of its lifelong residents, watermelons were sold on the sandy streets for a nickel each and oysters were sold by the bushel for a half-dollar.

Long before Oriental was settled by people of European descent, its creeks were the domain of several tribes of Indians. One of the first Indian villages explored by Arthur Barlowe in July 1585 was Aquascogo, believed to have been at the present site of Oriental. It was here that the first act of violence by English people toward American Indians took place, when Barlowe's explorers burned homes and crops because of the theft of a silver cup.

As the first wave of white settlers began claiming prime lands along area waterways in the late seventeenth century, the two disparate civilizations clashed. Almost overnight, the seeds of hatred and contempt were sown that eventually exploded into bloodshed.

Once the Indian wars were over, increasing numbers of settlers found the five creeks and the fertile lands along them very attractive. Magnificent stands of virgin cypress and juniper trees provided ample supplies of lumber, which were used to build wharves and homes on the waterfront. However, no concentrated settlement developed in the area prior to Reconstruction.

Perhaps the safe anchorage afforded by the complex maze of creeks and backwater was the drawing card for the famous pirate. Maybe it was the isolation that lured him to this point of land on the Neuse. Whatever the reason, Blackbeard maintained a hiding spot within the present corporate limits of the town of Oriental. He reputedly left a beautiful foreign princess at this hiding spot after taking her as a prize in one of his last forays against shipping off the North Carolina coast. His rendezvous with destiny at Ocracoke intervened, and Blackbeard never sailed the waters of the Neuse again. In time, the stranded princess married and remained in the area for the rest of her life.

None of Blackbeard's treasure has ever been found in Oriental. If there was any, it may have washed away long ago, or may now be claimed by the waters of the Neuse. But if the digging that has gone on throughout this century is any indication, there are many people who believe that some of the pirate's lost treasure remains stashed somewhere under the streets of Oriental or along its creeks.

For many years, much of the treasure hunting centered around a large, old live oak near the waterfront on a farm between Smith and Greens creeks. Some treasure hunters believe that old brick foundations near the tree, called Teach's Oak, are the remnants of an underground passage. A large three-story house once stood farther back from the water. Known as "the Great House," it was most likely in existence during Blackbeard's time, as suggested by its hand-riven heart-of-pine construction. Many a spade has dug into the earth at this site in the quest for hidden riches. Local legends and frightening tales have added to the aura of mystery surrounding the place. (For more information about Blackbeard, see The Great Dismal Swamp Tour, page 55, The Ocracoke Tour, pages 253–57, and The Northern Pamlico River Tour, pages 291–94.)

The founding of Oriental took place by accident—or fate, as some would call it. On a spring day in 1871, Louis B. Midgette, a twenty-four-year-old resident of Roanoke Island, was on a boat trip from his home to New Bern with a load of salt fish when a horrendous storm blew up. Midgette was caught on the Neuse River. To avoid certain death, he steered his craft to the nearest shore, landing at the now-famous harbor at Oriental. Climbing ashore, he made a camp and marveled at the splendid natural beauty of the area while the storm ran its course.

Once the skies cleared, Midgette climbed a tree to survey the countryside. From his vantage point, he could see a fertile land blessed with copious natural resources. Before he left his newfound paradise, he envisioned a town rising on the Neuse waterfront at this peaceful harbor.

Midgette used all of his assets to purchase 250 acres at the site of his dreams. Near the waterfront, he erected a two-room dwelling, the only home within a 10-mile radius. To his delight, the town he envisioned soon began to take shape. Traders and fishermen were attracted to the fine harbor. Other prospective settlers were willing to take up residence in the town but were too poor to purchase land. Midgette gave such settlers a homestead.

As the village took shape, it lacked one essential ingredient: a name. One villager, eager to remedy the situation, choose Smith's Creek in deference to the local waterway. By 1896, a post office opened under that name here. But Louis Midgette, known to local residents as "Uncle Lou," was still not satisfied. He wanted a name that would express the beauty of his town.

Fate, it seems, once again played a hand in the town's destiny. Uncle Lou's wife, Rebecca, was combing the beaches on Hatteras Island one day when she came upon the nameplate of the *Oriental*, a Federal transport that had wrecked near Bodie Island in 1862. During her childhood in Dare County, the *Oriental* had once provided hungry local residents with a feast of raisins that had lasted for months. When she returned home, Rebecca suggested that the name of the town be changed to Oriental. Her husband concurred wholeheartedly with her idea, and so Smith's Creek gave way to Oriental.

Thought to be the original Oriental in the United States, the town now shares its name with at least twenty other towns. Uncle Lou's dream came full circle in 1899, when the town was incorporated.

With an apparently bright future on the horizon, Oriental ushered in the twentieth century as a progressive, vibrant town. Its businesses attracted patrons from many of the villages in Pamlico County. Oriental was the first town in the county to have a plant that generated electricity. Until 1928, Duke University operated the first resort summer school in the United States here.

Two firsts in North Carolina educational history took place in Oriental in the twentieth century. In 1917, the state's first motorized school bus, affectionately known as "the Benzine Buggy," began operation in Oriental. Then, in 1951, the first school integration suit in North Carolina—and only the second in the nation—was filed in Oriental.

While the rest of Pamlico County slowly recovered from the misery of the Great Depression, the economic chaos continued to reverberate through Oriental. Suddenly, there was no reason to visit the town.

There seemed to be little hope for the economic recovery of Louis Midgette's town until two Wake County judges were attracted to Oriental's boating possibilities in the early 1960s. They encouraged friends with boating interests to inspect the waterfront town. Everyone who came liked what they saw. Word spread far and wide, and the long-awaited recovery of Oriental began. In an instant, deserted houses were reclaimed. Marinas, motels, stores, real-estate agencies, and restaurants began to appear.

What has occurred here over the past three decades has been nothing short of a miracle. If Uncle Lou could stand on the highway bridge overlooking Oriental's harbor, he would be overwhelmed by the coffee-table-book vistas of the spectacular waterfront. Today, sailing enthusiasts from the world over call at Oriental. Every day, hundreds upon hundreds of magnificent pleasure craft, primarily sailing boats, line the shores of the creeks. Numerous marinas offer every service under the sun. Courtesy cars are even available for shopping excursions or sightseeing.

As Oriental's popularity among sailors has increased, the town has given birth to a variety of sailing organizations and schools. Several annual events and festivals showcase the beauty and maritime flavor of the town.

Most of commercial Oriental is clustered along the waterfront. Tourists are drawn to the interesting shops there. Elegant bed-and-breakfast inns are located in some of the historic homes that line the village streets. Overlooking the Neuse River, Lou-Mac Municipal Park on South Avenue provides a picnic area and a riverfront walkway.

To the gratification of visitors and residents alike, Oriental has been able to avoid many of the pitfalls encountered by fast-growing communities along the coast. Despite its popularity, the picturesque sailing town remains virtually unspoiled. Visitors often view it as a delightful blend of an old fishing village and an upscale yachting club. Oriental has found a happy medium. In terms of development, it is an world alien from what Uncle Lou envisioned more than a century ago. But as to its breathtaking beauty, Oriental remains the same.

From the bridge spanning the creeks which blend into the harbor at Oriental, you can enjoy one last spectacular view of the waterfront.

Proceed southwest across the bridge, where the highway becomes S.R. 1308. Approximately 2.9 miles west of the bridge, turn left onto S.R. 1302 and drive south 2 miles to the small river village of Janeiro.

Janeiro's magnificent waterfront location is enhanced by Dawson Creek, a navigable waterway which empties into the Neuse at the town. Public boat ramps are located on the creek, providing river access. A picnic area featuring a walkway to the shore is located on the north side of the creek.

With a mighty river at its front door and a navigable creek flowing up to its back door from the hinterlands, this town evolved into a substantial commercial center replete with lavish homes, a hotel, mercantile establishments, mills, gins, and wharves.

Until a post office opened as Janeiro in 1891, the prosperous village was

The Lou-Mac Municipal Park

TOURING THE BACKROADS OF NORTH CAROLINA'S UPPER COAST

known as Dawson Creek. The new name came courtesy of local seafaring men, who christened the town in honor of Rio de Janeiro, Brazil.

Bridge at Oriental

Once the mouth of the creek was bridged, freight boats no longer made regular runs to Janeiro, and the fishing village fell into relative obscurity. Yet there remain ghosts of the past, vivid reminders of a time when prosperous planters built exquisite mansions near the river.

Chief among the relics of the bygone days of prosperity is the China Grove House, located on the north side of the village on S.R. 1302. Listed on the National Register of Historic Places, this three-story Federal house is believed to be the second-oldest home in Pamlico County. It was constructed in 1790, presumably by Edward Carraway, a prosperous farmer and shipper. Named for a row of chinaberry trees growing near the house, China Grove was restored in the 1960s. Its massive double porch offers an outstanding view of the Neuse. Unfortunately, the house is not open to the public.

Leaving Janeiro, continue on S.R. 1302. It is 2.2 miles to an intersection with S.R. 1301. This is the location of Cash Corner No. 2, the community which shares a name with a Pamlico County community to the north. Continue on S.R. 1302 to the junction with N.C. 306 approximately 1.4 miles west of Cash Corner No. 2. Turn south on N.C. 306 and proceed 2.2 miles south to the end of the road at Minnesott Beach.

Dawson Creek Park

China Grove House

Just south of this resort town lies one of coastal North Carolina's most historic geographic points. Wilkinson Point, the southern tip of Pamlico County, extends into the Neuse River at the place where the river bends in a northwesterly direction toward New Bern. This spit of land is most likely the first place on the American mainland where the English colonists came ashore.

In his 1585 diary, Captain Arthur Barlowe recorded that an expeditionary force left Ocracoke on the "11th day of July . . . passed over the water . . . for the mainland, in which we discovered the towns of Pomeiok, Aquascogo, and Secotan."

According to the renowned early histories of North Carolina by Francis L. Hawks and François-Xavier Martin, the Indian village of Pomeiooc was probably located somewhere near Wilkinson Point. So impressed was Barlowe with the virgin forests, the sound, and the rivers near the current tour stop that he described the area as "the most plentifull, sweete, fruitful and wholsome of all the world."

Minnesott Beach, a small, scenic resort community nestled on the banks of the Neuse, traces its origins to the years following World War I. Consequently, it is the oldest resort in the county. Naaman Hardison, a native of the area who achieved success in the freight business, was the genius behind this watering hole, which remains the most popular resort in the county. Its unusual name comes from an Indian word meaning "land of sky-blue water."

Clean river beaches attract tourists to Minnesott Beach, while a temperate climate and an unhurried lifestyle lure growing numbers of retirees. Numerous privately owned cottages and a large yacht basin line the waterfront.

Three well-known summer camps are located near Minnesott Beach. Camp Don Lee, a facility owned and operated by the United Methodist Church, is situated on a parcel of land located between Dawson Creek and Wilkinson Point. Camp Sea Gull and Camp Seafarer are among the largest and most popular youth camps on the Atlantic coast. Both are located on high ground at Wilkinson Point.

Access to Minnesott Beach and other parts of southern Pamlico County from New Bern and the southern shore of the Neuse is provided by the state-owned Cherry Branch–Minnesott Beach Ferry. This ferry began operation in 1972 in response to public demand for a more direct access to the Cherry Point Marine Air Station, located on the southern side of the river. Crossing time for the twenty-vehicle vessel is twenty minutes. There is no fare.

From the waterfront at Minnesott Beach, you will have a spectacular view of the Neuse River, the water route used by settlers and commercial traffic since colonial times. From the ships of Sir Walter Raleigh and the pirate ships of the past to the military craft and pleasure boats plying its waters today, the Neuse has proven a vital waterway.

Minnesott Beach

Formed in western Durham County by the junction of the Eno and Flat rivers, the mighty Neuse flows southeast through Wake, Johnston, Wayne, Lenoir, and Craven counties. Near its mouth at Pamlico Sound, the 200-mile-long river forms a portion of the boundaries of Craven, Carteret, and Pamlico counties. Encompassing 6,192 square miles, and populated by a sixth of the state's population, the Neuse River Basin is the third-largest river basin in the state, and one of only three major river basins that is completely contained within the boundaries of North Carolina.

Arthur Barlowe named the river for the local Neusiok tribe. Among the

Tuscaroras, the river was known as Gowtano, meaning "pine in the water."

As with the other significant waterways of coastal North Carolina, the Neuse is not without its tales of lost treasure.

As war grew imminent in 1860, banking officials in New Bern became concerned over the safety of their assets. Ultimately, they made the decision to entrust the bank deposits, consisting primarily of gold, to a committee of honest men. This committee was charged with the responsibility of burying the gold in a safe place down the Neuse River. A burial site was selected somewhere near Wilkinson Point.

The ravages of the Civil War took their toll on the men of the committee. By the end of the war, no one was alive who knew the exact location of the bank treasure. No report has ever surfaced about its discovery. Perhaps some lucky camper at Sea Gull or Seafarer will one day unwittingly unearth untold riches.

To continue the tour, turn around and drive north on N.C. 306 to the village of Arapahoe, located 5 miles from Wilkinson Point. Arapahoe is one of the oldest towns in Pamlico County. Permanent settlers from Virginia arrived here in the latter part of the seventeenth century. Legend has it that the settlement was named for a local racehorse.

At Arapahoe, turn left on S.R. 1117 and drive 2.5 miles southwest to Beards Creek. This village is blessed with a magnificent waterfront location on Beard Creek and the Neuse River. Beard Creek is navigable for almost 6 miles.

Stories abound that the creek was named for Blackbeard, who is known to have frequented the Neuse River. With a broad, deep estuary inside its narrow mouth, the creek would have provided an excellent sanctuary for the pirate and his men.

Since World War II, a small recreational community has developed along the banks of the river and creek.

Retrace your route to Arapahoe, turn left on N.C. 306, and drive 6.7 miles north to the village of Grantsboro. Located in the heart of Pamlico farming country, this community was named for William Grant, a nineteenth-century peddler from New York City who settled here, married, and built a store. Grant's store building was subsequently moved from its original location to the intersection of N.C. 306 and N.C. 55, where it remained in operation until 1960.

Today, Grantsboro lies miles and miles from the sea, but there was a time when this area was located right at the shore. A sand ridge sixty feet above sea level runs directly through the village. Discernable not only on geologic maps but also to the naked eye, the ridge runs in a north-south direction across Pamlico County. This unusual geographic feature marks the ocean shoreline of many, many years ago. Because of the ridge, Grantsboro is perhaps the highest spot in the county.

To the north, the ridge crosses the Pamlico River in central Beaufort County, runs through Martin County, and disappears into the Roanoke River, only to surface again in Bertie County, whence it runs toward Virginia.

South of Grantsboro, the ridge, usually a mile or more wide, runs parallel to N.C. 306. Arapahoe is situated on the ridge as it makes its way to the river, where it becomes the tall banks of Wilkinson Point. From under the Neuse, the ridge reappears at Cherry Point in Craven County. It then runs through Carteret County and vanishes beneath the waters of Bogue Sound.

In times past, Pamlico residents living east of the ridge buried their dead on it.

At the intersection of N.C. 306 and N.C. 55 in Grantsboro, turn left, or west, onto N.C. 55. It is 7 miles to the small settlement of Olympia. This village lies at the western extreme of Pamlico County, separated from Craven County by Broad Creek, a significant tributary of the Neuse.

The site of Olympia had already been settled when the oldest towns in North Carolina—Bath, New Bern, Beaufort, and Edenton—were incorporated.

Until the 1970s, Olympia held a unique distinction: America's oldest holly tree, estimated to be two centuries old, grew here. It stood nearly a hundred feet tall. The tree and the surrounding three acres were purchased and fenced by the state in 1964. A subsequent storm destroyed the tree, from which gavels were made for local clubs and civic organizations.

The tour ends in Olympia. New Bern is located 6 miles to the west on N.C. 55.

Grantsboro

Appendix

Federal Agencies, Parks, and Historic Sites

**Alligator River
National Wildlife Refuge**
P.O. Box 1969
Manteo, N.C. 27954
919-473-1131

**Cape Hatteras
National Seashore**
Route 1, Box 675
Manteo, N.C. 27954
919-473-2111

**Currituck National
Wildlife Refuge**
P.O. Box 39
Knotts Island, N.C. 27950
919-429-3100

**Fort Raleigh
National Historic Site**
Route 1, Box 675
Manteo, N.C. 27954
919-473-2111

**Great Dismal Swamp
National Wildlife Refuge**
P.O. Box 349
Suffolk, Va. 23434
804-986-3705

**Lake Mattamuskeet/
Swan Quarter National
Wildlife Refuge**
Route 1, Box N-2
Swan Quarter, N.C. 27855
919-926-4021

**Mackay Island
National Wildlife Refuge**
P.O. Box 39
Knotts Island, N.C. 27950
919-429-3100

**Pea Island National
Wildlife Refuge**
P.O. Box 150
Rodanthe, N.C. 27968
919-987-2394

**Pocosin Lakes
National Wildlife Refuge**
Route 1, Box 195-B
Creswell, N.C. 27928
919-797-4431

**Wright Brothers
National Memorial**
P.O. Box 427
Kill Devil Hills, N.C. 27948
919-441-7430

State Agencies, Parks, and Historic Sites

**Coastal Reserve Coordinator
North Carolina
National Estuarine Research
Reserve**
7205 Wrightsville Avenue
Wilmington, N.C. 28403
910-256-3721

***Elizabeth II* State Historic Site**
P.O. Box 155
Manteo, N.C. 27954
919-473-1144

**Goose Creek
State Park**
Route 2, Box 372
Washington, N.C. 27889
919-923-2191

Historic Bath State Historic Site
P.O. Box 148
Bath, N.C. 27808
919-923-3971

**Jockey's Ridge
State Park**
P.O. Box 592
Nags Head, N.C. 27959
919-441-7132

Merchants Millpond State Park
Route 1, Box 141-A
Gatesville, N.C. 27938
919-357-1191

Museum of the Albemarle
1116 U.S. 17 South
Elizabeth City, N.C. 27909
919-335-1453

North Carolina Aquarium
at Roanoke Island
P.O. Box 967
Manteo, N.C. 27954
919-473-3493

North Carolina Division
of Archives and History
Historic Sites Section
109 East Jones Street
Raleigh, N.C. 27611
919-733-7862

North Carolina Division
of Coastal Management
P.O. Box 27687
Raleigh, N.C. 27611
919-733-2293

North Carolina Division
of Marine Fisheries
P.O. Box 769
Morehead City, N.C. 28577
800-682-2632

North Carolina
Division of Parks
and Recreation
512 North Salisbury Street
Raleigh, N.C. 27611
919-733-4181

North Carolina Ferry Division
113 Arendell Street
Morehead City, N.C. 28550
919-726-6446 or 800-BY-FERRY

North Carolina Travel
and Tourism Division
430 Salisbury Street
Raleigh, N.C. 27611
919-733-4171 or
800-VISIT-NC

North Carolina Wildlife
Resources Commission
512 North Salisbury Street
Raleigh, N.C. 27611
919-733-3393 or 800-662-7350

Pettigrew State Park
Route 1, Box 336
Creswell, N.C. 27928
919-797-4475

Somerset Place
State Historic Site
P.O. Box 215
Creswell, N.C. 27928
919-797-4560

Museums and Other Historic Attractions

Aurora Fossil Museum
Fourth and Main Streets
Aurora, N.C. 27806
919-322-4238

Belhaven Memorial Museum
P.O. Box 220
Belhaven, N.C. 27810
919-943-3055 or 919-943-2242

Chicamacomico
Lifesaving Station
N.C. 12
Rodanthe, N.C. 27968
919-987-1532

Elizabethan Gardens
P.O. Box 1150
Manteo, N.C. 27954
919-473-3234

Graveyard of the
Atlantic Museum
P.O. Box 191
Hatteras, N.C. 27943

Historic Albemarle Tour, Inc.
P.O. Box 759
Edenton, N.C. 27932
919-482-7325

Historic Edenton
P.O. Box 474
Edenton, N.C. 27932
919-482-2637

The Lost Colony
P.O. Box 40
Manteo, N.C. 27954
919-473-3414 or 800-488-5012

Nags Head Woods
Ecological Preserve
P.O. Box 1942
Kill Devil Hills, N.C. 27948
919-441-2525

Newbold-White House
P.O. Box 103
Hertford, N.C. 27944
919-426-7567

Ocracoke Island Visitor Center
N.C. 12
Ocracoke, N.C. 27968
919-928-4531

Port O' Plymouth Museum
P.O. Box 296
Plymouth, N.C. 27962
919-793-1377

Whalehead Club
N.C. 12
Corolla, N.C. 27927
919-232-2075

Chambers of Commerce and Information Centers

Aycock Brown
Welcome Center
P.O. Box 392
Kitty Hawk, N.C. 27949
919-261-4644

Belhaven Community
Chamber of Commerce
102 West Main Street
P.O. Box 147
Belhaven, N.C. 27810
919-943-3770

Camden County Manager
P.O. Box 190
Camden, N.C. 27921
919-338-1919

Chowan County Tourism
Development Authority
P.O. Box 245
Edenton, N.C. 27932
919-482-3400 or 800-775-0111

Corolla Business Association
P.O. Box 25
Corolla, N.C. 27927

Currituck County Manager
P.O. Box 39
Currituck, N.C. 27929
919-232-2075

Dare County Tourist Bureau
P.O. Box 399
Manteo, N.C. 27954
919-473-2138 or 800-446-6262

Dismal Swamp Canal Visitor
Center
2356 U.S. 17 North
South Mills, N.C. 27976
919-771-8333

Edenton–Chowan County
Chamber of Commerce
P.O. Box 245
Edenton, N.C. 27932
919-482-3400

Elizabeth City Area
Chamber of Commerce
502 East Eringhaus Street
P.O. Box 426
Elizabeth City, N.C. 27909
919-335-4365

Greater Hyde County
Chamber of Commerce
Route 1, Box 81
Engelhard, N.C. 27824
919-925-5201

Ocracoke Civic Club
P.O. Box 456
Ocracoke, N.C. 27960
919-928-6711

Outer Banks
Chamber of Commerce
P.O. Box 1757
Kill Devil Hills, N.C. 27948
919-441-8144

Perquimans County
Chamber of Commerce
P.O. Box 27
Hertford, N.C. 27944
919-426-5657

Town of Columbia
P.O. Box 361
Columbia, N.C. 27925
919-796-2761

Washington–Beaufort
County Chamber of Commerce
102 West Stewart Parkway
P.O. Box 665
Washington, N.C. 27889
919-946-9168

Washington County
Chamber of Commerce
701 Washington Street/U.S. 64
Plymouth, N.C. 27962
919-793-4804

Bibliography

Albemarle Genealogical Society. *The Heritage of Currituck County*. Winston-Salem, N.C.: Hunter Publishing Company, 1985.

Alexander, John, and James Lazell. *Ribbon of Sand: The Amazing Convergence of the Ocean and the Outer Banks*. Chapel Hill, N.C.: Algonquin Books, 1992.

Alexandria Drafting Company. *Salt Water Sport Fishing and Boating In North Carolina*. Alexandria, Va.: Alexandria Drafting Company, 1981.

Alford, Michael B. *Traditional Work Boats of North Carolina*. Harkers Island, N.C.: Hancock Publishing, 1990.

Allcott, John V. *Colonial Homes in North Carolina*. Raleigh, N.C.: Carolina Tercentenary Commission, 1963.

Anderson, Nina, and William Anderson. *Southern Treasures*. Chester, Conn.: Globe Pequot Press, 1987.

Arner, Robert D. *The Lost Colony in Literature*. Raleigh, N.C.: North Carolina Department of Cultural Resources, 1985.

Ashe, S. *History of North Carolina*. 2 vols. Raleigh, N.C.: Edwards and Broughton Printing Company, 1925.

Ball, Bonnie. *The Melungeons*. Rev. ed. Johnson City, Tenn.: Overmountain Press, 1992.

Ballance, Alton. *Ocracokers*. Chapel Hill, N.C.: University of North Carolina Press, 1989.

Barrett, John G. *North Carolina as a Civil War Battleground, 1861–1865*. Raleigh, N.C.: North Carolina Department of Archives and History, 1960.

————. *The Civil War in North Carolina*. Chapel Hill, N.C.: University of North Carolina Press, 1963.

Bell, Lester M. *As I See It*. Edenton, N.C.: *Chowan Herald*, 1994.

Biggs, Walter C., Jr., and James F. Parnell. *State Parks of North Carolina*. Winston-Salem, N.C.: John F. Blair, Publisher, 1989.

Bishir, Catherine W. *The "Unpainted Aristocracy": The Beach Cottages of Old Nags Head*. Raleigh, N.C.: North Carolina Division of Archives and History, 1983.

————. *North Carolina Architecture*. Chapel Hill, N.C.: University of North Carolina Press, 1990.

Bledsoe, Jerry. *Carolina Curiosities*. Charlotte, N.C.: East Woods Press, 1984.

Booker, Louise R. *Historical and Traditional "Tar Heel" Stories from the Colorful Central Carolina Coastal Plain*. Murfreesboro, N.C.: Johnson Publishing Company, 1968.

Bragg, Cecil S. *Ocracoke Island: Pearl of the Outer Banks*. Manteo, N.C.: Times Printing Company, 1973.

Brickell, John. *The Natural History of North Carolina*. 1737. Reprint, Murfreesboro, N.C.: Johnson Publishing Company, 1968.

Burns, Robert P., ed. *100 Courthouses: A Report on North Carolina Judicial Facilities*. Vol. 2, *The County Perspective*. Raleigh, N.C.: North Carolina State University, 1978.

Butchko, Thomas R. *On the Shores of the Pasquotank: The Architectural Heritage of Elizabeth City and Pasquotank County, North Carolina*. Elizabeth City, N.C.: Museum of the Albemarle, 1989.

————. *An Architectural Portrait: The Historic Architecture of Edenton, North Carolina*. Edenton, N.C.: Edenton Woman's Club, 1992.

Butler, Lindley S. *North Carolina and the Coming of the Revolution, 1763–1776*. Raleigh: North Carolina Department of Cultural Resources, 1976.

Byrd, William. *William Byrd's Histories of the Dividing Line Betwixt Virginia and North Carolina*. Edited by William K. Boyd. Raleigh, N.C.: North Carolina Historical Commission, 1929.

Cairns, Huntington. *This Other Eden: Aspects of the Natural History of the Outer Banks of North Carolina*. Manteo, N.C.: Times Printing Company, 1974.

Campbell, Elizabeth A. *The Carving on the Tree. A True Account of America's First Mystery: The Lost Colony of Roanoke Island*. Boston: Little, Brown and Company, 1968.

Carabelle Books. *Outer Banks Guide: An Historical Adventure from Kitty Hawk to Ocracoke*. Reston, Va.: Carabelle Books, 1983.

Carr, Dawson. *The Cape Hatteras Lighthouse: Sentinel of the Shoals*. Chapel Hill, N.C.: University of North Carolina Press, 1991.

Carter, Catherine T. *Ghost Tales of the Moratoc*. Winston-Salem, N.C.: John F. Blair, Publisher, 1992.

Cheatham, James T. *The Atlantic Turkey Shoot: U-boats off the Outer Banks in World War II*. Greenville, N.C.: Williams and Simpson, Inc., Publishers, 1990.

————. *Sailing the Carolina Sounds: Historical Places and My Favorite People*. Charlotte, N.C.: Delmar Printing and Publishing, 1993.

Corbitt, David Leroy. *Explorations, Descriptions, and Attempted Settlements of Carolina, 1584–1590*. Raleigh, N.C.: North Carolina Department of Archives and History, 1948.

————. *The Formation of the North Carolina Counties, 1663–1943*. Raleigh, N.C.: North Carolina Department of Archives and History, 1950.

Corey, Cindy. *Exploring the Seacoast of North Carolina*. Raleigh, N.C.: Provincial Press, 1969.

————. *Exploring the Lighthouses of North Carolina*. Chapel Hill, N.C.: Provincial Press, 1982.

Crosland, Patrick D. *The Outer Banks*. Arlington, Va.: Interpretive Publications, 1981.

Currituck County Historical Society. *The Journal of Currituck County Historical Society* 1 (1973).

————. *The Journal of Currituck County Historical Society* (1977).

Davis, Hubert J. *The Great Dismal Swamp: Its History, Folklore and Science*. Murfreesboro, N.C.: Johnson Publishing Company, 1971.

————. *Myths and Legends of the Great Dismal Swamp*. Murfreesboro, N.C.: Johnson Publishing Company, 1981.

Day, Jean. *Wild Ponies of the Outer Banks*. Havelock, N.C.: The Print Shop, 1988.

de Hart, Allen. *North Carolina Hiking Trails*. Boston: Appalachian Mountain Club, 1982.

DePanfilis, Jayne, and Nancy McWilliams. *The Insider's Guide to North Carolina's Outer Banks*. Manteo, N.C.: Insider's Guides, Inc., 1994.

Doolittle, Myrtle G. *Ocracoke Island: Peeking through the Keyhole of Memory*. Charlotte, N.C.: Herb Eaton Historical Publications, 1989.

Eastern Publishing. *Outer Banks Traveler's Guide and Souvenir Book*. Manteo, N.C.: Eastern Publishing Services, 1992.

Edenton Woman's Club. *Historic Edenton and Countryside*. Edenton, N.C.: Chowan Herald.

Edmunds, Pocahontas Wight. *Tales of the North Carolina Coast*. Raleigh, N.C.: Edwards and Broughton Company, 1986.

Ehringhaus, Ann Sebrell. *Ocracoke Portrait*. Winston-Salem, N.C.: John F. Blair, Publisher, 1988.

Farb, Roderick M. *Shipwrecks: Diving the Graveyard of the Atlantic*. Hillsborough, N.C.: Menasha Ridge Press, 1985.

Furr, Gene. *Images: The Outer Banks*. Chapel Hill, N.C.: Cinehaus Productions, 1981.

Gannon, Michael. *Operation Drumbeat*. New York: Harper and Row, 1990.

Gentile, Gary. *Shipwrecks of North Carolina from Hatteras Inlet South*. Philadelphia: Gary Gentile Productions, 1992.

Gillespie, C. Richard. *The James Adams Floating Theatre*. Centreville, Md.: Tidewater Publishers, 1991.

Gleasner, Diana, and Bill Gleasner. *Sea Islands of the South*. Charlotte, N.C.: East Woods Press, 1980.

Goerch, Carl. *Down Home*. Raleigh, N.C.: Edwards and Broughton Company, 1943.

————. *Ocracoke*. Winston-Salem, N.C.: John F. Blair, Publisher, 1956.

Goldstein, Robert J. *Pier Fishing in North Carolina*. Winston-Salem, N.C.: John F. Blair, Publisher, 1978.

————. *Coastal Fishing in the Carolinas: From Surf, Pier, and Jetty*. Winston-Salem, N.C.: John F. Blair, Publisher, 1986.

Graetz, Karl E. *Seacoast Plants of the Carolinas for Conservation and Beautification*. Raleigh, N.C.: UNC Sea Grant Program, 1982.

Hackney, Cay. *The Manteo Walking Tour: A Step Back in Time*. Manteo, N.C.: Roanoke Island Studio, 1987.

Hakluyt, Richard. *Hakluyt's Voyages*. Edited by Irwin Blacker. New York: Viking Press, 1965.

Haley, Dru Gatewood, and Raymond A. Winslow, Jr. *The Historic Architecture of Perquimans County, North Carolina*. Hertford, N.C.: Town of Hertford, 1982.

Harrington, J. C. *Archaeology and the Enigma of Fort Raleigh*. Raleigh, N.C.: North Carolina Department of Cultural Resources, 1984.

Hickham, Homer H., Jr. *Torpedo Junction*. Annapolis, Md.: Naval Institute Press, 1989.

Hill, Michael, ed. *Guide to North Carolina Highway Historical Markers*. 5th ed. Raleigh, N.C.: North Carolina Division of Archives and History, 1990.

Holland, F. Ross, Jr. *America's Lighthouses: An Illustrated History*. New York: Dover Publications, 1988.

————. *Great American Lighthouses*. Washington, D.C.: Preservation Press, 1989.

Hulton, Paul, ed. *America 1585: The Complete Drawings of John White*. Chapel Hill, N.C.: University of North Carolina Press, 1984.

Hyde County Historical Society. *Hyde County History: A Hyde County Bicentennial Project*. 1976.

Johnson, Archie, and Bud Coppedge. *Gun Clubs and Decoys of Back Bay and Currituck Sound*. Virginia Beach, Va.: CurBac Press, 1991.

Johnson, F. Roy. *The Algonquins: Indians of That Part of the New World First Visited by the English*. Vol. 2, *History and Traditions*. Murfreesboro, N.C.: Johnson Publishing Company, 1972.

————. *The Lost Colony in Fact and Legend*. Murfreesboro, N.C.: Johnson Publishing Company, 1983.

Jones, S. M. *A History of the Tri-County Area—Craven, Pamlico, and Carteret Counties—from Their Earliest Settlements to the Present*. New Bern, N.C.: Owen G. Dunn Company, 1981.

Kaufman, Wallace, and Orrin H. Pilkey. *The Beaches Are Moving: The Drowning of America's Shoreline*. Garden City, N.Y.: Anchor Press/Doubleday, 1979.

Keatts, Henry C., and George C. Farr. *Dive into History*. Vol. 1, *Warships*. Houston: Pisces Books, 1990.

Kirk, Paul W., Jr., ed. *The Great Dismal Swamp*. Charlottesville, Va.: University of Virginia Press, 1979.

Kraus, E. Jean Wilson. *A Guide to Ocean Dune Plants Common to North Carolina*. Chapel Hill, N.C.: University of North Carolina Press, 1988.

Kupperman, Karen Ordahl. *Roanoke: The Abandoned Colony*. Totowana, N.J.: Rowman and Allenheld, Publishers, 1984.

Lane, Mills. *Architecture of the Old South: North Carolina*. New York: Abbeville Press, 1985.

Lawson, Glenn. *Troubled Waters*. Swansboro, N.C.: Hadnot Creek Publishing Company, 1990.

Lawson, John. *A New Voyage to Carolina*. 1709. Edited by Hugh T. Lefler. Chapel Hill, N.C.: University of North Carolina Press, 1967.

Lefler, Hugh T., and Albert Ray Newsome. *North Carolina: The History of a Southern State*. 3rd ed. Chapel Hill, N.C.: University of North Carolina Press, 1973.

Lefler, Hugh T., ed. *North Carolina History Told by Contemporaries*. Chapel Hill, N.C.: University of North Carolina Press, 1948.

Leland, Elizabeth. *The Vanishing Coast*. Winston-Salem, N.C.: John F. Blair, Publisher, 1992.

Lemmon, Sarah McCulloh. *North Carolina's Role in World War II*. Raleigh: North Carolina Division of Archives and History, 1969.

————. *North Carolina's Role in the First World War*. Raleigh, N.C.: North Carolina Division of Archives and History, 1975.

Lewis, Taylor, and Joanne Young. *The Hidden Treasure of Bath Town*. Norfolk, Va.: Taylor Lewis and Associates, 1977.

Lonsdale, Richard E. *Atlas of North Carolina*. Chapel Hill, N.C.: University of North Carolina Press, 1967.

Loy, Ursula, and Pauline Worthy. *Washington and the Pamlico*. Washington-Beaufort Bicentennial Commission, 1976.

MacNeill, Ben Dixon. *The Hatterasman*. Winston-Salem, N.C.: John F. Blair, Publisher, 1958.

Manning, Phillip. *Afoot in the South: Walks in the Natural Areas of North Carolina*. Winston-Salem, N.C.: John F. Blair, Publisher, 1993.

Marsh, Kenneth F., and Blanche Marsh. *Colonial Bath: North Carolina's Oldest Town*. Asheville, N.C.: Biltmore Press, 1966.

McAdoo, Donald, and Carol McAdoo. *Reflections*. Manteo, N.C.: Island Publishing, Inc., 1976.

Merrens, Harry Roy. *Colonial North Carolina in the Eighteenth Century*. Chapel Hill, N.C.: University of North Carolina Press, 1964.

Meyer, Peter. *Nature Guide to the North Carolina Coast*. Wilmington, N.C.: Avian-Cetacean Press, 1991.

Miller, Helen Hill. *Historic Places around the Banks*. Charlotte, N.C.: McNally and Loftin, Publishers, 1974.

Mobley, Joe A. *Pamlico County: A Brief History*. Raleigh, N.C.: North Carolina Division of Archives and History, 1991.

————. *Ship Ashore! The U.S. Lifesavers of Coastal North Carolina*. Raleigh, N.C.: North Carolina Division of Archives and History, 1994.

Morris, Glenn. *North Carolina Beaches*. Chapel Hill, N.C.: University of North Carolina Press, 1993.

Naisawald, L. Vanloan. *In Some Foreign Field: The Story of Four British Graves on the Outer Banks*. Winston-Salem, N.C.: John F. Blair, Publisher, 1972.

Outlaw, Edward R., Jr. *Old Nag's Head*. Norfolk, Va.: Liskey Lithograph Corporation, 1956.

Parramore, Tom, and Barbara Parramore. *Looking for the "Lost Colony."* Raleigh, N.C.: Tanglewood Press, 1984.

Paschal, Herbert R., Jr. *A History of Colonial Bath*. Raleigh, N.C.: Edwards and Broughton Company, 1955.

Payne, Roger L. *Place Names of the Outer Banks*. Washington, N.C.: Thomas L. Williams, Publisher, 1985.

Perquimans County Historical Society. *Perquimans Historical Society Year Book 1970*. Hertford, N.C.: 1970.

Pilkey, Orrin H., Jr., et al. *From Currituck to Calabash: Living with North Carolina's Barrier Islands*. Research Triangle Park, N.C.: North Carolina Science and Technology Center, 1978.

Porter, Charles W., III. *Fort Raleigh National Historic Site*. Washington, D.C.: Government Printing Office, 1952.

Powell, William S. *Paradise Preserved: A History of the Roanoke Island Historical Association*. Chapel Hill, N.C.: University of North Carolina Press, 1965.

—————. *The North Carolina Gazetteer: A Dictionary of Tar Heel Places*. Chapel Hill, N.C.: University of North Carolina Press, 1968.

—————. *North Carolina through Four Centuries*. Chapel Hill, N.C.: University of North Carolina Press, 1989.

Price, Steve. *Wild Places of the South*. Charlotte, N.C.: East Woods Press, 1980.

Puetz, C. J., ed. *North Carolina County Maps*. Lyndon Station, Wis.: Thomas Publications, Ltd.

Puterbaugh, Parke, and Alan Bisbort. *Life Is a Beach: A Vacationer's Guide to the East Coast*. New York: McGraw-Hill Book Company, 1986.

Quinn, David Beers. *The Lost Colonists: Their Fortune and Probable Fate*. Raleigh, N.C.: North Carolina Department of Cultural Resources, 1984.

—————. *Set Fair for Roanoke: Voyages and Colonies, 1584–1606*. Chapel Hill, N.C.: University of North Carolina Press, 1985.

Quinn, David Beers, ed. *The Roanoke Voyages, 1584–1590.* Vol. 2. New York: Dover Publications, 1991.

Rankin, Hugh F. *The Pirates of Colonial North Carolina.* Raleigh, N.C.: North Carolina Department of Cultural Resources, 1976.

Reed, C. Wingate. *Beaufort County: Two Centuries of Its History.* Raleigh, N.C.: 1962.

Rights, Douglas L. *The American Indian in North Carolina.* 1947. Reprint, Winston-Salem, N.C.: John F. Blair, Publisher, 1957.

Roberts, Bruce, and Ray Jones. *Southern Lighthouses: Chesapeake Bay to the Gulf of Mexico.* Chester, Conn.: Globe Pequot Press, 1989.

Roberts, Nancy. *Blackbeard and Other Pirates of the Atlantic Coast.* Winston-Salem, N.C.: John F. Blair, Publisher, 1993.

Robinson, Blackwell P., ed. *The North Carolina Guide.* Chapel Hill, N.C.: University of North Carolina Press, 1955.

Robinson, Melvin. *Riddle of the Lost Colony.* New Bern, N.C.: Owen G. Dunn Company, Publishers, 1946.

Roe, Charles E. *A Directory to North Carolina's Natural Areas.* Raleigh, N.C.: North Carolina Natural Heritage Foundation, 1987.

———. *North Carolina Wildlife Viewing Guide.* Helena, Mont.: Falcon Press Publishing Company, 1992.

Saunders, Keith. *Outer Banks: Gem of the Atlantic Coast.* Dubuque, Iowa: Feature Services, Inc., Kendall/Hunt Publishing Company, 1978.

Savage, Henry, Jr. *The Mysterious Carolina Bays.* Columbia, S.C.: University of South Carolina Press, 1982.

Scheer, George, III. *North Carolina: A Guide to the Old North State.* New York: Burt Franklin and Company, 1982.

Schoenbaum, Thomas J. *Islands, Capes, and Sounds: The North Carolina Coast.* Winston-Salem, N.C.: John F. Blair, Publisher, 1982.

Schumann, Marguerite. *The Living Land: An Outdoor Guide to North Carolina.* Chapel Hill, N.C.: Dale Press, 1977.

———. *Tar Heel Sights: A Guide to North Carolina's Heritage.* Charlotte, N.C.: East Woods Press, 1983.

Sharpe, Bill. *Tar on My Heels.* Winston-Salem, N.C.: The Tar Heels, 1946.

———. *A New Geography of North Carolina.* 4 vols. Raleigh, N.C.: Sharpe Publishing Company, 1954–65.

Shears, David. *Ocracoke: Its History and People*. Washington, D.C.: Starfish Press, 1989.

Simpson, Bland. *The Great Dismal: A Carolinian's Swamp Memoir*. Chapel Hill, N.C.: University of North Carolina Press, 1990.

Snow, Edward Rowe. *True Tales of Buried Treasure*. New York: Dodd, Mead and Company, 1966.

South, Stanley A. *Indians in North Carolina*. Raleigh, N.C.: North Carolina Division of Archives and History, 1975.

Standard Oil Company of New Jersey. *The Story of North Carolina Esso No. 1*. Charlotte, N.C.: Herald Press.

Stick, David. *Graveyard of the Atlantic*. Chapel Hill, N.C.: University of North Carolina Press, 1952.

―――. *The Outer Banks of North Carolina, 1584–1958*. Chapel Hill, N.C.: University of North Carolina Press, 1958.

―――. *Dare County: A History*. Raleigh, N.C.: North Carolina Division of Archives and History, 1970.

―――. *North Carolina Lighthouses*. Raleigh, N.C.: North Carolina Department of Cultural Resources, 1980.

―――. *Roanoke Island: The Beginnings of English America*. Chapel Hill, N.C.: University of North Carolina Press, 1983.

―――. *The Ash Wednesday Storm*. Kill Devil Hills, N.C.: Gresham Publications, 1987.

Stick, David, and Bruce Roberts. *The Cape Hatteras Seashore*. Charlotte, N.C.: McNally and Loftin, Publishers, 1964.

Stick, David, ed. *Aycock Brown's Outer Banks*. Norfolk, Va.: Donning Company, Publishers, 1976.

Taggart, John, and Kathryn Henderson. *A Field Guide to Exploring the North Carolina Estuarine Research Reserve*. Raleigh, N.C.: North Carolina Division of Coastal Management, 1988.

Tate, Suzanne. *Duck Tales*. Nags Head, N.C.: Nags Head Art, Publisher, 1986.

―――. *Memories of Manteo and Roanoke Island, N.C.* Nags Head, N.C.: Nags Head Art, Publisher, 1986.

―――. *Whalehead: Tales of Corolla, N.C.* Nags Head, N.C.: Nags Head Art, Publisher, 1987.

Toops, Connie. *National Seashores: The Story behind the Scenery.* Las Vegas, Nev.: KC Publications, 1987.

Trotter, William. *Ironclads and Columbiads. The Civil War in North Carolina: The Coast.* Winston-Salem, N.C.: John F. Blair, Publisher, 1989.

Walser, Richard. *North Carolina Legends.* Raleigh, N.C.: North Carolina Division of Archives and History, 1980.

Walser, Richard, ed. *The North Carolina Miscellany.* Chapel Hill, N.C.: University of North Carolina Press, 1962.

Walsh, John Evangelist. *One Day at Kitty Hawk: The Untold Story of the Wright Brothers and the Airplane.* New York: Thomas Y. Crowell Company, 1975.

Washington County Historical Society. *Historic Washington County.* 1970.

Watson, Alan D. *Society in Colonial North Carolina.* Raleigh, N.C.: North Carolina Department of Cultural Resources, 1982.

————. *Perquimans County: A Brief History.* Raleigh, N.C.: North Carolina Division of Archives and History, 1987.

Wechter, Nell Wise. *The Mighty Midgetts of Chicamacomico.* Manteo, N.C.: Times Printing Company, 1974.

————. *Some Whisper of Our Name.* Manteo, N.C.: Times Printing Company, 1975.

Wescott, Lynanne, and Paula Degen. *Wind and Sand: The Story of the Wright Brothers at Kitty Hawk.* Eastern Acorn Press, 1983.

Wetmore, Ruth Y. *First on the Land: The North Carolina Indians.* Winston-Salem, N.C.: John F. Blair, Publisher, 1975.

Whedbee, Charles Harry. *Legends of the Outer Banks and Tar Heel Tidewater.* Winston-Salem, N.C.: John F. Blair, Publisher, 1966.

————. *The Flaming Ship of Ocracoke and Other Tales of the Outer Banks.* Winston-Salem, N.C.: John F. Blair, Publisher, 1971.

————. *Outer Banks Mysteries and Seaside Stories.* Winston-Salem, N.C.: John F. Blair, Publisher, 1978.

————. *Outer Banks Tales to Remember.* Winston-Salem, N.C.: John F. Blair, Publisher, 1985.

————. *Blackbeard's Cup and Stories of the Outer Banks.* Winston-Salem, N.C.: John F. Blair, Publisher, 1989.

Wheeler, John Hill. *Historical Sketches of North Carolina from 1584 to 1851.* Baltimore: Regional Publishing Company, 1964.

White, Robert W. *A Witness for Eleanor Dare: The Final Chapter in a 400 Year Old Mystery.* San Francisco: Lexikos, 1991.

Whitney, Dudley. *The Lighthouse.* New York: Arch Cape Press, 1989.

Wilson, Elizabeth Jean. *A Guide to Salt Marsh Plants Common to North Carolina.* Raleigh, N.C.: UNC Sea Grant Program, 1981.

Works Progress Administration. *The Ocean Highway: New Brunswick, New Jersey, to Jacksonville, Florida.* New York: Modern Age Books, 1938.

Wright, Sarah Bird. *Ferries of America: A Guide to Adventurous Travel.* Atlanta: Peachtree Publishers, 1987.

————. *Islands of the South and Southeastern United States.* Atlanta: Peachtree Publishers, 1989.

Index

Adams, James, 306-7
Adams, Ray T., 32
Adventure, 254, 293
Adventurers for Draining the Dismal Swamp, 47
Airships Industries USA, Inc., 67
Albemarle, 116, 117
Albemarle and Chesapeake Canal, 16, 45, 57
Albemarle and Pantego Railroad, 279
Albemarle Beach, 110, 121
Albemarle County, 3, 73, 79
Albemarle River, 85
Albemarle Sound: Batchelor Bay, 116; bridges over, 94-95; Dare County, 137; early maps of, 85; exploration of, 84; former ferry across, 122; geographical description of, 9, 84; Lake Phelps, 126, 130; Little River, 78; Oregon Inlet, 207; Pasquotank River, 53; Perquimans County, 74; Perquimans River, 73; Scuppernong River, 134; Tucker Lee's flight, 156; Viking route, 114
Albemarle Sound Bridge, 73, 94-95
Aldrin, Buzz, 192
Algonquin Indians, 115, 142, 185, 212, 267
All Saints' Church, 198-99
Allen, Abram, 308
Alligator, 110, 136
Alligator Creek, 136
Alligator Dismal Swamp, 137
Alligator Lake, 260, 278
Alligator River, 133, 134, 136-37, 138, 139, 141, 260, 261, 265, 266
Alligator River National Wildlife Refuge, 110, 140, 261
Alphonso Barco House, 17, 18
Amadas, Philip, 134-35, 152, 159, 324
American Society for Psychical Research, 297
Amity, 264, 265

Amity Methodist Church, 264
Anderson, Hull, 301
Anne, Queen, 92, 96, 296
Application of the Church Catechism, 291
Aquascogoc, 277
Arapahoe, 312, 336, 337
Arcadia, 185
Archdale, John, 52, 286
Armstrong, Neil A., 192
Aronson, Stuart, 294
Arps House, 89, 92
Asa Jones House, 171
Ash Wednesday Storm, 222
Ashby (Ashbee) Harbor, 172
Asher C. Havens, 232
Atlantic, 249, 258, 259
Atlantic Coast Line Railroad, 113
Atlantic Research Corporation, 33
Aurora, 312, 313, 315-18
Aurora Borealis (newspaper), 316
Aurora Fossil Museum, 313, 318-19
Ausbon House, 112, 119
Avon, 200, 201, 220-21, 222
Avon Fishing Pier, 221
Aydlett, 3, 18

Back Bay, 9
Back Creek, 255, 285, 291
Bagleys Swamp, 81
Bahamas, 283
Bald Head Island, 235
Bank of Manteo, 170
Bank of Washington, 296, 300, 310-11
Barco, 2, 15, 16
Barker House, 100, 101, 102, 103
Barker, Penelope, 99, 102
Barker, Thomas, 102
Barlowe, Arthur, 134-35, 150, 152, 159, 314, 324, 329, 334, 335
Batchelor Bay, 116
Batchelor Bay Game Land, 116
Bateman, A. J., 178
Bath, 97, 255, 283, 284-99, 309, 313, 315, 322, 337
Bath Creek, 285, 286, 287, 288, 291, 292, 297
Bath School, 287, 296-97

Battle of Plymouth, 113, 116-17, 118, 119
Battle of Plymouth Living History Weekend, 117
Battle of South Mills, 49-50
Batts Grave, 85
Batts Island, 85
Batts, Nathaniel, 85
Baum, Abraham, 165
Baum, Carolista Fletcher, 181
Baum, Thomas, 137
Bay River, 312, 323, 324, 325, 326
Bay Side, 65
Bayboro, 312, 313, 325
Bayley, 14
Bayview, 313
Beach Springs, 72, 83
Beacham Savanna, 315
Beacon Island, 238, 239
Beacon Island Fort, 238
Beacon Island Military Reservation, 238
Beacon Island Roads, 238
Bear Creek, 323
Bear Swamp, 83, 93
Beard Creek, 336
Beards Creek, 312, 336
Beaufort, 102, 111, 258, 293, 337
Beaufort County, 111, 261, 278-83, 284-311, 313-19, 320, 322, 337
Beaufort County Courthouse (former), 300, 309-10
Beaufort County Historical Society, 289
Beaufort Inlet, 26, 249
Bedfordshire, 246-49
Bee Tree Canal, 129
Beechland, 111, 140-41, 155
Belgrade (Perquimans County), 86-87
Belgrade (Tyrrell County), 128
Belhaven, 260, 261, 273, 279-83, 297
Belhaven Lumber Company, 280
Belhaven Memorial Museum, 261, 281-83
Bell, Joe, 257-58
Bell, John, 15
Belle Port, 280
Bell's Island, 3, 10, 15, 17
Belvidere, 81, 82

Belvidere Academy, 82
Belvidere Plantation, 82
Bennetts Creek, 37, 39, 256
Berkley Center County Inn, 245
Berkley Manor, 245
Bermuda, 48, 226
Berry, W. T., 275
Berry-Mullen-Edwards House, 89, 93
Bertha, 18
Bertie County, 337
Bethel, 326
Bethel Baptist Church, 83, 93
Betsy Tooley's Tavern, 56
Betty (Bettys) Town, 316
Beveridge, George W., 65
Beverly Hall, 100, 104
Big Colington Island, 186-88
Big Savannah, 110, 134, 135, 136
Billet, Daniel, 51
Billet's Ridge, 51
Billy Mitchell Airfield, 230
Bingham, Hiram, 190
Birds Landing, California, 220
Black Pelican Oceanfront Cafe, 195
Blackbeard: biographical sketch of,
    292-93; demise of, 253-55; dramas
    about, 52, 293-94; former houses
    of, 55, 291, 293; treasures of, 255-
    57, 315, 322, 329-30
Blackbeard, 52
Blackbeard Island, 255
Blackbeard: Knight of the Black Flag,
    294
Blackbeard's Revenge, 294
Blackstock, 68
Bladen County, 57
Bland-Overman House, 54, 61
Blount House, 121
Blount, Thomas, 122
Blounts Creek, 256
Bodie Island, 28, 191, 201, 202-6,
    207, 208, 214
Bodie Island Lifesaving Station, 208
Bodie Island Lighthouse, 28, 200,
    201, 203-5, 208
Bogue Banks, 208, 337
Bonarva, 128, 129
Bond Creek, 319
Bonner, Herbert Covington, 206,
    302, 308

Bonner House, 287, 291
Bonner, James, 308
Bonner, Joseph, 291
Boritz, William, 98-99, 105
Boston, Massachusetts, 269
Bray Store, House, and Inn, 17
Bray, Thomas, 17
Brent, Virgilia, 199
Brick House, The, 55-56
Brickhouse Landing, 77
Brickhouse Plantation, 47
Briefe and True Report of the New
    Found Land of Virginia, A, 163
Bristol, England, 292
British Cemetery, 234, 245-49
British Museum, 106, 164, 314
Broad Creek, 326, 327, 328, 337
Brooke, Rupert, 248
Brooklyn Museum of Art, 103
Brooklyn Navy Yard, 246, 248, 306
Brown, Aycock, 192, 246-47, 249,
    253
Brown Creek, 326
Buffalo City, 110, 111, 138, 139-41,
    158
Bullock, William J., 280
Buncombe County, 3, 123
Buncombe, Edward, 123-24
Buncombe Hall, 111, 123-24
Buncombe Landing, 124
Burgess, Dempsey, 52
Burnett, Peter H., 328
Burney, Robert, 327
Burnside, Ambrose, 149, 172, 302
Burrus Supermarket, 231
Buxton, 200, 201, 214, 222, 223-30,
    231
Buxton Woods (Cape Hatteras
    Woods), 201, 223-24, 228, 229,
    230
Buxton Woods Nature Trail, 224
Buzzard Bay, 188
Byrd, William, 9, 40, 43, 44, 46, 47,
    48, 105, 183

Cabin Ridge Plantation, 122
Caffeys Inlet, 2, 9, 23
California, 317, 328
Camden (Camden Courthouse), 27,
    36, 37, 50, 51, 52

Camden County, 15, 41, 43-52
Camden County Courthouse, 37, 50,
    51
Campbell Creek, 320
Campbell, John, 180
Camp Don Lee, 335
Camp Seafarer, 335, 336
Camp Sea Gull, 335, 336
Canadian Hole, 222, 223
Cape Hatteras: geographic descrip-
    tion of, 224-26; radio experiments
    at, 149, 222-23
Cape Hatteras Lighthouse, 28, 200,
    201, 204, 223, 224, 226-29
Cape Hatteras National Seashore,
    175, 176, 199, 200-233, 234-42
Cape Hatteras Water Authority, 224
Cape Lookout, 246
Cape Lookout Lighthouse, 28, 204,
    227
Cape Point, 222, 223-26, 229
Cape Point Beach, 224-226
Cape Point Campground, 224
Caribsea, 250-51
Carl Gerhard, 196
Carolina bays, 267
"Carolina Moon", 73
Carolina River, 85
Carova Beach, 34
Carroll A. Deering, 194
Carteret County, 111, 258, 335, 337
Cash Corner, 313, 323-24
Cash Corner No. 2, 313, 323, 333
Cashie River, 116
Caswell, Richard, 47
Catherine Creek, 256
Catherine Johnson, 311
Cecil B. DeMille Museum, 300, 310
Cedar Grove Methodist Church, 80-
    81
Cedar Island, 155, 259
Chancellorsville, Virginia, 323
Charles II, 186
Charles Creek Park, 65
Charles L. Harney House, 54, 61
Charles O. Robinson House, 54, 62-
    63
Charleston, Earthquake of 1886, 227
Charlotte Observer, 227
Charlton House, 105

Charlton, Jasper, 105
Cheatham, Frank B., 190
Cherry Point-Minnesott Beach Ferry, 333
Chesapeake Bay, 153
Chesapeake Bay Bridge-Tunnel, 53
Chicago, Illinois, 280
Chicamacomico, 215, 216, 219
Chicamacomico Historical Association, 216
Chicamacomico Lifesaving Station, 171, 201, 215, 216-17, 218
China Grove House, 33, 334
Chisholm vs. Georgia, 107
Chowan County, 50, 52, 77, 82, 83, 93-109, 122
Chowan County Courthouse (former), 78, 100, 106, 108
Chowan River, 84, 95, 96, 98, 256
Chowanoke Indians, 85
Christ Episcopal Church, 54, 59-60
Church Island, 2, 17-18
Church of England, 77, 83
Church of the Holy Trinity, 88, 92
Civil War: Ashby (Ashbee) Harbor, 172; Beacon Island, events at, 238; Belhaven, origin of, 279, 280; Bray Store, House, and Inn, 17; Cape Hatteras Lighthouse, 227, 229; Collins, Josiah, III, 127; Columbia, 135; Durants Neck, events at, 77; Edenton, events at, 99; Elizabeth City, events at, 57-58, 59; Hatteras Island, events at, 204, 207, 213, 215-16, 219, 232-33; Hertford, events at, 78; Maribel, origins of, 325; Merritt, origins of, 326; monument related to, 10; Nags Head, events at, 178, 199; naval vessels of, 15, 24, 116, 233, 302; Oregon, origin of, 319; Pettigrew, James Johnston, career of, 129; Plymouth, Battle of, 115, 116-17, 118, 119; Port O' Plymouth museum, 113; Quaker opposition to, 80-81; Roanoke Island, events at, 148-49; South Mills, Battle of, 49-50; Swan Quarter, events at, 274, 276; treasure related to, 21-22, 336;

Vandemere, origin of, 324; Warren, Dr. Thomas, 104; Wash Woods, 35; Washington, events at, 301, 302, 303-4, 307, 308-9, 311; Wood-McCallum-Winslow House, 92
Clansman, The, 8
Clark, 277
Clark-Chesson House, 112, 119
Clarks (Clarksville), 216, 219
Clay County, 50
Cleveland, Grover, 17, 278-79
Cluff-Pool Building, 54
Coast Guard Light Attendant Station, 17
Cobb Building, 54, 60
Cockle Creek, 243
Coffield House, 108
Coinjock, 2, 3, 16-17, 45
Coinjock Bay, 2, 15, 17
Coleman, A. B., 38
Colington Island, 174, 175, 186-88, 208
Collection of Many Christian Experiences, Sentences, and Several Places of Scripture Improved, 77
Colleton, John, 187
Collett, Map of 1770, 85
Collins, Josiah, 125, 126, 127, 128
Collins, Josiah, Jr., 126
Collins, Josiah, III, 126, 127, 130
Colonel Francis Toms' House, 89, 93
Colonial Assembly, 55, 79, 86, 87, 98, 288, 290
Colony House, 127
Columbia, 110, 111, 122, 133, 134, 135
Columbus, Christopher, 114, 168
Comberford, map of 1657, 5, 85
Continental Congress, 44, 52, 102
Cool Spring, 132
Coquina Beach, 202-3
Cora Daniels Basnight Bridge, 167
Core Banks, 249
Core Sound, 221
Corinth Baptist Church, 19
Cornell University, 119
Cornwallis, Charles, 97
Corolla, 2, 3, 9, 23, 24, 25-34, 191, 194

Corolla Academy, 32-33
Corolla Wild Horse Fund, 26
Coutanche, Michael, 288, 289
Cove Grove, 75
Craig, Stanley, 247-48
Craven County, 258, 320, 335, 337
Creecy-Skinner-Whedbee House, 89, 91
Creedle, A. L., 264
Creeds Hill Lifesaving Station, 231
"Creekers", 243
Cresville, 132
Creswell, 110, 111, 132
Croatan Sound, 84, 142, 145, 146, 147, 148, 149, 172, 220
"CROATOAN", 143, 154
Culong, 14-15
Cunningham, Thomas, 246-48
Cunningham, W. H., 316
Cupola House (Edenton), 100, 103-4
Cupola House (Shawboro), 14
Currituck, 2, 3, 10
Currituck Banks, 15, 23-35
Currituck Banks National Estuarine Research Reserve, 34
Currituck Beach, 24, 25
Currituck Beach Lighthouse, 2, 3, 25, 27-29
Currituck County, geographical description of, 8-10
Currituck County Courthouse, 3, 10-11
Currituck County Jail, 10, 11
Currituck County Wildlife Museum, 33
Currituck Inlet, 5, 10
Currituck Narrows, 18
Currituck National Wildlife Refuge, 34
Currituck Shooting Club, 24
Currituck Sound, 2, 3, 4, 7, 8-10, 15, 20, 22, 27, 28, 29, 214
Currituck wild horses, 26-27
Currituck-Knotts Island Ferry, 2, 3, 8, 10

Dailey, Benjamin, 223
Dailey, Richard, 223
Daniels, John T., 189
Daniels, Jonathan, 198

Daniels, Josephus, 253
Danson, John, 51-52
Dare, Ananias, 154
Dare County: Cape Hatteras National Seashore portion of, 200-233, mainland portion of, 136-45, 261-63; Nags Head to Kitty Hawk portion of, 174-99; northern resort communities in, 21-23; Roanoke Island portion of, 146-173
Dare County Regional Airport, 164
Dare, Eleanor, 154
Dare, Virginia, 75, 154, 159, 161, 162-63, 164
Davie, William Richardson, 125
Davis, Dwight D., 190
Davis, Jefferson, 116, 117
Davis, Walter Royal, 194-95
Dawson Creek, 332-33, 335
Dayton, Ohio, 188, 189
Deals, 35
Dean, Joseph, 328
Declaration of Independence, 91, 99, 102, 107
Defoe, Daniel, 292
DeMille, Agnes, 304
DeMille, Cecil, 285, 304-5
DeMille, Henry Churchill, 304
DeMille, William, 285, 304
"Devil Ike," 183
Diamond Shoals, 194, 225, 226, 227
Dimock, Susan, 310
Dinah's Landing, 299
Dismal Swamp (Beaufort County), 278
Dismal Swamp Canal, 37, 43-46, 53, 56, 57
Dismal Swamp Canal Welcome Center, 46
Dismal Swamp Natural Area, 46
Ditch, The, 243
Dixon, Henry, 49-50
Dixon, Mary, 50
Dixon, Thomas, 7-8
Dock One, 66
Dock Two, 66
Dr. A. L. Pendleton House, 54, 61
Dr. C. Winslow House, 93
Dowdy, Betsy, 3, 27
Drain Point, 262

Drake, Francis, 153, 187
Dred, A Tale of the Great Dismal Swamp, 48
Drumgoole, Edward, 15
Drummond, Edward, 292. *See also* Blackbeard
Drummond, William, 70
Duck, 2, 3, 9, 21-23, 192
Duke Swamp, 38
Duke University, 233, 297, 331
Dunes of Dare Garden Club, 186
Dunmore, John Murray, 27
Durant, George, 74, 78, 90
Durants Neck, 72, 73, 74-80, 90
Durham County, 335

Eagle, 248
Eagle Hotel and Tavern, 91
Easons Crossroads, 36, 37
East Bluff Bay, 260, 273
East Custom House, 108, 109
East Dismal Swamp, 110, 122, 124, 134
Eastern Courier (newspaper), 74
Eastham Creek, 322
East Lake, 110, 111, 137-38
East Lake Methodist Church, 138
Eden, Charles, 96, 98, 107, 109, 292, 315
Edenton, description of, 96-109; historic structures of, 98-109; history of, 98-99; map of, 100
Edenton Bay, 99, 105
Edenton Municipal Airport, 95
Edenton Tea Party, 97-109
Edison, Thomas, 149
Edmund B. Skinner House, 86
Edmund Hatch House, 108, 109
Edmundson, William, 75, 91
Edmundson-Fox Memorial, 75, 89, 91
Edward Wood House, 89, 91
Ehringhaus, J. C. B., 64
Elizabeth, Queen, 57, 152, 161, 162
Elizabeth City: Davis, Walter Royal, 194; description of, 53-65; Dismal Swamp Canal, 44; Dowdy, Betsy, ride of, 27; historic structures of, 53-57, 59-65; history of, 56-59; Knapp, Joseph Palmer, 8; map of, 54; Twine, S. J., 198

Elizabeth City Beach, 52
Elizabeth City Historic District, 59-64
Elizabeth II State Historic Site, 146, 147, 166, 167-68
Elizabeth Town, 57
Elizabethan Gardens, 146, 147, 151, 161-63
Elliott, Jesse, 298-99
Elmwood, 300
Emperors Island, 17
Engagement Hill, 181
Engelhard 260, 261, 263, 264
Ericson, Lief, 48
Essex Square, 170
Etheridge House, 15
Etheridge, Richard, 211-12
Evans, Mary, 289

Fairfield, 261, 265-67
Fairfield United Methodist Church, 266, 267
Far Creek, 263
Farmers Bank Building, 62
Farmer's Journal, 296
Fayetteville, 56, 107
Ferber, Edna, 298, 296, 307
Ferdinando, Simon, 1154
Fessenden, Builder of Tomorrow, 150
Fessenden, Reginald, 149-50, 222
First Baptist Church (Elizabeth City), 54, 61-62
First Colony Farms, 125
First Flight Airfield, 190, 192
First Flight Day, 190, 192
First Flight Society, 192
First Presbyterian Church (Washington), 300, 311
First Provincial Congress, 87
Fletcher, Inglis, 181
Fletcher-Skinner House, 75-76
Flora House, 15
Florence, 312, 326
Flyer, Wright brothers', 189, 192
Foreman, Mary Blades, 61
Fort Bartow, 148, 149
Fort Blanchard, 148
Fort Clark, 233
Fort Forrest, 149
Fort Hatteras, 233

TOURING THE BACKROADS OF NORTH CAROLINA'S UPPER COAST

Fort Huger, 148
Fort Landing, 110, 111, 136
Fort Morgan, 238
Fort Ocracoke, 238
Fort Oregon, 207
Fort Raleigh, 150-55, 158
Fort Raleigh National Historic Site, 146, 147, 150-55, 163, 164, 302
Fort Russell, 148
Fort Williams, 116
Foster, Charles Henry, 213
Fowle, Daniel G., 306
Fowle Warehouse, 300, 305
Fox, George, 75, 91
Francis Nixon House, 74, 75
Franklin, Benjamin, 98
"French Fry Row," 182
Frisco, 200, 201, 214, 230-31
Frisco Day Use Area, 230
Frisco Fishing Pier, 231
Frost, Robert Lee, 49
Fulcher, Joseph, 327

G. A. Kohler, shipwreck of, 220
Gale, Christopher, 96
Gallop, Hodges, 21-22
Gans, Joachim, 164
Garden Club of North Carolina, Inc., 161
Garrett, Alfred, 120-21
Garretts Island House, 119-21
Gaskill, James Baugham, 250-52
Gaskins, George, 278-79
Gates County, 37-43, 46, 47, 53, 256
George II, 96, 295
George Washington Bicentennial Commission, 308
George W. Beveridge House, 65
Georgia, 155, 255, 308, 325
Gettysburg, Pennsylvania, 129, 303
Gibbs, John, 12
Gibbs Point, 12
Gibbs Wood, 12
Glenn, John, 192
Gone With The Wind, 64
Goose Creek, 299, 322
Goose Creek Island, 313, 320-23
Goose Creek State Park, 284, 285, 299

Goose Creek Wildlife Management Area, 312, 313, 322-23
Governor Scott, 221
Grace Episcopal Church, 112, 117-18, 121
Granberry House, 10
Grandy, 3, 18-19, 156
Grantsboro, 312, 313, 336-37
Grant, U. S., 303
Grant, William, 336
Granville, John, 286
Graveyard of the Atlantic, 175, 176, 194, 196, 225-26, 233, 311
Graveyard of the Atlantic Museum, 233
Gray, Michael M., 316
Great Alligator Swamp, 262
Great Alligator Dismal Swamp, 124
Great Bridge, Virginia, 9, 27, 45, 87
Great Dismal Swamp, 13, 27, 36, 37, 38, 40-49, 53, 73, 91
Great Dismal Swamp National Wildlife Refuge, 46
Great Eastern Dismal Swamp, 124
Great Pyramids of Giza, 131
Great Smoky Mountains National Park, 214
Great Swamp (Beaufort County), 278, 284
Great Swamp (Currituck County), 2, 13, 15
Green, Edward, 171
Green, Paul, 159, 162-63
Green Swamp, 156
Greenfield Plantation, 96
Greenhill, 300, 301, 302
Greens Creek, 328, 330
Greenville, 256
Grenville, Richard, 152-54, 237, 240
Grice House, 54, 60
Grice-Fearing House, 60
Griffin, Charles, 68
Griffith, Andy, 160-61
Grimesland, 255
Guinea Hole, 124
Gull Rock Game Land, 273
Gum Corner, 14

Hack, map of 1684, 74

Haley, Alex, 212
Halifax Resolves, 102
Hall, Clement, 77
Halls Creek, 69, 70
Halls Creek United Methodist Church, 69-70
Hamilton, 116
Hamilton, Alexander, 225-26
Hampton Academy, 112, 119
Hampton Lodge, 18
hang gliding, 179-80
Hang Gliding Spectacular, 180
Harbinger, 20
Harding, Edmund, 289, 306
Harding Square, 306
Hardison, Naaman, 334
Hardy, Edward, 19
Hariot, Thomas, 158, 163-64
Harold, 319
Harper's New Monthly Magazine, 115, 178
Harper's Weekly, 302
Harrell House, 84
Harrell Swamp, 38
Harris, John, 90
Harvey, John, 86-87, 90
Harvey Point Defense Testing Area, 86
Harveys Neck, 72, 73, 74, 83-88, 93
Harvey, Thomas, 86
Harvey, Thomas, Jr., 86
Hatteras (village), 200, 201
Hatteras Inlet, 213, 231, 232, 238, 239, 245
Hatteras Inlet Coast Guard Station, 231
Hatteras Island, 156, 200, 201, 202, 204, 207, 208-33, 238, 302, 311
Hatteras Island Fishing Pier, 218
Hatteras-Ocracoke Ferry, 200, 201, 231-32, 233, 235, 236
Havana, Cuba, 283
Havens House, 305
Havens Warehouse, 300, 305
Hayes, 109
Hayes, H. A., 274
Haywood Bell House, 14
Hecklefield Farm, 77
Hecksher, August, 269-70

Henry, Patrick, 44, 47, 48
Herbert C. Bonner Bridge, 200, 201, 206-7, 208, 210
Hertford, 27, 71, 72, 73-74, 75, 78, 82, 88-93
Hertford Baptist Church, 93
Hewes, Joseph, 100, 101-2
Hewes Monument, 100, 101-2
Hickory Point, 312, 313, 314
Hill, Daniel Harvey, 303
Hinton-Pailin House, 54, 62
Historic Bath Commission, 289, 296
Historic Bath State Historic Site, 285, 286-97
Historic Shipwreck Preserve, 197
History of North Carolina, 114, 188
Hitler, Adolph, 246
Hoboken, New Jersey, 320
Hobucken, 312, 313, 320, 321, 322
Hoke, Robert F., 116-17, 119, 303
Hollow Ground Swamp, 134
Hollowell, Margaret, 66
Hollyday House, 300, 302-3
Hollyville, 322
Hollywood, California, 304
Holy Heart of Jesus, The, 98-99
Hooper, William, 91
Hornthal House, 112, 119
Horseshoe, The, 53
Horton, R. P., 326
Hotel Hill, 178
Howard Street, 234, 249, 250
Howard, William, 249
Huguenots, 5, 12
Huguenots Island, 5
Hume, Ivor Noel, 164
Humphrey, Hubert, 160
Humphries-Roberts House, 15
Hunter, Charles, 307
Hunter, James "Catfish," 90
Huron, shipwreck of, 196-97
Hyatt House, 307
Hyde County: mainland portion, 263-278; Ocracoke Island portion of, 234-259
Hyde County Courthouse, 276
Hyde County Historical Association, 277

Ice Plant Island, 166, 167-169
Idaho, 317
Indian Creek, 7
Indian Island, 312, 313, 314-15
Indian Kettles, 20
Ink Bottle House. See Octagon House
Intracoastal Waterway, 16, 17, 43, 44, 136, 261, 266, 277, 281, 320, 322, 323, 328
Iredell, James, 101, 107
Iredell, James, Jr., 104, 107
Isaac White House, 83
Island Gallery and Christmas Shop, 171-72
Island Inn and Dining Room, 257

Jackey Ridge, 180
Jack's Neck, 280
Jackson, 326
Jackson, Andrew, 48
Jackson, Thomas J. (Stonewall), 323, 326
Jacocks House, 77
Jacocks-Reed-Newbold House, 93
James Adams Floating Theatre, 64, 288, 306-7
James Bell House, 13
James Iredell House State Historic Site, 100, 107
James Iredell, Jr. Law Office, 104
Jamestown, Virginia, 147, 163
Janeiro, 312, 313, 332-33
Jarvis, Thomas J., 19
Jarvisburg, 2, 3, 19, 20
Jefferson, Thomas, 135
Jennette's Fishing Pier, 199
Jessamana, 284, 301
Joe Bell (gaillardia flower), 257-58
Jockey's Ridge, 175, 176, 178-182, 184, 197
Jockey's Ridge State Park, 174, 175, 179-82
John Barnwell, map of 1722, 85
John Birch Society, 80
John Gatling House, 83
John L. Roper Lumber Company, 279
John, Palemon, 62
John W. Garrett, 122

John White, map of 1585, 144, 277
Johnson, Lady Bird, 160
Johnson, Lyndon, 302
Johnston County, 335
Johnston, Samuel, 101, 109
Jones Bay, 320
Jones' Beach, 25
Jones House (Riverside), 75
Jones Island, 320
Jones, John Paul, 102
Jones, Sam, 245
Jonesborough, 51
Joseph Palmer Knapp Bridge, 16
Josiah Elliott House, 89, 91
Joyce's Creek, 44
Judge Isaac M. Meekins House, 54, 61
Juniper Bay, 276, 277

Kalola, 85
Kansas-Nebraska, Act of 1854, 264
Kelsey, Harlan P., 269
Kendricks Creek, 122, 123, 124
Kennedy, Joseph P., 20
Kershaw Creek, 328
Kickowanna, 85
Kilcocanen, 85, 90, 91
Kill Devil Hill, 183, 184, 186, 188, 189, 190, 191, 214, 230
Kill Devil Hills, 174, 175, 176, 182, 183-86, 188-92, 193, 195-96
Kill Devil Hills Coast Guard Station (former), 195
Kill Devil Hills Lifesaving Station (former), 34, 189
King Blount, 135
King, Elizabeth, 99
King of Kings, The, (motion picture), 305
Kinnakeet, 220
Kiskitano, 91
Kitty Hawk, 2, 21, 174, 175, 176, 191, 192-95, 196
Kitty Hawk Bay, 174, 188
Kitty Hawk Fishing Pier, 174, 194-95
Kitty Hawk Kites, 180
Kitty Hawk Lifesaving Station (former), 195

Kitty Hawk Methodist Church, 194
Knapp, Joseph Palmer, 5, 7-8, 9, 11
Knight, Amanda Marie Louise Label, 29-31
Knight, Edward C., Jr., 29-31
Knight's Publishing Company, 29
Knoll, The, 242
Knott, James, 5
Knotts Island, 2, 3-8
Knotts Island Bay, 4
Knotts Island Channel, 4
Knotts Island United Methodist Church, 5
Kyzikes, 196

Lake Drummond Hotel (The Halfway House), 47
Lake Landing, 265
Lake Mattamuskeet, 131, 260, 261, 264, 265, 266, 267-73, 278
Lake Mattamuskeet National Wildlife Refuge, 272
"Lake of Dismal Swamp, The," 48
Lake Phelps, 110, 111, 125, 127, 128, 129, 130-32
Lamb, Gideon, 52
Lamb's Ferry, 52
Land's End, 78-79
Lane, Ralph, 84, 115, 152-53, 172, 237
Lane, William, 69
LaRochefoucald, Alexandre, 48
Lassiter Swamp, 37, 39-40
Latham House, 112, 113
Latham-Brinkley House, 112, 119
Laura A. Barnes, 202-3
Lawson, John, 114, 188, 202, 285, 286, 291
Lee Creek, 317, 318
Lee, Robert E., 116, 323
Lee, Thomas, 123
Lee, Tucker, 156-158
Leechville, 278, 279
Lees Mills, 115, 123
Leigh, Gilbert, 78, 106
Leigh House, 106
Leigh, James, 78
Leigh's Farm. *See* Land's End
Lenoir County, 335

Leviathan, 169
Lewis, R. A., 49-50
Lewis Richardson House, 89, 91
Liberia, 301
Light Ground Pocosin, 325
Lighthouse Club, 29, 30
Liles, Sam, 53
Lilienthal, Otto, 179
Lincke, Paul, 317
Lindsay Warren Bridge, 136-37
Lindsay Warren Visitor Center, 151
Little Colington Island, 186
Little Dismal Swamp, 262
Little Kinnakeet Lifesaving Station, 220, 221
Little River, 36, 67, 69, 74, 77, 78, 80
Littlejohn House, 100, 105
Liverpool, England, 283
London Advisor (newspaper), 101
Longfellow, Henry Wadsworth, 48
Long Point, 17
Long Shoals Bay, 140
Lords Proprietors, 79, 84, 97, 187, 193, 286
Lost Colony, The, 146, 147, 159-61, 167, 171
Lost Colony of Roanoke, 141, 143, 147, 150, 152-58, 165, 186
Lou-Mac Municipal Park, 332
Louvre, 106
Lowe, John, 199
Lower Broad Creek, 327
"lower end," 173
Lowland, 312, 313, 320, 321-22
Lowry-Chesson Building, 54, 63-64
LST No. 471, 218
Lumber River, 131, 156

McArthur, Douglas, 19
McCarter, D. C., 324
McColter, Hezekiah, 328
MacKay Island National Wildlife Refuge, 2, 3, 4, 6-7
Mackeys, 110, 111, 122
Mackeys Creek, 122
Mackeys Ferry, 122
McLean, Angus, 214
McLean, George, 32

McMullen Building, 64
Macomb, Alexander, 44
Macon, Nathaniel, 104, 135
Madison, James, 108
Mager Woodhouse House, 19
Magnolia, 128
Maine (warship), 283
Mallison Building, 300, 310
Mamie, 20
Manning, Thomas Courtland, 107
Manns Harbor, 110, 111, 142-44, 260, 261
Manteo, (town), 3, 146, 147, 148, 149, 150, 161, 166-72
Manteo (Indian), 75, 152, 155, 164
Maple, 3, 15, 16
Maple Leaf, 15, 83
Maple Swamp, 13, 18
Marconi, Guglielmo, 222-23
Maribel, 324-25
Marriage Chapel of Harry B. Umphlett, 62
Marsh House, 300, 307
Marsh, Jonathan, 288
Martin County, 337
Martin, Francois-Xavier, 334
Martin, Josiah, 109
Martins Point Creek (Jean Guite Creek), 21-22
Mary Blades Foreman House, 54, 61
Mashoes, 110, 111, 142, 143, 144-145
Masonic Lodge (Camden), 51
Masonic Lodge (Elizabeth City), 54, 60
Maynard, Robert, 254-55
Mayo, Wiley, 320
Meekins, Isaac M., 61
Merchants Millpond, 37, 38
Merchants Millpond State Park, 36, 37-40
Merritt, 312, 326, 327
Merritt, Wesley, 326
Mesic, 313, 323
Messick, S. R., 323
Metropolis, 3, 24
Metropolitan Life Insurance Company, 7, 263
Metropolitan Museum of Art, 101
Mexico, 107, 253

Mexico City, Mexico, 253
Michieux, Peter, 145
Middle Bay, 312, 321
Middletown, 260, 264
Middletown Creek, 264
Midgett, 218
Midgett, John Allen, Jr., 218
Midgette, Louis B., 330-31
Mill Landing, 173
Mill Seat Landing, 322
Mill Town, 52
Millpond Access Area, 40
Milltail Creek, 139, 140, 141
Minnesott Beach, 312, 313, 333-35
Mirlo, 218
Mitchell, Billy, 230
Mitchell, Thoms, 64
Mitchell-Ward House, 82
Moccasin Canal, 130
Moccasin Track 53
Monck, George, 84, 96-97
Monitor, 233
Monroe, James, 48, 52
Monteray Shores, 24
Moore, Thomas, 48
Moores Corner, 312, 328
Moratoc, 115
Morehead City, 217, 246, 248
Morris Creek, 328
Morton, Hugh, 228
Moseley, Edward, 106
Moseley, map of 1733, 81, 85, 262
Moth Boat Park, 64
Mother Vineyard, 135, 146, 147, 165-
    66
"Mother Vineyard Scuppernong," 166
Mt. Olivet Methodist Church, 166-
    67
Mt. Zion Methodist Church, 19
Mountain Canal, 125
Mouse Harbor, 322
Mouzon, map of 1775, 180
Moyock, 2, 3, 6, 8, 12, 13
Muddy Creek (Beaufort County), 319
Muddy Creek (Perquimans County),
    79
Mulberry Hill, 95-96
Munden, Robert, 55
Murphy, 3, 166, 175, 226

Muse, William T., 101
Museum of the Albemarle, 37, 53-54,
    66
Myers House, 300, 307
Myers-White House, 84
Mysterious hoofprints at Bath, 285,
    297-99

Nags Head: description of, 175-83,
    196-99; history of, 177-78, 180-81,
    185-86; origin of name, 183-84
Nags Head Cottage District, 198
Nags Head Fishing Pier, 196
Nags Head Hotel, 177-78, 199
Nags Head Woods Ecological
    Preserve, 174, 175, 184-86
Narrow Shore, 18
Nash County, 14
National Air and Space Museum,
    189
National Audubon Society, 24, 273
National Audubon Society Sanctuary,
    24
National Oceanic and Atmospheric
    Administration (NOAA), 233
National Park Service: Bodie Island
    Lighthouse, facilities at, 202-6;
    Buxton, facilities at, 224; Cape
    Hatteras Lighthouse, plans for,
    228-29; Frisco, facilities at, 230;
    Kill Devil Hills, facilities at, 188-
    89; Ocracoke Island, facilities at,
    239-40, 243; Salvo, facilities at,
    220
National Park Service Visitor Center
    (Ocracoke), 236, 243, 252
Naval Battle of Roanoke Island, 149
Nebraska, 260, 261, 264
Nelson, Jack, 208
Neuse River: geographical description
    of, 335; treasure of, 336
Neusiok Indians, 335
New Begun Creek, 67
New Bern, 77, 87, 97, 102, 238, 258,
    290, 303, 328, 334, 336, 337
New Bethel Baptist Church, 83
New Currituck Inlet, 9
New England, 183, 255, 288, 306,
    317

New Hampshire 255
New Holland, 260, 261, 268-73
New Holland Farms, Inc., 269
New Holland, Higginsport, and Mt.
    Vernon Railroad, 270
New Hope, 72, 77, 80
New Hope Methodist Church, 77
New Inlet, 210
New Jersey (battleship), 230
New Lake, 278
New York City, 269, 336
New York Times, 159
Newbegun United Methodist
    Church, 67
Newbern's Landing, 20
Newbold-White House, 73, 87-88
Newby's Bridge, 82
Newbys Point, 92
Newfoundland, 110, 135
Newton, Wayne, 66
Nixon, Francis, 74, 80, 177, 181
Nixonton, 36, 37, 68, 69, 199
Noah Burfoot House, 51
Norfleet, Kinchen, 38
Norfleets Millpond, 38
Norfolk-Southern Railroad, 94, 122,
    123, 270
North Carolina (battleship), 228, 306
North Carolina Aquarium at
    Roanoke Island, 146, 147, 164-65,
    212
North Carolina Division of Archives
    and History, 20, 217
North Carolina General Assembly,
    23, 56, 57, 181, 259, 289
North Carolina Museum of History,
    101
North Carolina Nature Conservancy,
    34, 38, 181, 186
North Carolina Seafood Industrial
    Park, 173
North Carolina State Agricultural
    Society, 296
North Carolina State Fair, 296
North Carolina Wildlife Resources
    Commission, 116, 273, 322
North Carolinian Building, 62
North Landing River, 2, 4, 7, 8
North Pond, 210

North River, 4, 19, 50, 51
North Rodanthe, 216
North Swan Beach, 34
Nuova Ottavia, 194

Ocean Hill, 34
Ocean Sands, 23, 24
Ochapee, Florida, 220
Ocracoke Coast Guard Station, 234, 243, 245, 248, 252
Ocracoke Hotel, 238
Ocracoke Inlet, 213, 235, 238, 242, 252, 286
Ocracoke Island: description of, 234-59; ferries to, 231-32, 258-59, 276; history of, 213, 237-39
Ocracoke Lighthouse 234, 235, 251, 252-253, 257
Ocracoke Methodist Church, 249-50, 251
Ocracoke ponies, 235, 239-41
Ocracoke Pony Pen, 239
Ocracoke Preservation Museum, 234, 243
Ocracoke School, 252
Ocracoke (village), 234, 235, 242-59, 293
Ocracoke-Cedar Island Ferry, 259
Ocracoke-Swan Quarter Ferry, 259, 276
Octagon House, 265
Ogilby, map of 1671, 187
Old Bond House, 109
Old Buck, 219
Old Nags Head, 176-78, 183
Old South Rod and Gun Club, 320
"Old Table Top," 256
"Olde Christmas," 201, 218-19, 262
Olympia, 312, 313, 337
Opera House (Academy of Music), 64
Operation Drum Roll, 246
Orange County, 156
Oregon, 207, 316, 319
Oregon Inlet, 173, 201, 202, 204, 205, 206-8, 209, 210, 221, 242
Oregon Inlet Campground, 205-6
Oregon Inlet Coast Guard Station, 206

Oregon Inlet Coast Guard Station (former), 208
Oregon Inlet Fishing Center, 205-6
Oriental, 102, 210, 312, 313, 328-32, 333
Oriental, 331
Ormond, Henry, 288
Outer Banks: Blackbeard, 292; Cape Hatteras National Seashore portion of, 200-59; Currituck Banks portion of, 22-35; Dare County, 137; Edenton, 94; Nags Head to Kitty Hawk portion of, 174-99; Roanoke Island, 147; Southern Shores, 21; Stumpy Point, residents of, 262; Swan Quarter-Ocracoke Ferry, 276
Outer Banks History Center, 168
Outer Banks Mall, 176
Overman-Sheep House, 54, 61
Oyster Creek, 322

Page, Matthew, 105
Palmer, I. N., 303
Palmer, Margaret, 296
Palmer, Paul, 52
Palmer, Robert, 288, 296
Palmer-Marsh House, 287, 288-90
Pamlico, 312, 313, 327, 328
Pamlico County, 319-37
Pamlico County Courthouse, 325, 326
Pamlico County Historical Museum, 325
Pamlico Inn, 251
Pamlico River: access at Goose Creek State Park, 299; ferry across, 312, 313; geographical description of, 302
Pamlico River Ferry, 312, 313
Pamlico Sound: Belhaven, origin of, 280; Cape Hatteras Lighthouse, 229; Dare County, mainland, boundaries of, 137; Engelhard, 263; geographical description of, 9, 220-221; Goose Island, boundaries of, 321; Marconi, Guglielmo, 222; Ocracoke Inlet, 286; Ocracoke Island, boundaries

of, 235; Oregon Inlet, 207; Pea Island National Wildlife Refuge, 210; "Shad Boat," 138; Stumpy Point, 261; Swan Quarter National Wildlife Refuge, 210; Teach's Hole at, 253
Pantego, 280
Pantego Creek, 281
Pantego Swamp, 278
Pasquotank County, 41, 46, 52-71, 101, 199
Pasquotank County Courthouse, 54, 63
Pasquotank River, 2, 36, 44, 51, 52, 53, 57
Pasquotank River Bridge, 52, 53
Pea Island Coast Guard (Lifesaving) Station, 165, 211-12
Pea Island National Wildlife Refuge, 200, 201, 209-12, 215
Pearl Harbor, Hawaii, 245, 250
Peele, Frazier, 232
Pembroke Hall, 100, 104-5
Perkins Chapel Methodist Church, 14
Perquimans County, 27, 41, 47, 73-93, 177
Perquimans County Courthouse, 88, 89, 90, 93
Perquimans River, 36, 73, 74, 75, 76, 79, 89, 92
Perry, Matthew, 42
Perry-Spruill House, 112, 113
Person County, 302
Pettigrew Cemetery, 129
Pettigrew, Charles, 129, 133
Pettigrew, Ebenezer, 128, 129
Pettigrew, James Johnston, 129, 133
Pettigrew State Park, 110, 111, 125, 126, 127, 128-132
Phelps, Josiah, 131
Phelps Point, 90
Philadelphia, Pennsylvania, 264, 278, 293, 296
Picket, 302
Pickett, George, 129
Picot-Armistead-Pettiford House, 112, 118
Pilmoor, Joseph, 11

Pilmoor Methodist Church, 11
Pine Island, 24
Pine Island Hunt Club, 24
Piney Woods Meeting House, 80, 82
Plank Bridge, 51
Plum Point, 255, 291
Plymouth, 110, 111-19, 122
Plymouth, England, 154
Plymouth, Massachusetts, 114
Plymouth United Methodist Church, 112, 119
Pocosin Lakes National Wildlife Refuge, 124-25, 278
Poe, Edgar Allen, 48
Point Harbor, 2, 3, 20
"Pointers," 243
Pole Line Road, 23
Polk, James Knox, 129
Pollock, Thomas, 107, 268
Pomeioc, 324
Ponzer, 265
Pool-Lumsden-Peters House, 54, 60
Poplar Branch, 3, 6, 18
Poplar Branch Landing, 18
Port O' Plymouth Museum, 112, 113, 117
Portland, Maine, 290
Portsmouth Island, 221, 238, 273
Post Office Department, 25, 308, 320
Powells Point, 2, 3, 20
Poyners Hill, 2, 24
Poyners Hill Lifesaving Station, 24
Price, map of 1808, 183
Pricklove, Samuel, 90
Probst, Mrs. Robert, 248
Providence Baptist Church, 14
Providence United Methodist Church, 261, 274-75
Puget Sound, 221
Pungo Lake, 110, 124, 260, 278
Pungo National Wildlife Refuge, 110, 124
Pungo River, 260, 265, 277, 278, 279, 280, 281

Quakers. See Society of Friends
Queen Anne's Creek, 98, 100, 109
Queen Anne's Revenge, 315
Queen Anne's War, 292

Queen's Bell, 296
Quigley, Redding D., 232

Ragged Point, 321
Raleigh News and Observer, 198, 227
Raleigh, Walter: colonization attempts of, 147, 152-56; portrait of, 162; portrayed by Andy Griffith, 161
"Raven, The," 48
Raynor Swamp, 38
Reas Beach, 121
Redding, 57
Red House Fork, 81
Reed House, 89, 91
Reed, Lemuel Sutton, 79
Reed, Walter, 80
Reno, Jesse L., 49
Revolutionary War: Dowdy, Betsy, ride of, 27; Edenton, events at, 97-99, 101-2, 108; Great Bridge, Battle of, 27, 87; Great Dismal Swamp, events at, 48; Ocracoke Island, events at, 238
Revolutionary War Memorial Cross, 169
Rhodes, Arthur, 114
Richardson-Pool-Glover House, 3, 60
Rio de Janeiro, Brazil, 333
"Ripley's Believe It Or Not," 118
River Forest Manor, 261, 280-81
Riverspree, 64
Roanoke Inlet, 201
Roanoke Island: description of, 146-73; history of, 148-58, 159-61, 165-66, 169-70, 172, 173; map of, 146
Roanoke Marshes, 148
Roanoke River, 84, 111, 112, 113, 114, 115-16, 207, 337
Roanoke Sound, 84, 85, 146, 147, 158, 165, 174, 176, 177, 179 185, 186
Rodanthe, 200, 201, 209, 215-19
Rodman House, 300, 301
Rogers and Poor, 102, 190
Rogers, Will, 283
Roosevelt, Franklin D., 159, 214, 302
Roper, 110, 111, 122, 123

Roper (destroyer), 203
Roper, John L., 123, 279, 280
Rose Bay, (bay), 260, 277
Rose Bay (community), 260, 276, 277
Rose Bay Baptist Church, 277
Run Hill, 184
Rycroft, Mrs. Frank, 248

Sadler, Sam, 274-75
Saint Andrews By-the-Sea Episcopal Church, 198-99
St. Anne's Catholic Church, 107
St. David's Chapel, 132-33
St. George's Episcopal Church, 264
St. Paul's Church, 96, 100, 106-7
St. Peter's Episcopal Church, 300, 305, 308-9
St. Thomas Episcopal Church, 287, 295-96
St. Thomas Parish of Bath, 290
Salvo, 201, 216, 219-20
Sam Jones Castle, 245
Samuel Ferebee House, 14
Sanderling, 2, 3, 23, 24, 26
Sanderling Restaurant and Bar, 23
Sanderson House, 13
Sandy Point Beach, 72, 94, 95
Sanford, Terry, 8
Savannah, Georgia, 290
Savannah River, 307
Save The Lighthouse Committee, 228
Sawyer Cemetery, 52
Sawyer, Lemuel, 52
Scott Newbern House, 20
Scrag Cedar Hills, 241
Scranton, 260, 263, 277
Scranton Creek, 277
Scranton, Pennsylvania, 277
Scuppernong Farms, 128-29
Scuppernong River, 110, 125, 134, 135
Scuppernong Swamp, 132
Second Provincial Congress, 87
Secotan, 324, 334
Seven Sisters, 181
Shallop's Landing, 135
Shallowbag Bay, 146, 147, 148, 166, 169

Shaw, George Bernard, 226
Shaw, Henry, 14
Shaw, H. M., 149
Shaw, William, 14
Shawboro, 2, 3, 14-15
Shiloh, 2, 36, 37, 51-52
Shiloh Baptist Church, 37, 52
Shoofly, 325
Showboat, The, 285, 288, 306-7. *See also* James Adams Floating Theatre
Showboat (novel and play), 288, 296
Sikorsky, Igor, 192
Silver Lake, 234, 235, 242, 243-45, 246, 249, 257, 258, 259
Simpson-Blanchard House, 89, 92
Skinner Cemetery, 87
Skinner, Thomas G., 91
Skinner, William, 87
Skinner-Elliott House, 107
Skinner-Paxton House, 100, 104
Skyco, 172
"Slave of Dismal Swamp, The," 48
Sligo, 3, 15
Smith, Axson, 280
Smith Creek, 328, 330
Smith, John Maynard, 261, 278-79
Smith, Kate, 20
Smithsonian Institution, 189, 282, 318
Snowden, 2, 3, 13, 14
Snowden, Milton, 13
Society for the Propagation of the Gospel, 290
Society of Friends, 67, 68, 75, 80, 81, 82, 91
Somerset Place State Historic Site, 111, 125-27, 128, 129, 131
Somerset Canal, 128
Sothel, Seth, 78-79
South Creek, (creek), 314, 316
South Creek (community), 312, 313, 315, 319
South Mills, 36, 37, 43, 46, 49
South Pond, 210
South Rodanthe, 216
Southern Hotel, 62
Southern Shores, 2, 3, 21

Spanish American War, 326
Spanish Mustang Registry (Society), 26, 240
Sparrow, William, 265
Spikes Creek, 256
Spot, 20
Spotswood, Alexander, 253
Spring Creek, 326
Stanton, 319
State Bank of North Carolina, 104
Stick, David, 21, 169
Stick, Frank, 21, 214
Stockton, 80
Stoddard, William Lee, 59
Stonewall, 313, 325, 326
Stowe, Harriet Beecher, 48
Stumpy Point, 260, 261-63
Stumpy Point Bay, 261
Stumpy Point Lake, 262
Styron Hills, 236
Sumnerville, 76
Sutton-Newby House, 76
Suttons Creek, 76
Swan Beach, 34
Swan Quarter, 245, 258, 259, 260, 261, 274-76, 277
Swan Quarter Bay, 276, 277
Swan Quarter National Wildlife Refuge, 261, 276-77
Sycamore Plantation, 96
Sykes, James, 19
Sykes-New Bern House, 19
Symonds Creek, 36, 68, 69

Tadmore, 262
Tar River, 255, 256, 300, 302, 308
Tarkington, Benjamin, 130-31
Taylor Beach, 52
Taylor, Marble Nash, 213
Teach, Edward, 55, 253, 292, 294. *See also* Blackbeard
Teach's Hole, 253, 254, 256, 257
Teach's Light, 262
Teach's Oak, 313, 330
Temperance Hall, 89, 92
Ten Commandments, The (motion picture), 305
Texasgulf, Inc., 317-18

Thatch, Edward, 292. *See also* Blackbeard
Theodore S. Meekins House, 171
Thirty Foot Canal, 125
Thistleworth, 292
Thomas Hariot Nature Trail, 158
Thomas Jackson House, 89, 92
Thomas Newby House, 77
Thomas Nixon House, 80
Tiger, 237
Tillett-Nixon House, 54, 60
Timbucktu, 24
Timothy Nicholson House, 83
Titanic, 223
Tomes, Francis, 75
Tompkins, John F., 296
Toms, Clinton, 88, 93
Toms Mill, 76
Toms-White House, 93
Tooley, Adam, 57
Tooley, Elizabeth, 57
Towerson, Gilbert, 291
Tredwell House, 105
Trent (Dare County), 230
Trent (Pamlico County), 326
Trent Creek, 326
Trent Woods, 219
Triggvason, Olaf, 115
Trinitie (Trinity) Harbor, 188
Tull Bay, 12
Tull, Thomas, 12
Tulls Creek, (creek), 12
Tulls Creek (village), 2, 3, 11, 12
Tuscarora Indians, 98, 295, 315, 336
Twin Houses, 14, 15
Twine, S. J., 198
Tyrrell County, 61, 111, 128, 133-36, 169
Tyrrell County Courthouse, 134, 135

U-85, 203
U-117, 218
U-152, 231
U-558, 247
Union Chapel Baptist Church, 67
Union Hall Academy, 75-76
United States Army Coastal Research Facility, 22-23

United States Army Corps of Engineers, 22, 45, 221, 262

United States Coast Guard, 17, 24, 28, 32, 168, 205, 217, 218, 320

United States Coast Guard Station (Elizabeth City), 65

United States Constitution, 107, 108

United States Fish and Wildlife Service, 7, 46, 125, 210, 267, 277

United States Lighthouse Board, 28

United States Lifesaving Service, 168, 195, 216, 217, 229

United States Merchant Marine, 250

United States Post Office and Courthouse (Elizabeth City), 63

United States Supreme Court, 107

United States Weather Bureau, 35, 149, 231

University of North Carolina at Chapel Hill, 8, 69, 70, 71, 125, 129, 133, 160

"Unpainted Aristocracy" of Nags Head, 175, 198

Upjohn, Richard, 117, 133

"Upper End," 173

Vandemere, 312, 324, 325

Vandemere Creek, 324

Van Der Veer House, 287, 296

Van Der Veer, Jacob, 296

Verrazano, Giovanni de, 185, 220, 237

Vestry Act of North Carolina, 290

Village Green (Edenton), 97-99

Vinci, Leonardo da, 305

Virginia (battleship), 230

Virginia Dare Hotel, 54, 59

Wahab Cemetery, 249

Wahab, Stanley, 239

Wake County, 331, 335

Walker, Henderson, 107

Wanchese (Indian), 152, 164

Wanchese (village), 146, 147, 161, 172-73, 200, 260

Wanchese Harbor, 146, 173

War of 1812, 44, 101, 306

Warren, Lindsay, 190, 191, 214, 301-2

Warren, Thomas, 104

Washington: description of, 301-11; historic structures of, 300-311; history of, 303-11; map of, 300; the "original" Washington, 308

Washington County, 94, 111-33, 279

Washington County Courthouse, 112, 114, 119

Washington Creef (Bicentennial) Park, 169

Washington, D. C., 22, 32, 66, 129, 161, 216, 302, 308

Washington, George, 44, 47, 48, 91, 107, 225, 238, 308

Wash Woods, 35

Waterfront Park (Elizabeth City), 54, 56, 58

Waterfront Park (Plymouth), 112

Waterlily, 2, 3, 17

Waterside Theatre, 158, 159-61

Waves, 201, 216, 219

Way, Eva Blount, 282-83

Wayne County, 335

Webb, Clifton, 64

Weeks, Stephen Beauregard, 70-71

Weeksville, 36, 37, 67

Weeksville Brick Road, 67

Weir Point, 147-50

Welch, Robert, 80

Wells Meeting House, 81

Wessells, William H., 116-17

Wessington, 100, 104

West Custom House, 105

West Indies, 21, 115, 140, 305

West Virginia Pulp and Paper Company, 140

Westover Plantation, 121

Whalebone Junction, 199, 200, 201, 202, 203

Whalehead, 25

Whalehead Club, 3, 27, 28, 29-34

Whedbee House, 76, 77

White House, The, 283

White Island, 17

White, John, 141, 143, 153-55, 157, 162, 163-64, 168, 314

Whitefield, George, 294-95

Whitley, John Hay, 162

Whitmore, Ephraim, 296

Whittakers Creek, 328

Whittie, John, 187

Whortonsville, 312, 313, 326, 327

Wild, Edward A., 77

Wilkinson Creek, 277

Wilkinson, John A., 280-81

Wilkinson Point, 334, 336, 337

William B. Umstead Bridge, 146, 147, 148, 149

Williams (Glebe) House, 287, 296

Williams-Flurry-Burton House, 107

Williamson, Hugh, 44, 101

Wilkinson Point, 313, 335

Wilmington, 102, 107, 305

Wilson, James, 107

Wilson, John, IV, 170, 171

Winfall, 72, 81

Wise, Henry A., 178

Wise House, 313, 327-28

Woccon (Wacocon) Indians, 237

Wolfman Jack, 82

Wood-McCallum-Winslow House, 89, 92

Woodville, 72, 80

World War I, 5, 156, 203, 208, 240, 250, 334

World War II: Bodie Island, incident off, 203; Edenton Municipal Airport, origins of, 159; *Lost Colony, The,* performance interruption of, 159; Ocracoke Island, incidents at, 247-48, 250-52; Southern Hotel, use of during, 62; U-boat menace during, 42, 66, 203, 246, 251, 252; Weeksville, blimp facility at, 66-67; Whalehead Club, use of during, 32

Wright brothers, 183, 186, 188-92, 193-94, 195, 278

Wright Brothers Fly In, 192

Wright Brothers Monument (Kitty Hawk), 193-94

Wright Brothers National Memorial, 174, 175, 185, 186, 188-92, 214

Wright Kite Festival, 192

Wright Memorial Bridge, 3, 20-21, 25
Wright, Orville, 188-92, 214
Wright, Wilbur, 188-90, 194
Wynne, Richard, 264
Wynne's Folly, 264

Yeager, Chuck, 192
Ye Olde Pioneer Theater, 170
Yeopim, 72
Yeopim Baptist Church, 94
Yeopim Creek, 84

Yeopim Indians, 79, 91
Yeopim River, 74, 84, 85